RECREATIONAL SAFETY

Acknowledgments

No book is written without reference to others in terms of work cited or support generated. Recognition is made to the individuals and organizations who either lent assistance in providing information, actively obtained information, supplied illustrative cases or records, and anecdotal experiences which were utilized. For the most part, the research relating to the topic was made easier through the cooperative efforts of those persons or agencies who are listed hereafter:

Joseph W. Halper, commissioner of Human Services and Recreation, City of Long Beach, California; Joseph E. Curtis, commissioner of Human Services, New Rochelle, New York; Joseph Caverly, commissioner of Parks, Recreation, and Conservation, Westchester County, New York; Henry R. Agonia, director of Parks and Recreation, Glendale, California; "Tex" Ward, general manager, Conejo Recreation and Park District, Thousand Oaks, California; Harvey Roth, superintendent, Recreational and Community Services Division, Conejo Recreation and Park District, Thousand Oaks, California; Dr. David Sterle, professor, Department of Recreation, California State University at Northridge, California; Jessie Farrow, Rhulen Insurance Agency, Inc., Monticello, New York; Joel L. Pittman, Esq., Union, New Jersey; Joseph J. Triarsi, Esq., Roselle Park, New Jersey; John E. Riehl, Esq., Freehold, New Jersey; Harold Chipperson, Esq., Union, New Jersey; Francis J. O'Dea, Esq., Rutherford, New Jersey; William D. McGovern, Esq., Freehold, New Jersey; L. Kent Mays, Jr., forest supervisor, United States Department of Agriculture Forest Service, Green Mountain National Forest, Rutland, Vermont; Joseph H. Reinhardt, technical coordinator, United States Department of Agriculture Forest Service, White Moutain National Forest, Laconia, New Hampshire; Robert G. Hess, student intern, Agency of Environmental Conservation, Department of Parks, Forests, and Recreation, Montpelier, Vermont; George Plumb, recreation chief, Agency of Environmental Conservation, Department of Parks, Forests, and Recreation, Montpelier, Vermont; O. Dale Graham, deputy director, Cleveland Metroparks System, Cleveland, Ohio; Edward H. Stone, chief landscape architect, United States Department of Agriculture Forest Service, Washington, D.C.; Clifton French, superintendent, Hennepin County Park Reserve District, Hennepin County, Minnesota; Charles W. Christy, director of Community

Recreation, Department of Resources and Economic Development, Division of Parks and Recreation, Office of Recreational Services, Concord, New Hampshire; Ben Harris, recreational safety specialist, National Safety Council, Chicago, Illinois; James A. Cook, chief, Bureau of Park Operations, Division of Recreation and Parks, Department of Natural Resources, Tallahassee, Florida; James P. Hadaway, general manager, Recreation and Park Department, Los Angeles, California; Lawrence S. Garland, Jr., president, Snowcraft Corporation, Scarborough, Maine; Henry R. Morton, vice-president, Gladding Corporation, Wood and Youth Products Division, South Paris, Maine; Ken Schmidt, vice-president, Aqua-Matic Piers, Inc., Milwaukee, Wisconsin; J. Michelle Williamson Fitzpatrick, graduate assistant, University of Connecticut, Storrs, Connecticut.

Among the organizations which provided material assistance were:

The American Alpine Club of New York City; American Whitewater Affiliation, Jefferson City, Missouri; United States Consumer Product Safety Commission, Washington, D.C.; Commonwealth of Pennsylvania, Department of Environmental Resources, Harrisburg, Pennsylvania; United States Department of Agriculture Forest Service, Rocky Mountain Forest and Range Experimental Station, Fort Collins, Colorado; United States Department of Agriculture Forest Service, National Avalanche School, Reno, Nevada; University of Vermont, Agricultural Experiment Station, Burlington, Vermont; American Standard Association; National Safety Council; American Red Cross; Department of Health, Burlington, Vermont; Division of Environmental Protection, Montpelier, Vermont; United States Department of Health and Human Services, Washington, D.C.; Recreation and Youth Services Planning Council of Los Angeles, California; South Carolina Department of Parks, Recreation, and Tourism, Columbia, South Carolina.

I wish to thank Mrs. Phyllis Gormley for the time and effort spent in revising and completing the manuscript.

concerned about safety education as it applies to the field of recreational service in all of its ramifications. This volume is expressly dedicated to the techniques available to recreationists for eliminating accidents, preventing negligence, and ensuring the safety of patrons. It is not enough to say that practitioners or suppliers should not be negligent. This is belaboring the obvious. Assuredly, no one intentionally tries to be negligent, but somehow, certain individuals perform in ways that are negligent. This is the kind of behavior that is to be stopped. Something must be substituted that, when habitually applied, will virtually eliminate negligence from those who practice in the field of recreational service.

This is what the book is about. It offers comprehensive plans and methods to be followed for the elimination of negligence and the development of a safe environment in which people may participate in recreational activities. It does this without expunging the risk element from recreational experiences. It is the methodical and systematized practice of safety education within the agency until all employees are thoroughly imbued with and habituated to performing their functions with safety uppermost.

If the plans, policies, and procedures are followed and routinely reinforced, evaluated, and conscientiously reiterated, not only will the rate of accidents decline precipitously, but the probability of successful litigation against defendant recreational service agencies will become negligible. In fact, it could be said that the techniques offered here should produce a climate of competence so pervasive that the rare case that gets as far as a jury trial will assume the proportions of a classic example of what not to do and serve as a model for students and practitioners alike.

Preface

The standard of care owed to all those who participate in organized or sponsored recreational activities under the control of some agency must be consistent with legislative intent and judicial interpretation. In order to fulfill their mandate to see to the safety of participants, those involved in supplying or delivering recreational service need to know the requirements for reasonable and prudent operations.

This text is not about tort liability and legalism. Rather, it is designed to relieve all those who work in any aspect of the field of recreational service from the costs which accompany lost litigation. There is really only one sure way to escape the pressures, bad publicity, and possible monetary loss which lawsuits against recreational service agencies reflect—prevent them. The basic article of faith which underlies the premise that allegations of negligence can be successfully opposed rests upon the simple but central idea that education is the cure.

To be sure, we live in an era when litigation is brought against any organization or individual for real or imagined injuries. Even when there are no grounds for a suit, litigants will attempt to intimidate the alleged defendant by bringing suits. There are a number of reasons for these actions. The plaintiff was actually injured or had property damage and seeks redress. The plaintiff believes that the organization was responsible for a mishap, despite his or her own negligence, and seeks redress. The plaintiff is merely being a nuisance and hopes to obtain some monetary reward despite the fact that there has been no injury or damage suffered. In the latter, instance, there is no basis for a suit, but the plaintiff hopes that some out-of-court settlement in his or her favor will ensue or that the insurance carrier will be directed to pay off to forestall any unpleasant publicity. People are perfectly willing to bring suits at any time they feel that they have been imposed upon. Particularly is this true if the agency is somewhat vulnerable to such litigation by virtue of weak or questionable standardized levels of care which the agency owes to its patrons. Currently, many litigations are initiated against agencies and individuals for injuries suffered that would never have been brought to court if the plaintiff was unaware that the defendant was covered by insurance.

This material has not been developed to frighten suppliers of recreational services from carrying out their functions. On the contrary, it has been produced to make recreationists, and others associated with the provision of recreational service, cognizant of the complexities of fulfilling legal obligations they have to those whom they serve. Furthermore, although information is presented about tort law as it applies to the provision of recreational service, it is more important to make recreationists recognize their legal responsibility for patron safety. Protection of the health and safety of patrons and seeing to their welfare should be the standard operating procedure of all those concerned with the provision of recreational service. Such standardized practices and responsible approach, which must be ingrained into the work habits of all employees, will become the shield that protects recreationists and those to whom they deliver recreational services.

To this end, the orientation is from the aspect of safety rather than from defense against negligence or other substandard care. This stance, if scrupulously followed, will almost never result in recreationists leaving the field because they feel so threatened by litigation and the consequences of losing. There are thousands of suits brought against recreational agencies of all kinds, whether they operate in the public or private (commercial) sectors. Where safety factors have been placed uppermost in the operating procedures, defendant organizations and individuals rarely lose. Of course, there is no guarantee if the case reaches a jury. There are too many imponderables to include that can sway a jury. Even if there was no real basis for an allegation, it is possible for juries to reach adverse decisions. When this occurs, it may be because of the age of the person who was injured, the relative skill of the opposing attorneys, and the trial judge's charge to the jury. Juries are made up of people who can be persuaded by clever argument contrary to the facts. In a few cases, all of the facts indicate a complete lack of negligence on the part of the defendant who is, nevertheless, found guilty of negligence. Contrariwise, those defendants who are clearly negligent are sometimes found innocent. In such instances, cases may be appealed to higher courts. There is every reason to believe that appeals can be won when higher courts overturn a lower court decision or reverse a jury's wrong verdict. Surely, those instances do arise when neither justice nor the public is well served, but these very inconsistencies are integral to the American jury system. No one can ever be sure what a jury's verdict will be, regardless of the facts. Yet, the greatest likelihood is that when all of the evidence is in, juries will reach the correct conclusion about whether or not negligence was indeed present and who was careless so that an accident occurred. Be that as it may, it is better to know and understand the need for accident prevention than it is to have to worry about how to defend against allegations of irresponsible activity. For this reason, the material covered in this text gives the reader the wherewithal to acquire the skill and knowledge necessary to counter potential charges of less than acceptable behavior.

Most texts offer statements about tort liability and provide typical defenses which may be used to oppose allegations of carelessness. This book is

Contents

Salus est non casus

For Rhoda To Whom I Owe Everything

Associated University Presses
440 Forsgate Drive
Cranbury, NJ 08512

Associated University Presses
25 Sicilian Avenue
London WC1A 2QH, England

Associated University Presses
2133 Royal Windsor Drive
Unit 1
Mississauga, Ontario
Canada L5J 1K5

The paper used in this publication meets the requirements of the American National Standard for Permanence of Paper for Printed Library Materials Z39.48-1984.

Library of Congress Cataloging-in-Publication Data

Shivers, Jay Sanford, 1930–
Recreational safety.

Bibliography: p.
Includes index.
1. Recreation—Safety measures. 2. Sports—Safety measures. 3. Recreation—Management. 4. Sports—Organization and administration. I. Title.
GV181.3.S55 1986 790'.028'9 85-47630
ISBN 0-8386-3241-6 (alk. paper)

Printed in the United States of America

RECREATIONAL SAFETY

The Standard of Care

Jay S. Shivers

RUTHERFORD • MADISON • TEANECK
FAIRLEIGH DICKINSON UNIVERSITY PRESS
LONDON AND TORONTO: ASSOCIATED UNIVERSITY PRESSES

PART I

Fundamentals of Recreational Safety

1
The Language of Responsibility—An Introduction

Being the defendant in a suit is not an enjoyable experience. The allegations of incompetence, omission, or negligence against which the recreationist must defend are anxiety provoking, time consuming, and almost never laid to rest despite final acquittal. The damage done to the agency's reputation in terms of bad publicity and to the character of the person held to have been negligent lingers on regardless of whether or not the plaintiff's allegations were proved false. It is a sorry state of affairs when a professional is brought into court, or threatened with suit, for carrying out the duties and functions for which he or she is responsible.

The recreational facility is not only a place for enjoyment, it may be the starting point of injury that winds up in a courtroom. There are at least five thousand litigations against public departments or other deliverers of recreational services each year in the United States.[1] Some suits, where gross injurics have occurred, require the payment of millions or hundreds of thousands of dollars or minor awards to those parties that suffered. Nevertheless, the loss of time, public monies, or private profits in those instances where negligence occurred has caused irreparable damage to the image of the organization, the personnel involved in the action, and the person who was injured. These days, offering recreational services can be tantamount to inviting assertions of negligence. Instructing a class in some recreational activity, performing as a camp counselor, supervising a playground, or acting as a lifeguard often seems to lead directly to a jury trial.

THE QUESTION OF MALPRACTICE

Avoiding recreationist malpractice concerns a significant but all too neglected aspect of the field of recreational service—the delivery of wholesome, safe, leisure experiences, capable of satisfying and enriching the lives of those engaged in them—and the possibility of lawsuit, discharge, and court proceedings arising from misconduct. This is a subject that needs study. Whether the field of recreational service is indeed a profession is not a question. As far as the courts are concerned, recreationists may be guilty of malpractice.[2] Possibilities abound in terms of potential situations that arise in the conduct of organized or sponsored recreational activities. Recreationists are confronted by similar legal hazards that have generated thousands of malpractice claims against teachers, lawyers, and personnel in the health care fields. Occupational malpractice is becoming an increasing threat to recreationists.[3]

If malpractice is construed as any professional misconduct or unreasonable lack of skill or observance in professional conduct, then recreationists had better look to themselves. Recreationists, especially within the past twenty-five years, have begun to claim professional status for themselves and the field. To some extent the claim is justified for there are many similarities between practitioners of recreational service and other recognized professions. As self-proclaimed professionals, recreationists must also recognize that deviation from professional standards of practice embodies professional malpractice.[4] Furthermore, malpractice is the infringement of a professional mandate to act with reasonable care and in good faith without deceit or conspiracy. Therefore, the recreationist, like other professionals, is subject to legal action when substandard conduct occurs.

The purpose of this chapter is to alert practitioners who deliver recreational services to the legal possibilities of their decisions and actions. It is designed to assist recreationists and others to appreciate the results of their options. This is not a book of law. The aim here is to generate a better understanding in the recreationist of potential liabilities and thereby prevent expensive miscalculations of choices. This material should do much to alert readers to the draining experience of defending against liability suits. Legal missteps awaiting the unwary in the recreational service environment are emphasized. It is presumed that when the dangers are known they can be forestalled. The jargon of the law has been avoided so that basic problems and common questionable occurrences can be given attention. The real and present dangers of poor judgment and incompetent behavior are highlighted and explained.

One does not have to be a lawyer to recognize the meaning of conduct that falls below that of accepted professional standards. Surely, reason and prudence are the best defense against charges of malpractice. The field of recreational service is one of the great humanitarian undertakings of this society. Despite the litigious nature of those who participate within the offerings of public or private recreational agencies, lawsuits can be avoided or, if contested, they can be won.

TORT LIABILITY AND MALPRACTICE

This chapter is not a substitute for a law course on tort liability.[5] It will not provide much more than a superficial grasp of what constitutes a tortious act when a recreationist is negligent. However, the subject of tort liability is so important to the arsenal of recreationist knowledge that it has been included here. Moreover, it is necessary that recreationists think about and be aware of tort law so that they may be in a better position to prevent themselves from becoming embroiled in the toils of lawsuits.[6] The basic function of recreational service lays the practitioner open to greater than normal tort jeopardy. These risks, and a second of carelessness, can produce participant injuries and, subsequently, litigation. The law has its own terminology, meaning, and complexity. This chapter simplifies the concepts and offers information that is practical and intelligible.

WHAT IS TORT?

A tort[7] is any civil, not criminal, wrong that is not a breach of contract, and is immediately concerned with physical injury to others, damage to property, or the demeaning of another's character. For recreationists the law of torts involves participant injuries, substandard practice, and defamation of character. There are several kinds of torts. However, for those who are practitioners in the field of recreational service there is really only one category of tort suit that is of vital concern and that is *negligence*.

NEGLIGENCE

Almost always, the single assertion which is the basis for a lawsuit arises out of an allegation of negligence.[8] Essentially, negligence is conduct which falls below a recognized and established standard of practice. Four components are immediately discernable in acts of negligence. These are: (a) standard of care, (b) immoderate risk, (c) proximate cause, and (d) injury suffered.

Standard of care.[9] The courts have held that recreationists have the responsibility for providing a suitable standard or level of care for those who participate within the activities organized or sponsored by their agency of employment. Criteria dealing with the care of those involved with recreational activities are expected to be of a higher degree than would ordinarily be required of the average person concerned with responsibility for others. Recreationists who are charged with working with the very young and the very old or who instruct in activities that are considered to be inherently dangerous, i.e., gymnastics, football, soccer, some craft or shop work, etc., must maintain a higher standard than others.

Standard of care is directly associated with supervision. The higher the degree of care necessary (based upon type of activity) the more closely and continuous must be the act of supervision. The typical recreationist exercises what has been termed indirect or general supervision. He or she is expected to practice a broad and moderate standard of care over participants. However, recreationists who work with the very young or the very old or in high risk activities are responsible for maintaining a higher degree of care. These recreationists are expected to offer a much more direct and constant level of supervision over those for whom they are responsible than the indirect supervision provided by recreationists in areas of low risk.

Immoderate risk.[10] The second factor of negligence is immoderate or inappropriate risk. The courts have held that recreationists have the duty to prevent exposure of participants to an unreasonable risk. Recreationists should not place their constituents in situations that lead to an unnecessary risk. Thus, recreationists who are charged with instructing shop activities, physical activities, or other high risk activities must provide those who are participating with the best possible instruction, and provide appropriate supplies, materials, or equipment utilized in such activities that are in suitable condition. Anything less than optimum instruction and safe equipment and the risk level becomes unacceptable.

Proximate cause.[11] The third factor of negligence is proximate cause. Proximate cause is defined as the attendant development of a sequence of action between the recreationist's negligent behavior and injury to the participant or spectator. The recreationist's conduct does not have to be the immediate cause of injury or even the indirect cause. It must, however, be the proximate cause, i.e., the sequential steps must be closely connected insofar as time, space, or arrangement is concerned. Proximate cause is usually associated with improper conduct or failure of supervision. The major question, under these circumstances, is whether or not the injury or accident could have occurred or been prevented if the worker had been performing supervisory duties properly.

Real Injury.[12] The final factor in negligence is actual harm or real and evident injury. In tort law, there is little question about injuries that are of minor degree and that heal quickly without lasting effect. Real injury of a substantial nature is the kind that leaves the injured party with permanent damage, impairment, or disability. For negligence to have occurred, all of these factors must be present.

DEGREES OF NEGLIGENCE

Negligence is a matter of degree. Those who deliver recreational services in whatever capacity they perform, whether in the public or private sector, must recognize that negligence allegations are not clearly delineated cases. There are conditions or grades of negligence which need to be considered. Negligence may be defined as slight, ordinary, and gross depending upon how state laws are written.

Slight negligence.[13] This means that the practitioner failed to use great care.

This definition states that a higher standard of care existed and was necessary, given the conditions of the situation, and the recreationist failed to supply it. Those workers who normally perform their functions in activities or with age groups that require a higher standard of care than are typically necessary in most recreational activities could be held to be slightly negligent if they did not provide that additional measure of care that the standard requires of them.

Ordinary negligence.[14] Used to indicate failure to exercise ordinary care. This concept contends that recreationists are expected to conduct routine activities with ordinary prudence and reasonableness and offer an ordinary standard of care when compared to the theoretical reasonable and prudent professional.

Gross negligence.[15] The failure to provide even slight care. To be guilty of gross negligence, a recreationist's performance must be found to be of lower quality than that of an indifferent person. Essentially gross negligence carries with it the implication of willful misconduct, recklessness, or an apparent intent to cause harm.

As with all cases of negligence there are certain acts of commission, omission, or nonperformance that are used to determine the presence of negligence and the degree of negligence that can then be applied to the particular situation. Among the actions taken which fall below the standard required are those of malfeasance, misfeasance, or nonfeasance.

Malfeasance.[16] An act of commission with intent to harm, damage, or injure another. There is no legal justification for the action, and the individual involved has, with malicious intent, determined upon a course of action designed to cause injury to another or damage property through misconduct or an abuse of the power of the position held.

Misfeasance.[17] An act of commission so ineptly performed that it results in injury to another or damage to another's property. The activity has legal justification, but the provider is such an incompetent that harm is caused without malicious intent.

Nonfeasance.[18] The omission of a necessary act or failure to perform a legal responsibility that produces injury to another or results in damage to property. The failure to act is a consequence of incompetence on the part of the provider, but there is no malicious intent accompanying the failure.

In order to test the charge of negligence, the court uses the measures of reason, prudence, and foreseeability.

THE REASONABLE AND PRUDENT PERSON DOCTRINE AND FORESEEABILITY

In examining the facts of a negligence suit, the courts fall back upon the doctrine of reasonableness and prudence.[19] The recreationist's performance is compared to that of a reasonable and prudent person acting in the same set of circumstances. Among the features of the reasonable and prudent person doctrine are: intelligence, physical capacity, reflection and recall, and esoteric skills and knowledge.

Intelligence. That innate ability to learn or understand from experience; as well as the faculty for responding rapidly and successfully to new situations. This mental ability enables the individual to acquire and retain knowledge about the things, places, persons, and ideas with which he or she comes in contact. In short, intelligence concerns discernment, perception, and problem solving. The courts assume that the recreationist is of at least average intelligence—no brighter, but certainly not less perceptive than any other peer.

Physical capacity. Physical capacity, on the other hand, concerns those strengths, motor skills, and stamina necessary to function effectively and carry out the responsibilities that the duties of the job place upon the incumbent. The court is only concerned with whether or not the recreationist is able to perform the activity insofar as the demands of employment require certain physical attributes.

Reflection. This has to do with the fixing of the mind on some subject or object. It is the conscious awareness of objects or other information derived through the senses. The element of recall also plays a significant role within this rationale. Thus, recall deals specifically with the power of retaining or dredging up past thoughts, images, concepts, or situations. The individual must possess normal perception and memory. The recreationist should have the ability to perceive and revive ideas so that knowledge about conditions, potentials, and probabilities can be weighed before actions are undertaken. The court expects the professional person, or the employee of the organization, to have the normal capabilities both in mind and body that will permit reliance for the safety of anyone placed within his or her charge.

Skills.[20] The final factors deal with the particular skills and knowledge that should be commonly held by all those who are employed in similar positions or in the same field. This means, for example, that the crafts instructor is expected to have all of the skills and knowledge that other crafts persons have who function on that level or are concerned with the kinds of activities that are offered. In such instances, the crafts person will be held strictly accountable for any special skills or knowledge that he or she claims to have.

Foreseeability.[21] The element of forecasting, planning in advance, or estimating the probabilities of something happening, given a set of circumstances and personalities involved, forces the court to determine whether a reasonable person could have foreseen whatever incident actually occurred. The courts declare that it is not unreasonable for the reasonable and prudent person to calculate whether certain actions would lead to an inevitable accident. This is known as the doctrine of foreseeability. Actions of a so-called reasonable and prudent person are compared with the performance of the individual involved in the litigation. If a reasonable peer could have foreseen the accident and consequent injury, then he or she would have acted in a way designed to prevent the situation from taking place. The actions of the recreationist are examined in order to observe or discover the similarities or discrepancies between the hypothetical reasonable person and the litigant. If the worker acted in a reasonable manner, then he or she is probably not negligent.

The issue of foreseeability is the crucial point upon which any negligence suit hangs.[22] All of the above aspects of reasonableness really come down to focus upon this basic determination. Would not the reasonable and prudent person have the ability to foresee a participant being injured during the absence of an instructor or other responsible person in charge? Would not the crafts instructor, who was a reasonable and prudent person, foresee that participants utilizing unsafe machines or not having enough knowledge or skill to use dangerous machines or substances might be subject to a high degree of risk and potential accident and injury? Would not the reasonable counselor be able to foresee the potential for serious injury if campers were permitted to climb cliffs, white water canoe, or to engage in other hazardous activities without appropriate instruction, equipment, or practice? Would not the reasonable center director be able to foresee a person slipping on a wet floor in the gymnasium, diving into the shallow end of the swimming pool, or being subject to injury when uncontrolled crowds are permitted to congregate after an event is finished?

RESPONSIBILITIES TO PARTICIPANTS

The courts have consistently held that recreationists, or persons acting in the guise and/or capacity of recreationists, have several duties to perform with regard to those who are nominally placed in their care of charge.[23] The first requirement is to provide adequate supervision. The second requirement is to provide appropriate instruction, and the third requirement concerns properly maintaining buildings, grounds, and equipment so that accidents can be avoided.[24] These are parts of the degree of care necessary to avert unnecessary risk and avoid the eventuality of injury that so often accompanies careless or haphazard direction.

In Loco Parentis. Adequate supervision is closely associated with the standard of care required in terms of the age of participants, activities engaged in, and circumstances surrounding the activities that put them at low or high risk. In the case of children between the ages of five and seventeen who are invited to participate within the scheduled program of activities ranging from residential camps and playground activities to competitive athletic teams and shopwork the courts have held that counselors, instructors, and other agency supervisory personnel stand *in loco parentis*, or act as parental surrogates.[25] When children are attending some recreational activity sponsored or directly supervised by some recreational agency, recreationists or other agents of the organization are expected to exercise the same standard of care that a parent would exercise. For the most part, however, adequate supervision refers to indirect or general supervision.[26]

Supervision. For those recreationists who control activities that fall into a high standard of care category, adequate supervision becomes something much more special and consistant.[27] For the former instance, a recreationist conducting a glee club or chorus would exercise an ordinary or customary standard of care. Adequate supervision for this person would merely require his or her presence in the session and the use of prudence in dealing with participants. For recreationists who direct high-risk activities, adequate supervision is considerably more intense, close, and constant.[28] The recreationist should never absent him or herself from the place of activity, should always be alert to dangerous circumstances within the activity environment, and should closely supervise each participant as they take part in the activity.

Instruction. Appropriate instruction is the second basis that forms the support required of recreationists in carrying out their responsibilities to those placed in their charge.[29] The most typical kind of negligence suits involves improper instruction. Instruction is a vital element in situations where participants are learning a new skill or must handle potentially dangerous materials or equipment. Acquisition of information that is necessary to perform satisfactorily in some activity must be appropriate. When participants are injured in shop/crafts, physical activity, playgrounds, boating, fishing, shooting incidents, or other such activity forms, the essential questions that will be asked are: What specific kinds of instruction were given as opposed to what was actually needed? Was the participant appropriately instructed in the various gymnastic stunts or routines? Was the participant properly instructed as to the use of the kinds of power saws, drill presses, or belt sanders and their protective guards in the shop or crafts room? Was the participant appropriately instructed as to the procedure for rappeling down a cliff face? The idea of appropriate instructions can cover almost any piece of equipment or material used in a given activity. If the individual is injured while using such equipment, can it be proven that he or she received appropriate instruction in how to perform the activity or utilize the materials necessary for accomplishing the activity?

Maintenance. The third leg of responsibility concerns the place of activity and the maintenance of equipment used.[30] To avoid potential injury and reduce the element of risk, recreationists are obliged to perform environmental inspections so that unnecessary hazards are removed or eliminated and proper warnings are in place. This may mean the filling of chuckholes in the outfield of a baseball diamond, the erection of a barrier to prevent some person from walking into a pitfall, or the posting of prohibitory signs indicating hidden or obvious dangers. Of equal importance is the necessity of recreationists to be responsible for the proper maintenance of all equipment under their control. This is specifically urgent in those activities where equipment is of paramount importance if the activity is to be operated, played, or performed. Thus, sport and game activities, crafts, playground experiences, diving, sliding, aquatic activities, and a host of other recreational activities that use various pieces of apparatus and equipment should have routine maintenance. Recreationists or other agency employees should check for unsafe electrical connections, cables, and cords; broken light fixtures; broken windows; and similar physical defects of the plant.[31]

The courts hold recreationists liable if a participant is injured because equipment and other aspects of the physical plant are not properly maintained. This means that the department should develop a preventative maintenance schedule for inspecting both the equipment used in the various activities and the lands, buildings, and facilities being managed by them. It has frequently been suggested that inspections should be carried out at least four times each year insofar as the physical plant is concerned. Equipment inspections should be carried out frequently. The more the equipment is used the greater the danger of breakage. It may be that playground apparatus and devices have to be inspected on a daily basis in order to insure safety of participants. There are no instances when participants should be permitted to use equipment that is defective and, therefore, probably dangerous.

Age and Negligence. Children up to the age of seven years are held to be not negligent when, in fact, they are the direct causes of injuries to others. Young children may not be held legally responsible for the commission of acts, regardless of how vicious their conduct may be. The child younger than seven years is not legally responsible for stabbing another or for throwing an object that can blind, disfigure, or cripple another despite intent or previous history of such actions. That is why agency personnel who are charged with the responsibility for the behavior of children under seven years of age have a higher standard of care to maintain than do other personnel dealing with older participants. Moreover, the law *presumes* that children between the ages of eight to fourteen are not negligent. Children of these ages are thought not to know better when they engage in activities that lead to the injury of others or the damage of property. This presumption may be argued, but the burden of proof lies with the recreationist to show that the child actually knew better than to behave in the manner that resulted in injury to himself or herself or others. Between the ages of fifteen and eighteen children are held to be possibly negligent. This means that the burden no longer rests with the recreationist, but is upon the youthful offender. Older childen are held to a higher standard of conduct than are younger children, but not as high as the standards that apply to an adult.

NEGLIGENCE DEFENSES

There are a variety of legal procedures which can be utilized by defendants to prove that they were not negligent as the tort action claims. These defences are the primary means to avoid false assertions of impropriety insofar as adequate supervision, instruction, or prudent behavior is concerned. Among the defenses are: (1) contributory negligence, (b) comparative negligence, (c) assumption of the risk, (d) *Vis Major,* (e) immunity, and (f) trepassing.

Contributory Negligence.[32] Personal negligence of one's own safety occurs when the injured party acted in a manner that is clearly substandard to what is required. When an individual fails to perform properly or foolishly exposes himself or herself to danger and thereby contributes to the sustained injury, contributory negligence may be claimed. However, children below the age of seven cannot be found negligent in this way. Children between the ages of eight and fourteen must be proved to have acted in such a way as to bring about their own injury. Of course children can be shown to have been guilty of contributory negligence, but the courts are unwilling to find youths, even those over age fifteen, to be culpable of conduct on a lower level than is required for the activity.

Comparative Negligence.[33] The second possible defense concerns the negligence of more than one person's involvement in the injury sustained by the participant. Comparative negligence permits the plaintiff to recover for injuries received in an accident if the degree of negligence is less than or equal to the negligence of others named as defendants in the action. Thus, an individual who actually contributed to his or her own injury might still be able to allege that the defendant's negligence also contributed to the injury that was sustained. Where this can be proved, the courts apportion the damages among the negligent parties. If the recreationist is found to be guilty of a certain percentage of negligence, then that is the percentage which is assessed. To the extent that other defendants may also be involved, the proportion of negligence charged against them will have to be paid to redress the person injured. Under such circumstances, the amount to be awarded to plaintiff (if comparative negligence is proved) may not be 100 percent of the amount determined but will be alloted among the several parties who have been found guilty of negligence. This is a defense because it lessens the amount that any one guilty party has to pay.

Assumption of Risk.[34] This defense is associated with the idea of reasonable and unreasonable risk. Where an individual voluntarily engages in a situation with the understanding that there is some chance of injury during the course of the activity, it is said that that person may assume a reasonable risk. Thus individuals who participate in body contact sports and games or use or come into contact with hazardous materials or dangerous equipment knowingly assume a certain risk of injury. However, courts presume that participants have received appropriate instruction, if they are playing in leagues, tournaments, or are involved in learning skills sponsored by the recreational service agency. Additionally, such participants are expected to have used the best possible equipment if it is supplied by the agency. It may be that individual participants must supply their own protective equipment. Where this is true, the recreational agency cannot be held responsible if individuals played with inferior equipment. In the case of school-operated activities or where the sponsor supplies uniforms and equipment, the equipment must be of the best possible type. Failure to conform to this requirement or to the provision of adequate instruction when instruction is a primary prerequisite for performance will negate the assumption of risk defense. Some courts may impose an additional burden on this defense. When children are participating, the courts have held the participants cannot assume risks unless they are aware of the risk. This means that those who conduct the activities must inform participants of the possibility of being injured whether they use the best possible equipment or receive sufficient instruction. For all practical intents and purposes, it will serve the interests of all concerned if written notification is presented to those taking part with a copy signed by participants indicating that they recognize the potential risks involved.

The Last Clear Chance.[35] Even if contributory negligence can be proved, the plaintiff may be able to recover damages if he or she can show that the last clear chance doctrine was an operational factor at the time of the incident. The last clear chance doctrine assumes that both parties to the injury or property damage were negligent, and the negligence was a contributory cause to the accident. However, if it can be shown that the recreationist defendant had the last clear chance to avoid the accident and did not take advantage of this opportunity to prevent the injury or damage, he or she may be held liable despite any contributory negligence on the part of plaintiff.

Vis Major.[36] An act of God or an uncontrollable natural force, therefore completely unforeseeable, is another defense against negligence. It is regarded as an accidental occurrence caused by some superior and unpredictable force beyond human control and one that could not have been prevented even with reasonable and prudent care. For example, the proverbial bolt from the blue strikes and kills a player. It is an act of God. Nothing could have been done to prevent it. However, if the lifeguard on duty had seen a squall forming and did not order all swimmers from the pool, the lightning death would be held to be negligence, because the probability of such an occurrence could have been foreseen.

Immunity.[37] In those few states where governmental immunity attaches to the recreational service function, injuries sustained by participants in publicly organized and sponsored activities may not be pursued. Governmental functions are those performed by the state acting in its sovereign capacity or by a subdivision acting for the state and are considered essential for the protection of the state and for the general welfare. Under these circumstances the doctrine of *respondeat superior*[38] is evoked (let the master answer). If the state holds itself immune from liability, it will not permit itself to be sued in its own courts. While this situation is rapidly giving way to abrogations by the courts or enactments of state legislatures, where the doctrine exists it may still be possible to sue individuals who were involved rather than the commission, department, or managing board. Those who work in the private sector have no such defense.

Trespassing.[39] A trespasser is one who is in a given location without invitation or right to be present at that time. Trespass is a clear violation of the right of protection from interference with one's person or infringement on one's property through unauthorized presence.

An exception to the rule of nonliability to the trespasser is the attractive nuisance doctrine and it generally applies to children.[40] An attractive nuisance is any dangerous device, instrument, equipment, contrivance, structure, or condition of land that is naturally dangerous and is a continuing hazard. The attractive nuisance doctrine applies to children whose immaturity prevents them from exercising ordinary good judgment.[41] It is based upon the theory that the condition, which is naturally and usually attractive to children at play but which may result in injury, is both attractive and a nuisance simultaneously. Liability attaches because any reasonable and prudent person would be able to foresee that such a condition would attract a child and that such attraction might lead to injury or cause great harm. Since the courts are not disposed to hold children guilty of contributory negligence, the fact that the child was a trespasser will not serve as a defense. Furthermore, the doctrine of attractive nuisance in such cases holds that the unsafe condition actually drew the child onto the property and was, therefore, the proximate cause of injury.

Among the conditions that create liability involving attractive nuisances are: (a) probability of trespass by children or youth; (b) the trespasser will be unaware of any danger due to immaturity; (c) the attractive nuisance must be clearly and closely associated with its potential for harm; and (d) the individual responsible for the area knows of the high risk that such a condition has for any trespassing child.[42]

Waiver. A waiver is an instrument wherein an individual, usually a performer, agrees not to seek redress in the event of injury sustained while participating. It is a contractual form that my be required by a sponsor, organizer, or operator of a facility, agency, or place that conducts the events in which the performer participates. Generally, waiver is the voluntary and intentional relinquishment of a known right, benefit, or advantage. If the waiver is freely entered into by an adult or competent person, who has presumably read the stipulations of the agreement, the courts will hold that it is binding. Thus, the person who disposes of his rights to sue another party can do so under contract law.[43] This, despite the fact that such absolvement may protect the sponsor even though the injuries to the participant were the result of sponsor's negligence. The only time that such exculpatory agreements will not be upheld is when there is evidence of force, fraud, or deceit.[44] Enforcement of the contract will be permitted when the person who waives understands the terms of the release, was aware of the waiver because of its prominence and appearance, entered into the transaction freely and openly, and where the stated terms are appropriate to the specific improper behavior of the party whose latent responsibility is waived.[45]

Youth serving agencies, among others, invariably utilize waivers in hopes of offsetting any liability that might accrue in their operations. Camps, schools, recreational service departments, Y's, and clubs use the waiver as a preliminary filter for selecting or inviting individuals to participate in sponsored activities where there may be some risk of injury. Except when signed by people who are ignorant of the law or are easily intimidated by what appears to be legal language, the waiver, in these cases, is hardly worth the paper it is written on. If a minor signs the waiver, the courts will disallow it as not being applicable under the principles of contract. If parents or guardians sign the waiver, the courts usually state that the rights of minors cannot be abrogated before the fact.[46] At best, waivers may be used to inform parents or guardians that some event that may be inherently dangerous for participants is planned by a sponsoring agency. Having informed the potential participant's parent, any injury that occurs if litigation proceedings are brought, will be judged on the basis of all such claims; that is, foreseeability, assumption of risk, contributory or comparative negligence, and other pertinent factors that determine liability.

SAFETY MEASURES

Recreationists are expected to provide appropriate guidance, direction, and control of the various activities under their immediate supervision. They are trained to be thoughtful, to use good judgment, and conduct themselves in a reasonable and prudent manner. If they do not safeguard those within their charge, they lay themselves and their employer open to allegations of negligence with consequent suits to redress any damages or injuries that were sustained by plaintiff.

Recreational activities, wherever they are conducted, may involve several unpremeditated dangerous conditions or circumstances. Elimination of all possible hazards would be tantamount to the denial of the opportunity to participate in many recreational experiences. Recreational activity is so important to the growth and development of children and youth that all purveyors of the service should use every reasonable and prudent behavior to protect the participant at all times. The enduring satisfactions generated by recreational exposure are vital to the well-being of persons of all ages and, as such, deserve the support of all sectors of society. Nevertheless, the safety of all participants remains the key element if personal satisfaction and enjoyment are to be anticipated outcomes of such experience. To this end adequate supervision must be exercised with people; physical facilities and areas used for recreational purposes must be well maintained. Unsafe conditions have to be removed or repaired diligently. The performance of recreationists must be at a level consistent with the standards operating throughout the field. Incompetence or conduct that falls below reasonable and prudent levels can only be considered negligence. Failure to perform in ways that safeguard participants invites unacceptable risks and practically insures litigation. No recreational service provision can long exist where dangerous situations are constant and unremitting. The key to litigation-free enterprise is the preventive measures developed to avoid injury.

These introductory remarks should not be construed as containing all of the details and legal principles involved in tort liability. These concepts have been included to emphasize the need for care when dealing with those who participate in recreational activities under some sponsorship. Too many recreationists, whether in public or private concerns, are not aware of the impact of tort law and how it may affect them in terms of their on-the-job conduct. Recreationists should recognize the potential for participant injury or property damage without becoming so cautious that they can no longer perform or are afraid of every little minor risk. It is only with the application of reason and prudence that safe and sane recreational participation may be enjoyed. Recreationists must be conscious of what they do and how they do it so that safe practices become habitual. With raised sensitivity to the need for good judgment accidents will be avoided, and tort suits will no longer threaten the practitioner who supplies or delivers recreational services.

To reiterate, there is no absolutely sure way to make the recreational service agency or the recreationist invulnerable to charges of liability. The variety of court opinions, the several laws of the states, the vagaries of jury decisions, attorney competence, and other significant factors determine the outcome of each case. If, however, recreationists practice the safety measures that are necessary to insure the standard of care, it seems likely that allegations associated with liability will not only prove unfounded, but will have little chance of success.

NOTES

1. R. Strickland, J. F. Phillips, and W. R. Phillips, *Avoiding Teacher Malpractice* (New York: Hawthorne Books, Inc., 1976), 6. Also, E. T. Connors, *Educational Tort Liability and Malpractice* (Bloomington, Ind.: Phi Delta Kappa, 1981), ix.
2. *Ishmael v. Millington,* (3rd Dist) 241 Cal App 2d 520, 50 Ca. Rptr. 592; also H. Barry Jaocbs, *The Specter of Malpractice* (Colorado Springs, Colo: Nationwide Press, 1978).
3. Stanley M. Rosenblatt, *Malpractice and Other Malfeasances* (Secaucus, N.J.: Lyle Stuart, Inc., 1977).
4. Ashley Underwood and Stephen Holt, *Professional Negligence* (New York: State Mutual Book & Periodicals Service, Ltd., 1981).
5. Michael D. Bayles and Bruce Chapman, *Justice, Rights, and Tort Law* (Hingham, Mass.: Kluwer Academic Publishers, 1983).
6. Oscar C. Sattinger, ed. *American Jurisprudence,* 2d ed., vol. 57 (Rochester, N.Y.: The Lawyers Co-Operative Publishing Co., 1983), 1–322.
7. Robert E. Keeton and W. E. Keeton, *Tort and Accident Law* (St. Paul, Minn.: West Publishing Co., 1983); also *Dargie v. East End Bolders Club,* 346 III. App. 480, 105 NE 2d 537.
8. *Ft. Smith Gas Co. v. Cloud,* (DA 8) 75 F 2d 413, 97 ALR 833.
9. *Rea v. Simowitz,* 225 N.C. 575, 35 SE 2d 871, 162 ALR 999.

10. *Rappaport v. Nichols,* 31 N.J. 188, 156 A 2d 1, 75 ALR 2d 821.
11. *Price v. Neyland,* 115 App DC 355, 320 F 2d 674, 99 ALR 2d 1391.
12. *Watkins v. Meyers,* 12 N.J. 71, 95 A 2d 705, 36 ALR 2d 1330.
13. *Astin v. Chicago,* M & St. P.R. Co. 143 Wis. 477, 128 NW 265.
14. *Clemens v. State,* 176 Wis. 289, 185 NW 209, 21 ALR 1490.
15. *Oliver v. Kantor,* 122 N.J. L 528, 6 A 2d 205.
16. *South v. Maryland,* 18 How (US) 396, 15 L Ed 433.
17. *Little v. Hackett,* 116 US 366, 29 L Ed 652, 6 S Ct 391.
18. *Elmgren v. Chicago,* M & St. P.R. Co., 102 Miss. 41, 112 NW 1067.
19. *Herring v. Humphrey,* 254 N.C. 741, 119 SE 2d 913, 91 ALR 2d 1320; also *Williams v. Hays,* 143 N.Y. 442, 38 NE 449, later app 157 N.Y. 541, 52 NE 589.
20. *Spokane Trunk & Dray Co., v. Hoefer,* 2 Wash. 45, 25 P 1072.
21. *Milwaukee & St. P.R. Co. v. Kellogg,* 94 US 469, 24 L Ed 256.
22. *Thompson v. Ohio Fuel Gas Co.,* 9 Ohio St 2d 116, 38 Ohio Ops 2d 294, 224 NE 2d 131.
23. *Rea v. Simowitz,* 225 N.C. 575, 35 SE 2d 871, 162 ALR 999.
24. *Doughtery v. Graham,* 287 A 2d 382, 161 Conn. 248.
25. *Morgan v. Smith,* 429 Pa. 561, 241 A 2d 531; also *Lueck v. Janesville,* 57 Wis. 2d 254, 204 NW 2d 6 (1973).
26. *Goldberger v. David Roberts Corp.,* 96 A 2d 309, 139 Conn. 629.
27. *Selleck v. Board of Education,* 276 App Div 263, 94 NYS 2d 318.
28. Rhabb v. New York City Housing Authority, 41 N.Y. 2d 200, 391, NYS 2d 540, 359 NE 2d 1335.
29. *County v. Copeland,* 96 Tenn. 296, 34 SW 427; also *Everhart v. Board of Education (1981),* 108 Mich. App. 218, 310 NW 2d 338.
30. *Flom v. Flom (1980) Minns),* 291 NW 2d 914.
31. *Facey v. Merkle,* 148 A 2d 458, 147 Conn. 708.
32. *Balaas v. City of Hartford,* 12 A 2d 765, 126 Conn. 510.
33. *Holman v. Jones (Fla.),* 280 So 2d 431; also *O'Connor v. G & R Packing Co.,* (1980, 2d Dept) 74 AD 2d 37, 426 NYS 2d 557.
34. *Wendland v. Ridgefield Const. Services, Inc.,* 462 A2d 1043, 190 Conn. 791; also *McIntyre v. Cusick,* 247 Pa. Super 354, 372 A 2d 864; also *Nally v. Charlonneau,* 362 A 2d 494, 169 Conn. 50.
35. *Guilbeau v. Liberty Mut. Ins. Co.,* (La.) 338 So 2d 600, on remand (La App) 345 So 2d 79.
36. Pleasure Beach Park Co. v. Bridgeport Dredge & Dock Co., 165 A 691, 116 Conn. 496; also *Caron v. Guiliano,* 211 A 2d 705, 26 Conn. Sup. 44.
37. *Wysocki v. City of Derby,* 98 A 2d 659, 140 Conn. 173. also *Cartha v. City of Norwalk,* 145 A 158, 108 Conn. 697.
38. *Wests' North Western Digest,* 2d ed. vol. 20 (St. Paul, Minn.: West Publishing Co., 1971), 300–302.
39. *Reasoner v. Chicago,* P.I. & R.R. Co., 101 NW 2d 739, 251 Iowa 506.
40. *Harriman v. Incorporated Town of Afton,* 281 NW 183, 225 Iowa 659.
41. *Browning v. Eichelman,* 162 NW 2d 898, 12 Mich. App. 408.
42. *Checkley v. Illinois C.R. Co.,* 257 Ill. 491, 100 NE 942.
43. *Winterstein v. Wilcom,* 16 Md. App. 130, 293 A 2d 821 (1972).
44. *Wood v. United States,* 75 App DC 274, 128 F 2d 265, 141 ALR 1318.
45. *State v. Hocaha,* 193 NW 2d 484.
46. *Foote v. DePoy,* 126 Iowa 366, 102 NW 112; also *Brown v. Anderson,* 186 Ga. 220, 197 SE 751, followed in 186 Ga. 222, 197 SE 833; also *Hatch v. Merigold,* 119 Conn. 339, 186 A 266, 96 ALR 1114.

2
Safety Essentials in Recreational Service

Injuries that are profound, permanent, or fatal can and do happen at publicly and privately operated recreational areas. These tragic incidents can be caused by the substandard behavior of participants, incompetence of employees of the organization, negligence by operators, or a combination of these inappropriate acts. One outcome that may occur from injuries is litigation against the alleged fault of the agency. People are inclined to sue for punitive and other costs incurred from any injury that they received as spectators or while taking part in leisure experiences at facilities that are administered for recreational purposes. Changing social conditions, increased liberality of the judiciary, and a consideration that no one should suffer crippling harm from the misfeasance of others have led to the growing awareness on the part of business operators and public employees that they are constantly exposed to law suits.

Questions of competence, professional knowledge and skill, degree of care, elements of risk, negligence, and incautious behavior all derive from a poor understanding of safety practices that are essential to the protection of patrons as well as for those who administer recreational functions. Until a well-established pattern of safety education is combined with a system for safeguarding the patron, either from ignorant action or environmental hazards, conditions of jeopardy will prevail. Such jeopardy is unnecessary, and the accompanying deviant or substandard behavior on the part of agents of the organization in question must be eliminated at all costs. Surely, there are behaviors of the individual who has been injured that may have contributed to his or her situation, but an inclusive safety program together with wide distribution of information dealing with hazardous conditions can probably reduce both the injury rate and likelihood of successfully brought suits against those delivering recreational services.

FUNDAMENTALS OF RECREATIONAL SERVICE

Risk is a basic factor in nearly every recreational activity in which people engage. Even those activities not usually thought of as being risky can become unsafe to participants under certain adverse circumstances. Accidents are endemic to the delivery of recreational services, and the outlook for injuries to persons and damage to property cannot be taken lightly. Nevertheless, the reduction of accidents and the alleviation of behavior that can lead to serious injury can be achieved. Without purging the element of risk from recreational experiences, which is one of the reasons for participation, there is still much that can be done by professionals to prevent standard operating procedures and recreational events from degenerating into accident-producing situations.

Necessarily, two tasks must be performed if accident prevention is to become an established fact. Initially, there needs to be developed some conceptualization of what safety is, together with an undoubted commitment to its moral and legal responsibility. There must also be an assumption that environmental factors can be controlled. Through the administration of proper planning the likelihood of accidents may be reduced or avoided. This suggests that a broad safety program must be inaugurated and be the foundation upon which professionals take their own obligation. The program will be two pronged: one concerning environmental safety practices, the other an intellectual promise to instruct all those whose contacts and participation within recreational activities require a positive attitude toward personal safety. This requires recognition that recreators have a contribution to make in either maintaining personal security or not contributing to behavior that can lead to accidental injury.

THE SAFETY PROGRAM

Any safety program must be designed to set up safe conditions for various recreational experiences, to exhibit safe working conditions within the physical plant, and to stimulate safe practices and behavior of all patrons of any recreational agency. Safety planning may be initiated by executive policy, but its successful administration cannot be guaranteed unless all parties who may profit by it are concerned and actively assist in the planning. This signifies that employees of the enterprise as well as active performers and spectators should have something to say about what a safety program includes and how it will be executed.

All recreational service safety programs require acceptance by the governing authority. Whether this is a private board of directors, commission, elected or appointed officials, there will be the necessity for direct commitment to more than intermittent safety crusades or slogans. Sound safety practices may require certain construction, maintenance operations, rational policies and their dissemination, in-service training of staff, and public education. For the safety program to be effective the final responsibility for its operation should rest with the executive. Moreover, the program would be based upon psychological factors, probabilities, and elimination of injury. It then is vital that all concerned recognize one underlying truth. Individual attitude toward safety for others as well as for one's self is the foundation of accident prevention. To be sure, logical principles of organization, administration, and leadership must be effected. Research oriented to seeking out accident experience by all those who are patrons of or who supply recreational services will form an informational pool upon which safety practices can be performed. Initially, recognition of supervision as an essential part of the success of the program must be understood. As is required for any wanted end, evaluation will be valuable for determining the effectiveness of any safety program.

The Safety Officer

Recreational safety can be gained through a plan of action that comprehends the elimination of physical hazards. The promotion of policies and practices that are clearly identified, understandable, and used daily to maintain a safe environment is required. If necessary, one individual will be assigned the task of organizing the safety program and assuring its accomplishment. One reasonable goal is that all patrons and suppliers of recreational service should be responsible for their own safe conduct to the extent they have the competence for that responsibility. There will have to be an information program stressing safety skills and knowledge together with the development of positive attitudes geared for safe living. Finally, any plan must incorporate preparation for unavoidable or unexpected incidents. All personnel should have training in first aid. For greater expertise, paramedical techniques can be required.

Accident Prevention

Personnel engaged in accident prevention and the reduction of injuries must be aware that certain actions either cause accidents or avoid them. Indeed, it is specific behavior as well as environmental dangers that produce many accidents and results in severe injury. Accidents that usually occur at recreational places probably can be prevented. In order to promulgate an accident prevention program, study must be made to ascertain the variables that intersect so that remedial methods may be discovered. Not all accidents are caused by people. On occasion, chance or factors beyond human control will have been in effect. Accidents produced by natural forces probably cannot be mitigated. Human behavior will be found to be a determining element in nearly every accident. Human functions are less important without regard to particular material and intangible aspects. The factors of the activity engaged in, the time of accident occurrence, the character of social and emotional forces impinging upon the person at the time, and the physical features of the environment will all play a role. It may be stated categorically that with the typical human approach and environmental factors, an accident is likely.

Laws of probability have much to do with the function of such forces and their consequences. The nature of recreational activity and chance may combine to produce no injury at all or death. Therefore, no one may downplay the possibility for accidents as long as such potential exists. The most important areas for attention will be environmental states, poor judgment, questionable behavior, and other psychological and social forces that may have some influence upon accident causation. Underlying all of the correlations and statistical material that may be obtained in determining the cause of accidents and injuries there is the certain knowledge that blind chance also plays a role. Nonpredictability or random factors prevent the elimination of all accidents. There is an area of stability in the prediction of accidents that cannot be controlled or wiped out simply because of the combination of chance factors together with variable circumstances.

With such information as a guideline, there are valid assumption that can be made about recreational safety and the possiblities which practitioners may follow to avoid those accidents whose factors and variable conditions can be controlled. The abatement of accidents, if not their elimination, due to human error on the part of practitioners can be accomplished through the development of curative efforts that accompany any soundly conceived recreational safety program. These prophylactic methods involve a cumulative interrelationship of planning, instruction, and observation that, for the foreseeable aspect, takes the randomness out of almost all forces conducing to accident causation.

PLANNING FOR SAFETY FACILITIES AND AREAS

Planning, with application to facility construction, for example, implies the investigation of the physical environmental in all of its ramifications so that potential lessening in the range of judgmental deficiencies (by practitioners and patrons) and in the enormity of their outcomes is likely. Planning that eliminates built-in hazards or that tends to restrict some act of faulty judgment or potential human error deals with physical restraints that impede or prevent the probability of questionable behavior.

Instruction. Instruction seeks to impart skill, knowledge, values, and a sense of personal responsibility. It is an effective tool for modifying behavior and is widely used by recreationists for reducing injuries and accidents among practitioners and patrons. Instruction is concerned with motivation, changes of attitude, insight, cognition, psycho-social factors, and skill. Attitudinal orientation, perhaps one of the most significant elements to be considered insofar as accident causality and safe living are concerned, needs different methods for development or change. Such directed learning may be effected through pronouncements, publications, educational courses, and other appropriate techniques as the individual associates with recreational service enterprises. Constant and perpetual educational activities may have a remarkable effect in the modification of attitudes and behavior.

Observance of Regulations. Observance deals with conformity to rules, regulations, policy, and local, state, and federal legislation which pertain to recreational safety. For example, ordinances which support certain rules and regulations governing use of specific facilities should be enforced whenever they apply. Unless individuals recognize that noncompliance will be punished, those who break rules will continue to be thoughtless without regard for the rights of others and certainly not for their own or others' safety. Observance of all regulations relating to recreational performance, whether concerned with activity participation, *per se,* or the utilization of recreational facilities or equipment should have an immediate remedial effect. Observance tends to set limits on how people behave. People are much more amenable to proper behavior when they know that infractions carry the onus and retribution of punishment. Effective observation will have the desired effect of causing mature patrons to think about the consequences of unsafe behavior. This could prevent future accidents which arise out of nonconformity.

ACCIDENT SOURCES IN RECREATIONAL SERVICE

A sound recreational safety program is a matter of necessity if accidents and their consequences are to be avoided. However, before any broadly-based program of accident prevention is made operable, the source or sources of the problem must be examined and explained. Human behavior and environmental dangers are only superficial explanations for accidents. Other variables, including physical manifestations as well as those psychosocial forces which motivate human behavior, contribute to an almost inexhaustible supply of components which have serious implications for the health, welfare, and safety of recreators.

Ignorance. Lack of knowledge, inappropriate information, or careless behavior tends to provide people with a sense of security that is unwarranted. Armed with a false premise, individuals act in ways that not only lead them to the brink of disaster, all unknowingly, but sometimes permit them to fall prey to their own ignorance in catastrophic ways. Instead of being alert to possible danger signs, people blithly proceed on their way performing activities or acting in ways which must inevitably result in an accident and some level of injury. Even if the individual escapes serious injury or comes through unscathed, inadequate knowledge, unless corrected, is a continuing source of behavior that will eventually prove tragic. Ignorance is, indeed, bliss. The poorly informed person is much more likely to engage in activities in such fashion that only ignorance of the real situation permits enjoyment. Taking risks that would be looked upon as precarious at best and hopeless at worse is symptomatic. It is incredible to know that many people will dive into water when they cannot see bottom, do not know if any obstructions are present, and cannot know how deep the water actually is.

Inappropriate Behavior and Attitude. Carelessness, foolishness, laziness, and procrastination are characteristics that can be listed as origins of accidents when the circumstances are right. These habitual responses to stimuli are derived from attitudes and habits that are out of step with safe performance. This kind of orientation often attends reckless endangerment, i.e., performing in ways which are inappropriate for the situation. It leads people, both participants and employees, to take chances which can end sadly. Skiing downhill one last time, despite fatigue, using a trampoline without spotters, or failure to supply adequate protective clothing or gear in a scuba class, even if they are available, because it requires extra work, are examples of this attitude.

There are circumstances in which it is imperative to take risks. However, when one participates in recreational activity, it is foolish to take unnecessary and often dangerous chances. Practitioners are usually blamed for not taking timely corrective actions when a hazardous condition has been called to their attention. This can be a result of desultory work performance, indolence, or inability to decide. Any one of these unsafe actions may put someone in jeopardy. Perhaps recreational center entrance doors have been designed for maximum visibility by the installation of glass doors and adjacent glass panels. It is possible that thoughtless individuals will either walk or run through the glass partitions, particularly if they are rushing. Such persons will not be aware of any danger until they come in forceful contact with the glass. The recreationist can probably remove this hazard by having the glass etched in such a manner so as to call attention to its existence, by substituting panels of glass brick, or attaching some attention-getting device to the door. However, it is sometimes noted that practitioners will procrastinate about having the glass entryway altered even though he or she recognized the potential for an accident. This habitual practice will continue until someone is seriously injured or property is damaged.

Dangerous Behavior. Improper behavior with regard to situations produces at least 90% of all accidents that take place at recreational facilities. For some people, the controlled violence of handball has given way to the greater risks of racquetball, squash, or jai alai. In the latter activities the hand and arm levers have been augmented by high powered extensions that send an object many times faster than the hand and arm alone could. Still, many people persist in playing at close quarters without proper protective equipment such as safety glasses if not helmets. More than one person has been badly hurt when hard hit balls come in contact with vulnerable parts of the body. In fact, skull fractures, dislocations, blindness, and other injuries have been recorded in court games. Although the games have changed considerably, the players' response has not acknowledged the increased risks involved.

Scuba diving without a partner, lack of attention when utilizing machines or chemicals, not waiting until the previous user has finished his or her trip down a slide, inadvertent placement of fingers under a seesaw, ice skating too fast for crowded prevailing conditions are all examples of unsatisfactory behavior that emphasizes lack of precaution and inattention to conditions which violate normally acceptable standards of conduct.

Poor Maintenance Practices. One of the more unsuspected forms of danger to the recreator is the incidence of poorly carried out maintenance practices. The recreator believes that the recreational area is safe. Almost every participant thinks that ball fields, running tracks, waterways, or beaches have been carefully cleaned of debris and other obvious hazardous material. To a great extent this is true. However, there are a few instances where maintenance (the cleaning and repairing of physical facilities and grounds) has not been performed at all or so inadequately that a dangerous condition is created. Even when organizational manuals designate that certain places must be cleared of debris, chuckholes filled in, grass mowed, and other routine maintenance carried out—such activities are not undertaken. The result is injury to some participant.

Limited Performing Skills. Accidents often occur because individuals perform before they have gained the necessary skills. Many injuries result from attempts to perform difficult activities, for example, when an unskilled person attempts a complex movement beyond his or her capacity. Drowning victims are likely to be inadequate swimmers who have attempted something difficult, such as trying to get across a riptide or crosscurrent or have been caught in an undertow without understanding what they must do or not having the stamina and acquatic skills required. Novice skiers, divers, bicyclers, skaters, and others with minimal skills may try activities which are beyond their ability with dire consequences.

Lack of skill is only one of many factors which can reduce an individual's capacity to perform. Fatigue, illness, emotional instability, or the use of alcohol and drugs can undercut an individual's skill to the extent that what would usually be well within his or her level of performance becomes difficult thereby placing that person in jeopardy. Under the stress of extreme emotionality, intoxication, or drug-induced euphoria an individual may lose rationality and take foolish chances. Some people, somewhat immature it is granted, might act on a dare or seek attention by performing a complex stunt with injurious results.

Environmental Hazards. Of all the resources readily available none are more attractive than outdoor recreational places. But it is particularly because recreational areas are attractive that they also present a clear and present danger to potential users. The great outdoors attracts millions of people each year. An abundance of natural hazards awaits the uninformed. Activities such as mountain climbing, spelunking (cave exploration), white-water canoeing and kayaking, survival camping, and other experiences of similar types beckon the unwary. To natural perils are added man-made dangers from abandoned pits, open mine shafts, wells, land that has been stripped of ground cover or earth-retaining propensity as a result of heavy logging so that land slippage occurs, and other artificial traps which by their very existence add excitement to the prospect of participation.

Despite natural hazards, there is every prospect that recreators are injured most frequently because they do not pay attention to their surroundings and behave in ways which are inconsistent with safe living. To the environmental perils of noxious weed poisoning, animal mauling, bee stings, snake bites, falling off precipices, or other equally dangerous possibilities, entrepreneurs and recreationists have developed artificial lures for getting the recreator to the recreational facility. Thus, moguls are developed on ski slopes, unfenced walkways are laid right up to boiling natural springs, and the construction of ocean beaches may change tidal currents so that undertows or riptides are produced. All of these artificial additions simply add to natural hazards. It is only after a serious accident, and then under the pressure of bad publicity or a tireless nemesis that artificial barriers or hazards are taken away. With a logically developed safety program many hazards in the natural environment can be eliminated. When accidents occur they are almost always related to the fact that most people fail to conduct themselves properly or they act in ways that practically assure their injury or death.

Certainly, accidents can be expected in natural environments, particularly when participants do not appreciate the hazards that exist and have inadequate knowledge to avert any dangers which natural surroundings may have for them. But people have the ability to control the conditions which might affect them thereby reducing the potential for accidents to happen. Good planning can insure that safety features are part of a recreational site, practice can enable the individual to participate at a level which is well within the range of his or her ability, and conformity to rational views as well as regulations enacted to prevent misfortune from striking can be a force for the promotion of safety in recreational activities. In all of these situations, one must learn how to avoid both inappropriate behavior as well as environmental perils.

Variable Sources of Accidents. Often accidents appear to have multiple causes. In many instances, victims of accidents, by exercising a little effort could have prevented the incident. Many reasons may be raised to explain the possibilities. Poor work habits, procrastination, ignorance, emotionality, preoccupation, or laziness are only a few of the many possibilities that combine to become the source of an accident.

Supervision. In some instances, lack of supervision becomes a typical cause for accidents. Despite educational programs, there are a variety of situations where carelessness or the absence of supervision may be the cause of accidents. No matter how well educated the individual is, there are activities which require close supervision if risks of injury are to be avoided. As participants attain greater skills and more knowledge about safe living, many activities that would normally require supervision can have such oversight reduced. Of course, there are some activities which will always require direct supervision regardless of performer skill and knowledge. Failure to provide this kind of supervision is negligence.

Negligence. Failure to act in a reasonable and prudent manner, that is, performing in ways that contribute to personal injury, becomes an essential feature in the cause of recreationally-inspired accidents. Sometimes it is not the negligence of authorities, but rather the personal negligence of the individual who will not take responsibility for actions. Unless the individual is forced to face the need for being responsible for behavior that proves incautious or absolutely dangerous, then even the best safety program is undermined.

Poor attitudes, unsafe habits, lack of skill or knowledge may all contribute to accident occurrence. Any of these factors may be the culprit, but frequently several of these variables operate simultaneously. If individuals did not habitually take risks with their life and safety, there would be less chance that they would attempt to perform activities that clearly require skill levels far above their present capacity. They would not perform with poor information about the inherent risks accompanying particular activities. Because there are built-in risks in many recreational activities, it is only the well-informed person who can make valid judgments as to whether the assumption of risk is either worthwhile or the degree of risk is minimized or eliminated due to his or her level of skill.

While it is not always possible to identify the specific attitude, skill deficiency, or characteristic responsible for an accident, every possible inclination should be investigated to determine the traits that have a tendency for exacerbating personal susceptibility to accidents. Counseling efforts may then be used to assist people in recognizing and mastering the weaknesses that endanger them.

3
Foundations for Recreational Safety

Safe living does not suggest the elimination of all activities that can be potentially hazardous. The desire to participate with some risk motivates some people performing recreational activities. Even a superficial look at the causes of accidents points to techniques for preventing their occurrence. The approach that will best satisfy the requirements in modern life is educating people to modify their customary ways of behaving. It also means instruction so that people can obtain the information, skill, and understanding necessary for associated attitudinal change. When knowledge of safe living is supplied and internalized, people may be more likely to perform in ways that negate environmental dangers and inherent risk to be encountered in recreational experiences.

Safety Education. It is a moral responsibility of recreational service agencies to develop safety programs which benefit all who participate within the agency. It is futile to offer information without being sure that such knowledge is acquired and practiced. Unless people are stimulated to develop and practice resistive skills, until they habitually adhere to well-known and specific safety principles, they will not have learned to live safely. the safety education program should motivate every person to protect him or herself from potential danger in all situations containing both recognizable and unfamiliar dangers.

Personal Responsibility. A safety program has one great disadvantage. It is trying to do remedial work with individuals whose personality traits and emotional needs are set. Attempting to change habits and attitudes is a huge task and may not always be successful. Nevertheless, the recreational service agency must make the effort. The optimum place to initiate safety instruction is with young children. Begun at an age when attitudes and personality are still relatively plastic, instructional methods may be oriented to obtain the goals of safe living. The young need clear, direct information with which to acquire self-understanding, self-control, and outlets for acceptable self-expression. It is important that safety education be based upon a group model as the technique for instilling desirable values. Any aspect of personal adjustment will more nearly be acceptable to the child when the peer group shows itself to favor safety practices and condemns foolhardy behaviors.

Young people usually obtain greatest satisfaction from the admiration of their peers; probably more so than from parents or other adults. If the safety program can teach a sense of responsibility in young people, these attitudes, habits, and knowledge will pervade all of their contacts and may prevent the formation of negative traits or daredevil behaviors that might end in injury or death. No safety education program will be able to overcome inappropriate attitudes and poor performance habits. It is possible that some individuals might be helped to recognize their own vulnerability and proneness to accidents. However, this is a time consuming process. The safety education program must, nevertheless, work with all those who use the recreational service agency. Applied effort may assist individuals in learning how to protect themselves so that they are not unnecessarily exposed to environmental hazards or their own innate tendency for making poor performance judgments. If such individuals can learn to think defensively they may have the potential for finally determining just what it is that causes them to incur personal loss through accidents.

Safety education cannot be only the publication of rules and regulations concerned with appropriate conduct. A well-conceived program will consist of identifying environmental hazards, motivating proper conduct for maximum enjoyment and personal satisfaction, and developing the kinds of performance habits and attitudes that stress safety. Recreational safety should be a basic function of all organizations that deal with the provision of recreational service delivery. It can only serve to help the agency and those who seek its benefits through participation or observation.

BEHAVIORAL PATTERNS

Individuals differ widely in physical and mental ability. Intelligence should play some role in the avoidance of accidents. Coordination, flexibility, strength, and speed should enable those who possess them to avoid accidents more often than those who are not as blessed. However, physical condition is not the sole answer for accident prevention. Motivation is the most significant factor. Although intelligence and good physical condition can affect the severity and number of accidents a person has, behavioral responses tend to influence how and whether an individual will be vulnerable to environmental hazards and will make personal adjustment to critical situations which call for speed of reaction if injury is to be avoided.

Perception. Sensitivity to the physical environment is important because it permits the individual who confronts the environment to consider what will be potential hazards. Awareness of one's environment plays a real role in establishing a sense of safe and unsafe situations and acting accordingly. Lifeguards, for example, are required to observe the way in which swimmers and divers behave. Lifeguards with developed perceptions can usually anticipate those persons whose actions are such that they will come to grief in the water. By noting these individuals and calling attention to their actions the lifeguard may prevent accidents. Expertness in any recreational activity allows the recreator to perceive certain actual or potential dangers in time to avoid them.

Motivation. How to be safe in recreational situations may be taught and learned. Generally, interest may be stimulated and sustained through evoking one or more fundamental drives. Of particular value are:

1. An appeal to survival: Perhaps the most compelling of all drives is that of self-preservation. Thus, stress should be laid upon the damage to the individual rather than upon the cause as such. A variety to media may be utilized to underscore the seriousness of such injuries which arise from accidents. Care must be used so that negativism is not emphasized to the exclusion of the real message, i.e., that individuals have a need to be cautious when participating in recreational activities. Accentuation of caution, rather than fear of injury must be the premise on which this aspect is founded.
2. Extrinsic reward: All ages will respond to an appeal that is based upon some form of recognition or reward. Reward for most will be in man-hours saved, medical bills which do not have to be paid, insurance premiums which are not raised, and other monetary inducements. For younger persons there may be appointment to some advisory committee which is a much sought after honor. It is also possible that other values may be recommended. An annual banquet, public acknowledgement, values may be recommended. An annual banquet, public acknowledgement, and other tribute may serve to motivate safe conduct.
3. Group dynamics: Peer pressure and interpersonal relationships derived from belonging to a group may encourage acceptance of safety habits in recreational activities. The whole idea of fair play, rule abidement, and the generation of loyalty to an identifiable group may serve as a promotor of safety.
4. Implication: The use of implication is necessary to arouse feelings of identification with the idea being presented. It is a subtle form of flattery in that it indicates to those receiving the message that they are important to the development of some movement or practice. It conveys that there is an association between the listener and his or her own values and those which are being promulgated. Those who listen tend to identify themselves with the thoughts that are offered and convince themselves that there is something worthwhile to be gained by joining in and exhibiting the practices which are being called for. Implication promotes affinity. It encourages commonality and stimulates individuals to adopt ideas, attitudes, and it is hoped, safe actions when participating in recreational events.
5. Rational persuasion: An appeal to reason is based upon compiling precise, factual information, and then transmitting the facts of the situation in such a manner that the outcome is inevitably inclined toward the cause which is being espoused. In order to reach this point of

irrefutable logic, investigation of all alternative courses of action must be undertaken so that their consequences may be foreseen. This requires the collection and examination of detailed information relating to the concept of safety practices in recreational settings. Pertinent data must then be analyzed as it concerns the problem of overcoming inertia, apathy, poor attitude, faulty habits, and errors of judgment. The recreationist will have to refine the material which he/she has gathered for the most clear, comprehensive, and comprehensible presentation which can be made. Thorough study of possible objections to safety concepts will also determine the probable means for undermining such objections. Enhanced with this knowledge, the recreationist is prepared to offer a rational frame of reference on the issues. Logical persuasion is a direct appeal to those who will listen by means of public speaking, debating, literature dissemination, and publicity through the mass means of communication. In this instance, however, it is primarily directed toward recreational patrons and users of facilities or equipment, rather than toward a mass public. The use of facts and figures designed to appeal to the senses has invariably proved valuable when accurately utilized.

The appeal to reason is a significant factor in obtaining attention and interest. Those who hear or see the message, if they have any intelligence at all, must perceive it to their own advantage to accept and act upon such a persuasive argument.

6. Repetition: Repeated pronoucement dealing with the concepts or facts concerning recreational safety are necessary if such information is to be impressed upon others. The validity and reliability of this technique has bee illustrated by its constant employment over decades. Educators have long used repetition of facts to make students relate particular bits of knowledge to other fragments. Children, for example, first learn their language and the social order from constant familiarization with the same idea before they are able either to communicate intelligibly or to recognize those about them. It is drill and incessant practice that may determine the acquisition of habit patterns and particular ideas. Since the recreational service practitioner deals with a "captive" audience (i.e., only those who actually use facilities or participate in programs), confronting the client with the same safety rules, regulations, and performance standards carries the probability that they may eventually be assimilated and become part of the behavioral pattern.

   Repetition should not be thought of as dull or negative methods whereby specific information is transmitted to a select audience. The information delivered can be packaged and disseminated in ways that are very attractive, stimulating, and of varied intensity so that they do not become merely irritating. Repetition, which means continual reiteration in various modes, is clearly necessary. The presentation of an idea which is unfamiliar or quite new to some should be given precisely. The idea must then be explained in some detail, the presenter adding embellishment, color, and emphasis as the information is offered. After the exposition has been stated, the idea should be repeated in varied form or language. The idea, if it is at all understandable, has a sound probability that it will be accepted by those who hear or see it.

7. Emotionalism: Directing ideas toward the emotions is relatively easy because the instigator needs only to appeal to the basic fears, insecurities, or ignorance of those who are swayed by such tactics. However, this approach is difficult to control. Any emotional identification must, therefore, be of a positive type, i.e., dealing with altruistic, familial, or personal reputation positions. For example, an appeal for the concern of, "those you leave behind," or "those who must care for you in the event of serious injury," can be an effective thrust. Additionally, such appeals can be made to the individual on the basis of health care costs, higher taxes, higher insurance rates, and other inflationary outlays which directly stem from accidents and injuries. Finally, an appeal can be made to fear on the basis of death, disfigurement, crippling injuries, and the pain which accompanies the latter three consequences. Fear or desire for profit plays a large part in influencing people through emotionalism. Emotional behavior is of short duration, however; it must be periodically restimulated if the desired response is to be continually elicited. Without a systematic stress upon emotional issues, the response to such an appeal soon loses its impact.
8. Ego-involvement: Initiating action toward a desired objective requires involvement of the target audience in some manner so that they may identify with the ideas, stated aims, or practices which are being tendered. In order to do this, potential victims of unsafe behavior must be allowed, even stimulated, to participate in the development of plans, policies, procedures, and objectives for safe living within recreational environments. As participating members of a group enterprise, individuals are more likely to take action. When individuals feel that they have been made part of a group's effort and that their presence contributes directly to the success of the project at hand, they will be encouraged to move in a direction that is satisfying to them. All goals must have a personal appeal for individuals so that they may identify themselves with the goal and thereby seek to achieve it.

RECREATIONAL AGENCY OBJECTIVES

In the field of recreational service, the objectives of recreational safety define the type of program and information to be presented to and for the public. Programs cannot be planned merely for the sake of having them. They must be developed with an eye toward meeting the needs of people whom the agency serves. Satisfaction of needs, in this instance, really means the development of attitudes and habits which are complementary to avoiding injury and being active in a safe and satisfying way. Activating a drive for recreational safety is not all that difficult. If potential participants can be made to understand that it is to their benefit, as well as to that of the community which the agency represents, to comply with safety practices as promoted by the system, then all will probably be well. When individuals understand that safety, competent supervision, healthful recreational experiences, and personal satisfaction are all tied together, they will more readily identify with the need for such a program. Once this identification is established, action often follows.

The entire function of directed action hinges upon motivational elements in human behavior. Goal motivation has to do with threats to the individual, to his or her ego concept, or to basic needs. Goal objects have meaning for the individual in terms of intrinsic values and symbolic values. Thus, the goal object may not only represent economic gain or aesthetic, cultural, social, educational, or physical enhancement but it may also represent mastery, prestige, affection, reputation, or the manifestations of psycho-physical needs. When the goal can be related to some or many of these factors, and the individuals making up the potential following can be persuaded of the fact that unless they act upon the soundness of the idea or upon a particular plan the goal will be lost or they may be deprived of whatever it is they consider to be of value, action will most usually accrue. Where the goal is important to the individual, the loss or threat of loss by lack of action will bring about the desired participation.

RECREATIONAL AGENCY SAFETY INSTRUCTION

The difficulty of changing behavior, so that reduction of unsafe acts and breaches of common sense practices will be accomplished, is an important consideration. Even though children are subject to parental values in the home and may learn safe living, the instruction of safety is a primary responsibility of organizations established to supply recreational experiences. Unless the recreational service agency is prepared to perform this instructional change, a high number of unsafe activities at recreational places will become common.

Safety education should start with the very youngest children who are found at the various activities sponsored by recreational agencies. Operations may be organized by schools, private or sectarian agencies, or public recreational service systems. The responsibility for promoting safe habits remains with the agency. As the individual matures, there should be direct teaching of skills, knowledge, and attitudes. Children must learn about unsafe practices such as jumping on and off moving swings, following another too closely down a slide, or diving or jumping into water about which little is known. Similarly, high school age youth must learn about safety practices, rules, regulations, and policies, as well as skills. Supporting all of this instruction is the development of sound attitudes. Education for safe recreational living requires expert counseling and teaching.

PRINCIPLES OF RECREATIONAL SAFETY

Safety hazards in the recreational environment are constantly increasing. This plus the higher incidence of suits arising from allegations of negligence or other liability-associated conditions necessitates a well-planned safety program. Surely other agencies, besides those dealing with recreational service, will also be conducting their own teaching and informational campaigns, but insofar as safety promotion in recreational situations is concerned, the primary responsibility falls to the department or organization most directly involved. Although there is increasing recognition that training in accident prevention will reduce the number of injuries that occur on recreational facilities and save lives as well, there is some question as to what should be included within the safety program initiated by organizations providing recreational services. The following basic principles may serve as a reasonable starting point for planning a recreational safety program:

1. There are numerous dangers inherent in recreational activity and these make it imperative that sound safety practices and programs become a basic part of the agency's defense against negligence or inept performance.
2. A recreational safety program should serve the general aims of recreational service, i.e., the development of individual growth, satisfaction, skill, enjoyment, and ethical behavior.
3. All recreationists, on every level, should assume leadership in the promotion of safety practices which should color every aspect of the recreational program and its physical plant, and should, by their own attitudes and habits, epitomize optimum safety practices.
4. By offering day-to-day experiences in safe recreational participation, the program should guide all participants in becoming aware of and acquiring knowledge which will help in the development of, or reinforcement of, desirable habits and attitudes that will support them in all recreational environments throughout the life span.
5. The recreational safety program should be of a positive, not a negative type. It should encourage wholesome responses without instilling anxiety or creating an over-cautious or timid person. At the same time, the recreationist should make sure that participants know the difference between courage and stupidity.
6. Recreational safety education should develop the concept of social awareness among its adherents as well as social citizenship, personal responsibility and the value of human life and dignity.
7. The program should emphasize the most relevant problems of the group, but each facet of program activity should receive an equal exploration for logical progression to be made.
8. The individual participant should be the starting point and the focus of the recreational safety program.
9. Even while the recreational service agency is developing its own

response to safety questions and issues, it should coordinate its efforts with those of other community agencies in an attempt to complement and supplement the entire range of life behaviors which have a bearing on safe living.

10. The objectives of the safety program will apply to the emotional, social, intellectual, and physical needs of individuals involved.
11. Cooperation and coordination with all segments of the community in the promulgation of recreational safety is fundamental to the success of any safety program.
12. The essential factor to the conclusive success of the recreational service safety program is the recreationist on the line. The program will never be any better than is the competence and effectiveness of those practitioners who are actually responsible for the development, initiation, instruction, and evaluation of the program.
13. Of supreme importance is that the recreational environment is such that it can contribute to the desirable individual habits and performances of safe practice which have been offered throughout the patron's contact with the agency.
14. The recreational service safety program should be the subject of continuous evaluation. Formative and summative techniques of evaluation will be worked out and applied so that improvement of the program is always of highest priority.
15. Recreational service safety records, reports, investigations, and studies should be maintained for easy access and use by appropriate persons.
16. Recreational safety is based upon social, physical, and psychological aspects of accident and injury prevention.
17. Procedures for recreational personnel to report the existence of hazardous conditions and unsafe practices whenever they are observed will do much to offset potential dangers and institute corrective measures into the safety program.
18. The recreational service agency must devise a plan in which routine inspection of the entire physical plant, throughout the system, is performed periodically. A search for hazards and dangerous conditions, whether within a building or in the extensive grounds of the agency, would be a regular practice of the periodic inspection procedure.
19. The elimination of or repair of any defects or unsatisfactory supplies, materials, or equipment used by agency personnel and the clients of the agency would probably reduce settings for accidents to occur.
20. Routine conferences of all recreational personnel to assess the agency accident experience and devise techniques to prevent accidents should be systematized.
21. Rules, regulations, and ordinances must be developed and enforced concerning such diverse factors as traffic flow, either pedestrian or vehicular, use of facilities, behavioral expectations, and the elimination of certain behaviors or activities which are of such nature as to be the cause of accidents.

22. Competent supervision, either of the direct of general type, is to be provided for all recreational activities which by reason and prudence would require it.
23. Investigation of all accidents which occur throughout the recreational service system or organization should be carried out immediately.
24. An accident-reporting system and analysis procedure which would be followed by all personnel throughout the system should be activated as soon as the safety program is in place.
25. The active involvement of all recreational service personnel within the safety program so that appropriate information, warnings, and other precautionary activities are undertaken for the health, safety, and continuous protection of all those who come in contact with the recreational service system is mandatory.

These principles suggest the function of a recreational service safety program. However, no attempt is made here to overlook the persistent problems that affect every recreational service agency.

It has never been satisfactory only to transmit information about safe practice or behavior. Recreational agencies have been content to play a defensive role by passively issuing warnings. That role has proved to be logically inconsistent with the responsibility which recreational service agencies have in modern society. Recreational safety requires an aggressive posture. It is one that thrusts itself into the vision and attention of those who want to participate in any way. Therefore, only transmitting information is not effective standard procedure. The function of promoting safe behavior at recreational places requires active involvement in the direct instruction and supervision of people who make up the constituency of the enterprise.

Recreational service agencies are confronted by the need to fulfill certain responsibilities which have been placed upon them by legal mandate and public expectation. Recreational service agencies must do whatever is necessary to inform people about safety attitudes and practices. If recreators accept the knowledge and modify their ways from dangerous to wholesome, there will be mutual benefit. To the extent that accidents are reduced and injuries minimized or eliminated the safety program will have done its job. Sensitivity to environmental hazards as well as to actions which are unsafe is the best method for combating the tragic accidents which daily remind us of the indispensable need for effective safety programs in the recreational service field.

4
Establishment of Recreational Safety Standards

A standard may be defined as something used by common agreement to determine whether or not an object or behavior is as it should be. Standards are generally thought to be a type or example that has been established by usage and custom that serves as a pattern to be followed or a criterion. Finally, standards have been described as a level of excellence in performance or as a thing which is seen as a measure of adequacy or a goal to be reached. Standards are a level of performance below which effort is viewed as inadquate. Standards are the floor of performance and should not be considered as the ultimate achievement. In truth, no standards for recreational safety have either been offered nor have won widespread acceptance when such are articulated. A number of statements have been put forward as estimates or suggestions based upon empirical evidence and either good judgment or common sense. In fact, some of these concerning spaces and facilities have become the basis for standards because they are not out of line with those statements expressed generally by many authorities.

THE DERIVATION OF STANDARDS

In an interdependent mass social system, standards serve a variety of objectives. They become the basis for maintaining a safe environment and indicate just what it is that is required for competent performance. Standards indicate how well a recreational service agency is operating and whether or not its practices are safe. Standards prevent agencies from promoting activities or administering facilities which tend to be hazardous to those who participate or spectate. Standards create a safe recreational environment for broadest use of recreational services of all kinds. Standards serve both the peculiar needs of the private sector by making goods and services conform to a recognized level of achievement which militates against shoddy workmanship, poor advice, or incompetent counseling, and the more public necessities of people as the patrons of public sector resources.

The need for standards in any field is obvious but when it comes to the safety of people it assumes even more significant proportions. Fundamentally, standards exist to protect those who patronize agencies which supply services of a recreational nature or goods which can be used for recreational purposes. Sometimes litigation is necessary to create standards, but this has not been forthcoming as it concerns the field of recreational service, except that there are a variety of laws promulgated which, when taken in toto, tend to exert some pressure for standarization even if only in a peripheral manner. The development of standards has been left to the voluntary efforts of the associations which enlist the practitioners of the field and a generalization of performance levels which appear to have much in common with standards.

Standards also serve the public interest by stimulating competition among those who purvey goods and services. For example, if it is standard for a ski rental agency or a commercial ski shop to fit the ski, boot, and binding to each individual, then it is reasonable to assume that those who do not perform this service may be risking litigation if something should go amiss with the equipment. Additionally, patrons of such organizations will surely seek out those companies and/or sellers who do perform the service, thereby maintaining the standard generally acceptable to the industry. Whenever standards omit rather than include, there is an obvious bias for or against a certain product or the way in which a service is dispensed. If standards do not exist when there is a clear public need to save lives or reduce the risk of accidental injuries, there is the expectation that legislation will be forthcoming and that the public will be involved.

The field of recreational service, and by extension, those organizations which provide the goods and services directly associated with participation in recreational activities, should attempt to define the objective of a standard as well as establishing the process for developing standards. Once there is a need for a standard, the process indicates what is to be quantified and ordered. Because the introduction of standards for any field is a process that combines the expertise of practitioners and the advice of those whom the standards will effect, standards-making bodies must serve the public interest by educating the public about the need for standards as well as offering information concerning the nature, scope, purpose, and importance of standards in preventing accidents and promoting safety within the recreational environment.

In order to meet public interest needs and satisfy the criterion of safeguarding the public from incompetent practitioner behavior, inadequately performed services, or shoddy products each professional field should have a designated standards-making group undertake an investigative study of current procedures and practices and revise them to protect patrons under the following tests:

1. A standards-developing committee should be formed from among those organizations that organize and administer recreational services, those

who produce and distribute the supplies, materials, and equipment for recreational usage, those who use and participate in organized recreational experiences, and those legislative bodies whose interests reflect a universal view of the community without bias toward any group or segment operating in the field.

2. A public process should be implemented with far-ranging participation from those who will be greatly helped by the standards as well as those who will eventually have to comply with them. Fruitful attempts should be made to enlist only the most competent practitioners, who will serve as representatives of agencies concerned.
3. The outcome of the standards development process should be open to all interested persons. Any standards which are proposed should receive the widest dissemination possible, including the reasons for the setting of such standards, the desirability of the standards, and how they can be achieved.
4. It is the responsibility of professionals and their organization to develop standards dealing with the greatest cause of concern and prepare procedures for assessing the competence of those who will have to comply with the standards as they become accepted in practice.
5. It is incumbent upon professional associations to cause standards of practice to be established, published, understood, and evaluated so that the patron will be the beneficiary and the agency will have acquitted itself of any negligent act brought about by noncompliance with a commonly accepted standard applicable to the field.

Voluntary standards, as defined and determined by professional practitioner associations, tend to become mandatory with the force of law to undergird them because they are seen as that degree of care necessary for the safety of participants. Thus, even without legislation, the standards developed by discussion and agreement become enforceable through litigation or threats of litigation. For these reasons, it is required to have a process sufficient for developing them privately. If the standard has been offered and developed carefully, it is likely that the courts will look upon it with favor and indicate the need for compliance. In the absence of specific legislation that compels compliance, as for example, the proposed Camp Safety Law, professional association standard making may be construed as enforceable if the benefits to the public are of such magnitude that they may not be easily discarded without jeopardizing those persons who participate in the offerings of agencies that represent the public, private and quasi-public sectors of society.

For the present, legislation does not prescribe how any recreational service agency shall conduct its operation in terms of the safety of participants or observers. It merely indicates that agencies can or will operate certain facilities for the public good. While there is still time, the professional association, together with other interested parties should determine the purpose of standards and describe them accurately. Surely, no one can believe that recreational service agencies want to damage property or injure people in the normal course of operations. In fact, there are compelling reasons for an opposite conviction to be in place. Among the fundamental principles upon which the field of recreational service is founded is the ideal that people are entitled to recreational environments as safe as they can be within the constraints of the inherent risk of activities. While recreational activities contain risk, there is the belief that no organization or its agents should increase the hazard of activity performance through negligence, incompetence, ignorance, or unconcern for the safety of the respective constituency. No court would hold that voluntarily accepted standards, which exclude unsafe acts on the part of organizations supplying recreational services to the public, should not become the basis for determing whether or not an agency had indeed lived up to the degree of responsibility it accepted when organizing and administering recreational services. With voluntary standards enlightened self-interest, if not public opinion, will compel the local agency to conform to whatever standards are published by the field itself.

When there are standards commonly in use, but these are not adhered to and the public suffers in consequence, then a more stringent procedure must be found so that appropriate steps will be taken to legislate enforcement. Cognately, if privately developed standards fail to achieve the objective for which they are established, then some logical process should be instituted by which standards can be improved voluntarily. If such upgrading is not undertaken, then legislation may be required.

Formulating Standards

A standard is a detailed description designed to serve as a model for behavior or as a measure of kind, number, quality, or achievement which is to be reiterated in practice. Standards develop from custom or planning. Traditional ways of doing things, habitual methods of performance, or long usage tends to designate standard operating procedures. However, changing times, different needs, and a more liberal interpretation of citizen rights may require the modification of such standards. When this occurs, another developmental process is enacted. This requires a systematic examination of the needs, agency objectives, costs, and personnel involved and the formulation of well-conceived and feasible methods by which the mutual self-protection of the agency and the public can be gained. In planning for the promotion of safer services, the formulation of standards undergoes the scrutiny of behavioral analysis, property and equipment evaluation, and a methodological process by which maximized security for participants in recreational settings can be achieved. In order to accomplish this task, a detailed statement of requirements is written. Thus, by reducing the desired conforming behaviors, actions, or physical property descriptions to writing, the agency specifies what is necessary and satisfactory for performance on a continuing basis. This offers a tremendous saving of time, money, and effort since the process does not have to be repeated interminably. Once derived by rational means, the written statement becomes the guide by which the agency will operate.

The standard tells, in no uncertain terms, precisely what it is that is wanted insofar as behavior, goods, or services are concerned. To this end the standard has a communications function. By widely disseminating the information contained in the standard, both internally within the agency and externally to the general public at large, the organization is in the best possible position for determining whether or not operations and behaviors are in conformity with the requirements of the written standard. Having served its communications function, the standard now serves as an example for distinguishing between things that are suitable and things that are inappropriate insofar as the standard applies.

In either instance, whether as communication or as example, the standard should be so thorough and intelligible that it can be understood by all without further clarification. Those with the responsibility for the formulation of standards should always attempt to write in terms of specific quantitative measures or precise behavioral descriptions which may not be construed in ways that are inadequate or unacceptable. When such written descriptions defy facile expression, it will be necessary for the agency to avail itself of some prototype or case in point to serve as a foundation for comparison. Those who formulate standards should always try to discover the bases of measurement whenever it is possible to do so. In addition it will also be necessary to specify the kinds of behavior that are acceptable by those who are employed by the organization as well as those who wish to participate in agency sponsored activities. This detailed procedure cannot be successfully undertaken without required research.

Research as a Basis for Standards

The need to collect information and facts about diverse aspects relating to recreational service operations gives rise to the research function. Particularly is this true when recreationists disagree on how, what, when, where, or why specific things, services, or facilities must be processed, organized, or administered. Opinions should not be the basis for standards. In too many cases this is exactly what has happened in consequence of habit, tradition, or customary ways of doing things or acting. Without a factual substructure to support the opinion, one way is as good as another. However, opinions may supply inadequate bases for formulation of standards. Therefore, the generation of factual evidence requires research unhampered by bias or temporization.

Vigorous objective inquiry into the factors and conditions on which recommendations can be made to design standards for the satisfaction of the field's multivarious needs is complementary. Standardization is an important outcome of research. As investigations are made that deal with behavioral objectives, space sufficiency, equipment quality, and other goods and/or services, revisions of standards can be developed. Standard making that meets contemporary requirements should be formulated only on the basis of controlled experimentation, where such is possible, or on empirical evidence. In the development of new standards or the revision of old ones, those who perform the research will be in the most advantageous position to extract from scientific methods recommendations that will be immediately useful to those who need them for optimum practice. Those criteria will undergo modification as continuing research reveals new information that reflects changing conditions or the necessity for looking at current information in a new light.

Simplification, Routinization, and Standard Development

Simplicity is the method of stripping away superfluous ideas and subtlety, and devising a form or process that is straightforward, natural, and without affectation. Simplification is the result of problem analysis followed by the elimination of excessive elaboration. The outcome of simplification is the selection of the desired statement which can then be translated into practice and enforced. The consequence of simplification is the production of a standard.

Routinization is the regularization of a technique or procedure. It is associated with habitual ways for getting things done. Routine is introduced into the standard-making process by devising logical sequences of action in order to obtain some result consistent with the agency's aims and objectives. Routine is not merely the timeworn and stagnating practice of performing some function the way it has always been done just to maintain the status quo. Far from it. Routine should be regarded as the carefully planned, investigated, and tested method for achieving some end in view. Routine actually indicates what is to be done, where something is to be done, by whom it is to be undertaken, how something is to be accomplished, and what the expectations are once routine is completed. In short, through the perceptions of work simplification and routine procedures the outlines of standardization begin to emerge. It is only when excesses are eliminated and the technical proficiencies of the agency are coordinated and employed to their fullest utilization that standards become realized.

Regularized procedures, written and specified, reduce the element of uncertainty and thus unpleasant surprises that can cause waste in time, money, and manpower. Routine enables a degree of accurate prediction to be made. It omits the likelihood of faulty assumptions and misadventures when and if routines are followed. This is not to imply that recreational environments are unchanging and therefore require inflexible regulations. By no means. Rather, routine suggests that conformity to tested practices will produce a climate that is conducive to optimum performance and safety.

Finally, simplification and routine prevent deviation from desired practices.

They neatly circumscribe the type of behavior that is appropriate for the occasion, signify the kind of physical plant necessary for maximizing recreational experience safely, and specify the quality of supplies, materials, and equipment for the health, welfare, and safety of the performer. Any standard which is developed by the process of planning, analysis, appraisal, and examination should promote the achievement of the following insofar as safety is concerned:

1. The behaviors which are called for are the same for everybody involved.
2. There is replication of behavior and environment.
3. The situation is predictable and negates misfeasance and uncontrolled behavior in a given situation where certain actions are required.
4. The standard is applicable in program operation because it may be used to cause the desired outcome with a substantial level of confidence that the consequences will be as forecast.

A Practical Approach to Formulating Standards

Recreational service agencies that want to initiate a safety standards program will have to begin with a clear declaration of purpose as well as an intelligible definition of standards. What is really desired is a system that will perpetuate and improve reliability and, simultaneously, increase safety effectiveness and thereby productivity. All of this has a way of decreasing costs. When a program of safety standards is in effect, little in the way of man-hours lost by virtue of unsafe working conditions or on-the-job or job-related accidents and injuries will occur, and a great deal of money and time will be saved by preventing accidents and concomitant injuries to patrons. In this latter area alone, great savings may be anticipated from not having to defend against litigations. Even if a case is won, or it does not run its course in the courts, much money has to be spent in gathering evidence, calling in expert witnesses, if such are needed, and in other expenditures that might not otherwise have to be made. Of course, the greatest saving will occur if taxpayers' money does not have to be spent when juries return verdicts against the recreational service agency. If negligence or other liability-invoking functions can be proved against the agency, thousands and even millions of dollars will have been diverted from the public treasury to redress injuries suffered by plaintiff. Thus, safety standards and their adherence can be a huge cost/benefit plus for the agency. Really, the only way to lower costs as the system operates is through reliability. Standards produce reliability.

To assure that the standards formulation program will be of significance and generate maximum effectiveness, the following priorities should be settled as the program is developed:

1. The need for a clear, precise, and readily understood language. Many recurring problems are associated with semantic difficulties and unclear transmission or reception of orders, commands, or policy. The best

communication is the easiest exchange of ideas in a language comprehensible to all those who are practicing in the field.

2. The need to prevent duplication. Duplication of effort is costly because it wastes manpower, time, and money. Additionally, it often produces problems where none existed before. Duplication is not only ruinous because of futility in terms of efforts made, but also because it simply tends to confuse the issues and the personnel working in the problem area.
3. The need to eliminate nonproductive outcomes and time wasted on such outcomes.
4. The need for maximized, pertinent information acquisition.

Since the formulation of a standard depends upon the immediate situation of the agency, the logical place to start is with an outline designed to thoroughly cover all safety aspects that are generated by agency operation. Thus, working objectives might be classified as follows:

A. Objectives of Safety Design Standards
   1. To make more time available for innovative effort through cumulative evidence of information relating to physical areas and facilities.
   2. To simplify facility and space design and reduce the probability of built-in hazards.
   3. To eliminate environmental hazards which can be prevented by design techniques when establishing recreational sites.
   4. To develop permissible alternate designs.
   5. To furnish technical data on materials for construction purposes as well as to show availability of new materials which can eliminate vandalism.
   6. To furnish design data which will permit the safe and effective development of physical sites.
   7. To avoid any competitive effects between aesthetics and safe design.
   8. To avoid the extravagance permitted when practical design of physical facilities is underserved in order to cater to the comfort of potential patrons.
   9. To produce the most effective recreational designs while maintaining the necessary quality for highest safety performance and reliability.

B. Objectives of Safety Design Procedures
   1. To establish efficient communication between design and construction
   2. To provide for effective management and dissemination of safety specifications and requirements
   3. To maintain consistency in supplying graphic information by:
      a. Sharpness of details

   b. Easily understood technical terms
   c. Uniformity of specifications provided to construction units
4. To establish and retain quality and assurance by:
   a. Utilizing recognized standards
   b. Establishing new standards based upon professional knowledge, accumulated facts, and prior experiences
   c. Implementing evaluation procedures designed to maintain optimum effectiveness and reliability of safety practices
5. To establish procedures for obtaining safe equipment, supplies and materials at minimum costs.
6. To establish criteria and context for maximizing signs and symbols with regard to warning and information about the use of the system's facilities, participation in activities, and any supervision which is found to be necessary.

Safety standards which are developed in this way become mandatory and serve as guides by which the recreational service system will be operated. Any deviation from these standards, except in terms of greater stringency, cannot be tolerated. The essential reason for introducing safety standards and maintaining them is to prevent personal or environmental jeopardy and consequent trauma. All standards will be based upon nationally accepted criteria, technical developments, legal responsibilities, and previously established practitioner performance directly concerned with patron and employee safety.

5
Recreational Safety Standards

Because safety hazards in the recreational environment appear to be increasing due to uncautious behavior on the part of patrons, inconsistent observance of organizational policy supposedly designed to limit hazards, and some incompetence and/or negligence on the part of recreational service operators, the need for a well-planned safety program is evident. In order to implement such a program, it is necessary that standards concerning recreational safety be determined, enumerated, and utilized to offset incautious behavior on the part of workers or patrons that can lead to dangerous conditions or that can negate environmental situations, either of a natural or man-made type, that play a role in paving the way for accidents to occur. When the subject of recreational safety is brought up for analysis and introduced as policy by concerned agencies, some confusion and misunderstanding is likely to develop. Safety policy is not to be considered as a straightjacket for personnel or patrons. It is merely a guide for the kinds of behavior required for maximized enjoyment without tragic consequences. Recreationists at all agency levels sometimes have conflicting interests, areas of specialization, or lack experience in the development of safety standards. To overcome this deficiency, general observations of the field of recreational service have yielded a number of recreational safety standards now enjoying currency. These standards have been developed over a long period and have been accepted by those administrative practitioners whose responsibility it is to safeguard all patrons when they attend or participate in the sponsored programs or at the facilities administered by public departments.

RECREATIONAL SAFETY STANDARDS

1. The direction of the recreational service safety program is the responsibility of the administration of the organization or system concerned.

It is obvious that unless the administrator is held directly accountable for the operational safety of the organization for which he or she serves as chief executive officer, little will be accomplished in obtaining a pervasive policy with vigorous enforcement of all collateral rules and reglations that accumulate directly from whatever reasonable and prudent demands such accountability necessitates. One of the strongest factors conditioning the inclusion of a standard in any recreational service system is the belief in the basic value of the standard held by the administrator responsible for the program. Of course, it is well known that administrators are ultimately responsible for everything that happens within and under their jurisdiction. However, in order to achieve the greatest possible involvement by the individual who actually issues and executes the policy of the department, this area of responsibility must be strictly assigned rather than generally presupposed.

2. One administrative officer, preferably at the assistant administrator level, should be assigned direct responsibility for and given the needed authority to assume control of the system-wide safety program. The individual so chosen should be a professional with an intelligent understanding and appreciation of the values of a safety program in all of its ramifications.

While all personnel employed by the recreational service system should assume leadership in promoting safety by their own attitudes, habits, and practices, administrative oversight is probably the best contributer for the organization of enumerated safety procedures, techniques, and evaluation. Although it may be assumed that recreationists will act in ways designed to reduce or eliminate unsafe conditions or actions within the system's program and physical plant, there are other employees who may be less concerned with safety practices because they are relatively removed from programming and the patrons who constitute the agency's clientele. An administrator charged with carrying out the safety program will see that interest in safety will permeate the entire recreational program, and all divisions will faithfully follow and perform their respective functions in ways that support sound safety principles.

3. The individual patron should be the focus of the safety program.

The objectives of the safety program should be centered on the physical, social, and mental well-being of those who form the constituency of the agency. Whatever can be done to minimize hazardous environmental conditions, which may be a contributing cause to accidents and injuries, should be performed. Even more pertinent is the participating of people in the various recreational activities organized and/or sponsored by the agency. Without doubt, many recreational activities are inherently dangerous. It, therefore, behooves the recreationists in charge to see that individuals have the required knowledge, skill, or instruction about the activities in which they engage so that they can make informed choices as to whether sufficient skill has been obtained which will permit complete enjoyment without the added anxiety that fear of accident or injury can bring.

4. The recreational service agency should provide continuous instructional courses in every activity which has inherent danger during performance.

The recreational service department owes its clientele whatever measure of protection will accrue from instructional procedures that offer specific information about the activity as well as the skills required. To the extent that the individual is or becomes skilled in the activity there will be a lessened probability of injury through carelessness or incompetent performance. The instructional aspect of recreational service is an integral part of all programming. Much recreational activity occurs during the formal phase of instruction as individuals learn about their own abilities or lack of same. By organizing continuous instruction in all categories of the recreational program, the department is simply living up to its mandated responsibility for providing individuals with the wherewithal to take part in recreational experiences. Instruction may occur within any time frame, but a specific period determined to be the most appropriate for a beginner to learn activity skills which will serve both to keep that person from harm and enhance personal enjoyment must be available throughout the year.

5. Written policy should be promulgated which deals with all aspects of recreational safety throughout the system. Such policy should be concerned with patrons as well as with employees.

The formulation and issuance of policy is the single most persuasive method to establish agency commitment to a total safety program within the recreational service system. Unless there are carefully written, easily understood, and well-publicized recreational safety policies disseminated to all who are connected with the recreational service system there can be no full-fledged assumption of responsibility for maximized safety efforts. Written policy at least assures that all personnel will recognized and be aware of administrative expectations for safe practices and the use of technical knowledge and competencies in maintaining a safe environment as well as providing guidelines for the behavior of patrons in preventing unsafe behavior. Policy not only establishes effective working procedures for carrying out the safety program, but it is the most practical method by which adherence to desired behavior can be obtained and monitored. No employee has the excuse that he/she was ignorant of certain acceptable performance expectations if written policy is particularly circulated throughout all echelons of the system. Written policy prevents individual interpretation and leaves no room for speculation about what is required. The presumption here is that written policy is unambiguous and precise as to its meaning.

6. The design of all facilities, structures, and interior spaces must be formulated with the safety of patrons and employees in mind.

Design of the physical plant must screen out unsafe features. This has to do with defensible space (about which more explanation will be offered later), adequate illumination, ventilation, traffic flow, and the elimination of artificially emplaced objects which in themselves constitute a potential danger to users. Care must be taken to design recreational areas so that whatever environmental hazards exist are successfully minimized if not completely eradicated.

7. The design of outdoor recreational places must be of such nature that full advantage is taken of natural terrain features without adding hazardous conditions by artificial means.

Many physical activities that occur in the outdoors are inherently dangerous. There is no need to design facilities or spaces in ways which compound the probability of accidents occurring because of the way in which the shape, terrain, or other natural features have been employed. Natural hills whose slopes are conducive for coasting do not have to have rigid barriers added as this merely creates one more potential collision point that is unnecessary. In fact, any additional man-made devices inserted into natural areas may eventually lead to conditions where ill-conceived behavior can be detrimental to the individual involved as well as the agency on whose property the incident occurred. The use of dams on streams, dock or wharf construction, various bridges across otherwise impassable barriers, excavations, fills, or the modification of natural places through the construction of fields, trails, or buildings, with consequent damage to flood plains (or their elimination), may do much to create conditions that have the potential for taking lives if not causing great injury to unknowing people who use the areas.

8. Appropriate supervision is required when activities under the direct administration of the system necessitate broad oversight of participants to prevent accidental injury.

Appropriate supervision really means that employed personnel of the organization are in the immediate vicinity or have the activity in question under their control. The nature of the activity and the age and/or skill of the participants will dictate the obligation to offer generalized oversight so that pertinent regulations for the safety of participants and observers are adhered to. Generally, supervision will be of a general type when dealing with activities in which large numbers of people participate simultaneously and where simple directions for traffic flow as well as the regulation of behavior are called for.

9. Appropriate supervision is required when activities under the direct administration of the system necessitate the immediate and close

control of individuals so that injurious behavior or foreseeable incidents do not contribute to injury to participants.

In ceratin circumstances, the organization of program activities requires that direct control over the actions of participants be closely guarded. This means that supervision cannot be general nor proximate. The supervision must be focused on the individual who is performing so that any potential miscalculation, fatigue, or uncoordinated action does not result in injury to the individual or those within the immediate vicinity. Under such conditions, the employee must be highly skilled in the activity, able to provide instruction to the participant, and act in ways which will prevent untoward mishaps from occurring. This latter instance can be prevented by anticipating the probability of accident due to the nature of the activity being controlled and being prepared to act in ways which are intended to stop the activity, reduce the likelihood of injury, or safeguard the participant from unskilled or unknowledgeable performance.

10. Complete and continuous safety records, including accident reports, should be kept in the office of the system administrator and be made available to employees who have a need to know about the causes of accidents and injuries and the required steps to reduce or eliminate them.

Among the safety records which will be necessary to maintain are those termed accident reports. Accident reporting is especially valuable in states where legislation permits litigation for recovery action following accidents. Worker's compensation covers most injuries to employees and may require extensive records to be kept. The analysis of such records may do much to reveal how and why accidents occur and what may be done to take remedial measures. In some instances the events leading to the accident, with consequent injury to person or damage to property, may be apparent. Sometimes, however, the proximate cause of accidents remain hidden, and only a thorough analysis of meticulously collected information concerning the behaviors of all involved as well as the physical conditions of the environment in which the accident took place may reveal the essential reasons for the occurrence. Periodic dissemination of accident summaries and their analyses should be sent to the various divisions of the agency for study. In this way all employees may become informed about them. These reports provide superior case studies around which the safety program of the agency may be organized. The recording of accidents permits the safety program to be adjusted so that the immediate needs of patrons and employees may be handled. Furthermore, such records provide the basis for in-service staff instruction as well as patron guidance. The study of records enables modification of the physical plant as well as the use of all structures and grounds if such becomes necessary in consequence of the information generated by examination of the records. Of course, the maintenance of records may materially assist the system in defending against liability suits stemming from accident cases as well as preserving the reputation of the system from adverse publicity when accidents do occur.

11. To the extent possible, all employees should be competent to undertake the duties and responsibilities that their respective positions within the organization require them to perform.

All employees of the system should be examined for physical and mental capacity to undertake the responsibilities that the nature of the job requires. All recreationists should be carefully screened for professional preparation, i.e., graduation from an accredited professional college or university program in recreational service education, with additional experiential work in similar agencies either on a full-time, seasonal, part-time, or voluntary basis. All specialists employed by the organization should have the requisite skills and knowledge necessary to provide the kinds of supervision mandated by the nature of the activity and the maturity of the participants. All technical, paraprofessional, ancillary, or other staff employees, not directly involved with the recreational program, should be trained in those skills and functions for which they are employed. Examination of such employees to determine competence to perform should probably be of a written, oral, and practical type so that the potential employee is enabled to demonstrate, to the satisfaction of the employing authority, that required knowledge and skills are possessed. Furthermore, some judgment should be rendered as to the potential employee's stability and ability to function in emergency situations when called upon to do so.

12. All recreational structures should be constructed of fire-resistive material and be in compliance with NFPA codes.

Although the incidence of fire damage and injury to patrons is extremely low within the field of recreational service, there are instances where fire due to the use of chemicals, faulty wiring, or even vandalism caused damage to the structure because fire-resistive materials were not used in the construction. Moreover, when accidental or premeditated fires occur, there is always the danger of personal injury and even loss of life if the building has not been designed to retard the rapidity of flames.

13. All recreational service buildings should be designed for quick and easy egress from the building within three minutes or less.

Rooms, corridors, stairways, and doorways should be of such sufficient size and number and be obstruction free so that rapid exit may be accomplished without undue loss of time and the potential injury that can be inflicted if people are caught within a burning building without easy access to the outside. This means that the structure should be designed so that ready access to stairways, which are to be fireproof, can be accomplished. All standard stairways, should be developed as fire escapes and no room exit should be more than one hundred feet from a fire escape or stairway.

14. Every recreational structure should be built, equipped, and maintained for safe activity experiences by patrons.

Not only is the system concerned with correct architectural design and the use of materials which can eliminate or reduce accidents, but all equipment utilized within the structure should be of a kind that is appropriate for the activity or support performance for which it is applied. This requires that health and safety equipment, from fire extinguishers to first aid supplies, be adequate and of sufficient number to serve when required. All supplies, materials, and equipment in use within the activity program should be of a quality that permits sound safety practices without infringing upon the enjoyment of the participant. Good tools, apparatus, and protective materials designed to enhance the safety of participants engaged in any of the programmed experiences sponsored by the agency must combine the intrinsic characteristics of high performance, durability, and effectiveness when cared for correctly.

The maintenance of building interiors and exteriors insofar as cleanliness is concerned should be of a high quality and be performed as necessary so that safety hazards do not accumulate. Any trash accumulation, stuck fire valves, clogged doorways, or other equally dangerous and inappropriate situations, e.g., poorly maintained tools and equipment, can be potentially hazardous to patrons. Daily maintenance inspections can do much to alleviate these problems while presenting a healthy environment for patrons. This also includes the replacement of lights for good illumination in rooms, corridors, and stairwells. It also means the repair of structural damage due to natural forces of wear, erosion, or use and the immediate repair of damage caused by vandals. Structural damage to buildings or the ruination of supplies, tools, equipment, or apparatus may have a negative effect on the safety of users and cannot be tolerated. Good maintenance procedures will do much to eliminate these problems and may even serve as a deterrent to continued vandalism.

15. Outdoor maintenance is an absolute necessity in order to effect quick repair of recreational devices which have been damaged through abuse, normal wear and tear, or natural causes.

Unless daily inspections are carried out to determine whether or not heavily used supplies, materials, and equipment are standing the strain of continuous exposure to people and nature there is the potential for objects to rust, wear out, or otherwise become mechanically inoperable with consequent danger to users. Thus swings, slides, and other such devices should be checked daily in order to be assured that they are in safe working order. Vandalized facilities, particularly lighting, playground devices, fences, or any other outdoor object used by people who participate in the recreational service program must be periodically and routinely examined to determine whether repair, replacement, closure, or continued operation is necessary. Inspection of swimming, boating, diving, and fishing facilities, playground areas, shooting ranges, golf links, outdoor gymnasiums, bicycle paths, and a host of other special activity areas must receive this scrutiny to prevent dangerous conditions from remaining and to insure that the public is not exposed to potential hazards which can be corrected if known. In all events, either remedial measures must be taken immediately upon notification of such unsafe conditions or the activity must be shut down with notice given for taking the object or device out of service.

16. Preventive maintenance practices must be observed to forestall environmentally dangerous conditions which develop when vandalism, uncleaned areas, or degraded recreational areas are permitted to exist without immediate remedial measures taken.

Routine maintenance operations normally deal with keeping all recreational areas free of debris (trash or garbage), mowing of lawns and all grassy areas used for games, picnics, or other recreational activities, the discovery and filling of natural or artificially made holes in playing fields that might interfere with recreational activities or contribute to accidents and injuries. Maintenance must also be concerned with replacement, repair, or cleaning of signs, fencing, or other recreational places which have been deliberately littered or where amenities, e.g., toilet facilities, benches, or tables have been overturned, pulled apart, marred, or damaged so that they create unsafe conditions. Agressive maintenance has to do with seeking out potentially unsafe conditions or anticipating rather than reacting to obvious maintenance problems, e.g., trash accumulation, broken windows or lighting fixtures, potholes, or missing directional signs.

17. Fencing, either to prohibit entry or to guarantee that patrons will not be exposed to dangerous environmental conditions, i.e., hidden or sudden drop-offs, boiling springs, or similar situations, must be of a type that is high enough, and suitable so that it fits into the area without appearing out of place.

The utilization of fencing designed to withstand the assault of vandals has not yet been devised. Individuals who are determined to gain entry into areas that are not patrolled and that have only the fence to indicate that the area is out of bounds for recreators, can force the fence using any number of tools. Thus, bolt cutters may be used to slice out a section of fence. However, the individual who cuts his/her way into a restricted area has already forfeited any protection which the fence may have offered. Any injury sustained by such a person will be solely attributed to contributory negligence. If there is something of value behind the fence, such as construction supplies, materials, or equipment, the fence alone will not protect pilferage. A uniformed patrol or other employee observers will have to supplement such fencing. When an area is fenced in order to protect potential users from injury because of dangers to be found within the area, then manning is unnecessary. The fence must simply be of a height and strength to make climbing over it difficult. Additionally, the use of keep out signs will also warn would-be scalers that their actions are prohibited and the risks they are taking will forfeit any protection that litigation for redress would have had. In some instances, low fencing or other appropriate barriers will serve the purpose of preventing potential accident victims from endangering themselves simply by existing.

18. Signs, signals, publications, or other notices of warning or direction must be erected and/or brought to the attention of patrons at various prominent places on the property to be used.

All notifications of warning that danger exists must be prominently displayed at sites that will cause patrons to recognize that some hazard exists and that they are to act accordingly. Whatever notice, edict, or symbol is used it must be of an appropriate type so that it can be easily seen. Furthermore, such warnings should be repeated at intervals so that there can be no mistake concerning the prohibitation which the organization is imposing. Whereever access is available, there too, signs should be prominently posted. Patrons must be made aware of the kinds of behavior expected by them within the recreational facility and warning or directional notifications are the best means to do this short of having an interpretative program for newly arrived visitors. Since the latter experience is not compulsory for patrons to attend, signs and other publications may be the best means for informing the public about environmental and other hazards or nonjudicious behavior which will not be tolerated by the agency in question.

19. All food service installations shall meet mandated health care standards with regard to food handling and cleanliness of the premises in which food is served.

Whether recreational service agencies perform their own food handling or permit concessions to operate, the maintenance of refectories should reflect hygienic operations in all food handling and preparation. Proper refrigeration of perishable items and sufficient cooking of foods which require heat should be a condition for continued operation. In addition, the premises should be cleaned as needed. This means that a continuous mopping and washing of the food handling area must be performed. All sanitary procedures should be vigorously applied so that the possibility of food poisoning and other illness-producing possibilities do not stem from any food service operation conducted or sponsored by the recreational service agency.

20. All activities within the recreational program sponsored by the system should be beneficial to the individual who participates. That is, the activity can in no way be inimical to the health, welfare, or safety of the individual involved.

All recreational activities are devised to enhance the physical, social, and emotional health of the individual. There can never be programmed activities which are maliciously inspired, that is, offered so that participants will inevitably be injured regardless of their degree of skill or knowledge of the activity. It seems almost absurd to imagine that recreationists or agents of a recreational service agency would perform in ways that could lead to patron injury or death, but there are instances where incompetent individuals act in ways which directly contribute to the death or injury of participants. It may also occur that these same thoughtless individuals permit or incite activities to take place which are negative in all respects, having no other purpose than to hurt the individual engaged. Activities of this type can never be allowed to occur and those charged with responsibilities for the oversight of participants should reflect the highest caliber of professional practice thereby preventing or eliminating the occurrence of negative experiences.

21. All employees who work with patrons should be skilled in first aid procedures.

It is necessary that all personnel who come in contact with patrons of the agency be skilled in first aid techniques so that they may administer to any person injured while attending or participating in an activity sponsored by the system. Common sense indicates that the application of first aid techniques, skillfully performed, will do much to alleviate complications, reduce further injury, and/or mitigate the pain which accompanies most injuries. Such skilled performance may result in life saving if carried out speedily. Of course, emergency procedures should be followed with timely notification of medical specialists, emergency vehicles (if available), and other contingency plans which may be expected to take effect under circumstances which elicit such response.

22. All equipment, wherever it is situated within the system, must be inspected before patrons are permitted to utilize it.

If any person is injured while using damaged equipment (apparatus or other paraphernalia), there would be little doubt that the agency would be at fault. Safety inspections are an absolute responsibility that must be carried out diligently and routinely. It is also the duty of employees to make sure that no patron is allowed to use any potentially dangerous facilities or equipment when a responsible person, either volunteer or employee, is not present. The simple expedient of posting warning signs which prohibits such use cannot be considered as a substitute for adequate supervision; unless some physical barriers are erected to actively prevent usage, signs alone will not exempt the agency from its mandated responsibility.

23. All activities which require physical skill taught under the sponsorship of the system demand adequate supervision to prevent unskilled individuals from attempting moves that may be beyond their capacities and therefore constituting a clear and present danger.

No person should be permitted to participate in an activity until he/she has been trained to do so safely. Particularly is this true for children. When an individual is injured during the performance of a particular activity that involves or necessitates a high degree of skill, strength, or knowledge, and that person was enrolled or otherwise under the control of a recreational service department sponsored experience, there will be questions concerning whether the individual knew that the activity was beyond his/her ability. Activities such as gymnastics, rock climbing, scuba diving, skiing, and similar experiences requiring a great deal of practice, instruction, and awareness of personal limitations invariably place the individual in jeopardy if sufficient knowledge requirements and skill attainment have not been met. Failure on the part of those responsible for courses or activity instruction to meet the minimum requirements of knowledge and skill for participants and permit them to engage in activities that are beyond their present level of competence endangers those for whom they are responsible and, therefore, such responsible people are acting in a negligent manner with probable consequences of liability.

24. Competent employees of recreational service systems must be capable of anticipating the likelihood of injury being sustained by individuals engaged in specific activities. It is the responsibility of recreationists to foresee the probability of accident and injury when supervising certain individuals in particular activities.

Recreationists should be able to anticipate the probability of accidental injuries received as a direct result of participating in some form of recreational experience due to the nature of the participants involved rather than the inherent danger of the activity itself. When working with children or youth, recreationists should always be aware that persons who are immature may sometimes act in ways that are thoughtless, destructive, or malicious thereby causing damage to property or injury to others unless this misconduct can be avoided or prevented by appropriate action. Even the most observant professional cannot always prevent incautious behavior resulting in injury. However, if the employee in charge tried to control indiscrete behavior and failed to do so, the likelihood is that no negligence could be charged. Since this is always a question of the degree of supervision necessary, the courts might hold that when all reasonable attempts fail to head off dangerous behavior in which children engage, no negligence applies. But rules and regulations must be made and enforced so that immature persons will be on notice as to the kind of behavior which is expected of them. It almost goes without saying that whenever a recreational service agency is dealing with immature individuals, a sufficient supervisory presence must be maintained so that good order and discipline on the organization's property will occur. Failure to provide such regulatory notices and/or proper supervision or both is tantamount to acting negligently.

25. Craft shops, where power tools, equipment, and dangerous chemicals of various kinds are present and in use constitutues a potential danger. Those participants in craft activities must be thoroughly prepared in the proper procedures and carefully supervised to be assured that instructions for safe handling are scrupulously followed.

Craft rooms and shops, because they contain a variety of power tools and equipment as well as dangerous substances, e.g., acids, flammable liquids, Bunsen burners, or other high heat producing equipment, require a good deal of thoughtful planning so that participants in craft activities reap the fullest satisfaction and enjoyment from the activity without consequences such as burns, fractures, lacerations, or cuts that might result from unsafe conduct or unskilled performance. To avoid liability for an injury incrued by a participant under his/her supervision, a craft instructor must always be sure that all dangerous machines are equipped with proper guards which will always be used during operation. Equally important is the provision for complete instruction of the participants before they are allowed to operate the tools or use hazardous materials. Concomitantly, close and immediate supervision is required to make sure that all instructions are consistently and correctly followed.

26. All excursions conducted under the sponsorship of the recreational service department must be planned meticulously so that no injuries to participants will occur.

Recreationist have the discretion and latitude to plan and take participants on off-ground trips or excursions. These may be in the form of hikes, bus trips, hosteling, or some other form of field excursion that is an accepted aspect of a well-rounded recreational program. The recreationist or volunteer who is responsible for the safety of the participants is mandated to safeguard all persons taking part during the trip. Whether the group is bicycling cross country, going rock climbing, camping out, going fishing, or taking a boat trip, there are certain hazards which attend these activities. In order to prevent accidents and injuries, the responsible person/persons (depending upon the number of people involved) should prepare participants carefully by informing them of potential dangers, instructing them in correct behavior or procedures to take during the activity, and providing direct and immediate supervision during the outing. If a participant is injured, the employee or volunteer may be held liable. Of course, everything revolves upon the incident which may have occurred, the circumstances, and whether the employee acted as a prudent and skilled person should have.

27. The transportation of participants in other than departmentally owned or operated vehicles can place those being transported in some jeopardy as well as create liability for the driver or owner of the vehicle. Under these circumstances, no private vehicle should be permitted to be used for the transportation of patrons of the department.

Almost all liability cases involving recreational service personnel are concerned with accidents in which recreational participants have been transported by private vehicle to some departure point for the beginning of an off-grounds activity or where the transportation is an integral part of the recreational activity itself. Every employee of the recreational service agency should recognize the potential liability which accrues when a personally owned vehicle is used to transport participants to or from recreational activities. Should an accident occur, not only the driver may be held responsible, but whoever owns the vehicle may also be made to bear the burden of liability. Litigation may be based upon the doctrine of *respondeat superior.* In order to avoid entanglements of this kind, the operating agency must develop a systematized plan for the transportation of recreational participants in privately owned vehicles, if no other means can be found for using public carriers or agency owned, leased, or rented vehicles for the purpose. It is probably better not to permit privately-owned vehicles to be used for transporting participants. The only time this rule is to be suspended occurs when participants have their own vehicles and assume the responsibility for attending a recreationally sponsored activity on a voluntary basis.

28. Recreational service agency sponsored programs which attract mass audiences must be handled in ways which avoid congestion and the loss of control of the crowd as a result of inappropriate or malicious behavior on the part of those participating.

Several actions are necessary for the recreational service agency and its employees to avoid being liable in the case of accidents when certain activities draw large numbers of people to the attraction. If the agency sponsors a mass audience event where tickets are sold, it must be on a reserve seat basis. No event which is likely to draw ten thousand or more people to an auditorium or other indoor arena can be on a first come, first served basis. This will only lead to congestion, highly aggressive conduct on the part of a rowdy few, and a disdain for common courtesy. Particularly is this true when entrance to the event is minimized so that stub collection can be made easier. The tendency for hundreds and, perhaps, thousands, to push, shove, and trample upon those in front so that they may gain entrance and a selection of seats is always a possibility. Many people can be hurt or even killed when this senseless behavior occurs. Crowd control to avoid congestion and the potential danger that such proximity brings may be developed by (1) selling all tickets on a reserved seat basis; (2) opening many entryways so that congestion at any one entry is minimized; (3) having a sufficient number of staff available to give general supervision as necessary; and (4) having the event take place on time. Many problems arise with young people when activities do not take place at the scheduled time. The audience has a tendency to become obstreperous, and sometimes other antisocial behaviors will be noted. All of these actions generate a serious negative attitude which soon permeates the entire crowd. When this happens, one or more problems will then arise which can result in injuries. Where rock concerts are the basis for special events, the audience expects some paid security force to be employed for the event to prevent the crowd from becoming a mob. The sponsoring agency must make sure that an adequate number of well-trained guard personnel are on hand to control the crowd and to forestall any threatening behavior or blatant rowdyism.

29. Whenever a recreational agency sponsored activity occurs in a relatively hard-to-reach area, emergency vehicles capable of traveling in the area should be immediately available to transport injured persons to places of safety or where additional medical treatment may be found.

When recreational service agencies operate recreational areas which are situated at some distance from roads or streets or when they are located in remote places such as ski hills, bodies of water, rock climbing areas, or wilderness regions, the department should station vehicles which are capable of negotiating the kinds of terrain that ordinary vehicles might find impossible to travel on in the event that an accident occurs which requires transportation of the victim to some medical facility or where medical treatment is readily available. These off-road vehicles could be motor powered sleds which would be able to carry an accident victim from a snow-covered slope relatively quickly or a "dune buggy" which could traverse loose sand in order to pickup a person who might have been injured in a wilderness area. Departments which operate marinas, beaches, or other water-based facility should have power boats and other kinds of craft readily available for the transportation of boating accident victims or the pick up of near drowning victims. Lack of such vehicles might mean the death of accident victims or a worsening of injuries received from participation in recreational system sponsored activities. Common sense dictates that such emergency vehicles should be a part of the stand-by equipment necessary for the preservation of life and the security of patrons involved in experiences where ordinary vehicles are neither appropriate nor available.

30. Illumination for indoor and outdoor recreational areas and facilities should conform to accepted standards as developed by a recognized body such as the Illuminating Engineering Society. Effective illumination can do much to reduce the incidence of accidents which occur in hallways, stairwells, gymnasiums, shops, and other similar places when people using these areas are unable to see. Outdoor illumination not only permits the use of recreational facilities and areas after dark, but does much to remove factors of insecurity which park patrons sometimes experience as a result of poor lighting.

Many accidental injuries occur because people cannot see obstacles or in consequence of misjudging distances. Many forms of recreational activity require good lighting so that participants can perform intricate movements of a gross muscular type or manipulate tools and other devices. Poor lighting may be one of the primary factors in injury. In order to prevent accidents where poor lighting is a direct cause illumination levels must be correctly maintained. In outdoor areas and facilities, proper illumination is an absolute necessity. Unless people can see what they are doing insofar as recreational participation is concerned, there will be no attendance. No system can expect people to attend outdoor facilities after dark unless they are well illuminated. Moreover, high levels of illumination will do much to deter vandalism and other criminal activities that usually take place under cover of darkness. Furthermore, well-illuminated facilities tend to attract large numbers of people and enhance the personal security of those who attend.

Good lighting is also required to indicate where hazards or artificial dangers exist. Any excavation performed by the system or its agents must be clearly marked by lighted signals to warn people away. Naturally, it is expected that barricades will also be used in conjunction with lighted signals.

31. All recreational service systems should have communications equipment connected at each outdoor area or throughout buildings which attract large numbers of people. These loud speaker systems are useful in providing directions, controlling crowds, and issuing timely warnings concerning behavior.

Indoor audio systems are useful in maintaining order and discipline or issuing directions. It is also helpful in controlling user traffic and preventing accidents which might accompany the outbreak of fire or other emergency condition within the facility. Loud speaker systems serve their best purpose in outdoor areas where many patrons are congregated. Issuing vehicular and pedestrian traffic control, providing directions to and from recreational activities, and guiding crowd behavior necessitate the acquisition and use of audio equipment.

The development of, agreement on, and implementation of standards concerning all aspects of recreational safety are vital to the operation of all recreational service agencies. Recreational safety standards are the best current practices which have achieved widespread acceptance and are significant in determining the degree of deviation from the norm when claims of responsibility arise about levels of care. Standards provide the guidelines below which conduct of recreational operations are considered to be irresponsible, harmful to, or potentially injurious to the clients served by the recreational agency. By adhering to the safety standards generally recognized throughout the field of recreational service, agencies who offer such services will inevitably remain free of liability that accrues from negligence or the improper performace of required acts.

PART II

Operational Behavior and Policy Making

6
Organizational Safety Policy

All policy is either reactive or anticipatory. Policy is a definitive statement which comes in response to internal or external organizational conditions that may be corrected through remedial practices. Policy that is formulated prior to forecastable or expected situations is of a preparatory nature and is used to guide behavior before the fact or to determine what the conditions of agency organization will be so that negative actions will not develop. The term policy, as used throughout the field, usually connotes any general rule that has been devised for the organization to inhibit the discretion of subordinates or to provide authoritatively disseminated rules established by top management that describe and prescribe the practices and behaviors that will be observed throughout the agency.

It must be understood from the outset that policy arrived at under legislative fiat carries certain ethical values that are the responsibility of those in a legislative position and answerable to the constituency that either elected or appointed them to office. Such policy is based upon factual evidence and the alternatives which are available insofar as objective consequences are concerned. Legislative policy is broadly construed as carrying out certain value judgments and philosophical orientations based upon the democratic derivation of balancing constituent needs and demands with the realities of facts and ability of the agency to actually carry out policy.

Administrative policy is formulated in response to community values, legislative request, law, and the varied resources by which the agency will execute its mandate. All administrators have a hand in offering the legislative body expertise—both in terms of facts to be presented and personal value judgments—on which subsequent policy may depend. However, administrative policy is more often developed in terms of meeting agency needs or in consequence of forestalling or averting situations which result in the discredit of the agency. This does not mean that all policy is construed as preventing negative conduct or action, although this may be the very outcome which occurs and is desirable. Policy that is positive, ethical, and correct can have as its aim the satisfaction, enjoyment, and benefit of those who will stand to gain from its execution. Nevertheless, such policy really does inhibit, reduce, or retard the probability of personal behavior or practices which are, indeed, ill-timed, ill-conceived, mismanaged, or in some other ways incompetently or negligently carried out. It is with an eye toward the prevention of such negative activities that policy of a restrictive or enhancing type is promulgated.

THE DEVELOPMENT OF RECREATIONAL SAFETY POLICY

Each of the fifty states has adopted laws dealing with the organization of recreational services. Thus public recreational service systems are established at every level of government as well as by private and quasi-public organizations, all intent upon offering services of a recreational nature to those who constitute the membership, patronage, or constituency of the agency. There are certain common features which are shared by the diverse agencies which offer recreational services. It is not the purpose to describe characteristics that are mutually shared, but to offer the one element that should be an integral function and responsibility in all agencies which purport to provide recreational services—the standard of care which each person is presumed to receive by those agencies which organize, administer, or purvey recreational services.

Every recreational service agency reflects the aspirations of those who support it. Recreational service objectives are formulated into policy, either written or corroborated by usage, and are brought to life in the daily operation of the recreational service agency. The legislative policies which have been developed exert greater influence over the operating agency's administration than any other combination of factors because the derivation of such policies is founded upon an assessment of constituency needs, demands, and the value judgments made by those who are responsible for carrying out the mandate that becomes the basis for present and future recreational expectations. In the private sector, with few discrepancies, the same outcome is generated by market expectations. Policies are formulated in terms of the supply of and demand for recreational experiences. It may be that safety policy will be overlooked, but the consequences of such an outcome will be very damaging to the business when redress or restitution has to be made. It may be that profit becomes the chief guide for business policy, but well-run businesses have to confront consumer rights sooner or later and weigh the difference between losses that occur because of deviations from acceptable standards and the profits that might accrue if such standards were kept without the concomitant loss which litigation and a bad press will certainly inspire. Therefore, whether policy is made in the public or private sector of the economy, all operations will be directly affected and governed by legislative (board of directors, trustees) policy. Efficient legislative bodies usually attempt to be consistent in their decisions regarding repetitive events. Being aware of this fact, administrators should be able to anticipate the decisions a legislative body would make under a particular set of circumstances and conditions.

Policy Formation

Policy formation incorporates the decision-making function and the collection and analysis of information in a system that has pervasive significance, long-range influence, and employs essential resources for achieving timely objectives within an unstable environment. Policy formation is a powerful social process in which a rational transaction is enclosed. Policy formation activities are associated with the entire organizational system. Policy is expected to affect the total organization for a prolonged period. In order to exploit opportunities to the advantage of the agency, thereby implementing policy, crucial resources of a personal, financial, and material nature are mobilized so that the agency may achieve influence or control of an environment which is quite volatile.

All policy formation rests upon those intellectual processes which require acquisition of information, analysis of evidence, and selection of competing alternatives that relate to such policy factors as agency mission, comprehensive organizational objectives, and fundamental values which tend to construct agency philosophy and orientation. Policy formation is a continuous procedure in response to changes that occur in the agency's resources and environment.

Basic Mission. The development of policy must be concerned with the interrelationships between use of limited resources and the potential opportunities, threats, or benefits perceived in a doubtful environment. Based upon information about such situational factors and considering the interest of the organization's intent as well as that of those who administer the operation, decisions will be made in terms of the basic mission or orientation of the agency. The mission is defined as the range of operations necessary to provide the services for which the organization was created. Thus, the provision of recreational services to the agency's constituency requires a number of policies to be devised. These policies will represent the direction that the agency will take in meeting the responsibility of its basic mission.

System Goals. Organizational goals or objectives are essentially based upon mission fulfillment. They can be determined by careful investigation of the environment in which the agency is situated, the internal capacity of the agency to carry out its mission, or they may be issued without any reference to other considerations by legislative mandate or managerial edict. In whatever way the aspirations of the agency are defined they become the target to be achieved through the development of policy. Since policies are broad guidelines for all employees in the achievement of objectives, it must be recognized that policies derive from fulfilling objectives. For example, an objective quality for providing enjoyable recreational activities may have a policy of prodigious inspection of all activities and facilities. Of course, each objective may require more than one policy in the attempt to satisfy it; therefore, another policy stemming from the goal of providing enjoyable recreational activities may be the decision to inaugurate and implement a complete program of safety in all of its ramifications.

In this way, the reader may observe the ladder effect in basic mission, goals, and policies. The extensive inspection of activities and facilities was a *policy* designed to achieve the goal of recreational service. All such policies become strategic steps in the fulfillment of basic mission and organizational goals. Each determines the shape, scope, and pervasiveness of the hierarchical sequence, and each is directly related to the other.

What is often unrecognized by policy planners is that any policy issuance implies substantive actions that must be undertaken if the policy is going to be implemented. The pronouncement of a broad or generalized statement designed to guide the activities of the agency inevitably leads to the generation of detailed rules, regulations, and directives so that rational performance can result. These details pervade the life of the agency and have ramifications affecting the daily operation of the agency to an extent that is almost never foreseen by those who make policy. In some instances this is a positive development, as in the case of safety practices and standards. The command to take all necessary action to prevent accidents, injuries, and/or damage to property requires the initiation of a complete series of descriptions of work to be performed as well as the establishment of the ways and means by which such work will be monitored, examined, and made to conform to the expectations of those who first realized the need for such a safety program.

Safety policy touches every facet of the recreational service organization. From the design and development of the physical plant to such disparate functions as emergency procedures for treatment of injuries, fire protection, and evacuation procedures—whether from structures or vessels—the application of procedures which execute the announced guidelines require the cooperation and understanding of every member of the employed force. As with all implied powers that develop in consequence of responsibilities taken on through assumed functions by the recreational service agency, the list of desirable procedures to follow grows and infiltrates all elements of the organization. This is precisely the outcome which rationally-based safety policy should encourage. It is only in this way that the agency can hope to reduce or eliminate unsafe behaviors and those artifically-created hazards must also be recognized and compensated for. In the main, however, it will be human error that produces the climate in which accidents occur. To counter this unproductivity, the administration of safety policy must be scrupulously applied. The potential for successful litigation arising from failure to comply with safety policy increases proportionately with the deviation from required standards and the severity of the injury incurred. To the extent that the agency applies itself diligently to the promotion and compliance with its safety policy the probability of successful litigation in liability claims will be negligible or completely negated.

SAFETY POLICY—GENERAL STATEMENT AND SPECIFIC IMPLICATIONS

It is the particular policy of the recreational service system to take all necessary action to prevent personal injuries and property damage to all patrons and employees of the system while they are using agency facilities or participating on agency property. This responsibility and commitment will be paramount in all operational practices and in the design of recreational areas and structures. It is the unalterable belief of the agency that recreational experiences must be as free as is humanly possible from undesired dangers. Through the implementation of a comprehensive public safety and personnel safety program, the system intends that, wherever possible, accidents will be prevented. The system also expects that its safety education efforts will make patrons and its employees aware of potential hazards and, therefore, careful in their participation in all of the experiences within the system's jurisdiction.

This public safety program applies to existing facilities and future developments as well. This policy statement defines a responsibility and commitment to the general public who enter onto any area or use any facility for any reason in an attempt to prevent accidents. Accidents can be reduced or prevented through the application of a sound safety program.

Safety is the responsibility of all agency personnel. Facility directors are responsible for insuring that all personnel recognize safety regulations within the recreational facilities operated by the system. Safety training and safety meetings are part of the functions undertaken by the facility director. The facility director may, at his/her discretion, appoint a safety coordinator.

Minimum safety requirements for each recreational facility include public safety, pesonnel safety, and equipment safety. Facility directors or their safety coordinator(s) may supplement the requirements depicted within this statement in any way necessary in order to provide an efficient working safety program in the individual facility.

Regular maintenance of recreational facilities is to be carried out on a daily basis. Safety inspections will be conducted by the facility director or his/her designated representative on a daily basis and by central office personnel in conjunction with staff visits. All inspections by the central office staff will include each item checked at the regular daily inspections by the facility directors or their alternates.

Potential Developments

Facilities which are planned for future implementation or existing facilities being improved will always include safety features in the plan. Future developments will be established on the needs of each area and will come under the jurisdiction of the central office. The regulations in the following statement should apply to extant facilities and will be initiated immediately throughout any system, if not already in practice.

The following safety precautions are to be observed scrupulously in the system's holdings for the activities specifically identified.

A. Bicycling
1. All rental bicycles are to be equipped with a red (day-glow) safety flag or pennant mounted on a raised aerial so that it is visible during the day from behind any reasonable obstruction to sight.
2. All bicycles rented to users will undergo daily inspections for appropriate maintenance and good condition. Particularly, the inspection will determine wheel stability, a well-secured seat, tight handlebars, a guarded chain and sprocket, properly inflated tires, correct lubrication, and properly attached safety pennant.
3. All bicycle rentals will stop one and one half hours before dark. All bicycling will be discouraged after dark.
4. All recreational areas where bicyclists and motorists use the same roadway will post conspicuous signs warning motorists to be careful of bicyclists. Such signs will be erected on roads in campgrounds, picnic areas, beaches, and on all vehicular roads.
5. Safety posters will be displayed at rental locations and at such places where they will serve to best advantage. Poster messages should include the following for bicyclists:
   a) When riding on roadways, keep to the right and as close to the shoulder of the road as is possible.
   b) Always ride with the traffic flow, never against it.
   c) Always give pedestrians the right of way.
   d) When entering a roadway, always watch for parked cars.
   e) Never hitch rides.
   f) Always ride in single file.
   g) Never carry more passengers than the vehicle was designed to transport.
   h) Use correct hand signals when turning or stopping.
   i) Ride appropriately.
6. Patrons who bring their own bicycles to the facility must be advised that they will have to conform to the same safety guidelines that apply to renters. Facility personnel should inform patrons that bicycles may not be ridden after dark unless properly equipped

with lights and reflectors. Such information may be imparted to patrons at appropriate times and place.

B. Boating

1. Explicit warning signs will be placed at all areas where possible hazards exist. Such signs will inform the patron about:
   a) Slippery surfaces such as launching ramps, rocks, or piers.
   b) Safe practices when loading fuel for motorized boats.
   c) Safe boating practices in general.
   d) Maximum speed limits, especially in confined areas.
2. Signs will be posted to explain the following specific policies and to advise patrons of the unstable nature of canoes and sail boats in inexperienced hands:
   a) Water skiing is allowed only in designated areas.
   b) Life jackets are required for each passenger of rental boats.
   c) The number of passengers in any rental boat may not exceed that which has been deemed appropriate for the boat.
   d) The weight carried in a rental boat may not exceed the specified weight carrying capacity of that boat.
3. General maintenance of rental boats will include daily inspections to insure safety. Special attention will be given to seams and riveting on aluminum craft, supporting joints on boat seats, condition and operation of rudders, condition of motors whenever they are rented, stability of sailboat masts, and other points of stress. Any unsafe feature of a boat must be corrected before the craft is permitted out. Additionally, boating areas will be scrutinized daily for floating debris. All such debris must be eliminated immediately.
4. On large water empoundments and ocean or open water areas, standard small craft warnings will be raised in the event of inclement weather. During the day, commonly recognized flags will be flown; during the night, standard illumination will be utilized. Particularly will such warnings be given at all marinas, docks, and other launching areas.

C. Camping

1. All campsites must be maintained properly. It is required that the following functions will be performed:
   a) Routine clearing of the area around each campsite, particularly noxious and/or poisonous, plants, rubbish, and other debris.
   b) Routine clearing of surrounding or overhanging brush near fire places within a radius of ten feet.
   c) Routine clearing of vegetation around water faucets and of trails leading to faucets.

d) Daily trash collection (in season).
e) Daily cleaning of all toilets and other sanitary facilities.

2. Posted notices and personal contact will be utilized to gain patron conformity to good camping practices. Signs will also be used to indicate trails and identify sanitary facilities.
3. At least one centralized bulletin board will be erected in each campground. The bulletin board will contain a map showing all activity areas, maintained trails, and roadways with distances between designated points. Each bulletin board will also carry the emergency procedures to be used in the event of injury, fire, robbery, illness, or other problem. The emergency measures will indicate who to contact, how such contact may be made, and what to do until assistance comes. Emergency telephone numbers will also be posted. If there is no telephone at the campground, the location of the nearest phone will be given. Posting of such relevant information will be conducted wherever there are large concentrations of patrons.
4. Frequent patrols by facility personnel will be conducted into campgrounds. Such patrols are designed to prevent vandalism and theft and will serve to provide assistance to patrons in need.

D. Field Sport Activities

1. Appropriate maintenance of sport fields will include the regular cleaning of debris from fields and daily inspections to make sure that fields are free of holes, pits, or other erosions. Such depressions will be filled immediately.

E. Fishing

1. Fishing will be prohibited near swimming areas and from bridges except where bridges are designed to accommodate fishermen in a safe manner. Also, trolling will be prohibited near activity areas such as beaches, marinas, docks, ski areas, dams, and dam spillways. Signs will be erected indicating where these prohibitions exist.
2. Hooks inserted deeply into the flesh of fishermen should be only attended by a physician. For minor hook injuries park personnel should follow First Aid practices only if:
   a) A doctor is unavailable.
   b) The injured party requests treatment.
   c) There appears to be no other reasonable alternative to safeguard the immediate health of the victim.

F. Hiking

1. A master map of each park will be developed showing all existing trails whether maintained by the park or not. Such a map will be

available only for park personnel use. It will aid in finding lost hikers and in planning new or improved trail locations. Trail maps may be made available for hikers.

G. Horseback Riding

1. When renting horses the agent will try always to determine the rider's riding abilities, age, and horse temperament preference. If the renter is in a group, the rental agent will ascertain the number of the group, the ages of the group members, whether or not a parent or guardian is with the group, and whether or not there are experienced riders among the group members.
2. The rental agent will use discretion when renting to individuals who are very young or very old and to persons who are attired in clothing which could prove hazardous. Specifically, the rental agent will watch for persons wearing sandals or tennis shoes or who are barefooted, as bare feet, tennis shoes, and sandals tend to slip in the stirrups. Discretion will be used in renting horses to persons who wear loose fitting or flopping clothing, because the free movement of such clothing can startle a horse. Long, flowing hair should also be considered a possible hazard as such hair can become entangled in trees and pull a rider from a horse.
3. Before renters are allowed to approach the horses, they should be instructed to:
   a) Not approach the horses from the rear.
   b) Mount only from the horse's left side.
   c) Not kick the horse once the rider is mounted.
   d) Never apply continually hard pressure to the horses mouth by excessively hard pulling on the reins.
   e) Stay single file while riding and never attempt to pass.
   f) Always follow the instruction of the park personnel accompanying the riders.
   g) Follow other good riding practices as indicated by the rental agents.
4. Each renter should be individually assisted in mounting his horse.
5. All rental parties will be accompanied by two park employees. Park employees who ride with the renters and assist in training and caring for the horse and equipment will be well trained, have had at least two years experience with horses, and be at least eighteen years old.
6. All horseback riding equipment will be properly maintained and thoroughly inspected at the beginning of each day. Saddle pads will be checked during the day to make sure they are not wrinkled. Cinches will be tightened on each horse after the first ride each day.
7. All saddles will be of the western style and should have a high horne. Stirrups will be made of wood; where openings exist be-

tween leather covered wooded stirrups and the stirrup coverings toe guards will be inserted so there is no chance of catching the feet in the opening.

8. All horses used for rental purposes must be as calm and gentle as possible. Skittish, nervous, disobedient horses will not be used. It will not likely be possible to always obtain very gentle and calm horses; however, every effort will be made to acquire these types of animals. Though some riders may prefer spirited horses, the cost and seriousness of a horseback riding injury may be far greater than the intangible benefits received by the relatively few who might prefer spirited horses.
9. All rental horses will be rested or swapped out for more obedient and controllable horses at least every six months. The length of rest periods will be determined by the stable master.
10. All horse trails will be marked so that hikers will not use the trails. If hikers do use these trails, they will at least be made aware of the presence of horses through proper signs.
11. All horse trails will be inspected daily and debris and fallen timber will be removed. Low hanging branches and dead trees and limbs will be removed from the horse trails for a heights of at least twelve feet.
12. Signs will be placed in plain view at the rental stables warning riders of the possible dangers of horseback riding.
13. All individuals who rent horses will be required to sign responsiblity waivers where the renter acknowledges that the system will not be held responsible for any injury that may occur during, before, or after the ride.

H. Hunting

1. Hunting will not be allowed on system lands because these are designated wildlife sanctuaries.
2. Firearms will not be permitted on system lands.
3. Special periodic inspections of system lands where hunting could become a potential problem will be undertaken by agency personnel with assistance from state game officers.
4. Signs indicating the above restrictions will be prominently posted throughout each park.

I. Picnicking

1. All picnic areas will be provided with one trash container for at least every two tables. The trash container will be equipped with a lid and should be free of all rough edges.
2. All trash containers will be emptied at least once a day in the peak season and otherwise as needed.

3. Daily inspection will be made of all picnic areas by employees who will also make sure all tables are mounted securely, free of chips and cracks in the concrete, and free of exposed metal. Wooden tables will be inspected to make sure they are free of cracks and splintered areas. Facility personnel will make sure that all glass, debris, and dead limbs and trees are removed from the area. Facility personnel will take special care to look for the nests of wasps, bees, or animals that may pose a possible hazard.
4. The immediate area around each table and trash container will be free of excessive vegetation, especially poisonous plants. All grill and fire pit areas will also be cleared of underbrush and hanging vegetation for eight to ten feet.

J. Playground Activities

1. Playground equipment will be concentrated in basic playground areas, but will not be so close together as to be crowded. It will be helpful to physically separate the playground equipment areas from other open playground areas if possible.
2. All playground equipment will be firmly and permanently anchored in concrete settings so that the tipping of equipment will not occur.
3. All metal playground equipment will be brightly painted so that children's attention will be focused on the playground and not on surrounding potential hazards, such as roadways. Multiple colors will be used.
4. Sliding boards should be placed in shaded areas or face the north to reduce heat build-up on the slide surface. Swing seats will be of the curved saddle type, as these seats grip a person better than bench seats and may prevent falls. Swing seats will be set at two different heights so that different age children can be adequately accommodated. All teeter-totter boards (seesaw boards) will have six-inch-high blocks attached to the undersides at each extreme end so as to prevent the crushing of feet when the teeter board touches the ground. All teeter-totter fulcums (pivot points) will be protected so as to prevent fingers from being caught during pivoting.
5. Landing areas of sawdust or sand will be continually maintained at the bottom of all sliding boards.
6. All playgrounds and equipment will be inspected daily for cleanliness, proper maintenance, loose or protruding bolts, rooted areas, and other potential hazards.
7. All holes or pits in the ground surface will be promptly filled in as they occur.
8. All playgrounds will be kept clean of glass, dead limbs and trees, and other debris.

9. All playgrounds will be covered where practicable with a maintained grass lawn.
10. All trash containers in play areas will be firmly mounted, covered, and have all rough edges removed. Trash containers will be regularly emptied.
11. No motorized vehicle will be allowed in playground areas, and signs should be erected to that effect.
12. Areas which by their very nature attract children and at the same time may be harmful to children, such as construction sites, are called attractive nuisances and are unauthorized play areas. These areas will be barricaded and signs erected indicating such areas are not open to the public.

K. Swimming

1. All lifeguards will be properly supplied with necessary lifesaving gear and be properly trained. It is required that all lifeguards be at least eighteen years old and have received Water Safety Instructor training from the Red Cross or comparable training from organizations designated by the system. Each lifeguard will be required to have completed at least one Red Cross course in first aid and will be fully acquainted with the proper and safe use of resuscitation equipment. It is mandatory that lifeguards be on duty at all swimming areas during all operating hours. The number of lifeguards necessary will depend on the number of swimmers and the size of the swimming area, but on weekends lifeguards should be on duty in greater numbers. All lifeguards will be required to wear a readily identifiable swimsuit. Each lifeguard is required to have a whistle around his or her neck on a chain, and the lifeguard stand will be equipped with an umbrella to provide shade, a megaphone, and a surf board which can be used as a water stretcher. A first aid room will be designated at each swimming area. A copy of *Lifesaving: Rescue and Water Safety* is to be used as the official lifeguard reference manual. Each swimming area will have rescue stations strategically located around pools and along beaches. Each station will have a ring buoy, of a material other than Styrofoam, with a fifty-foot retrieving line and a reach pole.
2. The public will be adequately informed by signs as to safe swimming practices and possible hazards they may encounter in the swimming area. These signs will be erected indicating that:
   a) Wrestling and running around pools or on beaches is not allowed.
   b) Glass containers are not allowed on beaches or in pool areas.
   c) Swimming is allowed only in designated areas.
   d) Swimmers will obey the lifeguards at all times.

e) Swimming is allowed only when lifeguards are on duty.
f) No more than one diver at a time is allowed on a diving board.

3. Special practices and policies will be followed by park personnel to insure safe swimming conditions:
   a) All drownings and near drowings will be handled as quietly as possible to prevent panic and fear among other swimmers.
   b) Reasonable capacity limits will be established for each swimming area and, if necessary, these limits will be enforced to prevent dangerous overcrowding of facilities.
   c) Also, where appropriate the beach will fly a large three-by-five-foot pennant where riptides exist and use flashing red beacons to indicate the hazard. Loudspeaker communication of the hazardous condition will likewise be used. It is possible that use of the pennant could be confused with small craft warnings, but this appears unlikely due to past public acceptance of this policy.
4. General maintenance practices for swimming areas will include removing of debris, glass, and other hazards, and the regular checking of diving areas to make sure siltation has not caused diving areas to become dangerously shallow.

L. Other Recreational Activities
Only activities most likely to be provided at system facilities are covered in the above. If parks have activities which are not discussed, the same overall type practices will be followed in order to insure system safety and an awareness of potential hazards. In all cases the intent is to avoid any impression of negligence on the part of the park employees and to give the impression of park employees being highly concerned about the health and welfare of all park visitors, with taking active steps to avoid accidents.

Policy Issuance

When the commitment to safety is settled, the chief executive together with his or her closest advisers and other employee representatives will develop a policy statement. The policy will probably be broadly expressed, i.e., the chief objective is to provide a safe environment thereby preventing accidents, injuries, and protecting the lives and welfare of patrons and employees of the agency.

The issuance of policy is accomplished with the codification of all policies in a manual, transmitted throughout the agency, and bound in a way which permits additions and deletions as situations change requiring new or modified policies. Effective bodies develop policy manuals or cause them to be developed. These policy manuals are almost always printed and available for distribution throughout the agency and to those who have a need to know. It is probably best to formalize policies into a manual form. This prevents misunderstandings on the part of those who are designated as having the responsibility for executing or conforming to policy decisions and negates the possibility of using ignorance as an excuse for not having performed in ways which are regarded as necessary in order to provide a safe and satisfying service. The publication of a policy manual incorporating both legislative and administrative policies represents the understanding of decision-makers with respect to those areas being delineated by policy and clearly specifies the intent of the organization in terms of its devotion to a particular objective, condition, or operation. No policy statement can be ambiguous. It must be unequivocal and enunciate precisely what is to be done, by whom, for whom, and in relation to what degree of care of known standard of practice is current.

With codification of policies there is also developed a substantial body of information which includes the techniques and methods most appropriate and desirable in carrying out policy mandate. These ramifications typically comprehend all organizational practices which have some bearing on safety. The safety manual will ordinarily contain specific information dealing with the separate divisions of the organization and the functions which have safety implications. These are introduced by activity and further amplified by rules, regulations, and ordinances.

Rules. The establishment of guides that determine conduct in the ordinary course of daily operations. It is a decision handed down by the administrative authority of the agency as a method or procedure to be followed by employees as they go about the business of carrying out the functions of the organization. Rules are based upon policy and prescribe the ways and means for adhering to the policy.

Regulations. Regulations are promulgated to control or direct the behavior of patrons within the jurisdiction of the recreational service system or those patrons buying services offered by private companies, corporations, or associations. Regulations are designed to apply uniformly to all those who participate in the program or utilize the facilities of the system. It is a limitation placed upon the behavior of those who are served by the agency so as to make the operation capable of maintaining the health and safety of patrons.

Ordinances. A statute enacted by the legislative authority of the jurisdiction involved, publicly posted or made readily available to those for whom the ordinance is directed. It usually forbids certain activities or behaviors and carries with it notice of penalties which can be applied for infractions. Obviously, ordinances may only be passed and enforced by local governmental units. They are generally used to enforce policy and prevent patrons from misadventures by prohibiting or restricting the would-be user from actively engaging certain experiences or entering on or into areas that are clearly posted, fenced, or otherwise declared dangerous.

Gaining Compliance to Policy

Education is the surest means for obtaining compliance to safety policy. However, it is also the technique which requires the longest time investment, and the lessons may need considerable repetition before they are finally learned. Nevertheless, education is the process by which personal commitment may be acquired and the basic understanding for safe practice internalized. The recreational service agency must provide an instructional program which is integrated, in fact inseparable, from the activities with which people want to become involved. This is a painless and unobtrusive process which becomes ingrained with time and effort. As the individual becomes more skilled in the activity of choice, it is reasonable to assume that safety knowledge and skills will also be acquired.

For employees, as well, educational techniques may be applied with the same expectation of acquisition and use. But the instructional practices do not have to be camouflaged to the same extent as does that which is provided to patrons. The safety instruction must be a part of the on-going development of workers and may never be left up to happenstance. In this way, safety performance and behavior will become second nature to staff members. Only the most recalcitrant, psychologically unsuitable, or deliberate misfeasant will not accept the safety teachings—either for themselves or for those for whom they are responsible. In such cases other measures must be taken to gain policy compliance. If there are workers who refuse to follow sound safety practices and their deficiency produces accidents or injuries, they must be called to account. Loss of pay, allowances, or other amenities may be one alternative, and this should be called to the attention of all employees periodically; or final termination from the position may be necessary. In the latter instance, it is possible to move that individual to another job that can be performed adequately without such contact. That is always the better procedure than abrupt termination. In the last analysis, if the individual still cannot comply with established safety policy, it is best for the welfare of all concerned that such a person be removed from the agency.

One other medium is also available to ensure compliance to safety policy. The publication of ordinances that are drawn up by and legislatively passed under the powers of the local legal subdivision in which the public recreational service is located may do much to prohibit serious infractions of agency safety policy and actually punish deviant behavior. Sometimes it is not only necessary to publish ordinances, but to enforce whatever penalties their infraction requires. For most sensible people, it is sufficient to deter certain activities or behaviors by posting timely notices or warnings to indicate that specific areas are dangerous or that a particular act is either prohibited or potentially harmful to the perpetrator. To those few who insist upon ignoring warnings or posted notices, enforcement of the ordinance's penalties may be salutory. This is especially valid where an activity that is actually hazardous to participants has long been practiced with only half-hearted remonstrances or lip-service paid to the potential danger by authorities. The lack of enforcement by prohibition and/or imposed penalty is brought home when an accident occurs and a serious or killing injury occurs. Nothing deters the would-be infractor more than active and speedy enforcement of penalties that ordinances explicitly affirm.

The following example, based upon an actual case concluded in New Jersey bears out this premise:

> A twenty-three-year-old man was injured when he dove into an unposted pond, located within a recreational area operated by a county park commission. The young man sustained a fracture of the neck after striking his head against an underwater obstruction and is now a quadriplegic with no hope of recovery of the use of his upper and lower extremities.[1]
> The area in question was acknowledged to have been used by local residents and other visitors to the area for more than forty years. Although the park commission passed an ordinance which specifically prohibited swimming in unauthorized places, the public's ignorance of this ordinance (since it was not conspicuously posted) and the commission's failure to actively enforce the ordinance's prohibition by penalizing offenders materially weakened the defendant's case that they were not guilty of comparative negligence which directly led to the accident and injury. Although the case went to trial before an empaneled jury, defendant's counsel capitulated and decided to settle the case without further trial. Plaintiff received a lump sum payment of $125,000 in cash and a lifetime annuity which should generate between $13,000 to $14,000 per year for the rest of plaintiff's life.

There are any number of other reasons why the defendant park commission's case was weak, but a significant defect in the defense was the fact that although an ordinance had been passed against certain activities, no steps were taken to enforce the law despite the fact that authorities charged with its enforcement knew that the ordinance was being violated and had been breached repeatedly over a number of years. When ordinance violators were apprehended, they were simply reprimanded and asked not to swim, wade, or dive into the restricted pond. Obviously, no one paid any attention to these ineffectual measures, and the tragic incident ensued with considerable financial stress for the park commission.[2]

Even policy which is logically contrived to answer the needs of the organization is futile unless the concept is translated into action. All that policy does is to articulate the intention of the agency. As with all good intentions, mere wish or pronouncement will not fulfill the programmatic or operational requirements of the system. The proof of policy is in the implementation, not declaration. Unless policy is systematically analyzed and its meaning interpreted to the several components which make up the personnel force of the agency, nothing will be done. It is in the execution of policy that the real ideas by which the agency is guided are produced.

NOTES

1. *Dambro v. Union County Park Commission, et al.*, 130 New Jersey *Superior Court Reports*, p. 540, 11 October 1974.

2. George Hjelte and Jay S. Shivers, *Public Administration of Recreational Services* (Philadelphia: Lea & Febiger, 1978), 168–80.

7
Risk Management in Recreational Service

The reason for establishing a risk management program is to heighten employment of money apportioned to the recreational service agency through effective control of loss. Loss in this instance refers to loss of productive worker hours on the job without sickness or accidents and the most efficient use of available capital for recreational purposes—not payment of injury claims. Risk management, or reducing losses to controllable proportions, has as a primary objective the correction of actual or potential hazards which may result in monetary loss. More significantly there is an essential focus for reducing or eliminating personnel loss to the agency by acting safely. Each employee has a personal responsibility for initiating the kinds of behavior necessary to insure maximum efficiency. This means performance on the job without time off for industrial injuries, destruction of materials, or patron-related injuries which might produce court action.

It is the function of the chief executive officer to establish and maintain a safe and healthful environment within the system. Regardless of work site, whether in the field, the shop, or the office, the administrator must insure that policies and procedures are developed and complied with by all personnel so that injuries can be minimized, vehicle accidents will be reduced, liabilities controlled, and material guarded from waste.

In order to implement risk management practices within an agency there will be a need to direct the attention of all personnel to the major objective of maintaining sound loss prevention policies as a first consideration in every operation. Therefore, every staff meeting will have time allocated to review incidents that contribute to agency losses and undertake those positive plans which reduce such losses. Obviously, whatever actions are taken must be based upon the number and seriousness of losses and the incidence of dangerous activities with which each agency division is routinely involved.

Each employee's injury or accident record will be reviewed periodically to determine why and how such loss occurred. This analysis can then serve as a basis for retraining the employee and assist in alleviating environmental hazards, assuring supervisory competence, or finding grounds for negligent employee termination. There must also be compliance with OSHA standards in facility construction and plant maintenance. Participation in risk management committee meetings and the promotion of aggressive and effective loss control are part of a constant and unremitting effort designed to maximize efficiency and eliminate loss.

SAFETY POLICY ADMINISTRATION

Since the executive is responsible for the safe and efficient accomplishment of the agency's mission, administrators must recognize the inclination for thought and action to present contrasting extremes. First, because of time and money constraints it will probably be impossible to prevent all the potential accidents that might occur. Sources of dangers may not always be perceived, and the most enigmatic factor, that of human error, is inevitable. Yet, administrators must constantly strive to coordinate all elements of the managerial system in order to gradually reduce, if not eliminate, hazardous exposure with the concomitant sources of accidents.

Administrators must be assured that their subordinates will act in compliance to safety directives. This requires that all supervisors will behave in ways that promote safety practices, serve as models for their subordinates, and expect that all employees will observe the rules, standards, and procedures established for safety.

Safety Committee

Successful safety programs not only require active involvement of the executive, but participation by all those who are directly affected by the implementation of safety standards and practices. To this end, safety committees composed of personnel from the various work units of the agency in large systems or a committee representing both workers and management in smaller agencies should be established to formulate rules and provide advice to top administration concerning ways in which work-related hazards can be eliminated and the ways in which the total environment can be made safer for potential patrons and participants.

There seems little doubt that employees of the system have the greatest benefit to gain from close adherence to safety practices and behavioral approaches which lessen the possibility of accidents and injuries to them. Moreover, employees have the most intimate knowledge of the environmental hazards and accident producing situations which can occur during work. Unless employees are specifically concerned with the reduction and/or prevention of unsafe activities and conditions, the most comprehensive safety policies developed by administrators will fail. By involving employees in the basic procedures out of which will come all-system policies and standards of safety, there is a greater chance for the successful implementation and execution of safety policies.

Among the functions of the safety committee will be:

a. Making routine inspections of the various working areas and suggesting corrective measures to eliminate physical hazards.
b. Studying work methods and making self-analyses in order to detect potential accident problems.
c. Observing patrons utilizing the various facilities and calling to the attention of appropriate authorities any improper behavior or dangerous actions that might be potentially injurious.
d. Correcting and/or eliminating whatever environmental hazards are observed during work—if they can be corrected by the person who observed them.
e. Suggesting safety practices that may be incorporated into any in-service safety training program for employees.
f. Assisting in the development of safety campaigns that may be a part of the overall in-service staff development program.
g. Maintaining an on-going reportorial accident and record-keeping system. This will assist in determining where, why, how, and to whom accidents are occurring.
h. On the basis of accident reporting and other analysis of the information dealing with injuries to persons or damage to property, a definite safety program should be designed and forwarded to the administrator responsible.
i. Periodically reporting to the administrator charged with promoting safety throughout the organization concerning progress being made as a result of safety measures instigated.

The organization and functioning of a safety committee is reliable testimony to the commitment that safety policy is not merely lip service. Since the safety committee is made up of those who will ultimately have to perform and carry out the mission of the agency in a manner that will offer satisfaction to all those who participate, it becomes intimately involved with every factor that conduces to safe operations. The safety committee not only has the blessing of administration, but answers directly to the administrator who has the responsibility for the maintenance of safety throughout the system. Many problems that might not ordinarily surface even with the use of the services of a safety engineer will be brought to light when those who are most deeply and personally concerned have a hand in shaping agency policy and assisting in the development of policies that will eventually affect them on the job. The presumption is that employees will also be concerned about those whom the agency serves and will want to offer the safest environment to them.

Safety Education for Personnel

In-service staff education is one of the chief components of a comprehensive safety program within any agency. It provides the methods, materials, and an organization that actually compels employees to be present at a variety of instructional activities intended to alert all concerned to the potential dangers that the work situation reveals and the techniques that can negate such hazards. The in-service safety program is the responsibility of first line supervisors. It is part of their function to provide employees with both information and practices that can make them more competent, effective, and efficient. To this end, safety education is one of the areas that can enhance greater productivity on the part of workers by reducing time-off-the-job by virtue of injuries due to accidents while at work.

Periodically, at least once each month and more frequently if need be, supervisors will convene members of their immediate unit and conduct reviews of the safety program. This may include discussions based upon accident reports within the unit or throughout the system. Among the methods particularly suited to the presentation of information leading to the reduction or elimination of accidents and the enhancement of safety are:

1. Audio-visual presentation. This includes such aids as mock-ups, motion pictures, film strips, slides, models, and other graphics.
2. Didactic presentation. This technique involves the introduction and development of information by lecture.
3. Discussion. This method requires input from members of the unit insofar as they are able to bring up pertinent problems that confront them on the job in relation to safety procedures and practices.
4. Literary presentations. This method includes the assignment of reading materials, e.g., books, pamphlets, reports, individualized instruction sheets, or specific articles that have been collected for this particular purpose.
5. Visitors from other units or extra-agency speakers. Through the process of cross-fertilization members of units within the agency may learn what other elements are doing to promote safety. Safety experts featuring various types of knowledge may be brought in to lecture and discuss specialized topics.
6. Role playing. Unit members are assigned particular roles and then spontaneously act out the role. A typical example might involve a variety of situations that employees encounter on the job. These can be between employees or patrons and concern unsound behavior or ignorance. Through this form valuable information can be conveyed.

In addition to the above methods, periodic review of first aid techniques, fire drills, and emergency evacuation procedures should be undertaken by those units for which such steps are suitable and necessary. While office workers, for example, might be required to evacuate the building in which they work, it is less likely that they will be required to know or practice first aid. The utilization of in-service education programs should be appropriate for the employees receiving them.

The safety of patrons should be an integral part of every staff meeting. A portion of every meeting should be concerned with the general topic of safety and the ways and means by which patron safety can be promoted and implemented. The supervisor of the unit in question should always have a formal agenda planned in which the problem of patron safety is clearly defined and where whatever remedial measures to be taken to insure safe behavior are pronounced. This should not be left to chance or spontaneous reference. A purposeful presentation concerning safety of patrons will reinforce one of the primary responsibilities that the agency assumes.

Safety Education for the Public

Providing an effective program of safety education for the public is difficult, but nonetheless, a responsibility of agencies which offer recreational services. Although some members of the public are reached by the formal requirements of instruction in schools, there are many who are beyond the jurisdiction of educational institutions and must be reached through the informal means of safety notices. However, recreational service agencies practically have a captive audience of those members of the public who visit facilities or participate in the various activities that are programmed for their enjoyment. Once the visitor is within the precincts of the park or other recreational facility, he/she is subject to the regulations and ordinances that the agency promulgates for his safety. Furthermore, the agency may develop a comprehensive safety education program primarily aimed at those who participate.

Recreational service agencies have several methods that will prove highly effective in reaching the public consciousness. These include interpretive programs about the facility or area interspersed with pertinent safety information; posted regulations and ordinances that carry out the safety policy of the agency; signs and other directional or warning devices that provide some safety information; and instructional activities carried on under the direction of employees. Whether the employee is teaching the rules, strategies, or techniques of a game, explaining the intricacies of using tools, machines, or other equipment, providing instruction for the use of apparatus, supplies, or other material, safety practices and procedures are an integral subject for inclusion. It is in this way that the most successful programs of safety education may be inculcated. Additionally, there has been enrollment in a wide variety of recreational activities that have as their basis the provision of safety. Thus, hunting, aquatics, first aid, rock climbing, skiing, gymnastics, and many more require that an individual who wants to learn first be instructed in the safety ramifications which undergird these experiences.

Supervisory Function

Supervisory consultation and attempted in-service staff development should be a constant stimulus toward the evolution of a work force that is capable of following safety procedures and carrying out the intent as well as the spirit of safety policy. Supervision may be furthered through well-timed and considered inspections of the areas and facilities under the jurisdiction of the supervisor—together with other members selected to accompany the supervisor on formal or informal inspections. It must be remembered that inspections are carried out to determine whether a physical property or thing is in its proper place and working in an effective and efficient manner. This also relates to the condition of land or places in and on which recreational activities occur.

Thus, inspection to determine whether fire extinguishers have been recently charged and are in working order, whether the playgrounds and playfields operated by the department are free of obstructions, potholes, or other potentially dangerous nuisances, or whether first aid equipment is available are some of the determinations that will be made by inspecting the various areas, apparatus, materials, supplies, and equipment that the department owns and operates.

Supervisory observation of workers as they perform their assigned tasks is another technique designed to indicate compliance with or deviation from standard operation procedures and safety policy. In this connection the supervisor periodically, but at irregular intervals, visits the site where employees are working and actually observes how they execute their responsibilities. It is not uncommon for a supervisor to visit a center, playground, swimming facility, or other recreational property to determine if staff are performing in ways which are expected. The observation provides material for use in supervisory conferences and weekly staff meetings. It is a way to discover adherence to preferred safe work habits. In addition, it affords a ready check on workers and insures that deficient or meritorious work will be verified and suitably acknowledged. Finally, supervisory visits are scheduled in advance with the intent of evaluating worker performance and, perhaps, offering suggestions for greater effectiveness or increased competence at that time. Naturally, the supervisor does not break into an activity to remonstrate with nor correct worker deficiency. If necessary, this will be accomplished at a time and place removed from curious eyes and ears. Unless the worker is in flagrant violation of agency policy or is actually endangering a patron's safety, intervention during activity sessions is uncalled for and may reduce worker morale with concomitant loss of productivity and/or effectiveness.

System Safety Officer

In order that the patron safety program is properly implemented on a system-wide basis, the agency will appoint a Safety Officer. The Safety Officer is responsible for making periodic inspections of each area. The inspections will include all items covered below.[1] The Safety Officer will review all accident reports for completeness and accuracy and will make personal follow-up investigations on all serious injuries and fatalities. The

Safety Officer will review all new development plans for safety considerations in layout, design, and construction. The Safety Officer is responsible for keeping all safety records for the system, coordinating all educational programs, and preparing an annual safety budget for the agency. The Safety Officer will work very closely with the individual facility safety officers in carrying out the assigned responsibilities in aiding the facility safety officers with problems peculiar to their situation, including acquisition of safety equipment. Also, the Safety Officer will be responsible for preparing and distributing public information brochures warning of hazards. The Safety Officer will make sure informative signs and posters are used in each recreational area, that signs are properly placed, and that adequate emphasis is given to educating the public about safe practices.

Organizational Commitment

When recreational service organizations recognize their responsibility for the safety of their constituency as well as that of the employees of the agency, they will develop risk management policy that reflects such recognition. The policy statement does more than define the ways in which the goals of the system will be carried out. It actually commits the organization to practice in ways which will preclude unsafe operations or inappropriate behavior. Risk management policy is a guide to the kinds of behavior expected by all employees in order to obtain the safest conditions possible in the provision of recreational services. This really means that the agency has formalized the practices and procedures which are required so that a safe environment becomes routine.

Resource Allocation

Policy also commits the agency to set up a system of priorities by which the allocation of its resources will be utilized to further the purposes toward which the agency has responsibility. Provision of recreational service carries with it certain substantial needs for personnel support, material reservation, and monetary encumbrance to carry out the intent of policy. Risk management programs and the creation of a safe environment does not develop merely by stating that it exists. A great deal of time, money, and effort must be disposed so that the tangible rewards of reduced environmental hazards, eliminated potential accidents, and uninjured patrons and/or employees are the outcome. This means that administrators and their subordinates consciously and literally are involved in producing a climate where safety practices are mandatory and express behavioral codes are imposed upon all employees so that this responsibility is executed.

Sometimes agency administrators cannot see the long-term advantages for having a sound safety program and its necessary commitment of monetary resources and personnel to it. Perhaps there is such a call for recreational activities and the various services which are directly associated with them that other elements are skimped upon. This is almost always an error of judgment. Even when there is an economic retrenchment movement impinging upon agency performance, it is better to eliminate some recreational activities temporarily than it is to stop the allotment of money, material, or personnel to the practice of safety or the curtailment of any facet of the safety program. The reason for this is obvious. Public clamor for the restitution of popular recreational activities may require the fiscal authorities to reinstate funds that will permit the programming of recreational experiences that were previously cut. Recreational activities that have few or no constituents may be reasonably pruned without loss to the productivity of the agency. However, any reduction of the safety program within the agency may give the appearance of short-term economy, but sooner or later that diminishment will be counterproductive. Since accidents can happen at any time, the disappearance of supervisory personnel, the failure to provide good maintenance and physical plant upkeep, the discontinuation of sign replacement after vandalism, or other negligent practices must inevitably lead to someone's injury with litigious consequences. One lost liability case can be more financially wearing to the agency (and its public image) than whatever money was "saved" in cutting back in safety practices. Myopic vision on the part of political officials or agency executives can be devastating to the agency. Little economies may provide the voters with a sense of saving that is not real. Many times, some minor expense is warranted even at the expense of recreational programming. Eventually, that expenditure for some heightened protection may pay off if, despite all effort, an individual is injured. The fact that such efforts were brought to bear will generally be reflected by a verdict of no negligence. Thus the community and its recreational agency (or the private promoter) will be spared the extravagance of court proceedings, and the cash outlays that invariably accompany jury or forced out-of-court settlements in losing cases.

It is probable that a carefully thought out risk management program, sound construction of facilities, well-maintained property, the employee safety program, a public informational program, and the employment of competent persons in the various positions necessary to the operation of a recreational service agency will more than compensate for the loss of one life or the permanently crippling injury suffered by an unsuspecting patron who might have been spared if only the department had performed its functions in a timely manner. The old adages of "penny wise, pound foolish," and "forewarned is forearmed," surely apply here.

Safety Education

Once an organization realizes the need to eliminate unsafe practices and offer a suitable environment for the preservation of the safety of patrons and employees, a number of procedures take effect. A safety education program with complement risk management procedures must be instituted throughout the agency so that employees will be habitualized toward the elimination of environmental hazards, the discontinuance of unsafe practices, the omittance of inappropriate conduct, and the development of positive actions that are necessary for the maintenance and administration of safe recreational services. A variety of rules, regulations, and other behavioral guides must be defined, developed, and posted. The implementation of special safety plans dealing with physical property as well as human practices must also be undertaken. Awareness of potential hazards and a preventive attitude toward accidents and injuries should be imbued within the consciousness of every employee.

The commitment of agency personnel and resources to the establishment and maintenance of a safe environment and program of activities will institutionalize safe practices and techniques, cause an aggressive seeking out of potential dangers and the elimination of causes before they become hazards. But even more significantly, commitment means that the agency will do everything that it must to operate safely. It may require the investigation and analysis of all property owned and operated by the agency to determine how potential sources of danger can be eliminated, and the development of an informational program that will attempt to educate the public toward safe conduct.

Ultimately, organizational commitment to safety requires the foundation of a risk management program that will:

1. Provide safe work places for its employees.
2. Provide safe recreational places and activities for patrons.
3. Provide information that will offer safe directions for patrons.
4. Provide instruction to participants that can effectively reduce or eliminate accidents and injuries that might occur.
5. Increase personnel effectiveness by reducing errors that lead to property damage, personal injury, time loss, and excessive costs due to litigation proceedings.
6. Consistently link safety with the prime mission of the agency.

NOTES

1. See *Infra,* Appendix pp. 310–19.

8
Design for Safety

In its comprehensive sense, the term design incorporates the total reasoning process from invented conception to satisfactory conclusion. In turning an idea into a finished product, the process includes basic inclination, agency policy, and particular details concerning the project being planned. The safe design of recreational places takes account of spatial relationships, physical sites, terrain features, expected appearance, functional use, and the various materials that will be used to give shape, texture, color, and boundaries to the construction or setting. Design is a process which focuses attention on the special elements associated with a unique environment, making them mutually interdependent, determining which will be applied, and then combining these into the most meritorious enhancement for the projected plan. The design is offered through a series of drawings, models, and written descriptions with accompanying diagrams, costs, specifications for all materials to be utilized, and all of those safety features required to prevent or diminish the probability of accidents. Through design, a given environment can have safety considerations built in to the development. Unless these factors are accounted for the opposite development may occur—i.e., hazards or artificially created dangers may actually be installed. Good design does not permit unsafe areas or objects to be introduced into structures or outdoor areas.

SAFETY DESIGN FACTORS

In each recreational development a variety of elements are present and must be arranged or adjusted so that the greatest harmony of site, facilities, and space can be produced. It is the function of design to bring these elements into conjunction without great disruption of the physical qualities of the site and to organize a recreational situation that exploits all natural advantages, but maintains the cohesiveness and integrity of the landscape in terms of its proportions, appearance, intended functions, and commitment to safety for users.

In planning recreational places consideration must be taken of the physical conditions affecting those who will eventually participate, the personnel employed, the departmental organization, and other elements that are also important to the outcome of an attractive environment. Of intense interest, therefore, will be special environmental factors that influence both the work and the recreational place.

The Personal Environment

All recreational agencies employ a disparate group of professional, technical, and ancillary personnel to perform the work for which the organization was established. These employees do the jobs that are in keeping with the objectives previously determined upon. Essential to the efficiency and effectiveness of the agency is the execution of responsibilities for administration of the program, facilities, and the system as a whole. Some personnel will be assigned to program operations. Technicians may be employed to assist professionals in a variety of ways. Some staff will devote their entire effort to management procedures. Each of these groups will be in contact with one or more environments during the period of their working life. For maximum performance environmental elements should not only contribute to the maintenance of an enjoyable occupational situation, but should also provide a climate of safety so that productive efforts will not be disturbed in consequence of time off the job due to major or minor injuries.

Employed personnel should have a working place which is conducive to the production of meaningful operational outcomes and be free of distraction and disruption. The immediate environment that forms the vocational areas of the work force and in which they most often function should be as comfortable and as safe as the organization can make them. This means that illumination should be such that it is appropriate for the worker's needs in order to sustain his working assignment. Stairwells, for example, should be well lighted. Stair treads should be skid proof. Office floors and hallways should be uncluttered, provide easy access to desired areas, and thereby control traffic patterns. Exits from structures should be such that they permit egress without hindrance. The structure itself should be free of fire hazards and meet all local building code regulations insofar as fire protection is concerned. These few items are just a brief listing of elements which are involved with the personal environment of employees.

Exterior Environment

All of the area around a given structure and the immediate neighborhood in which the recreational place is situated comprises the exterior environment. Any deliberation with design must first consider all factors that are directly concerned with the physical environment. Additionally, attention must be focused on the interrelationships between the elements that are juxtaposed because of the ways in which they affect each other. The ability to assess the part played by spatial factors in the achievement of the fundamental objectives of the organization on a systematic basis will also influence design. Actually, the concept of designing safety features into the physical property rather than introducing hazards is something for which each organization must be held accountable. It is not unusual for a planner to locate artificial structures in recreational areas because of aesthetic considerations, despite the fact that these constructions represent potential dangers to users. In many instances, the planner is preoccupied with how an area looks instead of the dangers that his/her handiwork presage.

Certain separations must be made between specific activities in order to prevent accidents and injuries. However, the type of barrier will have much to do with the prevention or allowance of such accidents. There are always extraordinarily safe ways for preventing participants from becoming entangled with one another. If space prohibits wide separation of activities, then soft barriers may be erected with safety. Unfortunately, soft barriers are sometimes thought to be unpleasing to the artistic eye. In these instances the designer may allow art to take precedence over common sense and safety. There is, sometimes, a tendency to cause the construction of hard, immobile objects that stand as barricades between activities. They may be pleasant to look at, but they are definite hazards to potential participants. Their presence will eventually result in a more or less severe injury when a body comes in contact with the object—especially if momentum is involved.

A case in point is that of an eight-year-old child, whose tobogganing mishap occurred when she struck the lower portion of a split-rail fence that had been used to divide a snow hill. One half was used for skiing and the other was used for coasting (both sledding and tobogganing). Although there was gross incompetency and negligence displayed by the county department operating the recreational facility, the injuries to the child may not have happened if the barrier separating the two areas had been composed of something other than rigid fence posts and rails. The net result was that the child was very nearly decapitated, suffered monumental neck and head injuries, and is, today, blind, deaf, and paralyzed from the neck down. An award of $5.3 million was made in this case.[1]

FACTORS OF RECREATIONAL ENVIRONMENT

For purposes of analysis and better understanding the various elements that constitute the environment must be artificially examined on an individual basis. It is clear that all environmental factors are inseparable and in actuality would be a synthesized environmental unity. While each integral portion is unmistakably interrelated and interacting with all other aspects of the physical surroundings, analysis is undertaken to assure easy identification and an indication of how each might affect design. Environmental components may best be described as groups of factors lumped under the general classifications of biological and psychological.

Biological

Biological factors encompass those elements of the environment that directly influence physiological stability, functions, and reactions to physical stimuli. Heat and cold, light and dark, humid or dry interiors tend to affect sensory reactions that either further or inhibit comfort in the normal operation of a recreational structure. What is true for the recreationist is also valid for the participant. Recreational activity is enhanced or retarded, in many cases, by the interior environment of a given room or space. High temperatures in summer or low temperatures in winter materially affect whether or not safe work habits will be promoted or inhibited. The same is true for active participation in a variety of physical activities (or any activities for that matter).

Interior climate is significant because it influences the individual's ability to accomplish little or much in the way of work and promotes or denies opportunities for people to freely participate in wholesome surroundings. Illumination, for example, not only includes lighting fixtures, but other concomitant features such as indirect lighting, reflected lighting, shadows, glare, color, tone of light. Placement of and storage for the areas in which craft activities will occur has much to do with the enhancement of physical comfort and safety insofar as chemical explosions or fires are concerned. A swimming facility in the building can be the cause of odors from chemicals utilized to make the water clear, clean, and safe. Wet slippery surfaces are ever prevalent in shower, toilet, and locker rooms and are the likely cause of accidents. The following case illustrates this condition: "An individual suffered a brain concussion when he fell on the 'wet, filmy, and slippery' washroom floor of a municipal swimming pool. The individual was awarded damages despite the fact that there was no permanent injury sustained. Moreover, the court found the municipality negligent and was upheld by a 6-0 decision of the Superior Court Appellate Division when the city apealed that it was immune from liability on the basis of governmental function. The court found that the hazardous floor conditions had existed 'for some time.' "[2]

The sense of touch also plays an important role in terms of physiological affectability. The tactile quality of materials prescribes how they will be interpreted by the brain, i.e., warm, cold, hard, soft, rough, smooth, resilient, rigid, or potentially dangerous when in contact with the body. Space allocation for each form of activity, whether of participation in recreational pursuits or carrying out the work of the agency cannot be so restrictive as to prevent needed movement from one point to another; nor so congested as to be potentially dangerous.

Psychological

How a given area appears to one individual will depend upon his/her psycho-physical balance, ability to appreciate certain structural relationships, colors, and so forth. Whether the interior surroundings seem suitable, closed in, or have more than enough room is determined on both actual and apparent scope, length, breadth, height, and mass of the enclosed area. Laboratory experiments have conclusively indicated that the human sense of balance may be distorted by juggling vertical lines and right angles. Geometric errors could conceivably be produced in structures thereby causing poor depth perception, spatial mistakes, and feelings of anxiety. Any room may be given a sinister or friendly cast by light and color arrangements. A psychological effect of a particular area can be modified by knocking out walls and adding dimension, utilization of different color tones, illumination, windows, optical tricks, and other techniques. A small room may appear larger if its walls are covered by light paint tones. Windows and mirrors also seem to enlarge a closed space. Both physical and mental elements are at work in relation to the individual's appreciation of what he/she sees or feels or thinks he perceives about interior environments. Essentially, if distractions and other environmental irritations can be eliminated from the work place, there will be fewer accidents recorded.

NOTES

1. Mark Boada, "Paralyzed Girl Wins a Lifetime Settlement," *Newark Star Ledger,* 2 February 1978, pp. 1, 26.
2. *Weeks v. City of Newark,* 34 N.J. 250, 168 At12d 11 (1961).

9
Supervision

Without doubt, supervision may be the single most significant element concerned with the elimination, or at least the reduction, of accidents and injuries that occur at recreational places. While it is true that some injuries cannot be avoided, due to the nature of the accident or the unpredictability of the behavior that resulted in injury or damage, even if competent supervision is immediately present and available, there is little question that the kinds of accidents that result in permanent injuries can be prevented by supervision. Eternal vigilance remains the greatest interdictive process against negligence on the part of employees who have responsibility for the safety of patrons.

THE NATURE OF SUPERVISION

Supervision is a process whose intent is to cause improvement in the behavior, skills, or competence of those who come within the jurisdiction of the person charged with the responsibility for providing it. Essentially, it is the oversight of activities and the conduct exhibited by participants in those activities so that the most competent performance in conformity with appropriate behavior is elicited. This means that the supervisor may have an instructional role to play or one that requires the restriction of certain acts as being inadmissible, dangerous, or unsuitable for the environment in which it is being performed. The supervisory process attempts to upgrade technical ability, knowledge, and conduct by obtaining close cooperation of those who are being supervised. Fundamentally, all supervision must rely upon leadership to develop the necessary rapport that produces cooperative effort.[1] In this manner, the recipient of supervision is called upon to offer personal commitment or identification through ideas, suggestions, or questions whenever the individual has the capacity to do so.

In some instances, supervision is simple custodianship. The relation between the supervisor and those supervised need not be one of democratic purpose. In this latter sense, supervision becomes a prohibitory activity whose function is to prevent behaviors from going beyond the bounds of common sense, a situation that can result in damage to property or injury to persons. This form of supervision must be imposed on those who either are not mature enough to adhere to standard expectation of conduct or fail to acknowledge dangerous situations and environments.

When dealing with personnel of the organization, it is obvious that supervision must be of a more personalized relationship. This is required if managerial authorities believe that motivation and authority are legitimate consequences for increased productivity. Personnel supervision can no longer rely upon a concept of authoritarianism. Instead, individualized counseling becomes the basis for the supervisory relationship. This mandates the need for leadership rather than headship. Each supervisor must appreciate the fact that all workers have different strengths and weaknesses and that they have to be considered as individuals. This outlook permits accomplishment of organizational objectives without compromising agency needs. Personnel who are unable to meet job expectations are to be assisted in every possible manner to remediate whatever deficiencies they have. In return, the worker will have to cooperate by making appropriate efforts toward improved performance.

This is not to be construed as a milksop approach. Far from it. It merely recognizes the reality that some persons are outstanding workers and others exhibit deficiencies in particular skills and aptitudes, both occupational and social. This orientation attempts to obtain valid knowledge about each worker, to determine skills possessed and aptitudes, and to place the employee into an appropriate job within the organization based upon that determination. If a worker's inadequacies can be corrected, the organization will bend every effort through close supervision so that the individual is motivated to become more effective. Good supervision attempts to place people in jobs that more nearly conform to their social and occupational skills. Thus, supervision as a leadership process reinforces the concept that employees who are happy in their work and associations will also exhibit greater loyalty to the organization and be more highly productive in the work that they do. Such supervision also recognizes the need to help employees develop whatever potentials they have, thereby satisfying personal needs for achievement in association with the duties and responsibilities they hold.

Orientation to Safety

All supervisors orient newly inducted workers into the procedures and expectations of the organization. Generally, such an orientation includes the history, philosophy, work methodology, other pertinent practices, and personnel policies that guide the performance of the agency. Such an orientation is designed to introduce the employee to coworkers, familiarize that person with the standard operating routines, and provide specified written materials in the form of worker manuals against which the employee can determine acceptable behaviors and other information. Included in any orientation procedure must be a concern for the safety of all personnel and the clientele that the organization serves. Here is a most suitable time for safety policies, practices, and concepts to be inculcated. From the very beginning of employment, the worker must be imbued with the idea that the safety of patrons is at least as important as is furnishing satisfying and enjoyable recreational experiences. One of the primary purposes of safety education is to disseminate information to prospective recreators as well as their nominal supervisors so that they may live safely in their environment. Safety of patrons involved with recreational activity is a combined responsibility of supervisors, recreationists, and administrators. Competent leadership and supervision is required at all times—depending upon the circumstances and the maturity of recreators. The ultimate success of any accident prevention program relies upon the effectiveness with which the program is administered. There are some situations in which supervision is not required, but these are only in circumstances in which the agency has never supplied supervision and is not mandated to do so. However, once the agency offers supervision, this factor weighs heavily in maintaining an accident-free environment.

Accidents can be prevented by employee alertness, which can best be achieved by diligent attention to the probable areas of trouble. Recreationists have the responsibility of including accident prevention in their instructions to participants as well as being certain that all safety rules are enforced. It is their responsibility to perform all recommendations of their supervisors that are expected to improve safety conditions. In their own function as supervisors of recreators they must be careful observers so that foreseeable problems do not erupt as injuries. Further, recreationists must be prepared to offer suggestions to their supervisors to improve safety conditions when this appears necessary.

Supervisory Characteristics

What are the qualifications and attributes of those who are given supervisory responsibility in recreational service delivery systems? How can it be determined whether or not an individual is capable of assuming the role of supervisor where the safety of others is concerned? Answers to these questions revolve around the concepts of professionalism and expertness, as well as those of personality and the virtue of having good sense. It is reasonable to assume that recreationists have certain characteristics in common and that these are developed through exposure to higher education preparatory programs in accredited institutions. The recreationist has the credentials that accrue with a bachelor's or higher degree in one of the specializations of the field of recreational service education. Moreover, the recreationist has acquired a personal philosophy or orientation concerning the obligation of offering disinterested service to those who are the clientele of the employing organization. Thus, professionalism arises inseparably from the idea of unquestioned competence in dealing with the technical skills that comprise the practice of recreational service delivery.

Individuals who are appointed to supervisory positions have the trust and confidence of the authority that appoints them. Presumably such trust develops from the observation of the recreationist over a period of time as the individual performs the functions of assigned duties. When an individual shows by aptitude, skill, maturity, and effort, a stable and reliable aproach in carrying out the requirements of the position, it is likely that a supervisory rank may be conferred.

A supervisor is selected for a given special ability or fitness to lead a particular cooperative endeavor. A supervisor has ordinarily demonstrated some ability or control better than the ability of other peers. Furthermore, the supervisor has the ability to initiate an environment of serious, critical examination of problems and procedures as well as a sympathetic insight into the mental processes of other individuals with whom he/she works or comes into contact. Above all, the supervisor must show by consistent behavior that impartiality and democratic techniques undergird his or her dealing with others.

For our purposes here, supervision is traditionally viewed as inspection of physical plant, the equipment utilized, and the manner in which participants comport themselves. Additionally, supervision necessitates both the training and guidance of persons for whom the supervisor is responsible in order that the latter's skills, knowledge, or appreciation of the activity in which they are engaged is improved. Except when interacting with other employed personnel, that is precisely what the supervisor's job consists of. In developing the best working relationships with peers and other subordinates of the organization, the supervisor sees cooperative, participatory relationships as most important. Such interactive relationships are essential if productivity and loyalty to the agency are desired.

The traditional view of supervision becomes the sole standard to which the the supervisor must adhere. The supervisor is granted authority by the employing organization and must carry out the duties and functions that tend to emphasize control over participants and the regulation of behavior so that it is appropriate for the occasion. The supervisor must have a general knowledge of and continued oversight of the property and facilities used by the agency to deliver recreational services.

The employing organization wants an individual who is responsible, reliable, competent, and of a mature outlook so that the activities engaged in will be safe as well as enjoyable for clients. Insofar as employee safety and working environments are concerned, the organization presumably wants its supervisory staff to instill the correct safety practices and principles that will prevent accidental injuries or property damage from occurring.

Nonpaid Personnel

Many recreational service agencies of all kinds depend, to a greater or lesser extent, upon the services of volunteers. These individuals, by virtue of interest, skill, and available time, freely grant their talents and experience to the department without pay. These persons perform a wide variety of duties and functions and tend to augment the service which the department can provide. Several questions arise as a result of the use of volunteers, student field-workers, or other nonprofessionals:

1. May a recreationist ever leave the supervision of participants in the hands of nonprofessional personnel?
2. If nonprofessional personnel may undertake supervisory functions of participants, regardless of age or skill, what are the legal restrictions on their use?

Where there is no declared statutory authority, it would appear that the recreational service agency may utilize such assistance in the provision of recreational services as are necessary to supply an effective level of opportunities to those who wish to take part in the recreational activities offered by the agency. Thus, volunteers and student field workers would be covered under whatever authority existed within the public category to employ, without payment, those individuals who want to donate their services. In the private sector, any liability assumed by the organization for recreational offerings would attach to those auxiliaries authorized by the agency to volunteer. In any event, some legal agreement, plus insurance coverage in the event of injury to persons or damage to property might also be wise tactics.

Insofar as the public sector agencies are concerned, the general authority under which they operate would empower them to employ, in a voluntary capacity, nonprofessional personnel; and, by extension, it surely appears permissible to allow a volunteer to supervise a recreational activity.[2] Under these circumstances, it would not seem to be negligent for a recreationist to leave participants under the supervision of nonprofessional personnel in normal circumstances, and the recreationist will not be held liable for the single reason that that has been done.

Nevertheless, the correctness of the use of nonprofessional personnel has its limitations. In the first place, the recreationist must personally exercise control over those activities that carry with them high risks of injury; this may not be properly delegated to nonprofessionals—regardless of the latter's skill. This principle applies wherever there is more risk of injury than in the normal recreational situation.

Secondly, the person selected by the recreationist or by agency policy must be qualified to perform the function or responsibility. Thus, persons who do not have the ability or capacity to maintain appropriate supervisory control of participants, for whatever reason or reasons, should not be left alone in a supervisory position. To permit such handling would be negligence on the recreationist's part. Only where the nonprofessional has the ability and stature to maintain supervisory responsibility for participants, in a low-risk recreational situation, is it permissible for the recreationist to leave the nonprofessional alone.

It may be stated that even in the absence of any statutes concerning the use of nonprofessional personnel, the recreationist will not be held liable, and by extension neither will the agency, for participant injury simply because the recreationist has assigned a student field worker or volunteer to supervise the participants.[3] Of course, if the activity was one of high risk or if the recreationist believed that the person assigned was not able to maintain proper control of the existing situation and an accident occurred, liability would attach.

Supervisory Responsibility

Although it is difficult to pinpoint the precise set of circumstances that tend to produce litigation, it is probable that the chief concern for those who deliver recreational services will come from a failure to supervise properly. Some aspect of supervision, either improper performance or absence of supervision will be the primary allegation for litigation. Recreational malpractice is performance that falls below the professional level and can be viewed as negligence. Depending upon the nature of the necessary supervision involved, i.e., general or specific, a single instance of recreationist obliviousness may result in the personal injury to one for whom there is responsibility, and this becomes the basis of a lawsuit.

Civil actions or tort liability cases concerning supervision stem from three fundamental categories: (1) failure to supervise, (2) incompetent or improper supervision, and (3) failure to warn of dangers inherent in the activity. Recreationists have the objective responsibility of supervising class activities, if instruction is one of the job functions, and additionally the effectiveness of the recreationist's behavior may be examined. There is a legal duty to act, and the action must be correct or reasonable. Recreationists, especially when placed in instructional positions, are required to act with the highest standard of care that a professional would ordinarily espouse. Recreationists have a legal duty to perform with extreme precaution—not merely in terms of what a reasonable or prudent citizen of the general population would do, but as one who possesses special skills and education. Negligence is conduct that falls below this standard, and such conduct may result in monetary redress against the recreationist, the employing agency, or both. Failure to act may be the basis for liability. Recreationists are required to act in a manner that is consistent with how a peer would normally act when confronted by the same or similar situation.

Neither the recreationist nor the employing agency is an insurer. No one can guarantee that accidents will not occur. Nevertheless, a reasonable standard of care requires that any foreseeable injury will be anticipated and must, therefore, be avoided. The scope of this supervisory responsibility is not so much a detriment as it is an opportunity for the recreationist to become alert to his or her responsibilities for preventing unsafe situations and protecting patrons—even against themselves.

Supervision may be classified as direct or indirect, reactive or anticipatory, instructional or custodial. Sometimes direct supervision is termed close, immediate, or specific. Indirect supervision may be looked upon as loose, remote, passive, or general. Reactive supervision occurs after the fact. Once some incident occurs and injury or damage accrues, then policy and practices are developed to prevent whatever negative behavior or inappropriate action that took place from recurring. This type of supervision is always late. It takes place after the damage is done. The accent is on cure rather than prevention. This form of supervision may assist in preventing future accidents with consequent injury to persons or damage to things, but it cannot undo what has already happened. Thus, reactive supervision is essentially remedial in scope.

Anticipatory supervision, on the other hand, foresses potential danger in situations or conditions in which people recreate, or it is concerned with the prevention of accidents before they happen. To this end, whether the supervisor is dealing with departmental personnel or patrons, the recreationist analyzes the setting for recreational activities, the recreational activities themselves, the possible kinds of behavior that might be exhibited by participants, or the work habits and performance of employees of the department. Such analysis provides the basis for constructive changes to be made, if necessary, so that dangerous activity, environmental conditions, or faulty habits are not allowed to interfere with the provision of recreational services. These preventive measures do not eliminate the adventurousness, inherent risk, or fun that is integral to recreational participation. Rather, it focuses on the prohibition of substandard behaviors and the eradication of environmental conditions that can be controlled through inspection and corrective efforts.

Custodial supervision is that which is present and controlling the behavior of individuals who may not be able to distinguish between appropriate and inappropriate behavior. It stands, as it were, between the person and the foreseeable danger. It is entirely prohibitory and utilizes admonitory warnings and penalties in enforcing safety. Of course, custodial supervision may simply inhibit substandard behavior by preventing potential participants from having access to dangerous places or situations. This requires that activities will be limited to some secure area so that participants are not exposed to environmental hazards. It also requires strict observation of individuals who are in charge so that they may not do anything that will bring injury to themselves or others. Sometimes this may mean the use of physical restraints, the use of protective covering, headgear, or other items of clothing so that the chance of physical injury is lessened or eliminated entirely. For example, a severly mentally retarded person may attempt to harm himself by hitting his head against resistent objects. This behavior can be offset by placing a football helmet on the person's head. This effectively prevents injury.

As a case in point, the absence of general supervision in the following instance illustrates the concept.

> A young child, while on a sledding activity with his father, struck a tree head-on after sleighing down a hill located on the Galloping Hill Golf Course, Union, New Jersey. The child, 5 ½ years old at the time of the accident, sustained severe head injuries, a fractured rib, and complete loss of hearing in his left ear. The following information seems pertinent to any analysis of this incident:
>
> 1. The Union County Park Commission did not post warnings concerning the use or prohibition of use at their premises at Galloping Hill Golf Course.
> 2. There is unrestricted access to the course rather than controlled access. The condition is clearly a deviation from standard recreational service practice in that it prevents good personal supervision from taking place and permits dangerous behavior to occur.
> 3. No maintenance person provides any supervision to patrons using the sledding slope at the golf course.
> 4. Police supervision is inadequate and generally not of a nature required of recreational service departments. Police officers may be useful for crowd control, traffic control, and the protection of life, limb, and property, but they almost never offer the kind of close personal supervision to patrons of recreational places that recreationists provide. Such supervision is concerned with behavior and activities not illegal, but that might be hazardous to the individuals involved. Clearly the lack of supervision by recreational service personnel is an intolerable situation and violates good recreational service standard practice.
> 5. Lack of supervision may be underscored to the extent that the records for the day of the incident in 1969 show eleven patrolmen for an average of 2500 park users on a three-hundred-acre facility. Additional investigation shows that at no time were more than six to eight police available for direct crowd control. The others would have been performing traffic functions.
> 6. Whatever standing operational orders the police personnel received on 12 February 1969 were verbal. It is a basic tenet in the field of recreational service to produce written policy regarding departmental safety practices particularly as such practices concern the health, safety, and welfare of patrons. There were no written rules or regulations regard-

ing safety practices concerning the use of the golf course facility for winter activities in 1977 nor were there in 1969. This is a deviation from standard recreational service practices.

7. Weather reports for the days immediately prior to 12 February 1969 report some precipitation and the fact that there was from five to eight inches of snow on the ground. These reports indicate the likelihood of icy ground conditions due to the impacted snow on the hills at the golf course as well as the rapid thaw-freeze temperatures on the two days prior to the incident. It is probable, therefore, that icy surface conditions did exist and that the facility should have been closed to prevent mishaps. The fact that the facility was not closed is another example of faulty practice. Both expert witnesses make statements as to the icy surface conditions present on the day of the incident.
8. Lack of access barriers and planned entrances that would have created better conditions for crowd control and user pedestrian traffic were lacking. Winter facilities require limited access rather than unrestricted access so that patrons may be directed more expeditiously to use areas and kept away from reserved or prohibited areas. That this was not in effect on the day of the incident is a substandard practice.
9. There was no attempt made to educate the public through a planned public relations and educational program about the correct use of snow facilities at the golf course, nor has there ever been any effort to define safe patron conduct and present this to the public. Such efforts at public education are generally supported practices in the field.
10. It is a mandatory responsibility for public authorities who operate any kind of recreational facility to mark, post, or otherwise buffer potentially dangerous areas. It is patently ridiculous to either buffer or mark every tree and rock, but with controlled user access and the marking of dangerous locations as well as prohibitory or directional signs, placed conspicuously at intervals, entire sections may be closed to use while other areas are open. This prevents misuse and forces the public to use protected and controlled places. No such posting was in effect on the day of the incident.
11. Given these facts and the circumstances of the case as it is now attested to through depositions of the various witnesses, it must be concluded that the Union County Park Commission did not act in a manner consistent with the standards of practice in effect in the field of recreational service concerning the supervision of and safe use by patrons at a public facility. The question of public operations by professionals in the field does not permit the evasion of responsibility or the shifting of said responsibility to those acting *in loco parentis* or to actual parents of minors when a facility is open to the public. Under such circumstances of operation reasonable and prudent care must be exercised by the professionals who are responsible. It may be shown that such care is considerably higher than that which would normally be required of the layman or minor under the same conditions because of the presumed expertise of the professional.

Subsequently, this case was settled in favor of plaintiff, and a considerable sum of money was provided as redress.[4]

Instructional supervision is closely associated with developing the recipient's skill, knowledge, and appreciation of whatever is of interest. It is concerned with teaching the participant whichever technical skill is involved in an activity, providing that person with an atmosphere conducive to learning, motivating the individual to continue to practice, and enabling the individual to achieve satisfaction through safe performance. Nearly every recreational activity has an instructional aspect, and it is at this point that the recreationist can best inculcate the fundamental ideas of safe performance as well as a sense of achievement as skills are developed and the person becomes familiar with and knowledgeable about the techniques involved in participation. Perhaps no other aspect of supervision is as important to the provision of safety as that of instructional supervision. It relies upon proper attitude development, knowledge of the methods required to obtain satisfaction, and is based upon the stimulus one receives from a sense of self-respect, self-reliance, and personal growth. Whenever possible, instructional supervision should be the basic approach utilized by recreationists to provide the motives that encourage safe living.

Recreationists who are placed in supervisory positions have a direct duty to those in their care. A recreationist involved in any instructional procedure has the duty to supervise in a manner sufficiently unflagging to prevent participants from facing unreasonable risks of injury. This means that the recreationist occupies a position in relation to those with whom he supervises comparable to that of a parent to children (in the case of youngsters) or at least to that of a reasonable and prudent person when dealing with young adults or adults. The recreationist has the responsibility to instruct and warn participants of any dangers of which he is aware or in the exercise of ordinary diligence should know are present in the immediate setting and to instruct them in techniques that protect them from these dangers, however they arise and whatever their cause. A failure to warn participants of such dangers or to instruct them in the means of avoiding such dangers is negligence.

INDIRECT SUPERVISION

The need for a recreationist to be in attendance at an activity, exercising general oversight of participants, and being at hand in the event of need has been termed passive or indirect supervision. It mandates that a recreationist be in the vicinity of the activity so that a participant can be reached and assistance rendered. Thus, a foreseeable incident that might result in injury can be prevented. There are a number of recreational situations where passive supervision is applicable because of the nature of the activity, because participants are of such age and capacity that they are able to have recognizance over their own activity, or due to the fact that the recreationist has no reason to believe that the situation presents the possibility of serious injury to anyone participating in the event. Additionally, passive supervision is required when participants have the maturity and understanding to assume the risk of the activity in which they engage. When participants have been properly instructed in the techniques, procedures, and regulations of the activity, the recreationist will, unless there are specific circumstances to the contrary or because of special need, not be required to offer close or direct supervision. In such instances, there may not be a need for the recreationist to continuously observe every aspect of the activity as it is being conducted.

Passive supervision is more likely to be given for activities involving beach or pool lifeguarding, playground games, field sports, picnicking, court games, small craft activities, such winter activities as coasting or sledding, tobogganing, skiing, or skating. In many situations it is usual for no supervision to be given with the exception of beach and pool lifeguarding. For the most part, indirect supervision tends to reflect the traditions of the agency, the type of activity in question, the age, maturity, and usual behavior patterns exhibited by participants, and whether or not the agency assumes responsibility when it permits the use of its facilities *only.* There are circumstances where an agency does not conduct activities nor does it offer any supervision. For example, an organization may own facilities that it rents or leases to another agency or group. The lessor only furnishes the facility. The users provide whatever supervision is deemed necessary.

Passive supervision requires that a recreationist be present at the facility or area where activities occur. It is negligent for the worker to be stationed inside a building while participants are outside, even if the worker can observe the activities from a window. Moreover, if the worker is absent from the immediate area of activity, it is no excuse that the worker is performing some other required assignment, such as registering late-comers, collecting equipment, or supervising another area. Naturally, the employee will not be held personally liable in cases where the administrator has assigned him to be in two places at once, but he will be held liable if too many responsibilities are undertaken at his own discretion.

Conforming to the necessity that there be supervision is the requirement that there be a reasonable number of qualified supervisors. One of the questions that may be remanded to a jury for decision is whether or not a particular number of workers to participants (when children are involved) constitutes adequate supervision. Once more, liability for the assignment of too few workers for the supervisory function would fall upon the administrator; however, it is obvious that the recreationist should consider carefully before leaving his assigned post and asking another staff member on duty to assume the responsibility.

As always, the question of inadequate supervision is inevitable in terms of determining the proximate cause of an injury—that is, whether the worker should be held liable because of absence when one participant negligently or maliciously injures another. The worker will be held liable when the absence of supervision permitted a dangerous situation to ensue, and the injury occurred from the activities comprising that dangerous situation. Thus, recreationists could be held liable for injuries to participants that resulted from rough play or inappropriate behavior, such as a child standing on a swing or slide or attempting to scale a fence. Further, recreationists could be made to pay for injuries produced from malicious acts that are not immediate, such as assaults.

The basis for determining liability is whether the recreationist's presence would have permitted him time to observe the questionable activity and to stop it before the injury occurred. The recreationist will not be held liable when the negligent or purposeful act of a participant was instantaneous and unexpected. Such sudden acts would preclude anybody from acting in time to prevent an accident. Thus, no liability accrues when participants are injured while playing basketball, when someone fell due to a playful shove, or when a participant intentionally fouled another player or failed to stop and ran into a spectator.

Typical of this kind of situation is one that arose from an accident that occurred when children left a playground.

> The director of the playground had assigned staff to supervise the children. The center building was open, although no one was on duty inside. Two children left the playground, entered the building, and started to wrestle on the gymnasium floor. As they struggled, a small crowd of their playmates gathered to watch. At one point one of the wrestlers threw his head back violently to escape a hold and struck it on the floor sharply. He died a short time afterwards. The child's estate instigated litigation against the recreational department for wrongful death, claiming that lack of appropriate supervision and negligence was the proximate cause of the child's death. During the proceedings, the court noted that had supervision been mounted, the supervisor would have stopped the wrestling when it occurred. Therefore, it was the reasoning of the court that since the dangerous incident would have been halted as soon as it had began, the accident was viewed as foreseeable in consequence of the development of disorderly behavior, rather than a sudden, unexpected fall.[5]

It must be clearly understood that the responsibility of supervision requires more than the formal appearance of a sufficient number of qualified employees at the scene. Supervisors are required to take positive steps to protect those under their care. Supervisors must, therefore, warn those for whom they are responsible about any existing dangerous conditions of which they are aware. Furthermore, the supervisor has the express duty to implement published rules or regulations, stop disorderly behavior, and not lead participants in hazardous activities.

If the supervisor is moderately industrious in his remote supervision and takes positive steps to correct unsafe situations, he cannot be said to be acting negligently; therefore, he will not be held liable for those unavoidable accidents that do occur. Once he has made participants aware of the rules and regulations that govern participation, he does not need to know what each person is doing at any given time during the activity, nor must there be a prohibition on normal activities that would take place at such a recreational place merely because there is some chance that an accident might occur. The courts require reasonable attention and common sense, not the ability to foretell the future.

Supervision of Formal Activities

Aside from permitting dangerous conditions to exist within the facility where a formal recreational activity is organized, two kinds of situations may develop that can result in litigation. The first occurs when the recreationist (instructor) is absent from the activity room and one of the participants negligently or maliciously injures another person. The second concerns an allegation that the instructor-of-record failed to protect participants from a known hostile or violent person.

The instructor who is absent from the activity room is not automatically liable for every injury that occurs during his absence. However, the courts have indicated a thin line between liability and nonliability. If an injurious act is unexpected and not prompted by some inflammatory behavior, the instructor will not be held liable, under the principle that the instructor could not have responded quickly enough to have prevented the assault. When, however, the injury came as a result of continually provocative behavior, it becomes apparent that the instructor would have been able to stop the disorderly conduct had he been present. Therefore, in the latter instance the instructor will be held liable for any injury which is sustained.

Two incidents, one on a playground and the other in a classroom, are instructive of how courts look at instructor absence.

> A playground participant claimed that he was stabbed as the result of no supervision. On this day the recreational worker was not on the playground when a contingent of young boys made their appearance at the facility. For the subsequent twenty minutes the boys ran around on the playground, engaged in pushing and shoving. One youth took out a knife, displayed it, and made stabbing motions with it for approximately five minutes. Finally, he stabbed the plaintiff.
> Defendant claimed that there should be no liability for the vicious act of the youth since no one could have known about his hostile tendencies and thus provided protection against them. The court agreed that there must be some kind of warning; however, the court decided in favor of the plaintiff on the grounds that had the worker been present as required, the build-up of horseplay would have served as sufficient warning. Moreover, the court indicated the worker's responsibility to disarm the youth. Since the worker would have taken the knife from the aggressor immediately, plaintiff would never have been injured.[6]

> In a parallel instance, a fourteen-year-old pupil was injured in a rough game in the school gymnasium when he was pushed into another pupil and fell on the floor. Roughhousing occurred while the teacher was out of the room

for twenty-five minutes. He had left the group of about fifty adolescent boys unsupervised during that time.

The pupil brought action to recover damages against the teacher and the city. It was alleged that the defendants were negligent in failing to provide rules to guide the class, in attempting to instruct an excessive number of pupils at one time, and in the teacher's absenting himself and exposing the plaintiff to an unreasonable risk of harm by leaving the class of almost fifty unsupervised. The defendants denied negligence and claimed contributory negligence on the part of the pupil in knowingly participating in a dangerous activity and in failing to follow his teacher's instructions not to engage in horseplay.

The trial court granted the defendants summary judgment. Summary judgment is a procedure designed to determine whether there are any disputed and material issues of fact. It discourages the practice of coercive settlement of an otherwise worthless or frivolous claim.[6] The case was appealed. The appeals court found that the trial court erred in that summary judgment should not have been rendered in this case. Insofar as the negligence allegation was concerned, the court stated the rule to be that the harm must reasonably be foreseen as probable by a person of ordinary prudence under the circumstances, if behavior contributing to harm is to be negligent, but it is not necessary that the actual harm that occurred from the conduct be foreseen. In this instance if the teacher could have foreseen the harm to some students in the class stemming from roughhousing as a consequence of his absence, it is immaterial that the injury that resulted was not foreseen by the teacher. Nor as a matter of law, was the rowdyism of the participants in the game a displacing cause of the pupil's injury. If the teacher's absence is negligence, and this question must be decided by a jury, the fact that the pupil's conduct or others in the game was also a major factor, does not excuse the teacher. A jury could find, the court said, that the teacher acted unreasonably in leaving his class unsupervised for twenty-five minutes, particularly in view of the testimony that the pupils were watching for the teacher, in which case his presence would have stopped the game.

The court further held that under the comparative negligence statute, except rarely, it is a jury function and not that of a court to decide the apportionment of negligence. In this instance, the court determined that this question of negligence was for a jury.

In rejecting defendants' contention that to permit recovery in this situation would make them the insurer of the city's school children, the court noted that while it has recognized that a teacher is neither immune from liability nor is he an insurer of his students' safety, he is liable for injuries arising from his failure to exercise reasonable care.[7]

The presence of an instructor is vital to those whom he supervises because, among his responsibilities, he owes a duty to maintain good order. The reasonably prudent worker would take additional precautions to protect participants from a known violent or hostile person. This is so although the instructor is not liable for sudden or unexpected behaviors of participants. Where an individual has known tendencies toward violent behaviors, it is obvious that there is less that is unexpected. All the instructor has to do is act reasonably. With that in mind, the worker should always ask himself: knowing the tendencies of a potential participant and the conditions of the activity, what methods would a reasonably prudent worker take to lessen the risk to others to an appropriate level? Where the worker has taken reasonable precautions he will not be held liable for a sudden act that could not have been stopped despite the immediate presence of the supervisor.

DIRECT OR IMMEDIATE SUPERVISION

During the course of recreational activities there may be occasions when participants are exposed to greater risk of injury than is usually present in less strenuous or potentially dangerous conditions. Almost all gymnasium and competitive athletic activities, as well as craft shop activities, are looked upon in this way. In consequence, the reasonable recreationist would not only perform the functions of general supervision of participants' activities, but would initiate actions that would bring him into close and relatively prolonged contact with one or a small group of performers. This immediate proximity, sometimes within a half arm's length of the participant in the case of certain gymnastic stunts, plus care in supplying the correct supplies, materials, or equipment to be used, as well as specific and detailed instructions concerning appropriate use of the materials, body movements, or proper behavior constitutes the essence of direct supervision.

The most typical instances of participant injury occur from a lack of or incompetent instruction. The recreationist must protect those for whom he is responsible from their lack of knowledge, or in the case of children, from their lack of maturity and judgment. Proper instruction includes clear information dealing with the skills or knowledge to be learned, the dissemination of safety rules that are peculiar to the activity undertaken, and also whatever cautions are necessary to make plain the magnitude of danger inherent in the activity. The courts have made it abundantly clear that any instruction that excludes information concerning the degree of danger and the seriousness of the injury that could occur from not conforming to safety directions is legally indefensible. The crafts instructor must spell out the hazards of placing unsuitable materials into a machine. When a participant is working on a potentially dangerous craft, such as a rocket, the crafts instructor is mandated carefully to inform the participant as to the proper use of his product. The recreationist must be prepared to fully explain the processes and procedures necessary to successfully complete the project. The courts have held that it is not unreasonable to assume that it is the duty of the supervisor of a craft activity, in the exercise of ordinary care, to instruct participants regarding the choice, combination, and use of materials with which dangerous experiments or potentially hazardous projects are to be accomplished.[8] Moreover, the recreationist must be the exemplar of good safety practices.

He must not violate the canons of safe instruction by exhibiting inappropriate behavior within view of those committed to his care.

The courts are extremely conscious about allegations of inadequate instruction; it is tremendously important for the recreationist to be sure that he has provided sufficient instruction for each person who participates. In activities that offer exposure to danger at a higher level than would ordinarily ensue, it is probably best that the recreationist maintain some kind of instructional plan detailing the topics covered during the session so that a written record is available. In this way, the recreationist could offer proof of the type of instruction, the contents of the activities undertaken by time and date, and the sequence of presentation. This should lend support to testimony of instructional adequacy. Of course, the instructor of record must be certain that participants are capable of and do understand the instructions.

Additionally, every recreationist is responsible for assuring participants of a safe environment—to the extent that this is possible. Although responsibility for providing suitable supplies, materials, and equipment rests with the operational management of the organizations, it is the duty of the recreationist to hold back any equipment that he has determined is in need of repair, defective, or inappropriate for the kind of activity to be offered. Wherever there is damage to protective equipment (goggles, helmet, padding, circular saw guard, etc.), that is, where the equipment is worn, broken, or where pieces are missing, the recreationist must not issue it. Whether offering instruction indoors or outside, hazardous areas, facilities, or material to be used that the recreationist should know about, must be inspected to safeguard potential participants. For example, it is negligence for a craft instructor to place an unlabeled, open bottle of caustic liquid where it can be easily obtained. Dangerous equipment should be locked when not being used. Storage closets, lockers, or rooms must be locked because it is not unforeseeable that some participants, especially young ones, will be particularly attracted to the contents therein. Even though the recreationist must maintain a safe environment, he will not be liable for injuries caused if stolen dangerous materials—poisons, acids, or flammable liquids—are used inappropriately. A locked facility is the proper precaution against theft.

There is a discernable movement for states to pass legislation that requires those who perform shop work to wear protective devices when handling hot, caustic, or explosive materials; when working with metal, or engines, or with machines that punch, saw, drill, or scrape. Such statutes do not relieve the instructor from responsibility. Rather, this kind of legislation connotes liability whenever the instructor fails to maintain their standards or displays poor judgment by not following the regulations himself.[9]

Where a recreationist does not conform to any of the aforementioned rules and has, by his actions, produced a hazardous condition, he will not be disassociated from liability simply because a participant acts upon the situation to injure another. For example, one court ruled that a crafts instructor who negligently failed to place safety guards for a machine was liable for the injury to a participant, even though that person was hurt when another participant started the machine before he was supposed to do so.[10]

When a recreationist has performed in a way that a reasonable recreationist would perform to offer a generally safe recreational environment, he will not be held liable for accidents. Shop, gymnasium, or other recreational facility supervisors have a responsibility of adequate supervision for those participants whom they are instructing. However, the instructor will not be held liable when an injury occurs during absence as a consequence of an unexpected, instantaneous act that did not develop in consequence of misbehavior or a dangerous condition. It must be clearly understood, however, that any supervisor would be held liable if he makes a mistake during the instructional session and an injury results from that error.

Gymnasium Activities

Because sports and games typically afford greater opportunity for injury than less active recreational experiences, the person in charge of the gymnasium owes added duties of adequate supervision to those under his care. The courts have held that not only would the reasonable physical instructor supply supervision, but he/she would also make sure that those who participate are properly prepared and the equipment appropriately arranged and inspected so that the possibilities of injury can be minimized or terminated. Surely the physical instructor is not the insurer of the safety of those in his charge, and will not be liable for injury when his actions were reasonably performed concerning his duties.

The physical instructor must not only provide adequate supervision, but must also give appropriate supervision to participants and supply suitable equipment to assist in the prevention of injuries. This really means offering competent instruction as to technique. The instructor must consider participants' physical capacities and experience, and further, he/she may not assign exercises that are too advanced for their abilities or that may worsen any recent injuries about which he knows. The physical arena must be carefully controlled. Protective gear must be worn or used, equipment must be securely anchored, padding must be placed wherever there are sharp projections, congestion of the activity area must be avoided. Although inspections of equipment to determine its usefulness is a part of supervisory responsibility, the instructor will not be held liable for sudden equipment failure that could not have been foreseen.

Certain activities have been found to be dangerous by several courts. Particularly have boxing, gymnastics, hockey, and combat activities been found to be inherently dangerous.[11] Under these circumstances only persons certified as physical instructors or those known to be highly skilled in the training or coaching of that activity should be given the responsibility for supervision. If persons other than those certified to provide skilled instruction are employed or volunteer and an injury ensues, the instructor will be held liable.

Supervision Prior to and after Formal Activities

The courts have not required supervision of participants on recreational grounds before or after formal activities, except during those times when a situation resembles the informal participation of audiences at a theatrical performance or sporting event.[12] If, under those circumstances, there is a dangerous condition present or the recreationally-sponsored activity is considered dangerous, then supervision is required.

Generally, supervision is not a requirement during the time when potential clientele have arrived for recreational activities but facilities, sessions, or grounds are not yet opened. However, there is a need for supervision when a dangerous conditon exists on the recreational facility grounds, since under such circumstances the likelihood of injury to the unwary is heightened. For example, supervision has been mandatedd if there is any open burning on the grounds or where, during the winter, icy conditions make the potential for getting hit by hardened snowballs quite likely and dangerous.

Excursions and Extramural Activities

The recreationist is held to the same standard of care whether the activity occurs at a recreational center or on a day trip, overnight hike, or off-grounds athletic competition. The supervisor is required to act prudently in overseeing the participants' activities, warning them of dangers known to him, and guarding them against their own inappropriate behaviors. As in the facility, the recreationist will not be held liable for injury due to sudden or unanticipated acts. There is no requirement to inspect department vehicles used for excursions, but the supervisor may presume that the department has provided a safe vehicle, if one is used.

Although the standard of care is the same, the fulfillment of that obligation may be quite different insofar as the conditions and situation permeating the atmosphere of the away-from-center trip. Individuals, especially youngsters attending an excursion, may be emotionally stirred by the prospects of visiting an historic site, climbing a bluff, hiking a trail, or attending a cookout. Under these circumstances, the reasonable and prudent recreationist would recognize the increased danger of injury and would provide a greater degree of vigilance then might be offered during the ordinary day at the home facility. Just how chary the recreationist must be, how many additional supervisory workers must accompany the group, how much direct supervison must be enacted, which areas should be avoided, etc., are not answered by the courts before the fact. Thus, the recreationist's best course of action is to continually ask himself the same question that will be posed if an accident occurs: what would a reasonably prudent recreationist in the same circumstances do or not do in order to avoid risking injury to those who are his responsibility? The fact that the recreationist is alert to this question will probably prevent accidents from happening.

Departmentally Sponsored Events

Because recreational service departments operate throughout the day and evening hours, depending only upon the work schedule of employed personnel, there is no sponsored event in which departmental personnel may not be held liable. Hours of operation may occur at anytime—within reason. Unlike school system operations that have a definite time for operations, recreational service agencies have no such fall back as "after hours." When the department has sponsored an event, regardless of where it takes place, it must accept the duty to provide adequate supervision. In a legal sense the department-sponsored street dance, parade, carnival, or holiday commemoration must be supervised so as to prevent injuries due to a buildup of obnoxious behavior.

In states that have laws concerning adequate supervision by certain agencies in carrying out their functions, such organizations must be concerned with every element that might possibly cause injury. In one case, a parade through town produced an injury.

> During a holiday parade, sponsored by the local recreational service department and several private companies, a spectator was injured when the coupling on one of the floats separated and the end of the float struck the plaintiff. He sued the department as well as the supervisors on the basis of inadequate supervision. After considering the evidence the jury found in favor of plaintiff. The defendants appealed. On appeal, the supreme court of that state upheld the jury's verdict. The court ruled that the department had a duty to supervise any of its sponsored events both on and off departmental property. Since the department had such duty by law, it was correct for the jury to find that the evidence disclosed negligence in the failure to supervise the float coupling.[13]

NOTES

1. Jay S. Shivers, *Essentials of Recreational Service* (Philadelphia: Lea & Febiger, 1978), 189–90.
2. *Segerman v. Jones* 259 A. 2d 794, 256 Md. 109 (1969); also *Cotton v. the Catholic Bishop of Chicago* 351 N.E. 2d 247 39 Ill. App. 3d 1062 (1976); Kan. 170 Sess. Laws, Ch. 278; Ky. Rev. Stat. Ann. 161. 180 (1970); and, Wash. Rev. Code Ann. 28.76-350.
3. *Ohman v. Board of Education of the City of New York* 90 N.E. 2d 474 (1949). Also Fagan v. Summers 498 P.2d 1227 (1972).

4. Communication from Joel L. Pittman, Esq., Attorney at Law, for the Plaintiff in *Kerr v. Union County Park Commission,* Superior Court of New Jersey Law Division, Union County Docket No. L-29299-74.

5. *Dailey v. Los Angeles Unified School District,* 87 Cal. Rptr. 376, 470 P.2d 360 (1970).

6. *New Jersey Mortg. & Invest. Corp. v. Calvetti,* 68 NJ Super 18, 171 A2d 321.

7. *Carillo v. City of Milwaukee,* 150 N.W. (2d) 260, Supreme Court of Wisconsin, May 9, 1967.

8. *Mastrangelo v. West Side Union High School District of Merced County* 42 P. 2d 634, 2Cal. 2d 540 (1935).

9. 52 Ala Code; 1 (12), Ariz. Rev. Stat.; 1290, Conn. Gen. Stat. Ann.; 115–258, Ohio Rev. Code.; and, 601, 24 Pa. Stat. Ann.

10. *Rodregues v. San Jose Unified School District* 157 Cal. App. 2d 842,322 P. 2d 70 (1958).

11. *Rosenweig v. State,* 5 App. Div. 2d 293, 171 N.Y.S. 2d

12. *Liginow v. Reford Jaycees* 349 N.W. 2d 153 (Mich. App. 1983).

13. *Ledmuth v. Longbeach Union High School District,* 53, Cal. 2d 544,348 P. 2d 887 (1960).

PART III

Recreational Places and Safety Practices

10
School and Community Playgrounds

No playground standards exist that, if followed, would automatically eliminate the hazards that active children and others expose themselves to in the normal course of recreational activity. The federal government has promulgated tentative safety standards for playground devices, but even these are open to question and do not cover such significant aspects as space requirements, carrying capacity, design or layout, basic installations, surfacing, or the need for supervision. Even the guidelines published by the Consumer Product Safety Commission dealing with playground safety are not endorsed as the answer to safe playground construction.[1] There are certain practices and concepts, well known in the field of recreational service, that constitute recognized methods of safeguarding the well-being of those who frequent playgrounds. Over the years, these operational practices have become sufficiently accepted so that they have assumed a quasi-standard status. This chapter is devoted to the explanation of these practices, the ways in which playgrounds can be made safer, and case examples of the types of incidents that can and do occur when proper care is not taken by those in authority or because of the incautious behavior of participants.

Playgrounds are recreational facilities designed for the use of children and other age groups. The smaller the facility the more likely the playground is to serve one specific age group. The playground is usually an enclosed or segregated area containing not less than ten thousand square feet and possibly ranging up to a space of five acres. The playground typically contains a variety of devices or apparatus that appeals to the imagination and physical prowess of young children. Larger playgrounds may also contain some form of shelter and formal court games spaces. The largest playgrounds may incorporate a softball or baseball diamond, horseshoe pitching pits, croquet field, picnic area, and other similar features. Playgrounds may be constructed as entirely separate facilities or may be contained in a section of a park or on school grounds that have been set aside for that purpose.

PLAYGROUND ACTIVITIES

Playgrounds have been constructed to attract participants, especially children. They are equipped and planned to enhance the recreational satisfaction

Brick, asphalt, and concrete playground—hard surfaces have a potential for injuries.

of those who come to the facility to indulge their varied interests. A good deal of the activity engaged in on a playground may be of the free play variety, where youngsters may, at their own discretion, utilize whatever apparatus, equipment, or space is available to them. They may also choose to participate in games with their peers. In fact, children are capable of finding amusement in almost any situation they wish to create on a playground.

Organized activities are also provided if the facility is considered large enough or if the operating authority has a system of playgrounds that it staffs with leadership personnel. There may be one or more recreational service workers assigned to a playground, depending upon its size and the number of participants it can accommodate, who are charged with organizing and supervising all who enter the playground. Thus, skills are developed in crafts, games, music, dramatics, and other activities that are appropriate for the age group in attendance.

A well-appointed playground will have sufficient space available for a number of different age groups to participate without intruding on each other's activities. Fixed playground apparatus will be emplaced so that it will not impede or obstruct team activities of older youth. Trees, shrubs, bushes, and other plants are used for making the playground an attractive setting as well as to segregate playing areas. There is no need for older youth to come into contact with young children, insofar as performance is concerned, unless such contact will prove beneficial to those involved.

Playgrounds are a place where youthful energy can be extended safely and with exuberance. No one will tell these young people to be quiet or restrict natural outlets. The only rules governing a playground should be ones of common sense dealing with safety. Unnecessary restrictions upon children running, jumping, climbing, or participating in sport and games of a group, individual, or team type should be eliminated.

It stands to reason that the playground must be skillfully designed, constructed, and maintained in order to provide recreational opportunities that are made possible by the existence of this kind of facility. Among the activities that will probably be included on a well-developed playground are:

1. Apparatus used for swinging, climbing, crawling, bouncing, sliding, and other vigorous exercise.
2. Courts for formal games such as volleyball, basketball, badminton, horseshoe pitching, and handball or modified racquetball.
3. Fields on which baseball or softball, soccer, football, or other team competitive games may be played.
4. Some kind of structure or shelter must be available for use during inclement weather or when it becomes very hot. Activities that may be offered might then include music, art, dance, dramatics, storytelling,

Creative design omits nearly all safety hazards.

table games, and similar experiences. If the playground building is commodious enough to contain sanitary facilities, offices, a crafts room, and perhaps a nature center or a small auditorium, it will provide the space for a wide variety of indoor events that may be scheduled at any time during the day or evening.

5. A large sandpile area together with a spray bowl may prove to be advantageous for highly informal and spontaneous activities during those months when the weather requires some respite from the heat.
6. Quiet areas, not designated for any particular kind of activity may be inviting to older youth and adults who might want to watch, have a picnic, or simply converse.
7. While the entire playground might be an outdoor laboratory for the nature study program, any nature-oriented activity may well take advantage of specific areas where plantings have been cultivated. Earth may be sifted and analyzed, or different rocks and pebbles may be gathered for study and exhibition. If the personnel are knowledgeable, it may be that an astronomical exhibit or evening observation of the sky might be a part of the activity.
8. Special events take form as playdays, tournaments, exhibitions, demonstrations of skills learned, talent shows, family nights, and other activities can be programmed by recreational service workers if interest is stimulated among the playground users.

The playground can serve an important function in any neighborhood of a community. It can provide essential space and equipment to afford opportunities for both organized and free play. It may become the focus of neighborhood cohesiveness and be the meeting place where different interests, skills, and appreciations may be expressed, both formally and informally. Above all, it must be a place where children and other youth may have safe experiences. All participants can be involved in exhilarating activities with a minimum danger of injury. Surely accidents can occur, but serious injury to anyone as a result of playground participation must be eliminated as far as it is humanly possible to do so. It isn't the function of the recreationist to insure the safety of the playground user, but it is the responsibility of the recreationist to foresee unacceptable and avoidable risks to those who do participate. Moreover, the design of the playground, the apparatus in use, the surface, and the upkeep of the facility must be such that dangers of injury due to poorly situated equipment, inadequate maintenance, or poor space allocation are eliminated.

PLAYGROUND DESIGN

Playgrounds come in all sizes and shapes. Some facilities are called playgrounds but are inadequate for the needs of the population to be served. Other areas are vacant lots, a section of a park, or a very small space on which has been placed some apparatus and that is designated as a children's

Slide built into the sand hill prevents impact injuries.

playground. Obviously, these are useful places that certain immediate needs of the age group to be served require, but they are not to be thought of in the same sense as the modern playground described in the above paragraphs. To adequately fulfill the function of a well-developed playground, sufficient space, apparatus, structures, and landscaping must be integral to the design.

There are no standardized plans that may be utilized whenever playgrounds are desired. Each neighborhood is different as are the communities in which they are located. Playgrounds may serve different needs and interests and therefore require individual planning based upon potential users. The amount of space provided in the planning, design, and construction of a playground should be capable of carrying at least several different age groups at the same time, e.g., preschool, elementary, and adult. It should be planned so that both active and passive experiences may be programmed simultaneously without interfering. There should be fixed apparatus, a wading pool or spray pool, a sandpile area, shaded areas, a shelter, sport and game field, courts, seating capability, and sanitary conveniences. There are basic properties that every neighborhood playground must contain. Variations and adaptation can be made as the number of anticipated users is smaller or larger. Sufficient space must also be given over to landscaping and pathways, although paths may not always be required.

Playgrounds may best serve populations when they are situated centrally. Any vacant land will not always be suitable for playground construction. The artificial hazards of heavily trafficked streets, industrial sites, railroad crossings, and the like make such a development poor choice. Natural hazards such as ravines, gorges, sinkholes, and other high-risk areas also preclude playground construction.

Layout

The design of a playground will need to take into account a number of diverse factors. Size, shape, and location of the site will determine allocable space for different activity areas. The amount of money set aside for the construction, development, and operation of the playground will constitute the single most important element in determining how the playground is to be equipped. A comprehensive playground will have apparatus for use by children. At least one climbing device, small and large swing set, slide, sand pile, seesaws, crawling or hiding places (usually sewer pipe or plastic blocks) that are cut out, hollow, and can be put together in a variety of geometric patterns. Even such recycled materials as old fire engines, airplanes, locomotives, trolley cars, automobiles, or wagons may be utilized as immobile but imaginative playground sculpture.

Every comprehensive playground should have a shelter building. This will be placed close to the main entrance and in proximity to those spaces that have been set aside for the very young. This permits close supervision of

Fine sand or other similar soft surfaces will do much to reduce injuries due to falls.

Typical big city school playground. Adequate fencing separates play areas, but asphalt and cement surfaces promote impact injuries.

children. The shelter may offer whatever sanitary and other needed interior areas the program calls for. Sport and game areas usually make up most of the playground's occupied space. These are segregated areas for organized athletic activities for older youth and sometimes adults. Landscaping typically supplies the natural buffer zones and controls traffic flow on the playground. Bushes and shrubs serve to fix boundaries between activity areas. Trees provide shade and protection from high winds while also making the facility attractive.

Surfacing

Turf continues to be the best surface for sport and game areas, while turned earth, sand, tanbark, or sawdust might be best suited for such game areas as horseshoe pitching or areas under slides, swings, seesaws, and other apparatus. Court games require a smooth firm surface such as that which is applied with asphalt. Artificial turf may also prove useful for a number of court games and is suitable for all-weather purposes.

Statistical records, based upon data developed at the 119 hospitals participating in the National Electronic Injury Surveillance System (NEISS) for 1984, indicate that both home and public playground equipment is involved in almost 120,000 injuries critical enough to require emergency room attention. One particular fact that is of considerable significance is that the most frequent hazard associated with playground equipment is falls. More falls occur from slides and climbing apparatus than for any other type of playground equipment. Three-quarters of all injuries occurred when children fell to the playground's surface or onto other pieces of equipment. Injuries sustained on public playground equipment most typically took place on raised apparatus. "Playground surfacing as well as the way the victim landed are factors in the kind and degree of injury incurred." More often than not, serious cases ". . . involved falls to asphalt, cement, or packed dirt playground surfaces."[2]

Although playground-based injuries tend to fall in a category not generally classed as permanently crippling, the nature of the injuries produce many head trauma cases that can result in a variety of permanent disabling effects ranging from minor brain damage to death. There is a real and present danger existing with each fall.

According to T. B. Sweeney, a well-known advocate for safe playgrounds:

> Although responsible supervision is necessary on playgrounds even the most diligent supervision cannot prevent injuries once a fall has taken place. All the supervisor can hope to accomplish is discourage the be-

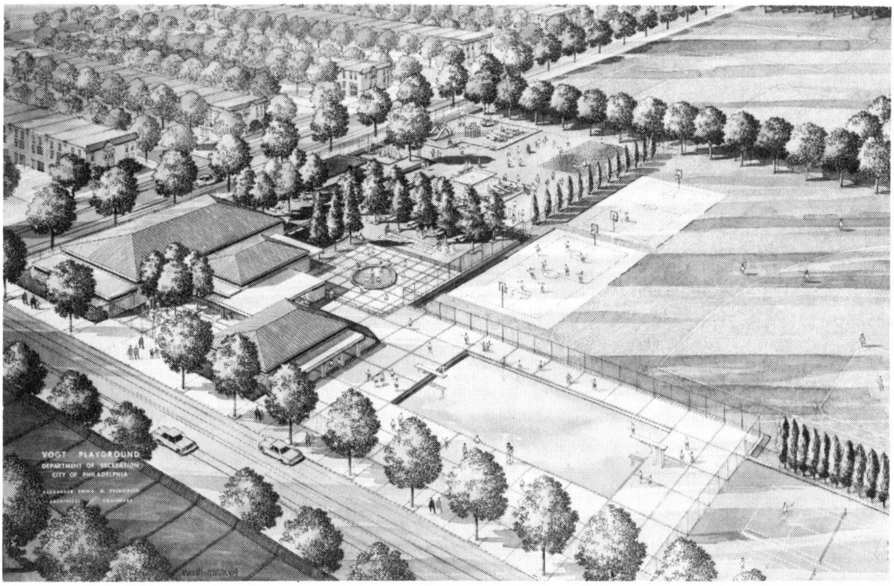

Community playground showing well-designed features and distinctly separated playground activities.

Resilient playground surface can prevent serious injuries due to falls.

havior which might lead to such accidents; a teacher standing right next to a slide, for example, will not soften the impact of the asphalt once a child has slipped from the equipment in question.

Consequently, the real issue in playground injuries due to falls should not be that of supervision, as necessary as it is, but rather whether or not the surface onto which the victim fell could possibly have absorbed the impact of a human being falling from a given height. It would seem that to install or maintain any playground apparatus over a non-energy-absorbing surface could be considered negligent on the part of the person or agency responsible for the property in question, given the immature judgment of the typical playground user.[3]

Attractive nuisance is the maintenance of any device, condition, or other instrumentality that is dangerous to young children because of their lack of judgment and inability to appreciate hazard and may yet draw them to its environs. The possessor of such an attractive nuisance has the responsibility to exercise reasonable care to protect such youngsters against the perils that probably exist by virtue of the attraction. Inattention of many school authorities and public park and/or playground officials to the subject of playground accidents occurring on their respective premises probably stems from having enjoyed immunity from tortious acts. It may be suspected that administrators, for so long protected, have come to believe that they are still immune. Without question, the incidence of playground equipment injuries is on the rise. Associated with such accidents are the risks of permanent and severe crippling to the young child. Under these circumstances, playground surfaces must be investigated carefully to insure that installation of playground apparatus is performed only on those surfaces that are best capable of providing the resiliency necessary to absorb and deter the shock that a fall produces on the human anatomy, especially the head and neck.

There are several products on the market that claim to provide the safety features necessary to insure an almost injury-free apparatus-related fall. Some of these manufactured surfaces are water permeable permitting play immediately after rainfall. Moreover the surface provides good resilience to reduce the injuries directly attributed to the impact of falls. However, it is imperative that any installation of these safety materials be made on nonconcretized, noncompacted earth, or nonasphalted surfaces that are not energy absorbing.

Fencing

Fencing is needed to prevent children from running off the playground and into the streets that tend to surround it. Furthermore, fencing will probably reduce the possibility of passersby being struck with thrown, batted, or kicked balls. There is also less likelihood of trespass because once the fence is closed and the gates locked, only those who are capable of climbing the fence and who know that it is wrong to do so will attempt to enter the playground.

Chain link fabric made of copper-bearing steel wire, galvanized after weaving, is believed to be the most satisfactory fencing and is most widely used. Boundary fences are usually six to seven feet high and are constructed of either No. 6 or No. 9 gauge wire with a two-inch mesh. If the recreational area borders on private property, a higher fence may be desirable, and if the fence also serves as a tennis court backstop, a height of twelve feet may be required.

Adventure Playgrounds

Adventure or Robinson Crusoe Playgrounds have been pioneered by European countries. The adventure playground is really a construction site. The main feature of this kind of facility is to allow youngsters to plan, build, and use whatever structure they can construct. Almost any type of building material may be employed in the construction of forts, scaffoldings, tree houses, and other imaginative structures in which youngsters climb about and employ in their make-believe world. As Cor Westland and Jane Knight state, ". . . adventure playgrounds consist of an environment primarily built and controlled by children. . . ."[4] It is a compelling concept and one that has

Resilient playground surface such as this artificial turf may protect against serious injury resulting from bad falls.

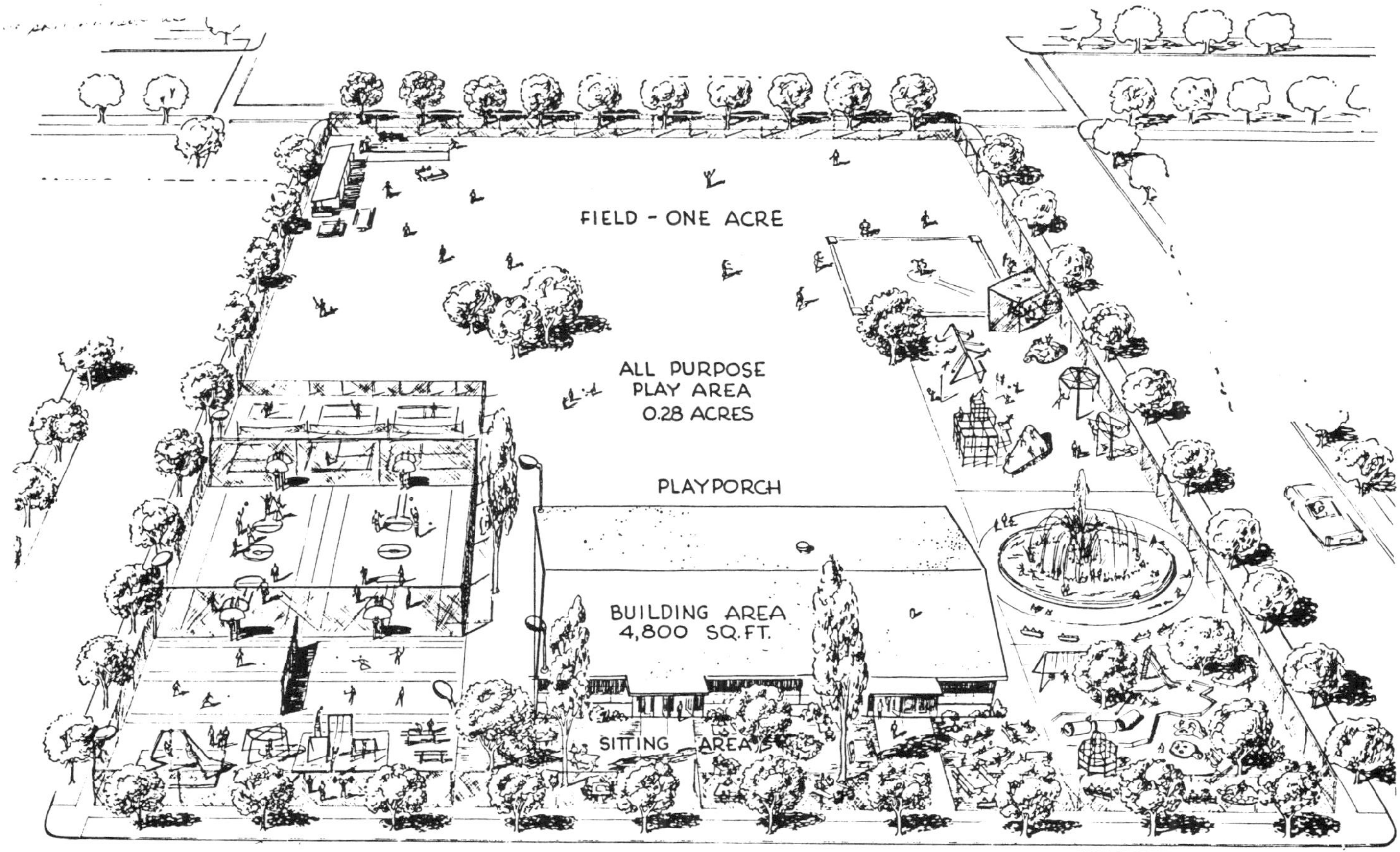

Attractive and functional recreational facility illustrates safety principles and separates users by age group.

seen its successful introduction to many parts of the world since its initiation in Denmark in 1943.

Adventure playgrounds need to be screened from passersby because they are often unkempt and relatively unattractive looking. However, the real reason for fencing is to prevent vandalism and the loss of building supplies and materials through theft. Children erect whatever their fancy dictates and play in, on, and around the area in a completely spontaneous manner. There are really no rules or regulations. Except for at least one professional playground worker, no adult supervision is given. Yet these playgrounds are as much a part of the community system as is any other publicly-owned facility. The big difference is that adventure playgrounds are run by and for children and all other playgrounds are operated by adults.

According to statistical summaries from those communities with adventure playgrounds, the number of serious or moderate injuries accruing to participants is comparable to those that arise on more traditional playgrounds.[5] However, the number of bruises and other nonserious injuries are more prevalent due to the kinds of activities engaged in by the participants. Needless to say, the use of construction tools, use of open fires, sand, and water contribute to the enjoyment and the probability of injury for participants.

PLAYGROUND SAFETY

Well-operated playgrounds are safe. Since playgrounds normally appeal to children and are attractive to them, if they are planned properly, it is the responsibility of recreationists and others to provide maximum protection to those who participate. Since the playground encourages several age groups to engage in active participation, it might be thought that accidents are inevitable. This is far from the truth. Organization and supervision can produce an unsurpassed safety record. Promoting safety on the playground is really a matter of supplying well-designed facilities and competent leadership. Stimulated by curiosity and activated by tremendous energy, young children are capable of falling victim to the various inherent dangers of a playground, if they do not invent new hazards themselves, unless the recreationist or teacher exercises continued alertness and immediately stops dangerous behavior. More importantly, it is necessary to help young people learn why negative behavior cannot be tolerated in the confines of a playground. Young children have the ability to learn appropriate behavior and will respect the consistency of a supervisor who is fair, sympathetic to their needs, and understanding. A recreational program that is organized to satisfy a variety of interests requiring skills within the participant's capacity and offers children opportunities to fulfill their desires for enjoyment and achievement can do much to prevent accidents and reduce unsafe practices.

Safety Education

A safe playground does not happen by coincidence. Safety can be secured only if competent leaders are employed. Children must be taught early that safe play is important to them. They must be encouraged to learn how to avoid injuring themselves and endangering others. The prime motive of safety education is to guide children into safe habits of play. No one can remove the inherent risks of recreational activities, nor should participation be discouraged simply because an activity could be hazardous. Well-instructed children can find enjoyment and satisfaction in the use of all playground facilities and within a program of stimulating activities. Of necessity, leaders must provide instruction dealing with proper playground behavior and the rules for the use of whatever apparatus, equipment, and activities are being provided and enforce them. The rules of safety need to be clearly explained as well as the reasons for their promulgation. Adherence to these rules should be so ingrained that violations of them will become a rarity.

Children should learn to use good judgment in determining where and how they will play. Instruction in playground safety needs constant reinforcement for as children grow older there is a rising incidence of accidental injuries that tops out between the ages of twelve to fourteen. If children are to be prevented from endangering themselves or others and participating in dangerous acts voluntarily, they must be offered every chance to develop a sense of responsibility for themselves and that of others while they are still young and impressionable.

Children should understand that game rules and safety regulations are necessary to see that everyone has a good time. The supervisor who explains these facts in terms that children can understand will find that youngsters are more cooperative and willing to play according to the rules. Playground rules and regulations that stress positive behaviors should be posted in highly visible places. Regardless of how well thought out and posted safety rules are, they cannot replace the guidance and counseling of competent leadership.

Every playground leader, when introducing a new game or even in organizing a familiar activity, should begin the session with basic instruction covering the rules of play and any methods that can eliminate or reduce the likelihood of accidents and injuries. There is no recreational situation in which the teaching and practice of skills will not be profitable or salutory for all concerned. Lack of skill, particularly in those activities that use apparatus or in which equipment such as bats, balls, or other implements are involved, will probably raise the chance of accidents and injury.

For apparatus activity, children should be taught how to mount and dismount, what bodily movements can be performed on a particular kind of apparatus, how to swing, grips to maintain, balance to hold, and other necessary techniques. Using swings and slides also brings up the concept of sharing and taking one's turn. Fair play, taught at an early age, will do much

Proper instruction and fine sand surface combine for safety.

to reduce the hazards that might come from pushing or shoving when waiting to use some piece of apparatus. It is obvious that organized games require instruction. Such basic elements as the rules of the game, tactics, skills in throwing, catching, hitting, kicking, sliding, running, and all of the other aspects that individuals must learn if they are to enjoy the activity are initiated through instruction. A few individuals may be able to gain sufficient skill simply by observing others perform. For the most part, however, skill instruction is required.

The need for a broadly based safety education program and a well-operated risk-management program may be seen from the following cases:

> On 23 June 1976 a five-year-old girl, Wendy Alker, visited Glenwood Park in Thousand Oaks, California. She attempted to play on a platform and slide device which was raised some 6½ feet from the ground. The child, in reaching for the chain prior to sliding down the incline, fell from the platform and received severe lacerations on and about her head, including a completely cut through bottom lip requiring plastic surgery. She also suffered a fractured jaw, and miscellaneous cuts and bruises. The child's guardian alleged that the fall was the result of the negligent and defective conditions, design, construction, and maintenance of the device. After an investigation of the incident, depositions were taken from those personnel responsible for the design, construction, and maintenance of the device. The case went to arbitration, and the following findings were determined together with the arbitrator's explanation and decision. Unfortunately, this is a matter which is not well adapted to the arbitration program in that where liability is seriously at issue there is often little hope of having the arbitration process terminate the litigation unless the arbitrator compromises the liability issue in the hopes of "settlement." I [the arbitrator] do not, however, see my function as a facilitator of settlement and have decided the matter accordingly.
>
> The plaintiff's theory of liability against the City of Thousand Oaks as presented at the abritration hearing was that injuries arose as a result of a dangerous condition which existed on public property. The essential prerequisites for tort liability for dangerous public conditions are that:
>
> a. The property be in a dangerous condition
> b. It proximately caused injury to the plaintiff
> c. The kind of injury that occurred was reasonably foreseeable as a consequence of the dangerous condition
> d. The dangerous condition was created by a public employee's negligent or wrongful act or omission within the scope of his employment, or the entity must have had actual or constructive notice of the condition a sufficient time before the injury occurred to have taken measures to protect against it.
>
> The plaintiff's testimony emphasized the existence of some rocks in the area where Wendy fell from an apparatus constructed for the amusement of children. There was also some question of the dangerousness of the apparatus itself in that there was no knot or ring at the lower end of the chain which was intended to be held by a child using the ride.
>
> Wendy's testimony at the time of the hearing was that she believed that an adult male was swinging the chain up to her and that although she believes

> she touched the chain she did not testify that she grabed on to it and attempted to swing with the chain. Therefore, any defect in the chain portion of the apparatus was not shown to have proximately caused the injury to the plaintiff.
> The real thrust of the plaintiff's theory dealt with the rocks which were partially imbedded in the sand beneath the apparatus. Obviously, the city would only be liable if they created that condition or had constructive notice of it for a sufficient period of time to remedy the defect. The uncontroverted testimony of Mr. Kenneth De Young (park supervisor) was that the apparatus in question had been set up some six months prior to the accident. He testified that new fill sand had been used as a cushion beneath the apparatus and that that was the material present on 23 June 1976. The sand was indicated to be approximately eight inches in depth and he had never received any indication that there were rocks in the area. I am satisfied from the testimony of Mr. De Young that the City of Thousand Oaks did not create the condition which injured the plaintiff. There remains the question of whether or not the City had actual or constructive notice of the dangerous condition.
> Again, the uncontradicted testimony of Mr. De Young was that prior to June 23, 1976 he had never received any report on rocks or debris in the area of the device. Furthermore, it was his policy to respond to notices of dangerous conditions immediately. Reports were phoned in to his secretary who then contacted work crews by radio for corrective action.
> Additionally, Mr. De Young testified that the park was inspected on a weekly basis by a crew leader. Furthermore, as Glenwood Park was a relatively new one, Mr. De Young himself would have "walked the park" at least once a month prior to the accident.
> In deciding this matter I have concluded that the governmental entity maintained and operated such an inspection system with due care and did not discover the condition complained of. There was no evidence with respect to the duration of the dangerous condition prior to plaintiff's injury and I was therefore unable to find any liability on the part of the City of Thousand Oaks.[6]

In the case of *Power v. City of Glendale,* an anonymous telephone call was received by the senior recreational leader in the central office of the Parks and Recreation Department of the City of Glendale, California on 6 September 1972. An inquiry was made about the department's knowledge of an accident that allegedly occurred to Kimberly Ann Power on 21 June 1972 at Verdugo Park. The recreationist advised the caller that the office had no record of such alleged accident and could therefore provide no information. The caller thanked the recreationist for this information.

On 29 September 1972 a memorandum from the Glendale City Attorney's Office to the Department of Recreation and Parks indicated that a claim for injuries sustained in a city park was being filed for plaintiff and requested information. The director of the department wrote the following response:

> Please be advised that our office has no record of any accident occurring to Kimberly Anne Power on the date of June 21, 1972. Further, we have checked with the Glendale Fire Department and they have no record of an

ambulance being called to Verdugo Park on this date which would tend to confirm a possible accident.

I personally inspected the area on Monday, October 2, 1972, to check the conditions outlined in the claim. I found a Thompson sprinkler head located beneath and slightly to the side of an overhead ladder, which the claim indicates the girl fell from. A diagram is attached showing the location of the ladder and the Thompson sprinkler head. It is further important to note that the Thompson sprinkler head is enclosed in a rubber cap and flanged and is located 1⅜ inches below the ground level.

We have contacted the Recreational leader assigned to Verdugo Park, and learned that he worked on the date of June 21, 1972, until 8 p.m. and that he was unaware of any accident occurring to persons at Verdugo Park on that date. In conclusion, it would seem somewhat unusual for this accident to have occurred as reported and there be no witnesses to the fact. Secondly, it would seem important that if the claimant truly is concerned about the City's liability, perhaps notice should have been given as to this condition as soon as possible and certainly not wait until the claim filing date of September 26, 1972.[7]

The claim for damages indicates serious injuries to the child. She sustained multiple fractures of the distal humerous cutting across the growth line; fractures of both bones in the left forearm; dislocation of the left elbow. Claimant fell several feet from a playground horizontal ladder, apparently striking her left arm on hard dirt ground and a hard rubber covered pipe extension several inches in diameter which was located directly beneath the playground equipment being used. A suit for damages was instituted against the City of Glendale alleging, "That the playground equipment used is an inherently dangerous device, negligently placed, located and installed.[9]

The case was investigated by the city attorney's office and in 1975 a resolution of the case was made. The city attorney's opinion is as follows:

The City used proper procedures in selecting and installing the subject equipment. Purchase of the specific equipment was approved by the City Council and its purchase authorized thereby. Although there have been other falls from the same equipment approximately a month before plaintiff fell, Mr. Biship confirmed that the equipment was installed over a proper surface and was not in a defective condition.

The main exposure in this matter is that the ladder was ten feet high and was not installed over sand or a comparable soft surface. As indicated to you in our letter of March 5, 1974, Mr. Wakefield, the representative of the Patterson-Williams Company, was not aware of any other installation in southern California over a hard surface such as dirt or grass. All other installations in southern California have been over sand or bark. It remains our opinion that this case is of doubtful liability, since the plaintiff has admitted that she traversed the ladder without difficulty at least once before falling when her hands became slippery. The fact that her parents permitted her to play on the equipment without their supervision will also be of assistance in establishing that they and their daughter were contributorily negligent. However, in view of the new comparative negligence rules in California, it is more likely under present law that the plaintiff may receive a reduced verdict, whereas under the old law her recovery would likely have been barred completely for her contributory negligence.

The fact of the prior falls from the same ladder shortly before the plaintiff's fall will also be of assistance to the plaintiff in establishing that although the ladder was purchased and installed with an approved plan in accordance with an approved plan and design, the City had acquired knowledge of its potentially dangerous condition without taking remedial action. Under the rule of *Baldwin v. State of California,* 6 Cal. 3d 424 (1972), the immunity for an approved plan or design is lost if conditions change so that the municipality is on notice that the public property is, in fact, dangerous.

Plaintiff's attorney indicated that he intended to consider the advisability of joining Patterson-Williams as a defendant based upon the design of the equipment and Mr. Wakefield's (company representative) supervision of the installation without recommending a softer surface under the equipment. I anticipate that plaintiff's counsel will not go to the trouble of joining Patterson-Williams unless he is satisfied that the plaintiff's injuries are likely to support a substantial verdict. We have arranged to have the plaintiff examined by an orthopaedic surgeon, on August 4, 1975. We will provide you with a copy of the physician's report as soon as it is obtained.

Based on the information currently available to us, it is our opinion that a verdict for the City is probable, although there is some risk of a verdict for the plaintiff under the rules of comparative negligence. A trial setting conference has not yet been set in this matter. We will advise you of all further developments.[9]

The case did not come to trial and was settled when the City Council of Glendale offered to compromise and settle the claim of Kimberly Anne Power. The City Attorney was authorized to pay a stipulated sum upon the entry of a dismissal with prejudice.[10]

Every effort must be taken to discourage small children from attempting to use equipment and apparatus that is obviously for older persons. This can best be done by designing the playground so that young children will have their own area with its varied installations. This will forestall any desire to approach and use such equipment. The attention of young children frequently wanders, unless they are engaged in something that is so fascinating that it holds their undivided attention. Supervisors should emphasize the need for children to keep their wits about them. They should try and assist children to be alert to what is happening around them when they are engaged in recreational activities. Frequently, a child is injured because he did not look where he was going, bumped into a moving object, or collided with another person. In the excitement generated by participating in some game, it is possible for children to act precipitously, thereby bringing themselves into danger and, perhaps, endangering others.

A PLAYGROUND SAFETY PLAN

In order to reduce the inherent risks that accompany almost all playground activities, administrators should call for designs that will lessen the possibility of accidents. Materials should be installed, surfaces constructed, and equipment emplaced that does not add to the possibility of injury to participants. Moreover, the playground should be planned so that supervision can be facilitated for those age groups that require constant observation for their own protection. The well-designed, intelligently proposed, and well-built playground will be the focus of few accidents. Safeguarding children and all other users of playgrounds against accidents is a major concern to recreationists. Employees who are assigned the responsibility of supervising playgrounds need to know why accidents occur, where they are most likely to occur, and the methods necessary for avoidance. Among the primary causes of accidents are poor design of the facility, installation of inappropriate and therefore dangerous apparatus, emplacement of structures that can exacerbate injuries, behavior of participants that is contributory to risk, defective playground devices, equipment, and supplies, nonmaintained or poorly maintained areas, no regulations governing playground conduct or nonenforced rules, and finally incompetent supervision.

Rules and Regulations Governing Behavior

It is probably best to teach by emulation than it is to remonstrate and concentrate on prohibiting negative behavior. Restrictions may be imposed on playground users if emphasis is placed on positive behavior to be observed. Instead of saying, "Don't do . . . ," it will be more palatable to indicate the proper or desired conduct to be observed. Although most of the rules are directed to the attention of younger children, there are some regulations that need to be aimed at those who are more mature. Thus, alcoholic beverages should never be permitted on a playground. Fires should never be lit, unless there is some programmed activity that calls for it.

Slides. The slide usually attracts many users at the same time and can be effectively held up by one person at the top. This is conducive to pushing, having several participants on the ladder at one time, or sitting at the bottom of the slide after the ride is finished. All of these actions should be restricted, corrected when observed, and eliminated wherever possible.

Whatever rules are issued should be explained in a way that will make the participants want to conform. Statements such as: keep hands away from sides, wait for your turn, slide only when clear, sit and slide feet first only, are some of the ways in which directions may be given.

Swings. Swings attract young people because they appeal to the child's need for movement and the apparent risk that comes from falling through space. However, there are dangers that must be eliminated and are eminently avoidable. Among these are the practices of throwing swings over the frame, standing on swing seats, jumping off moving swings, swinging sideways instead of forward and back, or throwing swings sideways when other children are swinging. It is possible to eliminate side contact with frames if the swing is designed in such a way that stanchions cannot be close to the arc of the swing.

Seesaws. The seesaw can be designed in such a way as to avoid injuries that might occur if children get their hands caught beneath the seat. This may mean installing a bumper beneath the seat or using a rocker-like frame on which two people sit facing each other. Mischievous children may attempt to get off the seesaw when the other participant is still up in the air; this must be prohibited. There are some children who want to stand rather than sit, and this, too, should be eliminated. Some rules that can be applied are: hold tightly to the handles, sit facing your partner, keep your feet from under the board when it comes down, try to balance so that both partners are touching the ground before getting off the board.

Sandpiles. Only the youngest children will play in sandpiles or sandboxes. It goes without saying that frequent inspection of the sand for debris is vital. The use of any glass object or sharp tools should not be permitted. Throwing sand should not be permitted. Children should not be permitted to eat food in the sand area. All playgrounds have sections provided for picnics or where food may be consumed. Indiscriminate food eating may cause rubbish, vermin, and other unnecessary or unwanted problems. Rules should stress sharing, building, and fun.

Apparatus. There are few playgrounds that do not have devices, either homemade or manufactured that attract some use. Apparatus should be used properly and not abused so that a dangerous condition is created for the next person. Apparatus should be appropriately placed and used for the age group it intends to serve. Common sense should play a paramount role in apparatus use. Most apparatus should never be used if it is wet because hands and feet tend to slip on smooth and filmy surfaces. The ground underneath apparatus should be soft or resilient so that falls are less likely to end in injuries.

Once apparatus is emplaced, it is difficult to control its use unless supervision is constantly maintained. Since this is rarely possible, it is better to follow a well-conceived plan prior to the purchase and installation of the device. Once the apparatus is installed, it should be set into an area that affords enough space around it so that crowding by participants will be eliminated. Depending upon the device, the surface underneath and around it should be appropriate for its use. If the apparatus has moving parts, it should be separated from the main flow of traffic by interior fences or shrubbery so that children are prevented from running into the path of moving objects.

Sports and Games

A number of personal injuries occur during the course of vigorous athletic activity normally found on any playground. For the most part, accidents happen because of poor judgment, carelessness, or thoughtless action. Players or spectators can be hit by thrown, batted, or flying objects. Sometimes spectators get too close to the playing field and may be injured when runners collide with them or when deflected or overthrown balls, stones, bottles, or other items strike them.

Participants can be injured if they are not properly attired for the activity. If a game calls for protective glasses, they should be worn. If there is a need for protective head gear or other equipment, then it is up to the supervisor to see that every player is suitably dressed for the game.

Some cases that illustrate the need for circumspection or that show what can happen if safety programs are not in effect follow:

> A five-year-old boy was injured on a defective playground slide. A suit was brought against all authorities directly or indirectly charged with the responsibility for maintaining the playground. It was dismissed by a lower court under the doctrine of governmental immunity from tort liability.
> The Minnesota Supreme Court upheld the dismissal of this action, but prospectively overruled the doctrine of governmental immunity as a defense to tort claims against municipalities, school districts, and other governmental units, except the state itself.
> Counsel informed the court that legislation was planned for the next session to give affected governmental entities a chance to meet their new obligations. Until then, the court felt that they had a right to rely on the immunity.[11]

This was a clear case of negligence on the part of the playground authorities. They were saved from having to provide redress only because the doctrine of governmental immunity was in effect at the time. The slide was defective; the authorities knew about it and had done nothing to repair the piece of apparatus that, when used, contributed to the child's injury.

> A pupil brought suit for negligence against the city and board of education for injuries received during the noon recess hour while waiting in the prescribed area to return to school. Her injury was caused when another pupil, playing basketball on a court developed by the school board adjacent to the area where she was waiting, ran off the court and collided with her. The trial court dismissed the suit, stating that the school board provided general supervision and that was all that was required.
> On appeal, the court held that there was evidence from which a jury could have found the board of education negligent in the layout of the basketball court, in directing the children to wait in an area so close to the basketball court, and in supervising the noon recess activities. The lower court finding was reversed and a new trial granted against the school board.[12]

> The school board and two teachers assigned to supervise the playground were sued for damages for injuries received when a softball player fell over a bench on the school playground. Benches supplied for use of the players were taken by spectators who overflowed onto the ground in front of them. Ropes and standards were available to restrain the crowd, but were not used.
> The jury found that the playground supervisors had been negligent. On appeal, it was found that the school board was liable for the negligence of its employees under the doctrine of *respondeat superior.*[13]

The need to establish and disseminate rules and regulations to guide the behavior of playground participants has always been an important tenet in any safety education program. Failure to perform this task is fraught with risk for those who are ultimately responsible for the well-being of their charges.

> A young boy was hurt while participating in an extremely dangerous game on a school playground. Both supervising teacher and principal of the elementary school where the incident occurred had observed the students playing this game on several occasions, but neither had stopped the game nor provided supervision for it.
> The parents of the injured child brought suit against the teacher and the principal for negligence. The teacher had not been present on the day of the accident and the complaint against him was dismissed. Responsibility was placed on the substitute teacher. The principal was held to be protected from suit by the doctrine of governmental immunity. On appeal, the Appeals Court of Michigan upheld the trial court's verdict in favor of the teacher. However, it ruled against the principal because she failed to establish and enforce rules against dangerous games or provide supervision to lessen the risk of injury to the students on the playground. Therefore, the principal, having ignored her responsibility to protect the pupils under her care could not claim protection under the doctrine of governmental immunity.
> The principal was found guilty of negligence.[14]

SCHOOL PLAYGROUNDS

School operated playgrounds, especially during recess periods, tend to provide supervision and no instruction in skills. It is only when the school playground is used during the physical education class that instruction in basic skills, which may include those for use of apparatus, is offered. Younger children are particularly prone to accidental injuries that occur on apparatus and in free play during recess or noon hours. To reduce school playground accidents, school authorities need to provide a sufficient number of adequate supervisors. Supervision, therefore, becomes a key issue in keeping children safe. The supervision should be appropriate to the size and nature of the facility, the kinds of apparatus installed, and the number and ages of the children on the playground.

Where young children have been injured on school playgrounds, failure to supervise adequately is a chief complaint. However, many playground injuries arise, not out of supervisory negligence, but due to causes not under the control of supervisors. In the following case, an allegation of negligence against a teacher was denied.

> A school board and a teacher were sued when a seven-year-old child was injured on a school playground. The pupil was struck in the face by a softball bat wielded by a seventh-grader when the child ran into the line of swing. At the time, the second-grade pupils were under the supervision of

their teacher. The teacher was unaware of the older girls playing softball. Rules established by the board of education stated that softball playing required supervision, a written request for the issuance of all equipment, and the presence of a teacher when the equipment was used. Although the older girls had obtained permission to play ball on the field, no written request was given for the use of the equipment that had been picked up where it was stored. The trial court found the jury verdict against the school board for five thousand dollars to be inadequate, and ordered the verdict to be set aside and a new trial held unless the board consented to increase the penalty to ten thousand dollars. Also set aside was the jury verdict of no cause of action against the teacher as contrary to the weight of evidence. Both the school board and the teacher appealed.

The appeals court ruled that there was sufficient evidence of the school board's failure to enforce its own rules for playing games on the playground and of its failure to supply adequate supervision to justify a verdict against it. The court ruled that the jury verdict in favor of the teacher should stand. The mere presence of older pupils in the area would not alert, necessarily, a reasonable and prudent teacher of young children to danger, and, therefore, under the circumstances of this case, the jury could find that the teacher was not negligent.[15]

In instances where spontaneous or unforeseen incidents occur resulting in pupil or participant injury, courts are not likely to rule that supervisors were guilty of negligence if they exercised reasonable and prudent care. Courts have repeatedly held that where injuries occur because of some unanticipated behavior on the part of the participant or another individual who hit, pushed, or pulled the injured person, that every action of every person cannot be predetermined and that supervisors are not required to maintain constant surveillance of each participant at all times.[16] This would constitute an unreasonable demand and is physically impossible to perform.

A fourth-grade male pupil, injured while running toward a playground area prior to a physical education class, sued the school district and his teacher. Another pupil pushed him into a basketball stanchion and the victim injured his two front teeth. The teacher had been locking the classroom door, arriving on the scene thirty seconds after the incident, just as the boy was getting up. The teacher had the responsibility for making sure that no one was in the classroom while it was unattended. A rule of the school district required supervision for children in the school yard.

No supervisory personnel was present when the accident took place. The suit against the teacher was dismissed before the case went to trial. The trial court found that the pupil was injured as a direct and proximate consequence of the negligence of the school district and found for the plaintiff. The school district appealed the ruling, contending that the evidence failed to prove inadequate supervision, and that the award to plaintiff was excessive.

The appeals court held that the proximate cause of the accident was the pupil who had pushed the plaintiff and not any reasonable supervision by the school district. A contrary view, insofar as the facts of the case warranted, would make the school district an insurer and necessitate constant supervision of all pupils at all times. This is not what the law demands. Judgment against the school district was reversed.[17]

In another instance, an injured pupil brought an action for damages against a school district, the school board, all administrative officers, and the teacher. The injury occurred when the pupil was hit by a rock thrown by another pupil.

> The school board and the school district moved for a dismissal on the ground of governmental immunity. They also contended that the complaint did not state a claim upon which relief could be granted. The court ruled that the dismissal of the action against all defendants was correct. The teacher was not the tort-feasor and the allegation that the teacher permitted the rock to be thrown did not state a claim against the teacher. The school district and the school board were not subject to suit because of the governmental immunity rule. The other defendants were not subject to suit because the dismissal of the claim against the teacher precluded action on the basis of *respondeat superior.*[18]

Avoiding Accidents

Poor planning on the part of administrative officers and supervisors is frequently cited as the basis for a negligence suit. Unless there is a concerted effort to develop and operate a logically conceived plan for the supervision of children on playgrounds, particularly during lunch or recess periods when children are required to wait in the playground area before returning to or entering school, the likelihood of accidents and damage suits will proliferate.

The school principal is primarily responsible for everything that happens within the confines of the school. It is his or her responsibility to organize the school and its faculty in such a manner that accidents will be reduced or eliminated. To do this, the principal must be aware of all of the areas outside of the school building that might lend themselves to opportunities for injuries if proper supervision is not maintained. A principal must have a complete safety plan for the physical plant within his or her jurisdiction All potential sites of accidents must be located. School districts have been held liable for accidental injuries occurring where pupils are prohibited from going as well as where they are directed to go.

The comprehensive safety plan will involve teaching faculty in its development as well as operation. After all, it is only by cooperative effort on the part of supervising teachers that the last clear chance for accident avoidance can be made. When trouble spots have been pinpointed, specific supervisory assignments must be made. Deploying the supervisory staff is part of the principal's responsibility.

> A pupil was injured as a result of having been assaulted by another pupil on the school playground. Action was brought against the board of education, the superintendent, the principal, the assistant principal, two teachers, and the other pupil.
> The trial court dismissed the case against all the defendants except the school board and the pupil who caused the injuries. The jury found the

> board of education not negligent because the fight occurred suddenly, was of short duration, could not have been anticipated, and could not have been prevented even if supervision had been given. On appeal, the judgment was reversed as to the school board and the principal. A new trial was convened.
>
> The appellate court found that since pupils were instructed to remain outside the school building during intervals between examinations, the principal had the duty to provide adequate supervision. Whether the principal had been negligent in not supplying adequate supervision and whether lack of supervision was the proximate cause of the injury were questions for a jury. Additionally, if the jury should find that the principal had been negligent, the board would be liable under the doctrine of *respondeat superior.*
>
> The court also held that the trial court had erred in not permitting the plaintiff to present testimony to show conflicting statements brought out by cross examination of a witness before the trial. It also erred in refusing to admit as testimony a report of the director of health and physical education on the ground that he had no personal knowledge.[19]

The playground itself, number of children utilizing the playground at any given time, unorganized informal games, the physical condition of the grounds, apparatus, equipment, and traffic patterns all must be considered and worked into a safety plan. Without doubt the number of supervisors available, where the school is located, the age and maturity of the pupils will all be factored into any equation that produces an organizational plan for accident avoidance.

Teachers, too, have responsibilities for acting in a reasonable and prudent manner when it comes to safety planning. Responsibility may ultimately rest with the principal, but teachers will also be involved in suits if they do not make every reasonable effort to prevent injuries from overtaking their pupils. This means that teachers are very much a part of any safety planning. Nor can teachers look to their own comfort when they are assigned supervisory duties on the playground. They must be alert, be constantly available, and provide the general oversight that the law demands.

Finally, good safety plans will standardize rules and regulations governing the posting of safety notices, advising students of high risk areas, and warning them against indulgence in prohibited activities that are potentially injurious to them. For example, bicycle riding on playgrounds during recess periods is a dangerous practice and should be prohibited. Failure to do this has been construed as negligence in past court decisions.[20] Warnings alone are insufficient. It almost always comes down to a question of the adequacy of supervision or the lack thereof. One school district was held to be negligent when a young child injured herself when she jumped off backwards from a five-foot set of bleachers in an unsupervised play area.[21]

Neither the school district nor the teacher will be held liable when supervision of playgrounds and the activities carried on on them is adequate and reasonable. When the standards of supervison fall below that which is required to prevent unreasonable risk to pupils, suits will ensue and liability will surely be fixed.

Informal play at recess or during the luncheon period must be supervised by competent personnel. This means a member of the faculty or one who has special preparation for working with children and is specifically assigned to the position. Significantly, the number of teachers assigned to a playground should be consonant with the number of pupils to be supervised. It is impossible for one teacher to supervise a large playground where fifty or more children of various ages are playing.

In the event that a pupil wanders away from the group during a recess period on the playground and subsequently injures himself as a result of an existing dangerous condition into which he thrust himself, the supervisor may be held liable for negligent supervision. However, when a pupil patently disregards a well-established rule against leaving the playground area, goes to a restricted area, and there injures himself, no liability will attach to the teacher or anyone else.

A good safety plan requires regular and routine inspection of the playground and all of the apparatus and equipment in use. When accidental injuries occur because of defects or poor equipment, school districts and their personnel may be liable for damages incurred. Some school districts are immune from liability suits because of their governmental functions. However, more and more states are lifting the immunity doctrine from school operations and declaring that negligent actions will be redressed.[22] Insofar as particular pieces of equipment are concerned, much depends upon whether adequate supervision could have prevented the injury from occurring and the state or condition of the equipment in question.

During playground recess, a second-grade school child was injured when the wooden handle of the jump rope she was using was jerked out of her teacher's hands when the child inadvertently stepped on the rope. The teacher was sued on the basis of negligence. The issue on appeal was whether the evidence was conclusive in determining that the child's injuries were the proximate result of the teacher's negligence or whether the injuries were due to an unavoidable accident. It was alleged that the teacher could have foreseen that the accident could happen and that in the exercise of reasonable care the teacher could have furnished a longer rope or one without wooden handles.

The court held that the evidence failed to show any actionable negligence on the part of the teacher. The jump rope was of standard manufacture, was the same used by children over many years, and was of a type normally used by children for that activity.

The court ruled that the teacher could not have foreseen that because the rope was no longer than six feet or because it was equipped with wooden handles or because the pupil might step on it while jumping and cause it to be pulled from an adult's grasp, the wooden handle would strike the child and produce injuries to her; therefore, the teacher had not been negligent.[23]

In another injury case, action was brought against a supervising teacher and the school principal on behalf of a child who was injured while riding a merry-go-round in the school playground during a recess period.

> The merry-go-round on which the nine-year-old child was riding was a circular wood platform resting on a cement base and supported by steel cross beams. The riding platform was approximately six inches off the ground. Movement of the device was furnished by riders who pushed against posts set into the platform and then jumped on the platform for the ride. The school had established a rule that children could ride only in a standing position. This device had a three-inch piece of board missing from part of the circular edge and a small hole through the floor near its center. This condition had existed for sometime and was known to school authorities. The defects had been reported to the maintenance department.
>
> Testimony as to how the child came to be injured was in conflict. The basic question was whether the child had injured himself by stepping through the hole, which he claimed was a dangerous condition that the teacher knew about, or whether a failure to warn him of it or prohibit the use of the device by any of the pupils where such a danger existed constituted the proximate cause of the injury.
>
> The supervising teacher testified that the child was injured because he was sitting or kneeling on the side of the device and dragging his foot over the side in such a way that it was caught under the center edge of the revolving platform. The teacher started for the child to correct this activity when the accident occurred. The child testified that his foot went through a board. The child's mother testified that the hole in the center of the device was large enough to permit the child's foot to go through. In view of this conflict of evidence in the case, the court held that whether the hole in the merry-go-round was the actual cause of the injury, and whether the existence of the hole would have caused a reasonable and prudent person to foresee risk in the use of the device were questions that would have to be determined by a jury under proper instructions. The case was remanded.[24]

In circumstances where pupils have been injured on equipment that was well maintained, inspected, and in standard condition for use, no damages would probably be permitted. Assumption of risk might be attempted as a defense against an allegation of negligence here, but it would be better to assert that the student sustained injuries that could not have been prevented and were not the fault of the supervisor. Courts have consistently held that specific supervision of each game and each piece of playground equipment would be an unreasonable requirement. Thus, pupils who have been hurt by falling off apparatus that was in good condition can attempt litigation, but it is highly unlikely that the case will merit serious consideration. However, if it can be shown that the surface beneath the equipment was itself hazardous, because of a hardened condition, it might be possible to allege negligence. The surface beneath playground apparatus should be resilient and energy-absorbing, i.e., soft.

It should be absolutely apparent that where children of all ages congregate on a playground, special precautions and vigilance should be taken to avoid accidents. Children develop at different rates and their coordination, speed, strength, and flexibility will vary. Some children will be more capable than others in performing on apparatus or using available equipment. There is always the presumption that some apparatus may be too dangerous for those who are immature and unskilled. Therefore to reduce or prevent accidental injuries on the playground adequate and competent supervision must be provided. Rules and regulations adopted for the control of playground behavior must be posted, verbally reiterated, and strictly enforced. Playground apparatus and equipment that contributes to the enjoyment and development of the user must be maintained in good condition. The playground itself must be designed and constructed so that hazards are not built into the installation. The playground area should be well maintained so that it is clean, and free of obstructions with all playing surfaces properly maintained.

Emergency Assistance

Even though a supervising recreationist is not empowered to supply medical treatment to a participant, he or she is responsible to administer whatever emergency assistance may be required. Thus, when a participant sustains an injury, the recreationist faces a difficult problem. The recreationist is caught in a dilemma that necessitates that appropriate steps be taken but that creates potential liability if too much assistance is rendered or not enough action is taken.

The recreationist-client relationship imposes certain protective duties upon the recreationist if an emergency should occur. Every recreationist should complete an approved first aid or CPR training course as a prerequisite for employment. First aid supplies should be readily available at recreational centers; along with emergency telephone numbers. Whenever there is a participant injury, especially if a child should be hurt, there is a need for immediate attention. It may be that the child's parents should be contacted so that they may consent to medical treatment. When parents cannot be reached in an emergency, the recreationist is required to summon a physician to provide first aid. Where it is apparent that time is of the essence, the recreationist has a duty to render first aid until a medical person arrives. First aid is defined as providing life support assistance in emergency situations where no competent medical person is immediately available. The first aider responds to a potential life threatening condition by stopping any hemorrhage, immobilizing fractures, assisting the victim to start breathing again, providing closed heart massage (when necessary), treating for shock, poisoning, or other endangering elements where minutes and, perhaps, even seconds count. The recreationist desists from supplying first aid as soon as a competent medical authority (usually a physician) reaches the scene and the victim.

In providing first aid, the recreationist is not required to perform in a manner such as one would expect from a physician, nurse, or paramedic. However, the worker should be reasonably prepared in applying emergency lifesaving techniques. Therefore, if the worker performs in ways that are completely unsound or acts in a manner that a reasonable person should know is unwise, detrimental, or medically unsound, he or she may be found liable for a negligent application of the duty to supply first aid.

> In taking a group of teenagers on a bicycle trip into the dry hills of California, the recreationist supervising the group did not take into account the effect that the sun would have upon the participants. Almost all of the bicyclists were sweating profusely. One of the cyclists became dizzy and nearly passed out on the trail. This young man had to be helped to the department bus that had been standing by to pick up the hostelers. After the group returned to the recreational center, the youth was taken to the health room, placed on a cot, and given first aid by the recreationist-in-charge. Since the worker was convinced that the case was simply one of mild heat exhaustion, he resisted suggestions by another worker that a doctor be summoned—even as the youth turned grey and lapsed into incoherence. Finally a physician was called, but by then the process had become irreversible and the young man died.
>
> After considering all the evidence, the court ruled that a reasonably prudent worker should have recognized that a serious situation existed and that such actions as were taken were improper and incompetent under the circumstances. The court ruled that the negligent actions of the worker were the proximate cause of the youth's death, because the worker's techniques materially denied the youth qualified assistance that might have saved him. Having determined that the worker was negligent and that the negligence was the proximate cause of the youth's demise, the court awarded damages to the estate of the youth and to the youth's parents.[25]

When a situation does not meet the test of an emergency, it is presumed that persons other than recreational service workers will handle the problem; in consequence, the recreationist does not have to call for a physician nor provide first aid. To the contrary, in nonemergency situations the recreationist does not have the prerogative to provide first aid to a child (the child is incompetent to give consent), and the recreationist may be held liable for treating nonemergency conditions.

NOTES

1. United States Consumer Product Safety Commission, *A Handbook for Public Playground Safety* (Washington: The Commission, 1980), 2.
2. United States Consumer Product Safety Commission, Bureau of Epidemiology, *Hazard Analysis:* Playground Equipment (April 1975), 3.
3. T. B. Sweeney, "Playground Accidents: A New Perspective," *Trial* (April 1979): 42.
4. Cor Westland and Jane Knight, *Playing, Living, Learning* (State College, Pa.: Venture Publishing, Inc., 1982), 63.
5. Bill Vance, *Adventure Playground Report* (Long Beach, Cal.: American Adventure Playground Association, 1979).

6. Communication from Frank O. Sieh, arbitrator, *Wendy Alker v. City of Thousand Oaks*, 14 December 1981.

7. Communication from J. M. Bishop, director, Department of Parks and Recreation, City of Glendale, California to the City Attorney's Office of that City, 4 October 1972.

8. Accident and Damage Claim filed by Geoffrey L. Power, Guardian *Ad Litem*, 26 September 1972.

9. Letter from Leonard M. Marangi, Esq., to the Senior Assistant City Attorney concerning *Power v. City of Glendale*, LASC Case No. NC C 5248 G, D/A 21 June 1972 (16 July 1975).

10. *Resolution of the Council of the City of Glendale, No. 18, 532*, 24 January 1978.

11. *Spanel v. Mounds View School District No. 621*, 118 N.W. (2d) 795, Supreme Court of Minnesota (14 December 1962).

12. *Webber v. The City of New York*, 292 N.Y.S. (2d) 574, Supreme Court of New York, Appellate Division, Second Department (8 July 1968).

13. *Domino v. Mercurio*, 234 N.Y.S. (2d) 1011, Supreme Court of New York, Appellate Division, Fourth Department (6 December 1962).

14. *Cook v. Bennett*, 288 N.W. (2d) 609, Court of Appeals of the State of Michigan (1980).

15. *Garmond v. Board of Education of Central School District No. 1*, 197 N.Y.S. (2d) 548, Supreme Court of New York, Appellate Division, Third Department (18 March 1960).

16. *Reithardt v. Board of Education of Yuha County*, 43 Cal. App. 2d 629, 111 P. 2d 440 (1941); also *Benedetto v. Travelers Insurance Co.*, 172 So. 2d 354 (La. 1965); also *McCloy v. Huntington Park Union High School Dist. of Los Angeles County*, 139 Cal. App. 237,33 P.2d 882 (1934).

17. *Woodsmall v. Mt. Diablo Unified School District*, 10 Cal. Rptr. 447, District Court of Appeal, First District, Division 2, California (17 January 1961).

18. *Carrol v. Fitzsimmons*, 384 P (2d) 81, Supreme Court of Colorado, En Banc (29 July 1963).

19. *Cianci v. Board of Education of City School District of City of Rye*, 238 N.Y.S. (2d) 547, Supreme Court of New York, Appellate Division, Second Department (18 February 1963).

20. *Buzzard v. East Lake School District of Lake County*, 93 P. (2d) 233 California (1939).

21. *Decker v. Dundee Central School District*, 151 N.E. (2d) 866 New York (1958).

22. *Muskopf v. Corning Hospital District*, 55 Cal. 2d 211, 359 P 2d 457. Cal. Rept. 89 (1961); also *City of Wilmington v. Spencer*, 319 A. 2d 199 (Del. 1978).

23. *Wire v. Williams*, 133 N.W. (2d) 840, Supreme Court of Minnesota (5 March 1965).

24. *Eastman v. Williams*, 207 A. (2d) 146, Supreme Court of Vermont (18 February 1965).

25. *Mogahgab v. Orleans Parish School Board*, 239 SO. (2d) 456 (La. App. 1970).

11
Parks, Forests, and Reservations

Parks

Without any question, a major portion of recreational activities occur in outdoor areas that have been set aside for such specific purposes. Parks are all of those land and water areas dedicated to passive and active recreational activities that occur in specifically delineated spaces. For the most part, parks are especially designed and landscaped areas that may include public parkways, boulevards, beaches, playgrounds, athletic fields, centers, open spaces, golf courses, and other publicly owned areas that have been acquired for the conservation of natural resources and participation in a variety of recreational experiences. Parks are generally designated as such by fencing, entryways, and appropriate signs, or simply by being the only landscaped or natural place within a given location. The fact that it is devoid of dwelling places, industrial structures, and other buildings tends to insure its separateness and indicates the general use to which it has been put. Parks may be of almost any size, shape, and contain varied topographic or geological forms. Most parks contain at least two acres of space and may be areas of up to ten thousand acres in certain cities. Of course, national and state parks may be even larger.

Parks contain diverse areas for almost any recreational use and participation. Except in extreme cases, all parks are open for year-round activities. Seasonal use of parks for appropriate activities and special sports, games, aquatic activities, caving, climbing, hiking, riding, hunting, fishing, shooting, or archery facilities may be found at local, county, state, or national parks, depending upon the extent of the area for such development and the permissiveness of the park authorities. In some of the largest parks zoological exhibitions, tennis courts, swimming pools, arboreta, band shells, playing fields, and boating marinas (where the park fronts an adequate body of water) may be found.

Forests

Forests, on the other hand, are large tracts of land set aside for the retention of tree cover. Forests are heavily timbered or wooded with one or more species of trees together with underbrush, varying geological and topographical areas, and the several habitats of game, fish, and other wildlife. One of the most important uses of forests is for recreational purposes. The recreational use of forests for fishing, hunting, trapping, camping, hiking, climbing, caving, and aquatic activities, where waterways cut through the forest, has attracted many millions of people each year. Forests tend to be less well developed than are parks. Few forest lands contain any of the formal sport and game facilities usually associated with parks and reservations. Forest recreational use generally falls within the area of natural resources that can most easily be oriented to activities without a great deal of construction for amenity or formal needs.

Forest recreational activities, aside from activities that can be carried on within a timbered section, would most probably be roadside picnicking, primitive camping, vacationing in a residential development, and those activities that require wilderness or undeveloped woodlands. Whatever natural sites are available will lend themselves to rock climbing, spelunking, orienteering, viewing unusual scenes, and a multitude of recreational experiences that can occur in the outdoors without any special construction.

Reservations

The reservation is a relatively expansive piece of land with scenic and geologic features maintained in its natural state. Some reservations have been developed into parklike areas, but for the most part, reservations are large tracts of land that have been acquired by governments for controlling and protecting stream valleys. It is typical to find such recreational activities as camping, hiking, picnicking, nature study, and seasonal sport and game activities occurring on reservations. Reservations usually contain thousands of acres, although there may be some with less property. The reservation is usually situated on the outskirts of the community, is held by the county or state, and therefore serves a regional need. Although it is desirable for these areas to be underdeveloped, i.e., maintained in a natural state, there are some reservations that contain not only primitive campsites, water and winter sports facilities, bridle paths, hiking trails, lookout points, and waterways for small craft use, but intensively developed recreational areas where shooting ranges, ball fields, tennis courts, craft shops, and other activity facilities are available. Perhaps, to the purist, reservations should remain as primitive as possible with environmental activities being the only experiences obtainable. However, when an area is as extensive as many reservations are, in excess of ten thousand acres, it may be perfectly permissible and necessary to serve both wilderness and highly organized recreational needs.

POLICY REGULATING BEHAVIOR FOR SAFETY

It is typical for authorities to control the conduct of patrons who enter outdoor recreational places. Such control is predicated upon two distinct bases, i.e., convenience of the authority and the preservation of the safety of the participant. Administrative convenience facilitates personnel scheduling and maintenance operations, and makes it easier to manage the area as well as to account for any fees or charges that are imposed on the public for its use of the facility. Safety rules, however, are designed to protect patrons from their own or someone else's poor judgment. The rules and regulations that are devised by recreational authorities have been developed over a period of time, usually in direct relation to experiences or observations that recreationists have had or made in similar situations.

UNIFORMED SAFETY PERSONNEL

The largest parks, forests, and reservations will probably have a uniformed patrol force. Sometimes the uniformed force is park police. In instances where park police operate, they are trained and qualified as police officers with all of the powers of arrest, interrogation, and responsibility that any municipal or state police agent would have in maintaining public security and safety and apprehending lawbreakers. Park police, therefore, are typically organized along the same chain of command and have the same or similar powers as do any law enforcement officers. Park and forest rangers may be given the same kind of police training and in some instances may be sworn in as law enforcement officers, but for the most part, rangers are prepared to enforce park, forest, or reservation public safety policies and may also act as guides and program interpreters and provide information concerning the flora, fauna, and environment in the recreational area where they are employed. Rangers may, of course, function in the capacity of police officers. Some public jurisdictions recruit personnel for the uniformed ranger force who will also be given police training, carry weapons, and operate in whatever capacity is deemed necessary for the situation.

The uniformed force should be well trained and competent to carry out the safety policies that are promulgated by the authority for whom they work. This means strict enforcement of any rules, regulations, or ordinances that are published and disseminated to the public by means of posting, announcements, or handouts. Recreational authorities must walk a tightrope when it comes to the use of police agents or those who act as law enforcement personnel. Sometimes, there is a tendency for rangers and police to become so preoccupied with maintaining the letter of every regulation that they lose sight of the chief function of the recreational service authority—to provide a setting where people may participate in a variety of experiences designed to produce satisfaction, enjoyment, and a healthy outlook. When uniformed forces focus their attention on some petty details regulating patron behavior, such as not allowing children to fly kites on grassed places or prohibiting picnicking in places not specifically designed for that activity, it is probably because such personnel have not been thoroughly imbued with the concept of recreational service. It may also mean that some rules, regulations, and ordinances are long overdue for change or deletion. At any rate, recreational service administrators would be well advised to indoctrinate their uniformed personnel with the ideas that tend to guide the practice of recreational service.

On some occasions and in certain situations, uniformed personnel can perform an invaluable function while carrying out their responsibilities. They can and should prevent patrons from behaving in ways that are detrimental to life and limb. Where there are posted areas prohibiting entry or use, uniformed personnel should strictly enforce such regulations. There are basic safety reasons for such posting. It may be that an area is hazardous because of sinkholes, wells, or other known, but as yet unmarked or unfenced sites. People should be kept out of these areas to prevent accidents. There are excellent reasons for prohibiting the use of certain waterways for swimming, diving, wading, or fishing. When these areas are posted, the enforcement policy should automatically follow.

For all practical intents and purposes, uniformed personnel, unless specifically trained and sworn in as peace officers, should not consider police functions as their primary responsibility. Rather, uniformed personnel will be designated as rangers, guides, or foresters and will consider their first duty to be the health, safety, and well-being of patrons utilizing outdoor recreational resource areas. The rangers' duties will include public relations, warning patrons of consequences when they behave contrary to recreational service jurisdictional rules or regulations, protection of patrons, and protection of flora and fauna found within the recreational resource.

AREAS, ACTIVITIES, AND HAZARDS FREQUENTLY FOUND IN OUTDOOR RECREATIONAL PLACES

Among the types of recreational areas designed for and constructed in parks or reservations are sport and game fields, archery fields, shooting ranges, hiking trails, bridle paths, and a variety of winter facilities for use during the appropriate season.

Recreationists, physical educators, coaches, and others who have the responsibility for supervising sport and game activities have an all-consuming requirement to protect the safety of those who are nominally in their charge. To do this such personnel must recognize the need to inform participants of any risks that they might face in activities, supply competent instruction, be assured that each participant is well conditioned for the rigors of the activity, make sure that athletic fields or other physical facilities are well maintained and in proper repair, and insure that whatever equipment is used is of the highest quality available. Having performed these prerequisite actions, they face only limited exposure to the allegation of negligence should any injury subsequently ensue as a result of participation.

However, there is no ironclad rule that automatically relieves an employee or organization from the liability resulting from sport or game activities that produce injuries. Such injuries may be the outcome of overly enthusiastic players competing at close quarters or in direct bodily contact. In some cases injuries will be sustained because of factors not ordinarily associated with actual play. In some circumstances, spectators may be injured. Each case is judged upon its own merits, although there are certain broad principles that apply in almost all of the cases. Thus, the most typical allegation of an injured party will be that the person or organization from whom recovery is petitioned was negligent. An example of this latter situation is the following case:

> A seventeen-year-old high school pupil was injured at a football game. She was standing by the sidelines when players violently collided with her during the course of play. At the time of the incident, the pupil realized that players might run off the field to where she stood and that safe seats were available in the bleachers.
> The pupil brought action for damages. A motion for summary judgment by the school board was granted. The decision was upheld on appeal. The court held that spectators at sporting events assume risks incidental to the game, especially where the spectator chooses to stay in an unprotected place despite the availability of safe seating.[1]

Football

Football is a game commonly played in parks. Where park authorities lay out, or develop formal football fields for the purpose of holding competitive activities, there are concomitant responsibilities that must be observed. Of course, many organizations may construct football fields both for developmental practice and competition. Schools, recreational service departments, industrial leagues, and similar organizations may utilize football fields for these purposes. Football is a contact sport, and every participant must be made to understand that injuries will occur. The essential need is for highly qualified and professionally competent personnel who will undertake the responsibility for coaching, instruction, and supervision of football players.

Any agency, department, or organization wishing to minimize injuries to participants and maximize safety will develop a set of operational policies to which all will conform. These policies are guides to desirable behavior on the part of participants and supervisors.

Safety policy dealing with football should constantly reiterate the necessity for warning would-be players of the potential dangers inherent in the game as well as the fundamentals for learning the skills required for participation. The organization should, by verbal admonition as well as published communications, repeatedly emphasize rules and procedures on the proper techniques to practice for maximum safety in the actual playing of the game. Among the skills to be learned that are required of all players will be those dealing with tackling, blocking, stance, body position, and instruction.

Tackling. Neither the head nor the helmet is ever to be used as a battering ram. Initial contact with an opponent is not to be made with the helmet. While contact with the helmet is often made during the course of the game, the technique of doing so correctly, when properly blocking or tackling an opponent, will be the best preventative of injuries. Tackling skill requires that contact be made above the waist, but not hitting the opponent with the helmet in a butting movement. Balance is important; the charging player should always maintain a straight back, with the knees bent, and the body leaning slightly forward. Initial contact with an opponent should be made by the shoulder. The head is held up. The helmet must be put as close to the body as is possible to avoid injury. Rules prohibit grabbing the face mask or edge of the helmet. All players must be impressed with such rules.

Blocking. Like tackling, blocking requires contact above the waist. Players must be prohibited from using their helmet as the initial point of contact. Balance and heads-up play will ordinarily prevent the risk of injuries. In blocking, the target area is as near the body as is possible with the main force of contact being taken on the shoulder.

Body Position and Stance. Contact with an opponent must be made with bent knees. It is important that all players understand the necessity for maintaining correct posture, balance, and body inclination. These points must be reiterated continuously during practice.

Equipment. Protective clothing including helmet, shoulder pads and hip, thigh, and knee pads must be properly fitted and used correctly. It must be determined that each player is correctly fitted, neither too small or too large. In these latter instances, the player who is incorrectly fitted with protective gear will be vulnerable to bruises, separations, or possible slipped spinal disks. Helmets must fit securely and tightly at contact points—front, rear, and the top of the head. The helmet must be safely labeled. The straps and pads of the helmet must be secured and be of the appropriate thickness to insure protection.

Instruction. Basic skill development and constant emphasis on proper techniques along with the reiterated warnings of the dangers that can occur if correct procedures are not followed is the responsibilityof every person who is charged with the supervision of football players. Of primary importance is the conditioning of athletes so that their bodies can take the shock of body contact without injury. The building of physical fitness through a variety of exercises and the development of strength, particularly of the neck, through various isometric and isotonic exercises will prove to be invaluable in the prevention of head, neck, and spinal chord, or shoulder injuries. Knee injuries can also be lessened through the use of weight training to strengthen the quadriceps and stretching exercises. However, body position and bent knees will probably offer the best means to escape serious knee injury.

CHANGING JUDICIAL OPINIONS AND THE BURDEN OF CARE

The assumption of risk doctrine has, until recently, been used as a defense against allegations of negligence when participants have been injured in athletic contests or during conditioning practices. The classic case is thought to be that of *Vendrell v. School District No. 260,* in Malheur County, Oregon. A high school football player was rendered a permanent paraplegic when his neck was broken during the course of a game. He had used his head as a battering ram while attempting to avoid tacklers. The player then brought suit, but the court denied redress. In this instance, the court took notice of the fact that the player had received extensive training, practice, and conditioning under the competent supervision and instruction of his coaches. Furthermore, the court stated that the reasons for the general rule of participant nonrecovery in football were that:

> The playing of football is a body-contact sport. The game demands that the players come into physical contact with each other constantly, frequently with great force. The linemen charge the opposing line vigorously, shoulder to shoulder. The tackler faces the risk of leaping at the swiftly moving legs of the ball carrier and the latter must be prepared to strike the ground violently. Body contacts, bruises, and clashes are inherent in the game. There is no other way to play it. No prospective player need be told that a participant in the game of football may sustain injury. That fact is self evident. It draws to the game the manly; they accept the risk, blows, clashes, and injuries without whimper.[2]

In this case the courts placed the burden on the injured player, by noting that the coaches had provided the proper instruction of skills, had required that players be physically capable and fit to participate, incorporated a vigorous training program, and instructed the participants in the correct techniques of using the protective devices to absorb contact forces. The court was simply restating precedent when it inquired into the responsibility of the coach to fulfill the duty to exercise reasonable care for the protection of those under supervision.

With a recent court decision in Seattle, Washington, the opinion of the courts appears to have shifted the burden of responsibility from the participant to those who provide supervision.[3] The assumption of risk doctrine is being redefined so that there is a higher duty of care owed to youthful participants by the organizing authority and its employees. Of immense importance, according to the courts, is the need to warn players of the risk of sustaining serious injury. It no longer is a self evident fact that players could be injured during a game. Such an opinion indicates that participants below the age of eighteen may not comprehend the possibility of being injured for their own actions as a participant.

Despite new court opinions, there are still situations where the sponsoring organization is, indeed, negligent. In 1979 a teenaged girl with no previous behavioral or disciplinary problems underwent a marked personality change as a consequence of being injured in a football game. She suffered a broken nose, a concussion, and an abnormal brain-wave pattern after being struck by an opponent in a powder-puff football game. The court held that the school was the sponsor of the event, despite denials by the principal. The girl was awarded sixty thousand dollars. The court found that the school was negligent in having failed to provide the necessary equipment to protect female competitors, failed to lock the gates that would have prevented the girls from coming onto the school grounds to play, and failed to stop certain teachers from coaching the activity.[4]

Baseball and Softball

Baseball and softball have many similarities, aside from the fact that both are played on diamonds, have standardized rules in common, and use equipment that is almost interchangeable. Of course there are differences in terms of the size of the ball, specific rules regulating the kind of game played, and pitching motions. However, the similarities of the game far outweigh the differences. Some hazards are also similar and may be divided into two parts: (1) those that are purely accidental, involving sprains, abrasions, fractures, concussions, and other impact injuries; and (2) those that are maliciously caused. Additionally, there may also be some spectator injury produced because of poor seating or protective arrangements, and miscellaneous accidents caused by unruliness or disorderly behavior by those attending the activity.

The second form of activity that may occur during a baseball or softball game is the malicious use of force against an opponent that is contrary to all the rules of the game and may result in injury. Thus, deliberately thrown "bean" balls designed to strike an opposing batter on purpose, attacks by a batter against another person, deliberately spiking an opponent, or some form of battery that produces an injury may all be settled in a court of law. In the latter instance, where injuries are produced as a result of poor sportsmanship and/or failure on the part of one player to observe even the most rudimentary rules of participation, the question of assumption of risk will probably be set aside. Indeed, when risks are such that they fall beyond what may ordinarily be expected to occur or inhere in the activity, then the risks would not be assumed by the participant to the degree that they did not conform to what was obvious, foreseeable, or expected.[5]

Finally, there are injuries that are produced as a consequence of facility deficiencies or lack of supervision of participants. Injuries that occur because operators have not been as careful as they might have been about how and where pieces of equipment are encountered by participants and spectators provide the basis for successful litigation in the following instance:

> Three children, all male, went to a neighborhood school playground one Sunday morning and began to play baseball. The youngest child was seated along the third base line on an emplaced bench. A pitched ball was batted by the child's older brother and struck the boy beneath the left eye. The child suffered an orbital fracture and some eye injury. Suit was brought on behalf of the child against the school board that operated the playground. In a court ordered settlement, the operating authorities were adjudged to have been negligent in permitting the placement of a bench so close to the third base line, for not having provided adequate protection for spectators, for not preventing access to the ball field at inappropriate times. The school board acknowledged their own negligence. The case was settled for six thousand dollars.[6]

The facts of the case are interesting for the lack of safety provisions and for the deficiency of facility arrangements that led to the injuries sustained by the plaintiff. This recreational playing field was constructed and operated with the express purpose of inviting children, and presumably others, to utilize the facility whenever they were personally motivated to do so. Although there was a fence partially surrounding the field, there were not less than three deliberately available entries that were apparently never closed in any way. Moreover, a section of the fence on the southwest side was dismantled and permitted easy access to the field by anybody. Finally, the playing field was completely open to entry on the northwest section because the fence line stopped and a vast opening occurred between the end of the fence and the school building. It was never the intention of the school authorities to deny access to potential participants. In fact, the facility was continuously open and available for use.

There is always danger that sports activities will cause injury to spectators when hit or thrown balls fly off at a tangent beyond the boundaries of the game. This is precisely what happened in this case. However, because of the age of plaintiff, it cannot be assumed that these children would normally recognize the risk that coexists with a spectator at such an activity. The "common knowledge" rule, that is, that the risks involved are so apparent that any person of reasonable intelligence could not possibly be unaware of their likelihood and must for that reason assume the risk of injury, in this case did not apply.

The most significant risk that a spectator will not assume is the risk that an operator of a facility in which competitive physical activities are organized, sponsored, or invited will fail to satisfy his/her duty of care. Operators of public recreational facilities are liable for conditions on their premises that cause physical harm to invitee-spectators if they know, or should reasonably

Proper facility design, adequate fencing, and appropriate seating arrangement are necessary for participant safety.

have ascertained, that a hazardous condition exists and that it puts forward an unreasonable risk of harm that the invitee-spectator will not recognize or protect themselves against and fail to take reasonable care for their own safety. Thus, the school board had the duty to maintain the premises at the playground in a reasonably safe condition to prevent injury. After plaintiff's injury, the school board removed the bench. They must have known that its location made it potentially hazardous, and that fact is borne out by the accident that did occur.

The school board failed to construct the facility in accordance with nationally known and generally recognized standards of safety. Although they constructed two official baseball (softball) fields, on a north-side axis, they deviated substantially from safety standards that are absolutely necessary if spectators and participants are to be protected from the very type of injury that occurred.

By emplacing a bench in such a way almost guaranteed that a sitter would be brought into close proximity to batted balls that might be deflected at odd angles. In this manner, the board of education acted irresponsibly and allowed a serious injury to plaintiff. The standard generally subscribed to is that players' benches or other seating must be situated behind protective screens or least sixty feet from home base and the base lines. Seating areas, unless protected by wire screen, should never be less than sixty feet from home plate.

It is essential that operators make reasonably thorough inspections of the seating areas on a routine basis to determine whether or not they are safe for use. If such inspections are not made in a timely manner or are performed in a perfunctory or improper manner, the operator will be charged with the knowledge that would have been gained had care been taken. It is questionable whether the school board or its agents ever made any such inspections. If they had, it is unlikely that a bench would have been positioned at an unsafe distance from the baseline and not protected by screening. Under such circumstances, the potential danger to anyone seated on that bench became actuality when the child was struck by the baseball.

By constructing an official baseball diamond without attending to arrangements that would have successfully protected the invitee-spectators from being injured, the board of education deviated substantially from generally recognized standards in the field of recreational service and physical education. By failing to place seating facilities correctly, installing seating facilities that were unsafe, and maintaining this unsafe condition over an extended period, the board of education failed to provide the necessary protection to invitee-spectators, failed to take reasonable and prudent action to prevent the injury from occurring, did not foresee the probability of injury to children utilizing this facility, and failed to take the appropriate measures required to eliminate the hazard that it caused to be produced. The school board's actions were the proximate cause of the injury.

Field Hockey

The game of field hockey is played on a field much the same dimensions as a football field. There the similarity ends. Two opposing teams are equipped with hockey sticks, and the ball is slightly larger than a baseball. Practice, conditioning, and stick handling technique are all part of the instructional procedure for participants. Among the prohibitions that carry with them direct safety implications are the following:

1. Sticks may not be raised above the shoulder at any time during the stroke.
2. No player shall ever strike the ball on the fly, into a player at close range, or so hard that the ball rises.
3. No player may undercut, i.e., use a stroke with the blade of the stick laid back.
4. No player may push, pull, trip, strike, or in any way place hands on an opponent.
5. No player may interfere with an opponent's stick in any manner.
6. No player may place her body between the opponent and the ball.

7. No player may use any part of the body to interfere with an opponent's play with the ball.
8. No player may force an opponent off-stride by running in front of her.

All of the regulations are designed to protect players from injury.

Lacrosse

Lacrosse is played by two opposing teams of ten players per side. The field is slightly larger than a football field. The ball is carried in the head of the crosse, and scores are made by causing the ball to enter the opponent's goal. The ball is kept in play by being carried, thrown, rolled, kicked, or batted with the stick in any direction, unless otherwise indicated by the rules or referee. The game requires superb physical conditioning, agility, balance, speed, and strength. Because the players use a lacrosse stick or crosse and a hard rubber ball, there is the need for protective equipment. This includes a helmet fitted with a face mask, heavily padded gloves, light shoulder pads, and arm guards. The game is played as a bodily contact sport. Among the techniques used are attempts to dislodge the ball from an opponent's crosse by striking it with the stick. This may sometimes lead to unintentional or deliberate fouls that could be injurious. In order to prevent such mishaps, coaches, instructors, and supervisors of contact activities like lacrosse must provide participants with the correct information about the game, offer the techniques that will enhance not hinder the contest, warn about the hazards that players may confront, and supply safety rules to which all competitors must adhere.

Among the rules of the game are those that enable an individual to perform effectively, but in a controlled manner so that random injuries will be lessened or eliminated.

Soccer

Soccer is not supposed to be a contact sport, but there are occasions when, in the heat of competition, players get too close to one another and trade kicks. Sometimes in tackling (the technique of kicking or trying to kick the ball away from an opponent) errors in judgment may produce an injury when inadvertent touching causes a player to take a sudden fall. Soccer requires the use of head as a vital defensive method. However, unless the player is quite expert in this maneuver, some facial injuries can occur. Except for shin guards, there is no protective gear traditionally worn for soccer. Now, however, there are heel guards to offset the probability of Achilles tendon damage.

For the most part, supervisors of soccer activities can do much to lessen the risk of injury occurrence by making sure that all participants are in excellent physical condition before play. Fundamentals of the game must be stressed, and practicing ball control, dribbling, and body position all form a significant part in keeping the participant from hurting himself, herself, or others. Soccer can be played safely. It is simply a matter of knowing the techniques of play, adherence to the rules of the game, and learning the limits to which the body can be put when attempting to kick, head, or tackle.

All competitive sports and games carry an element of risk not inherent in the activity itself. This is the risk that competitors run when opponents forget the rules of sportsmanship and intentionally foul a player. Thus, the so-called tactical foul may prevent a player from scoring. However, there are occasions when a tactical foul results in player injury. This is the risk that should not have to be assumed by participants. It is a fact of the contest, but is both illegal and contrary to the rules of the game. Coaches should be chary about advising their players to commit tactical fouls because negative attitudes about observing the rules might be instilled. In some instances, malicious intent to hurt an opponent is observed. But malicious intent is difficult to prove, unless there is some pictorial representation of the action, such as a videotape of the sequence. There are injuries that are proximately caused by the intent of one player to foul an opponent and disable the player in the process. When serious injuries, especially of a permanent nature occur, there is every likelihood that an allegation of negligence and/or misfeasance will be brought against the offending person and those parties or organization for which he or she competed.

When sports competitions become so heated that intent to do bodily harm is commonplace, then those who organize the activities as well as those competing in them need to be admonished for permitting such illegal and felonious actions to occur. Placing a player at risk by intentionally stepping on his heel thereby rupturing the Achilles tendon, intentionally kicking a player so that a fracture results, tackling an opponent in such a way to produce a high spinal chord injury, using a bat as a weapon, or other such assaultive behaviors cannot be tolerated. Nevertheless, malicious behavior in athletics is neither new nor unknown. Proving malicious intent may be difficult or impossible, but players who are seriously injured in consequence of personal fouls should not have to be penalized with permanent injuries without redress. Those who knowingly physically assault another competitor should face criminal charges. If coaches or supervisors of activities instruct their players to use illegal tactics, they, too, should be charged in terms of comparative negligence.

Nongame Activities

Among the other recreational activities that are found in parks, forests, or reservations will be those of spelunking (cave exploration), horseback riding, hiking, rock climbing, archery, and target shooting. All of these activities carry with them inherent dangers. Each of these hazards may be compounded by lack of skill, poor instruction, unfamiliarity with the terrain or other geological features, immaturity, lack of emotional control, and poor judgment. When such activities are under the jurisdiction of or sponsored by recreational service agencies of any type, then all of the responsibilities associated with the provision of appropriate instruction, guidance, or warnings are in effect.

Spelunking. The exploration of naturally-formed caves is popular with those who like to investigate holes in the ground. It is both recreational and educational, but it can also be dangerous. Most caves are formed by acidic water action on limestone. The likelihood of collapse is limited, but there is that small possibility. It is much more likely that water will be found the further into a cave system one penetrates. Most caves do not have the space to permit walking. Instead, there will be a mixture of crawlways, walkways, narrow fissures, gorges, arches, bridges, crevasses, and domes. The spelunker will have to anticipate climbing, crawling, walking, wading, sometimes swimming, in areas that require this form of forward motion.

Among the myths of spelunking is that cave collapse is imminent and frequent. This is simply not true. Cave collapse is rare, and the potential for such fracturing is easily observed. Dangerous animals are almost unknown, although some poisonous snakes have been found around the mouth of a cave. There are hazards that experienced spelunkers will recognize. These are the probability of rising water, slide areas down which cavers will need ropes, and the ever present problem of striking the cave roof with the head. An essential safety item, therefore, is the hard hat.

Hiking. Packing into wilderness areas or simply traveling on foot from one point to another has become a recreational activity that millions of people are enjoying. However, there are certain precautions that should be taken by participants and those who sponsor or operate programs where hiking is one of the activities of choice. Any kind of walking requires some physical conditioning, but hiking can be a strenuous activity especially if it involves backpacking. The participant's physical condition becomes a very significant factor if hikes are to be accomplished with satisfaction and without accident. To remain safe and healthy while on the trail requires thorough knowledge, skills, and appropriate and adequate supplies or equipment.

Hiking requires attention to detail and proper planning insofar as outfitting oneself for the activity. If a hiker expects to travel to a distant point, it may be necessary to pack food, water, supplies, and emergency equipment. If some incident should occur that requires outside assistance, the time and distance factors become crucial elements in an emergency. The hiker may have to be able to survive on the supplies that have been carried until help arrives. Thus, necessary supplies or equipment must be thoughtfully selected and properly packed for easy carrying and convenience when needed. Food is another item that must receive consideration. If a hiker is to travel more than one day from point to point, there will be a need for food. If anything delays the hiker while en route, it may be necessary for whatever food supplies there are to be stretched so that the hiker will be able to continue or until assistance is obtained. Additionally, food must be handled in such a manner that it does not become spoiled with resultant food poisoning for the hiker.

Participants should have a good understanding of what hiking is all about and have a correct idea of the trip as well as the ability to perform whatever skills are necessary. Walking is one thing, camping out along the trail is quite another. Only those who are highly motivated to perform the physical exertions required and who really want to take part in such an expedition should be permitted to undertake this experience. The single most important issue involved in the prevention of accidental injuries when hiking is supervision. The sponsoring agency should require that one experienced guide or supervisor should accompany every eight to ten participants. The supervisory staff should be completely familiar with the area to be hiked. This means that those in guidance or leadership capacities will have had previous experiences on the trail to be taken. All supervisory personnel will be thoroughly trained in first aid techniques and be prepared to render assistance to any participant in an emergency.

Being aware of what is happening while on the trail and recognizing the potential hazards to which hiking exposes participants will help in reducing the commom problems that sometimes occur. The group should perform at a level of skill and capacity well within each person's ability. No participant group should be allowed to hike without an experienced supervisor. This will prevent individuals from wandering away from the group, getting lost, becoming caught in storms, or impulsively striking out without any knowledge of the area to be covered.

Horseback riding. Horseback riding has become popular in many outdoor areas. Whether in camps, parks, reservations, or forests, horses may be used for riding for short or long periods depending upon the objective of the activity. Basic instruction should be given concerning the temperament of the horse and how best to work with it. Potential riders should be taught that horses need to be calmed and that the best method for calming a horse is to talk softly to it when approaching it. No participant should ever approach a horse from behind. The rider should speak softly, move quietly about the horse, and never make abrupt movements or sudden noises. (See pp. 87–88.)

Rock Climbing. Rock climbing deals with all of the techniques used to ascend a rock wall, traverse a crevass, scale a peak, or use any piece of equipment for support and safety. Rock climbing also includes scaling a rocky surface using only the natural features of the rock without any artificial aid whatsoever. Climbing requires a high degree of skill and sufficient practical experience to insure ability for dealing with any problems or difficulties that might ensue during a climb. Supervisory personnel must instruct all would-be participants in the hazards, techniques, physical effects, and personal responsibility that each person must recognize if such an activity is to be successful and without accident. Of primary importance is the physical condition of the climber. The physical demands of climbing are such that unless the participant is in top shape, the climb can lead only to exhaustion and, perhaps, injury.

All climbers must be made aware of the necessity for carrying food, water, clothing, and safety gear designed to maintain the security of the climber. Moreover, the need for rest periods to husband strength and the avoidance of life-threatening situations are part of the instruction that should be provided to anyone who wants to climb and is under the jurisdiction or sponsorship of some recreational service agency. Among the conditions to be encountered on any climb will be the dangers of hypothermia. Therefore, the clothing to be worn must be appropriate for the climb. Everything that the climber needs must be packed on his or her back. Whether the individual faces a natural climb, that is, without the use of support equipment, or will utilize varied equipment, will be determined by the skill, length of climb, surface to be traversed, and other variables to be encountered.

Shooting. Shooting, whether with pistols, rifles, or other guns should be confined to firearms ranges that are especially constructed for safety purposes. Weapons use can be dangerous when individuals are unskilled, thoughtless of others, or where proper facilities are not in use. Ranges, whether indoor or outdoor, can be constructed from plans developed by nationally recognized organizations.

Except in situations where individuals are not under the sponsorship of any organization, shooting ranges simply operate facilities for business purposes. The facility operator must make sure that the construction of the range is such that shooters will in no way harm spectators nor cause injury to themselves or other users by virtue of poorly constructed facilities. However, operators cannot be responsible for the type and caliber of firearms that the private user brings to the range. The operator's responsibility is to construct a range that will stop a bullet behind a target without ricocheting. Target retrieving must be accomplished by mechanical means and in such a way as to prevent bullets from rebounding. Operators have a duty of care that necessitates the taking of such measures to provide a reasonably safe place for the purposes of the invitation extended to participants.

Archery. Archery ranges, like shooting ranges, must be constructed so that casual walkers and observers are protected from inadvertently coming into the line of arrow flight. Either the archery range must be clearly visible from every angle, or it must be enclosed by protective fencing that will not permit anybody to be struck by stray or well-shot arrows. For best results in stopping arrows, a shooting hill may be constructed directly behind the target butts. Such a hill will admirably serve to stop any stray arrows that overshoot the targets.

Potential archers should be old enough so that they understand all of the safety procedures and can use the necessary equipment. More importantly, archers must understand the need for precautions to be taken in order to safeguard themselves, other participants, and spectators. Archery is an activity that can be open for almost anyone in any age group, both sexes, those who are able bodied, and those who have certain physical disabilities. What is really necessary is a physical capacity to learn how to use archery equipment and the maturity to do so in a reasonable and correct way.

NOTES

1. *Cadieux v. Board of Education of the City School District for the City of Schnectady,* 266 N.Y.S. (2d) 895, Supreme Court of New York, Appellate Division, Third Department (8 February 1966).
2. *Vendrell v. School District No. 26C,* Malheur County, 233 Oregon 1, 376 P. (2d) 406 (1962).
3. S. H. Adams, "Court Decision Hits Hard With New Liability Twists," *Athletic Purchasing and Facilities* 6, no. 5 (May 1982): 12–16.
4. *Lynch v. Board of Education of Collinsville Community School District No. 10,* 72 Ill. App. (3d) 317, 390 N.E. (2d) 526 (1979).
5. *Bourque v. Duplechin,* 331 So (2d) 40 La. App. (1976).
6. *Superior Court of New Jersey* Law Division in Union County, No. L 4285277, 15 June 1978.

12
Slope, Trail, and Sliding Activities

When the seasons change and cold weather sets in, many recreational participants look forward to skiing, sledding, coasting, ice-skating, iceboating, or ice hockey. These have been the traditional activities of winter. They are fun, exhilarating, and satisfying to both novice and expert. However, such activities carry innate risks of injury for participants. The nature of the activity contains the stimulation of potential injury even when the participant has no awareness of the possibility of danger. Many incidents and injuries occur at places that are presumably designed for safe winter activities. For the most part, such accidents and the injuries that accompany them may be ascribed to poor judgment, poor design of the facility, faulty equipment, lack of skill, fatigue, and sheer incompetence on the part of organizational agents. Not infrequently, the proximate cause of an accidental injury may be traced to laziness, procrastination, or unconcern for the safety of participants on the part of operational authorities. Sometimes the fault lies with participants who contributed to their own harm.

Winter recreational activities are growing popular with diverse agencies and groups sponsoring programs that include camping, hiking, fishing, snowmobiling, snowshoeing, and other well-known activities. Persons who participate in these experiences are frequently ignorant of the hazards of cold weather. Tragic occurrences may sometimes develop when individuals are not prepared for the debilitating effects of cold, wind, snow, and fatigue. It is important for sponsoring or organizing agencies to warn participants of the dangers that shifting weather conditions can have upon the body, what safety precautions need to be taken, and how individuals can prepare themselves for the rigors of outdoor winter recreational activities.

Supervision

Supervision of all participants, whether children or adults, is extremely important for the safety of all persons who are engaged in winter activities. Of course, individuals will always participate in their own voluntary activities without coming under the aegis of some organization; but for those who do perform within the jurisdiction of some agency, supervision is a significant factor in reducing accidents and injuries.

Snow Vehicles and Equipment

Sleds, toboggans, and snow discs are some of the equipment to which all age groups seem to take to find enjoyment and active fun during wintery weather when there is snow. Unfortunately, such equipment also contributes to thousands of accidents and injuries each year, and in some cases death may ensue. Of great concern are mechanical and structural deficiencies. These include breaking up while in use. Some sleds, discs, and toboggans are poorly manufactured and are constructed from materials that cannot take any stress whatsoever. Such items will not stand up to the bumping, thumping, and hauling that users often give to them. Hence, they fall apart with use.

None of these carriers can readily be steered in an emergency. Although sleds are guided by a front steering mechanism, it is not highly maneuverable nor can it change course suddenly to avoid collisions or danger spots. In fact, the sledder's legs and body must be used in conjunction with the steering element if any course change is desired. Toboggans and discs have no steering mechanism at all. Theoretically, toboggans are supposed to be steered by continuously adjusting the body's weight on the toboggan, but in actual practice this seldom offers desirable steering. In both of these latter terms, the rider is essentially unable to steer and must take any hazard that comes. Poor riding conditions and loss of control are a fact of life for users of sleds, toboggans, and discs. Any rut, ridge, hummock, rock, tree stump, or other debris hidden under a few inches of snow can cause the rider to be thrown out of the carrier or can overturn it. Icy conditions, hard-packed snow, slush, and bare ground can also cause loss of rider control and offer dangerous conditions for the rider. There is always the risk of running into another rider or a stationary object, with disastrous results.

Where sleds, discs, or toboggans are part of the recreational activity supervised by some agency, it might be logical to present a safety program covering the use of such equipment along with rules and regulations about the safe use of slides, slopes, or artificial runways. Recreational service agencies operating slopes for coasting should make sure that the slopes are clear of debris, trees, boulders, stumps, and other obstacles that might cause an accident. If obstacles exist on the slope and it must be used, then buffer the stationary objects in such a manner that collision with them will not produce injury to the rider. This may best be performed by using a sufficient number of hay bales stacked to an adequate height and depth in the direction that a coaster might possibly hit. Additionally, other barriers such as loose netting, berms topped with soft plantings, styrofoam-filled plastic bags, or other equally soft and impact-absorbing materials may be used as buffers.

Whenever an agency operates a coasting slope, it must provide supervision as well as visual signs of warning and posted rules and regulations for the slope's use. In this way potential accidents may be avoided.

In an illustration of unsafe facilities and poor supervision, the following case is presented:

> A young girl, age fifteen, went on a ski weekend with a group of approximately forty boys and girls from a parochial high school in New Jersey. The young girl, together with her friends, arrived at the ski lodge at 7:30 in the evening. A meeting was conducted by the operator of the lodge, and the manager informed the group where meal tickets could be obtained and where personal belongings could be stored, but neither he nor any other personnel gave instructions as to where tobogganing was permitted. There was to be no skiing that evening because snow was being made. However, there was no prohibition against snowmobiling, tobogganing, or ice-skating. A toboggan was rented. The young girl was seated in the middle of two other riders. On the way down the slope the toboggan hit a bump, throwing the third passenger off the rear. The toboggan carrying the two girls continued down the slope, ran over a bale of hay, and struck a fixed wooden structure situated in the tobogganing area, a short distance beyond the hay bale. The fixed wooden structure was concealed from view and was not illuminated, nor were there any signs or warning devices indicating its presence. The impact of the toboggan against the structure caused the girl to sustain severe facial and bodily injuries.

> An analysis of the facts produced the following:

> The ski lodge is situated across from a small lake. One must drive up a steep macadam road to reach the administration building. The area of inspection consisted of a main lodge, dining hall, and a ski rental shop, that also rented toboggans. The slope on which these structures were located was divided by a road leading to the parking lot. Looking down the slope, the property was bounded on the right by an intermediate slope upon which an aerial chair lift had been constructed. Almost directly in front of the ski rental shop is a slope that terminates abruptly in an eight-foot drop-off in front of a partially concealed building. Several standing pipes are situated on the slope. These presumably serve for hose attachments for snowmaking purposes. These pipes were buffered by hay bales.

> Standard operating procedures in the field of recreational service are vitally concerned with the safety of participants. The safety of patrons, particularly at a commercial facility, is essential. At no time should an activity be initiated or a facility operated without observing fundamental rules of equipment and facility inspection to insure the safety of participants. Operational policies should be developed concerning the performance requirements of patrons and standards of conduct required for participation. The signaling of participants verbally or through the use of clearly posted signs concerning any directions necessary and areas of use is mandatory and commonly practiced in the field. Warning signs and symbols or other devices are also utilized to protect participants from coming into contact with dangerous conditions.

> Standards of care currently existing in the field of recreational service

concerning the operation of facilities on which potentially dangerous activities occur require a high order of supervision in order to prevent accidents. Because the lodge catered to teenagers especially, it should have been understood by the management that direct supervision would be required whenever such participants were on the slopes. Employees of commercial resorts must exercise reasonable prudence in the performance of their respective duties at the site of the activity and pay scrupulous attention in carrying out procedures designed to insure participant safety. No evidence of any kind of supervision was indicated when the young girl was injured. Based upon an appraisal of the facility and several inspections of the area in which the incident occurred, the following conclusions were reached:

1. The area was improperly designed, planned, and constructed. Deviation from standard practices of design concerning safety hazards were obvious. The slope on which the accident took place terminates suddenly at a drop-off in front of a partially concealed building. The building is set into the slope, surrounded by trees, and is low lying enough so that it is, for all practical intents and purposes, camouflaged. There were no signs in evidence directing patrons to a specific tobogganing slope. There were no directional signs anywhere, and the original toboggan slope was in darkness. The darkness at the time of the accident and the general terrain precluded the tobogganeers from actually seeing the low lying structure that was probably snow covered. The pine trees which backed the building apparently made the likelihood of discerning it and any other hazard extremely improbable. There were no warning devices at all on the building.
2. Standard operating procedures were not followed in that there existed fixed obstacles in the path of the tobogganeers.
3. Improper design is also noted in that the convenience and safety of patrons was not a consideration on the part of the operators. In contradiction of the official brochure of the lodge, the rental of toboggans was transacted at the ski shop and not at the recreational hall. It is no coincidence that the injured party and her group would naturally be attracted to a convenient area, particularly when others were observed to be tobogganing there. Since there were no signs as to where toboggan slopes were located, it is quite logical that the girls would have used the slope that they did because it was almost directly in front of the building in which they rented and received the toboggan.
4. Lack of or improper supervision consonant with the prevailing conditions and the patrons were in contradistinction to standard operating practices of the field. The manager neither provided accurate or even cursory information that would possibly have avoided this accident and subsequent injury. Not one of the participants in this group heard or remembered any information being given that would have advised them as to where they may have tobogganed. The lack of signs directing users to the tobogganing slope or other visual aids contributed to the accident. There does not appear to have been any kind of ski patrol operating on the night of the accident.
5. Improper maintenance of the facility was evident from the fact that the operators appreciated that the abrupt termination of the slope in question could cause an accident and/or injury. This was inadequately

controlled by scattering a few hay bales across the area. No attempt was made to reduce the likelihood of injury to the users of the slope by erecting soft protective devices such as netting or other practical buffers. The implantation of standing water pipes in the path of slope users is a substantial deviation of standard practice.

6. Deviation from normal illumination procedures for night operations was evident from the fact that the toboggan slope was not then night-lighted in any way. The illumination utilized was insufficient for slope users to see any of the hazards that existed at the time of the accident and was a serious deficiency.
7. The condition created at the lodge was brought about because the operators performed in a less than appropriate manner. The unsafe design of the facility, the inadequate efforts to insure patron safety, the lack of convenience for patrons, poor maintenance procedures, inadequate illumination, failure to warn of risks, and the incompetent supervision, or lack thereof, was substandard in all respects. The owners and operators of the lodge by disregarding commonly accepted standards of practice and substantially deviating from well-known principles of the field of recreational service regarding levels of care, caused the conditions that resulted in the injuries to Anne L.[1]

One other incident further illustrates the need for protective barriers to be installed in places where coasting is encouraged. Unfortunately, few departments or private businesses concerned with winter recreational activities bother about safety planning for snow based activities. In the following case, a nineteen-year-old woman, sledding on a snow hill in a public park established for coasting, was injured when her sled struck a bump on the hill. The jarring caused the sled to veer left toward a snow fence. The bump threw Patricia over the steering bar of the sled, with consequent loss of leverage and control. Since the sled was on an icy patch fifteen feet from the snow fence, the distance was traversed rapidly, and Patricia hit the fence with sufficient force to shatter the bottom of the fence and receive severe facial injuries that resulted in permanent scarring and disfigurement. Patricia then walked toward the bottom of the sledding hill and was met by a Holmdel Township Park Commission employee who advised her to sit down at that point on the hill in the snow. Later an emergency vehicle arrived, and she was carried to the vehicle by stretcher. Holmdel Park is operated and controlled by the Monmouth County Park Commission and is part of a system containing several parks. It was noted that on the evening of the day of the incident, hay bales were used to buffer the snow fence at the bottom of the hill. There were no hay bales used to buffer any other section of the snow fence installed from the top to the bottom of the hill. It is also known that no person participating on a sled ever coasted as far as the hay bales located at the bottom of the hill regardless of the speed the sled attained. The presumption must be that friction and other distance absorbing impediments prevented sleds from traveling the entire distance from the top of the hill to where hay bales were positioned in front of the snow fence at the bottom of the hill. The following facts and concepts appear to be relevant:

1. Insofar as the facility at Holmdel Park is concerned the following commonly accepted planning principles in the field of recreational service apply. In the operation of any recreational facility, but particularly those that promote potentially dangerous experiences due to the nature of the activity performed upon them, a general principle of the field is to use foresight in order to prevent injury to participants. If there are conflicts between aesthetics and safety, aesthetic factors play a secondary role.
2. In the instance of the sledding hill at Holmdel Park, this generally understood practice was not met. Apparently aesthetic considerations were of paramount importance to the detriment of participant safety. The snow fence, which delimited the sledding hill boundaries, was illuminated by kerosine pots on poles. This may have been attractive, but could hardly have cast enough light for nighttime hill use with reasonable safety for participants. Better illumination of the sledding hill might have prevented the accident.
3. The utilization of a snow fence to specify the sledding hill area was unnecessary and probably constituted the most flagrant violation of safety practices. Park authorities should have foreseen that such a snow fence was a potential hazard to participants. In fact, Monmouth County Park Commission employees did recognize the potential hazard of the snow fence because they placed buffering hay bales all along the bottom of the hill to offset the possibility of coasters slamming into the fence with consequent injuries. Thus, the operating authorities at Holmdel Park obviously knew that the snow fence constituted a hazard because they anticipated impact type accidents. Evidence for the conclusion drawn is inferred from the fact that the Holmdel Park authorities particularly buffered the fence with hay bales to prevent participants from coming into contact with the fence.
4. The operating authorities at Holmdel Park deviated from accepted standards in failing to buffer the entire snow fence. More particularly, those places along the fence where it was logical to believe that sledders could potentially and unintentionally swerve into the fence. The fact that Patricia W. hit the fence at the point where she did is evidence that such incidents could occur.
5. Operation of a recreational facility before proper safety precautions were taken, i.e., buffering the entire snow fence, suggests incompetence to perform in accordance with reasonable standards. It is likely that had hay bales, at least two bales in width and height, been emplaced all along the length of the snow fence, the injuries sustained by Patricia W. would have been immeasurably lessened or nonexistent. Failure to observe even the most common safety practices contributed to the injuries received by Patricia W.
6. Holmdel Park authorities should not have utilized a snow fence to demarcate the sledding hill area. Rather, safer, more flexible materials could have been utilized that would have rendered the possibility of injury to participants impacting against same or coming into contact with the materials at a high rate of speed either negligible or nonexistent. For example, park authorities could have utilized crossed slalom poles to which warning flags could have been affixed. They could have utilized slalom poles connected by a single strand of rope or nylon cable at a height that would not have affected any sledder breaking the vertical plane of the rope. Employees could also have utilized netting

with the same expectations. In none of these instances would there have been any serious, or even minor, injury to one coming into contact with the slalom poles or the netting.

7. Standard operating practices in the field of recreational service are vitally concerned with the safety of participants. The safety of patrons at any recreational facility is essential. At no time should an activity be initiated or a facility operated without observing fundamental rules of administration for the safety of participants. Operational policies should be developed governing the performance of patrons as well as those guiding the behavior of employees.
8. There is a need for a high order of supervision at facilities where potentially dangerous activities occur. Recreational service employees must exercise reasonable care in the performance of their respective duties in order that injuries to patrons can be avoided. This entails alertness at the site of the activity and scrupulous attention in carrying out procedures designed to insure participant safety.
9. The operating authorities at Holmdel Park performed ineffectually insofar as they diverged from carrying out standard operating procedures concerning the supervision of participants on the sledding hill. Since the sledding hill was clearly established by park authority policy, because the hill was clearly set aside for sledding, and because park employees were enjoined to prevent persons from sledding on the hill outside of the snow fence area, Monmouth County Park Commission employees had a clearly specified supervisory function in that they were to warn potential users away from sledding beyond the fenced section. If they had a supervisory function, it is apparent that they should have been present to advise sledders to keep away from the snow fence by instructing them to coast down the middle section of the hill rather than using the right or left slopes. If such supervision had been available, it is probable that the accident would not have occurred.
10. The circumstances of operating the facility in a less than appropriate manner, the unsafe practices indulged in by not buffering the entire snow fence, the use of the snow fence to delimit the sledding hill, the lack of competent supervision, the failure to utilize softer and, therefore, safer barriers to define the sledding hill, and the failure of park authorities to act in a reasonable and prudent manner were both substandard and incompetent. By disregarding commonly accepted standard practices and acting in violation of basic principles extant in the field of recreational service, the operating authorities of Holmdel Park caused the conditions that resulted in injuries to Patricia W. that produced scarring of a permanent nature.[2]

Planning Safe Winter Recreational Sites

Thousands of people of all ages want to participate in winter activities. Any of these activities simply require a slope and some kind of vehicle on which to coast. Whether the facility accommodates organized groups or individuals who have spontaneously decided to participate in a brief period of winter fun, operators of cold weather facilities must plan and develop safe areas where people can participate without unreasonable risk. Today, many winter recreational areas containing open slopes are becoming dangerously congested. More people are utilizing slopes with uncontrolled toboggans, sleds, and plastic discs. These coasting devices are being used in increasing numbers on ungroomed, steep hillsides that can lead to the kind of injuries noted above and sometimes to fatalities.

Proper planning by public and private agencies before snow related activities are implemented will be beneficial for all concerned. Site selection and development should include consideration for slope inclination, potential or actual obstacles within the user's path, prevailing winds, existing ground cover, acreage available, annual snowfall, drainage and subsoil conditions, and the duration of the winter season. A winter resort or recreational area requires sufficient space for the planning, development, and construction of access roads, parking areas, service and emergency vehicle parking, lodge or central recreational building, and the activity areas where patrons participate.

Among the factors that have to be given attention are: parking space, service and maintenance facilities, any structures to be erected, and the various activity areas. Additionally, traffic circulation for pedestrians and vehicles will be plotted. This means access and service roads as well as walks and trails. Utilities for sanitation, light and power, water storage and sources, and health services will be included.

In order to assure that structures and other emplaced facilities never cause impact injuries to patrons, planning guides that are designed to remove barriers should be implemented. Safe design of winter recreational facilities must include features that segregate activity areas from traffic patterns as well as locate structures well away from recreator slopes. Main buildings such as the lodge or recreational center should be situated at the bottom of the slopes and distant enough so that there is no possibility of any participant ever hitting any part of the structure. Every slope should have a run-out area of sufficient distance so that the recreator will be able to stop safely. This also means that a retrograde strewn with hay should also be part of the slope. Pedestrian trails or walkways should be combined with service roads. A single access road, well down and away from activity areas, with appropriate space for parking will also prevent accidents. The vehicular drive will permit entrance and exit from the recreational site and permit access to service areas without forcing encounters between pedestrians and automobiles. At least one acre of slope should be available for every fifty recreators. One acre of parking should be able to accommodate three hundred vehicles.

Specific rules and regulations concerning slope use as well as patron behavior will prove invaluable in combating accidents, visitor confusion, and delays in getting onto the slopes and participating. Adequate supervision at critical points is vital. This means that some control at the top of the slopes will be maintained. It may also be necessary to have some kind of slope patrol. Simple, but explicit instructions and directions must be placed at

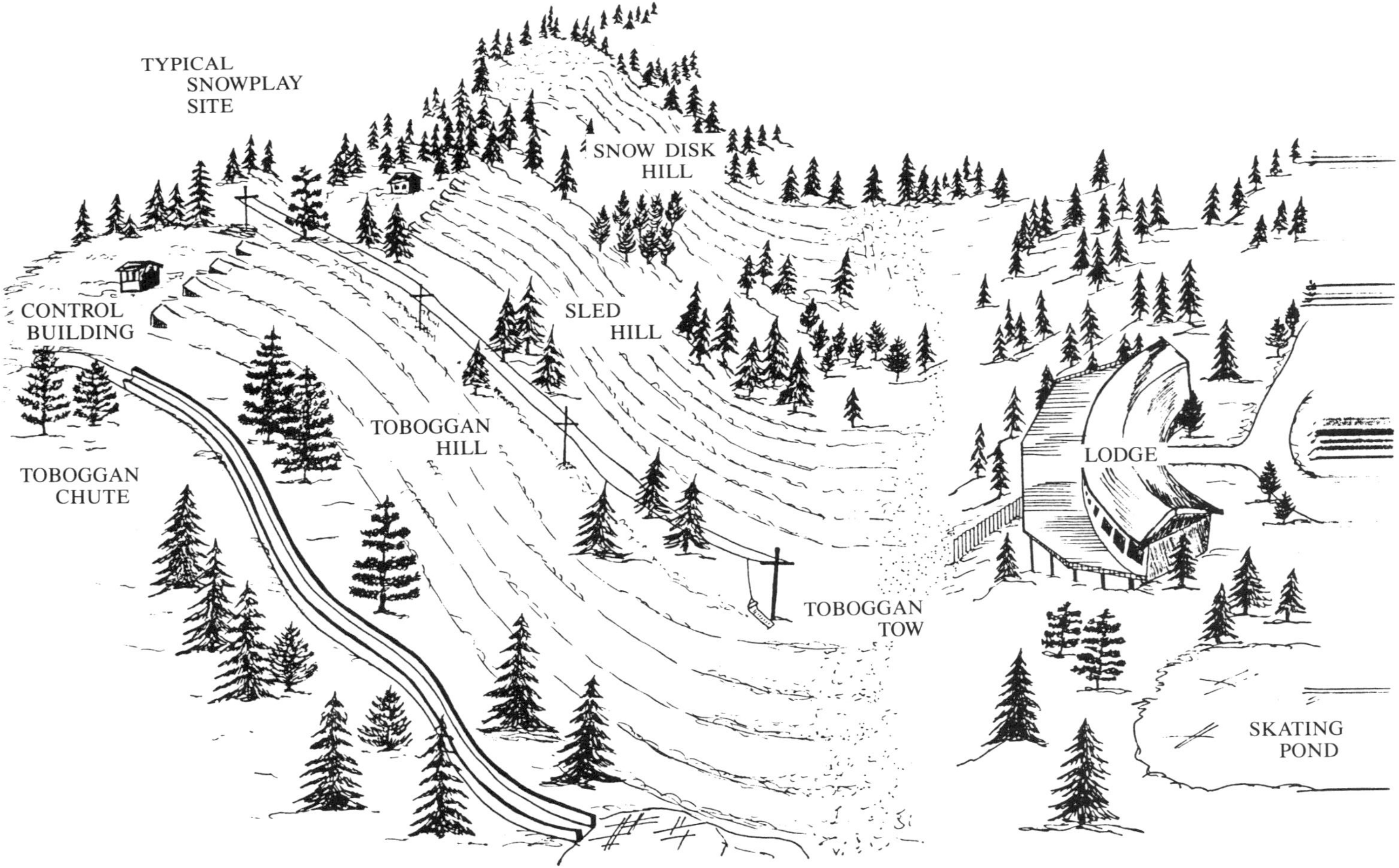

A well-designed snow activity area promotes safety.

strategic spots so that potential patrons know where their desired activity areas are located, where they can rent equipment, and other information may be obtained. Loud speaker systems are important and must be installed so that warnings, emergency broadcasts, and other significant information may be quickly transmitted. Maintenance management will be of a continuous pattern to keep up with use (impaction) and changing snow conditions. All activity equipment will be monitored through a checking and conditioning system. Inspection of all equipment will be accomplished after each day's use or prior to use on the following day. All rental equipment will be maintained in appropriate working condition. Where skiing or sledding is permitted and individuals have their own equipment, the user is at some risk in that the owner must see to his or her own equipment. No personal toboggans will be permitted on the slopes, especially if a commercial operation is in possession. Public areas may also disallow private toboggans from being used, unless certain precautions are taken.

Toboggan Slopes

Slopes that are dedicated to toboggan use may require that only rental equipment be permitted on the slopes. However, there are situations where private equipment can be used. When a slope is groomed specifically for toboggan use, chutes are sculptured from the snow. Each chute is built with a snow berm separating one chute from another. The chute is slightly wider than the toboggan. Since the steering capability of the toboggan is poor, the chute itself becomes the steering mechanism, and a long safe ride is accomplished. There is still the sensation of speed, risk, and movement enjoyed by the recreator, but in actuality real danger to patrons has been removed. Of course, a participant could fall off the toboggan, but that is unlikely to happen, and the operator would not be held liable for injuries sustained under those circumstances.

A number of toboggan slopes include electronically designed and operated release mechanisms that control the start of a toboggan at the top of the run. These slopes are chuted to accommodate the toboggan, but the starting mechanism is a ladderlike piece of equipment with a locking device and release brake that activate the toboggan's movement when the chute is clear. The electronic release is controlled from a central booth from which a supervisor may observe all chutes and see that the run is clear or being used. When the run clears, the operator electronically releases the lock mechanism on the starting platform. When the locking device is released, a signal light flashes, and the recreator then pushes the brake lever, and the toboggan is free to move. The starting platform is slightly raised at the back with the front a few inches above the snow at the top of the chute. The toboggan then travels down the chute until the run out or reverse slope is reached, and the recreator may then walk up the slope on an access trail, specifically designed

View from the top—a safe and well-designed tobaggan chute.

for such use, and take another turn. In some locations, toboggans are returned to the top of the hill by a powered return tow. Supervisors at the top remove the toboggans from the tow, stack them, and assign them to the next participant.

Artificial Slopes

One of the more attractive facilities utilized for tobogganing is the artificially constructed chute. This piece of equipment may be built where terrain is flat, thereby precluding tobogganing ordinarily. When the chute is constructed, it provides the necessary height and run-out distance to provide enjoyment to those who want the thrill of a rapid plunge. Artificial chutes may also be constructed into the sides of hills. Hills may also be constructed by fashioning a huge mound of earth, stabilized to prevent ground slippage, and then building the chute into the mound. In whatever way toboggan chutes are constructed, the safety factors required by operators remain an issue. Chutes are designed so that the toboggan is guided down the length of the slide by the chute itself. The chute's sides are raised so that there is no way that the toboggan can escape from the run. All the passengers have to do is hold on.

Of course, there will always be the danger of vandalism that may sabotage the chute, but this problem can be overcome by daily inspections of the facility and adequate supervision when the chute is operating. Recreator behavior must be carefully controlled so that dangerous antics, while the individual or group is on the chute, are prevented. Control of patron behavior, whether of children or adults, will probably prevent serious accidents from occurring. Since the chute will only accommodate one toboggan at a time, there must be strict supervision at the top of the run. This will prevent crowding and pushing to get ahead and prevent a second party from attempting to slide while another is still on the chuteway.

The artificial chute may be operational during anytime of the day or evening, if the temperature is cold enough and the chute is snow covered. There are chutes that have been developed that do not require snow. These are refrigerated chutes. When the temperature reaches fifty degrees, water is sluiced down the chute and a refrigeration unit quickly converts the surface to ice for a rapid trip. The same safety rules apply to the refrigerated chute as any other. Night lighting also makes tobogganing possible into the evening, thereby extending the period of use for the facility. The run out or bottom of the chute may lead either to a straightaway or be gently inclined to an adverse slope. Hay may be utilized to further impede forward motion, although if the chute length is sufficient, this will not be necessary.

The greatest danger to patrons will be in terms of the behavior of overenthusiastic or uncaring individuals. Supervision will play a chief role in keeping recreators orderly and regulating any congestion, confusion, or

AQUA-MATIC SLED SLIDE

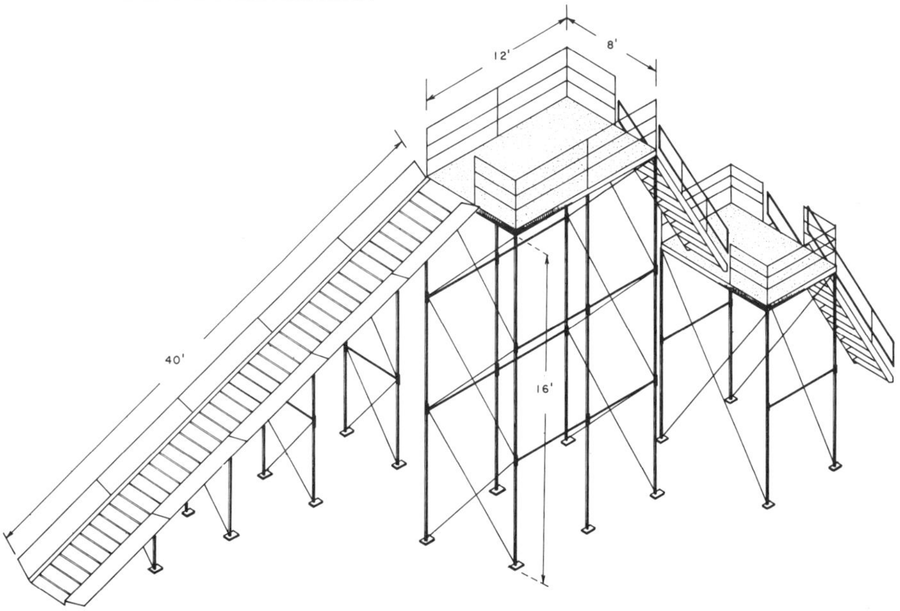

Toboggan slide for use where natural slopes are absent.

displays of unruly behavior. It is possible, but unlikely, that someone will try to navigate the chute standing up, but posted and verbal warnings by the operator should quell any attempt to perform in this way. However, when warnings have been issued and posted and the individual behaves in ways calculated to bring harm to himself or others, this will be construed as contributory negligence and provide an excellent defense against any allegation of negligence on the part of the operator.

Discs, sleds, skis, and toboggans should be separated. Discs or plastic saucers may utilize slopes that are not groomed or sculptured with chutes. However, free coasting on a saucer that cannot be steered, may sometimes prove dangerous to patrons. Therefore, shallow snow chutes may be the best protective arrangement for the disc users.

Because sleds do have steering mechanisms, there is little need for the sled to use a chute. However, patron behavior must be rigidly controlled on any hill operated by a public or commercial enterprise. There are always individuals who perform dangerously, such as cutting off another coaster, colliding with other users, or swerving suddenly into the path of another. All of these antics make the sled more hazardous due to the potential for impact injuries. Such behavior may be eliminated or greatly reduced through the use of strict supervision.

Ski Slopes and Runs

Ski slopes have their own problems, far beyond that which is typical of coasting. Downhill skiing is a dangerous activity because it requires a high degree of skill, good physical conditioning, and a reasonable outlook toward fatigue factors. A number of accidents occur at almost all skiing facilities every year. Some are unquestionably the fault of the skier. Most of these include skiing on slopes that are beyond the ability of the skier to use safely. Faulty binding release mechanisms that fail to operate thereby producing boot-top fractures are common. A variety of fractures, tendon tears, and joint dislocations as a result of falls taken while on the slope are recorded continuously.

In recent years, operators of ski slopes have been hard hit by a number of law suits stemming from injuries that were formerly assumed to have been part of the assumption of risk undertaken by the skier. This is particularly true of alpine or downhill skiing and falls from aerial trams, lift chairs, or gondolas. If the participant is possessed of full legal capacity and understands the nature of the risks inherent in the activity, then the general rule of risk assumption is likely to be applied. For example, skiers have begun litigation against resort operators because they were struck by other skiers who had lost control on a downhill run, because they struck an uneven spot on the slope, or because they hit a tree in a stand of trees growing in the middle of a slope. This latter aspect is deliberately designed by the ski slope operator as a protection for skiers against prevailing head winds.

In order to limit the ability of skiers to obtain awards for participant-related injuries, several state legislatures have passed broad assumption of risk statutes that the skier is responsible for injury to person or damage to property associated with participation or the use of lifts.[3] In cases where there is unreasonable risk to the participant, such as when one skier fails to behave in a manner consistent with common courtesies and expectation of those enjoying downhill skiing, the injured party will certainly be able to seek and probably gain redress for any injuries suffered. The likely target of the suit will be the person causing the injury rather than the slope operator; although in today's climate, attorneys advise their clients to sue everybody and anybody connected with an incident.

The most considered danger that will not have to be assumed by participants is that which is created by the negligence of others who have a specific duty of care toward invitees. Typically, suits are brought against operators of facilities in or on which activities occur. This is usually the case of actions against ski resort operators. When redress for injuries is instigated, the question will generally turn on whether the operators have met their obligations to the participants utilizing their facilities. As invitors, operators are subject to the same legal responsibility incumbent upon other land owners.

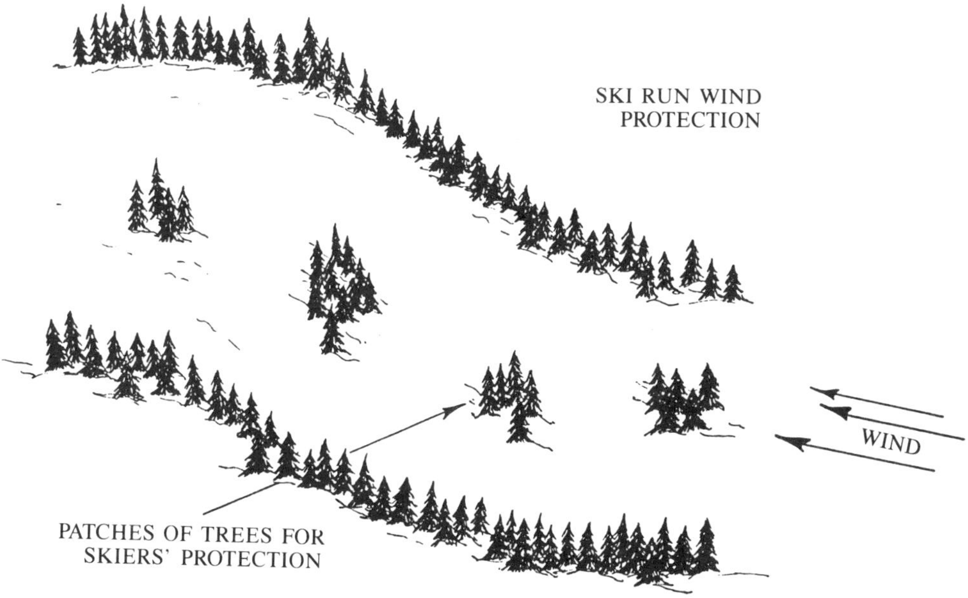

Ski hill design showing tree coppice as a windbreaker for skier protection.

Operators, therefore, will be liable for conditions on their property that cause physical harm to their invitees (recreators) if they know or should reasonably have known that the danger exists. To compound the issue, the hazard must have constituted a clear and present danger and threaten an unreasonable risk of injury that the recreators would not ordinarily recognize or protect themselves against, and the operators must not have exercised reasonable care for protection of the recreator. Incorporated in the standard of care is the obligation to maintain the property in a reasonably safe condition, to supervise the conduct of patrons, to provide instruction that is competent when offered, and to advise participants of safety instructions.

In a now classic case, a skier successfully sued a ski resort when he snagged a ski tip on some brush lying just beneath snow cover at the side of the downhill slope on which he was skiing. The court ordered redress for the serious and permanent injuries that the individual received. In this instance, the assumption of risk defense was put aside in favor of the degree of care owed to the skier by the resort operators. In failing to maintain the property in a manner consistent with the principle of unreasonable risk posed by the negligence of others who have a specific duty of care to fulfill, the courts ruled that the brush constituted a danger to the skier that the operators should have recognized and removed.[4]

Slope design and the elements that go into the production of an attractive and well-maintained area are well known. There are basic considerations that must be given to the development of slopes, the placement of lifts or tows, the separation of runs by degree of skill, and the grooming and maintenance of slopes. Everything from ski lift waiting lines to the knowledge of prevailing winds needs to be recognized by operators and assigned a proper place in the construction of a skiing facility. For example, the parallel lift loading system is more efficient and safer than is the right angle system. Operators should be cognizant of this fact when utilizing any lift system.

Ski slopes are divided into at least three and, perhaps, four types of runs. The easiest to traverse and the one with a gradient of from ten degrees to twenty-five degrees will be the practice and beginner slope. Approximately one-third of the ski run should be developed for the beginner. The slope itself should be of a gradual transition and the width should be as wide as possible. It is extremely important to avoid terminating or intersecting the beginner slopes with advanced runs.

For intermediate skiers, the acreage developed should be approximately 50 percent. The degree of steepness for intermediate slopes should be from twenty-five degrees to forty degrees. It is important to widen out short steep pitches where the pitch exceeds the maximum gradient. Some variety in the slope gradient should be offered to make the downhill run more stimulating. For advanced skiers, at least 25 percent of the area will be developed to accommodate this group. The degree of steepness for advanced skiers can run from forty degrees to sixty-five degrees. Variety of slope gradient is very important. For the experts, at least ten percent of the area should be graded and developed at a steepness and variety that will prove acceptable. The slope should probably incline from fifty degrees to eighty degrees. Of necessity, neither expert nor any other slope should intersect or terminate and join. If this design formulation is heeded, there will be less likelihood of impact accidents caused by skiers coming into contact with one another.

Designing ski slopes is both an art and science. Downhill trails tend to deteriorate quickly. A sharp turn on the run produces snow scrape off because the metallic-edged ski digs in during braking and skidding. Narrow trails cause congestion and, therefore, faster erosion. Wider trails will not completely resolve the problem but can reduce surface erosion considerably due to better maintenance. There are environmental restrictions to the widths that can be rationalized as aesthetic or economic. Cross trails should "out-slope" so that water collected from snowmelt will not pool in the center or inside of the trail.

To provide for skier comfort and preserve aesthetics, aerial rides should have a low profile and not protrude above tree height. In any trail design, work roads should afford easy access to vital sites with consequent elimination of as much vehicular traffic as is possible. If operators fail to follow these simple procedures the results can be costly and, perhaps, dangerous for users.

Trail Construction. Ski trail development requires the clearing and logging of a selected slope, stump removal, rough grading, cultivation of the soil in a manner commensurate with any soil tests and fine grading with placement of water bars plus the surface application of fertilizer, seeding, and mulching that are necessary to prevent erosion and the exposure of rock. The entire procedure for constructing ski trails should await the proper season, after snowmelt and when the watershed has had a chance to dry out.

During the initial construction, it is necessary that machinery operators maneuver carefully at the edges of the trail so that trees and shrubs at the edges will not have root systems broken or exposed. If this happens, the soil stabilization and shelterbelt capabilities will have been destroyed needlessly. Moreover, brush and other debris should be removed from the body of the trail as well as the edges so that unwary skiers will not be tripped up by hidden snags. A well-maintained grass cover will prevent erosion and offer skiing with a minimum of snow. This tends to lengthen the skiing season. Bare rock ledge must be mulched heavily so that snow is trapped and the surface remains fit for skiing. Mulch can be old hay, straw, wood chips, or other suitable material.

Ski operators should mow all slopes as part of a yearly maintenance program. Forests have a major role to play in any attempt at ski slope management. Wind resuction caused by trees in shelterbelts and forests have been measured at 20 to 60 percent of the wind speed blowing across open spaces. Differences are determined by tree height and crown density. Softwoods reduce wind velocity to a greater extent than do hardwoods because of greater crown density. The higher the tree at the edge of the ski trail and the narrower the trail, the more snow is collected and retained.

Risks and Precautions. With ski slope development and proper maintenance of trails, the incidence of accidents to recreators will be considerably reduced insofar as unsafe skiing conditions are concerned. The hidden root, tree limb, bush, or exposed rock will be eliminated from the path of the skier. Of course, there will still be accidental injuries caused by the skier's inability to perform, but that is part of the risk inherent in the activity. It is unlikely that liability will be attached to ski slope operators when skiers fall and injure themselves as a result of personal inability, poor physical conditioning, or lack of skill. This is part of the assumption of risk that the participant accepts.

Where aerial lifts or other carriers are utilized to transport skiers from the bottom to the top of the run, ski resort operators have an additional responsibility for the safety of patrons because they become common carriers. Whenever a fee is imposed for the transportation of skiers from one point to another, the operators of such lifts owe a duty of highest care to those being transported. They must do whatever is necessary to safeguard the passage of their patrons. Thus, where passengers are distressed because of equipment breakdowns, where they fall from the lift, or where skiers are stranded aloft, it is probable that liability will attach.[5]

Snowmobiling

A snowmobile is a motorized sled with ski-like attachments extending from under the front part of the vehicle to several feet in front of the sled. It obtains its motive power from a revolving belt or tread driven by a small engine. The driver (and passenger) sit on a cushioned seat directly over the motor. The ski attachments are steered by grips or handles easily accessible to the driver. Snowmobiling has become immensely popular in the snow-belt states with annual sales in excess of one billion dollars. More than eight million people currently participate in snowmobiling.

A number of concerns have surfaced about the use of snowmobiles. Some of these are environmental, others deal with the safety of recreators, and still others are focused upon the erratic or inappropriate behaviors exhibited by some snowmobilers.

Criticisms directed at snowmobiling invariably include environmental problems directly indicting the machine for its impact upon flora, fauna, and the land itself. Among the more obvious arguments against snowmobiling are the excessive noise produced by the machine, wildlife harassment, parking violations, trail behavior and etiquette, dangerous contacts with automobiles on roadways, trespassing, snow compaction, and other impaction that tends to create erosion as well as other environmental degradations.

The snowmobile manufacturers have been forced to acknowledge these criticisms because they are so blatant, continuing, and generating adverse political and social pressure that tends to threaten the development of this activity. If legislation is enacted to curtail the growth of the industry, based upon documented evidence of damage, destruction, and injury, the manufacturers would be financially hurt. In order to minimize such pressures the industry has responded by reducing some of the negative factors. One example has been to reduce the high decibel level to more moderate noise levels. Furthermore, the industry has attempted to organize snowmobiling clubs. Such clubs are valuable as information disseminators concerning the proper use of the machine and for enforcement of ordinances and other legislation regulating the use of snowmobiles, through the use of peer pressure on members who may act inappropriately and bring the club and its membership into disrepute. Such self-regulatory functions serve as a supplement to the public agency's managerial and enforcement program.

The snowmobiling activity does present some problems with the safe operation of the machine as well as environmental hazards that frequently exist where the recreator travels. The snowmobiler should be physically fit and mentally prepared to meet the conditions that may tend to put the recreator at risk during participation. The snowmobiler needs to know something about first aid and wilderness survival if he or she is to enjoy the experience in back country areas or in sparsely populated snow-belt regions. If the machine breaks down and the recreator is miles from any population center, there is a need to know how to fix the machine and have the right tools to do the job. Snowmobiling experts recommend that only the most experienced snowmobilers venture into wilderness areas without a guide. Snowmobilers should always travel in pairs to maximize safety, especially when traveling any distance from a main disembarkation point or trail head.

Snowmobiling is much like automobile driving, although no licenses exist for snowmobile machine use. The implication is that governmental agencies enforce certain rules of the road, that the driver of a vehicle is responsible for his own conduct and safety, and that any accident or injury sustained by the recreator is substantially assumed by the participant, unless negligence can be proved against the machine manufacturer,[6] another individual,[7] or an agency operating snowmobile trails. In order to prevent accidents and injuries occurring through snowmobile use, several states, notably Utah, have passed legislation dealing with off-highway recreational vehicles. The legislation's primary purpose is "to promote the safety and protection of persons, property, and environment in connection with the use, operation and equipment of snowmobiles, all-terrain and other recreational vehicles and promote uniformity of laws and to adopt and pursue an educational program and develop trails and other facilities for the use of these vehicles."[8]

Many states that have climates that permit varied winter recreational activities, including snowmobiling, have begun to plan, develop, and operate extensive snowmobile areas within the state's boundaries, with trail head snow removal, trail head and trail signing, safety and enforcement management. Where it is most feasible, particularly due to major utilization of sites, trail grooming has also been undertaken. Whenever public agencies perform these tasks, they may be subject to some risk of liability if recreators are injured while using the groomed trails and some aspect of grooming may have led to an accidental injury, if negligence can be proved.

A number of problems arise in connection with the development of snowmobile areas. Among these are:

1. Availability of the physical space to permit snowmobiling. The resource may exist; but environmental factors, skills required by the recreator, potential conflict with other activities, e.g., cross-country skiing, or prohibitive legislation, may not provide opportunities or accessibility.
2. Environmental considerations. The depth of the snow to support the weight of the vehicle as well as the movement of the sled without damaging the environment. Snow consistency, and minimum depths of wet snow as opposed to powder for cushioning effect on what the snow covers are vital concerns.
3. Duration of the snowmobile season. The impact of people attracted to an area and the consequences for the environment will be a factor in determining the desirability for planning a trail.
4. Potential dangers to the recreator. Any planning for snowmobile use must include such safety problems as road accessibility; parking areas; safe, groomed trails; and the trail head itself.

Signing becomes extremely important because of environmental hazards that may be integral to a given area through which a trail passes. Snowmobilers must be warned about actual dangers and be provided with information that should insure the safety of responsible drivers. Trail signs are useful in regions with heavy snowfalls because they can reduce such hazards as drifted cornices, sidehills, and disorientation because of blowing snow. Wherever there are obvious dangers, public agency planners and managers may close trails and prohibit their use. Thus, when potential or existing hazards such as dangerous traffic conditions in road access, insufficient and limited turnaround and road shoulder parking, hazardous slide areas at the summit, and conflict of use between skiers or watershed resources exist then for the purposes of maintaining safety for all, snowmobiling will be prohibited.

It is always possible for private enterprise to become involved in the servicing of public recreational areas. When the state or county government contracts out such services as trail head and trail grooming, signing, and amenity functions, then the private sector will assume the burden of liability in the event of accident or injury to recreators—if negligence can be proved.

When states have attempted to plan and develop recreational sites for winter activity use, they may find that private property must be crossed in order for any linear facility to be fully used and offer the satisfaction that the skier or snowmobiler seeks. It is critical for winter outdoor recreational activities that legislation be enacted in terms of "Hold Harmless Laws" to protect the cooperating private land owner from liability when that person wants to make property available for public outdoor recreational opportunities. As with automobile users, snowmobilers must be made to comply with existing regulations concerning reckless driving, speeding (unless during programmed races), trespassing, consumption of alcoholic beverages while using the snowmobile, and other unsafe practices that can be controlled through strict inspection and enforcement of safety practices.

Ice-skating

Ice-skating is a universally known recreational activity that may occur either indoors or outdoors. It is a method of locomotion on ice by utilizing sharpened steel or plastic blades attached to a shoe. The skater alternately slides one foot and then the other forward so that movement occurs. Highly expert skaters not only move extremely fast, but may also dance, perform a variety of acrobatic stunts, and cut figures as well. Of course, as with all such activities, sport and games experiences may also be enjoyed.

Although ice-skating can take place indoors, on artificial rinks, the typical skater usualy finds some frozen waterway for use. Outdoor skating on natural aquatic areas contributes as much to recreational skating as do all of the indoor rinks in existence. Wherever public jurisdiction extends to include empounded water, there the problem of safety and the control of recreators is a concern. There is always a question about the point when a pond, lake, or other empounded area becomes safe enough to skate upon. It would be impossible for public jurisdictions to oversee and properly supervise all of the numerous small lakes and ponds that lie within its jurisdiction. It may be that such facilities have been used by neighborhood skaters for years and have become known as the local skating pond. All that public officials can do is post an area they wish to proscribe.

When a public agency wants to permit skating at an area, it generally constructs amenity facilities, sets up skate rental concessions, and otherwise provides some supervision to prevent fractious behavior that might result in injury. Typically, outdoor ice-skating areas are used by adults and children who need to know when ice is safe for recreators. If a public department or an owner wants to test the thickness of ice to insure the safety of invitees or the casual trespasser, small holes may be cut in several places so that a measuring device can determine the thickness. The frozen surface may be strong enough to support the weight of one person, but unless the ice is at least four inches thick it will not accommodate an unlimited number of skaters. Public authorities should never permit anyone to use an ice-skating area unless a minimum of four-inch-thick ice is present. Although thinner ice would support the weight of a small group, it is difficult to estimate the numbers that might be attracted to the facility if anyone were on the ice before the desired thickness was attained. Therefore, an excellent policy to follow is no admission until the ice can support everybody who wants to skate. The four-inch minimum is for hard, clear ice, not frozen slush or air filled crusted ice.

Snow covering lakes or ponds will not permit the ice to increase in thickness due to its insulating quality. If ice-skating is wanted, then the snow should be removed from the ice surface. If snow is permitted to accumulate on the ice before it is strong enough to support the weight of an individual and it is not removed, then it is likely that the surface will remain unused because thickness has not been able to increase and the safety hazard will remain.

Ice will accumulate fairly rapidly at low temperatures. Water freezes faster when humidity is low. Ice melts more slowly when there is high humidity. The larger the impounded water area the longer it takes the water temperature to reach thirty-two degrees Fahrenheit.

Chart 1. Rate of Ice Thickness Increments

Thickness of Ice	*Time to Freeze Clear Water at Air Temperature*			
	+14°F.	−4°F.	−20°F.	−35°F.
1 inch	2.10 hrs.	1.15 hrs.	40 min.	35 min.
4 inches	17.20	16.50 hrs.	11 hrs.	8 hrs.
6 inches	48.00 hrs.	24.00 hrs.	16 hrs.	11 hrs.
10 inches	120.00 hrs.	60.00 hrs.	35 hrs.	30 hrs.
12 inches	176.00 hrs.	88.00 hrs.	58 hrs.	48 hrs.

Protective and Warning Devices

When a public agency determines that ice-skating should be included as part of its recreational program opportunities for the general public, it must devise a system of signs, signals, or prohibitory measures that will safeguard the participants. Warning signs are one obvious way for the agency to inform patrons about regulations that govern the use of the ice-skating facility as well as the appropriate conduct expected. Certain ideas may have to be reiterated in order for them to be assimilated and to gain compliance. Among the admonitory statements should be those dealing with traffic flow of ice users. Normal traffic patterns should be observed, especially if large numbers of people are expected to participate. It may also be necessary to caution skaters not to race when the facility is congested, nor to play dangerous games such as "crack-the-whip." Aggressive behavior, such as pushing or purposely bumping into others cannot be tolerated. These few regulations, plus scheduled times for use may be all that is necessary. Of course, the classic qualifier message of "skating at your own risk when facility is not supervised" should also be included.

A few simple rules, clearly spelled out, and unequivocally enforced can do much to prevent injuries from occurring. A common sense approach to regulating the conduct of recreators, especially youth, will probably prevent all but the most minor injuries that stem from a lack of skill. There is little that the public organization can do about that. The formation of instructional classes to teach ice-skating skills should be a part of every winter program, but novices will always fall and there is a chance that injury may accrue. To the extent that proper supervison will reduce or eliminate accidents and potential injuries that might occur because of malicious behavior or poor judgment, the agency may well lessen the possibility of litigation based on negligence.

The first concern of any department that conducts an ice-skating activity on a natural area is the thickness of the ice and its weight-bearing capacity. When the ice is of sufficient thickness so that many skaters can be using the ice simultaneously, there may still be certain areas that have not attained correct thickness or that will always remain ice free. These areas should be closed to public use. Barriers must be erected to prohibit access to those areas that are actually or potentially unsafe for recreators. The barriers may consist of wooden, metal, or plastic rails affixed to which are warning lights for night illumination and pennants or small flags that can easily be seen during the day. Additionally, it might be wise to place a warning sign in front of the barrier. The sign should be simple, clear, and concise. Typically, the words danger, open water, or thin ice will be sufficient to alert the skater of imminent jeopardy.

Despite all of the warnings and barriers that are designed to prevent access, there will always be one or more incautious persons who are attracted to the dangerous area. Therefore, a sound system should be available to supervisory personnel so that when some skaters are drawn to the hazard they may be warned away by an announcement over the loud speaker. Nevertheless, there will still be one individual who disregards all warnings and proceeds into the danger area. Under those circumstances, it will be part of the agency's preparation to have an emergency rescue plan ready to operate in the event of any mishap. Ropes, ladders, reaching poles, and scuba gear (with properly insulated suit) can be available in case of a break through in the ice. Some departments even have hydraulically operated cherry pickers that can be wheeled to the accident scene for rescue purposes. An established emergency plan, which includes the local fire department station, should be worked out and coordinated so that when a call comes through, the fire department will know what rescue vehicle to use. It may be that the police emergency squad is better equipped for ice rescues. Then the department should coordinate with the police department. In any case, the public department should be prepared with its own rescue plans, and all personnel assigned to any natural ice-skating area must be trained to take whatever action is required to alleviate the situation.

Ice-skating may also be conducted by organizations that establish artificial ice-skating rinks in the outdoors. Typically, night illumination and warming huts, or even well-constructed recreational buildings, may serve as shelters for artificial rinks. Skating facilities are usually scheduled in the late afternoon and evening hours, but on weekends may be opened eleven or twelve hours from morning to late at night. Weather determines the exact dates of outdoor rink seasons. Depending on the location of the community, in terms of its latitude, the actual days of operation may average between fifteen and sixty.

To provide proper outdoor ice necessitates temperature in the low twenties for several days. The ground on which the rink will be established is first sprayed with water to develop a water soaked layer. This creates a frozen barrier and prevents water from seeping into the ground. Next, water is sprayed on the rink surface in successive layers. If the weather does not produce cold enough temperatures to freeze the water quickly, the water will penetrate the ground and form a faulty ice base. This causes "white ice" or air pocketed thick ice layers. Such conditions are poor for skating and may lead to many falls and injuries.

Ice rink maintenance is performed after each day's operation. During the night, the maintenance crews renew the top layer of ice by spraying additional water. Snow is removed by plowing and then brooming with a large rotory brush mounted on a truck. Rough areas are patched. Some departments have the financial capability of employing a Zamboni or ice-making machine. This machine is often used in covered outdoor ice-skating rinks, but more usually with indoor rinks.

Safety Considerations and Rink Operation

In order to insure ice-skating safety and prevent injuries from occurring, departments establish personnel manuals that detail policy, duties, functions, emergency procedures, and regulations for the guidance of patrons participating at the facility.

As usual, all personnel are required to be at their appointed stations at least fifteen minues before the scheduled starting time, but this varies with the needed functions that must be performed to get the facility opened and ready for operation. Sometimes, if a great deal of preparation must be made, personnel are enjoined to be at their respective posts thirty minutes before opening. Each staff person will sign in. Depending upon the number of personnel employed at each rink, the following responsibilities are assigned:

Ice Rink Supervisor

1. Arrive early enough to open the rink prior to the starting time.
2. Sign in all other staff personnel.
3. Supervise facility safety check.

4. Record any corrective actions taken.
5. Check all first aid supplies.
6. Open all exits and entrances.
7. Illuminate the facility as necessary.
8. Supervise staff enforcement of rink regulations.
9. Deal with all patron problems:
   a. Receive reports of rule violations.
   b. Discipline all patron offenders.
   c. Expel rule offenders when necessary.
   d. If a child is to be expelled, make a home call to explain the situation to the parent. Hold child until the parent arrives if requested to do so.
   e. Refer any patron failing to cooperate in serious behavioral situations or when safety considerations are jeopardized to the police.
   f. Make clear and accurate reports on accidents, incidents, or maintenance functions as they occur. These should be brought to the attention of the appropriate authority as soon as possible.
10. Make sure that restrooms and shelter structures are patrolled. Maintain a clean rink and shelter house. Report any abnormalities promptly.
11. Maintain the alertness of the rink staff in watching for patrons in difficulty. Respond immediately when emergencies arise.
12. In the event of an accident, follow the following procedures:
    a. Make the injured person comfortable, but do not move the victim if there is danger of further injury.
    b. Treat for shock, if necessary.
    c. Obtain from victim his or her name, address, telephone number, and the individuals to notify. If victim is a minor, call parents.
    d. Perform standard emergency procedures (if coordination with fire or police department has been developed, call for emergency assistance from one or the other).
    e. Fill out an accident report clearly and completely.
    f. Obtain the name and address of any witnesses, preferably adults.
13. Begin clearing skaters from the rink approximately ten minutes prior to actual closing time.
14. Make sure that no child is ever left at the area or locked out of the warming hut. It is the supervisor's responsibility to see that everyone leaves the facility safely. It may be necessary to telephone parents to pick up children.
15. Check all reports on facility use and any incidents that may have occurred. Check against any vandalism to the facility.
16. Make sure that the facility is closed and locked against intruders.
17. Make sure that the facility is cleaned and well-maintained before turning off the lights.

Other personnel assigned responsibilities at the rink may have such titles as skate guards, rink guards, or rink maintainers. Whatever the staff title, these personnel play an important part in minimizing accidents and reducing the probability of injuries due to unsafe conduct. Inappropriate behavior of ice rink patrons must be controlled quickly. It is up to the staff person to deal with behavioral problems. Some behavior is merely thoughtless, non-malicious, and only irritating to others. This can be stopped with little difficulty. Serious behavioral breaches may have malicious intent to hurt someone or damage property. It is this latter behavior that causes safety hazards. The rink staff person must be mature enough and able to deal with patron conduct at all times.

One important consideration is making physical contact with a patron. No patron should be touched unless the patron is an accident victim. If a patron must be physically accosted, the rink supervisor should be consulted first. If there is no time for consultation, then the rink staff must be able to justify whatever actions are taken, especially to forestall any complaints about overreaction, brutality, or assault and battery.

Skating rink staff should never leave their post without permission. Conversation with patrons should be minimized unless it is to answer questions about rules, regulations, instructional activities, ice rink business, or injuries. Additional responsibilities invariably deal with the cleanliness and safe maintenance of the facility. Certainly, rink staff will have emergency functions to fill in the event of an accident as well as administering first aid when necessary. As with all other bureaucratic organizations reports and records concerning incident, accident, and vandalism must be made out promptly and accurately.

Ice Hockey

Ice hockey is a contact sport. The requirements of excellent physical condition, technical proficiency, strength, speed, and precision of the player make this activity one of the fastest exercises and inherently dangerous to participants. Injuries can arise from the use of the hockey stick whether on offense or defense, body checking, collisions with the side boards enclosing the rink and with other skaters, and being hit by the puck. Any of these mishaps can result in serious injury, sometimes of a permanently disfiguring or crippling nature.

The intent of the game is to propel the puck by using the hockey stick so that it enters the opponent's net or goal. The hockey rink is a rectangular ice-surfaced arena two hundred feet long by eighty-five feet wide. It is divided into three zones: two end zones and a neutral zone. In play, only the team that is defending that half of the rink on which the attack is made may use body contact. Such body contact is used against the player in possession of the puck.

Essential protective equipment needed for play includes shin pads, elbow pads, gloves, helmet, tendon guards for the skates, and pants that are especially reinforced to ward off upper thigh injuries. It is apparent that skates are the most significant item of equipment to be used. The skate should be of a type that is durable, provides support for the ankle and arches, and has the blade of the skate machined to provide both speed and maneuverability. Sharpened skates afford greater ability to maneuver, but are also dangerous because of the possible contact that could occur to the exposed body of another player. The sticks are of different lengths, depending upon the needs and position of the player. However, no stick may be longer than fifty-two inches. Laminated sticks insure strength and durability. The blade of the stick has a slight upward curve so as to permit greater blade contact with the puck.

There are a number of shots that may be taken with the stick to pass, maneuver with, or attempt to score. In almost all of these shots, the puck is hit strongly enough to rise off the ice. Since the puck is hard and relatively heavy, when propelled by the force of the stick at high velocity it can produce devastating injuries. Even with protective equipment, some players may receive a variety of contusions, fractures, cuts, and other injuries. Of course, competition can also produce illegal activities that increase the likelihood of injuries.

Despite all of the advice and counsel given to participants, equipment now being used or actively tested still permits injuries to occur. However, these injuries can be foreseen, and those who want to participate in ice hockey had better accept the fact that in all probability injury will occur sooner or later. Nevertheless, it is is not to the expected risk that accompanies playing in the game that attention is drawn. Rather, it is the unprovoked or malicious assault that sometimes erupts due to competitive aggression or overt hostility by one player toward another. There must be little question that those who participate in the game of hockey must anticipate contact that could be interpreted as assault upon their persons. Body checks are the most frequent contacts made and in the heat of a game may become too severe thereby causing emotions to go out of control. Under these circumstances, officials have the responsibility for separating the parties involved and penalizing those who have broken the rules of the game. Even by consenting to the idea that body contact will be made in numerous ways, that injuries could result, or that the individual player assumes the risk of accident, there are principles that can be applied to reduce or prevent many injuries.

Coaching. Good coaching is not only concerned with the fundamentals of play, stick handling, practice sessions, physical condition of the athletes, and the tactics of the game, but also with the transmission of rules, regulations, and principles of sportsmanship that must be imparted to each player. Coaches who deliberately call for illegal activity or teach the players to use techniques that are fouls at best and attempts at malicious injury at worst are guilty of malfeasance and negligence. Of course, the best coaching is concerned with the players' well-being as well as winning. Among the ideas that the coach constantly emphasizes are warnings to players about the risks involved and how best to avoid them. Thus, stick technique must be reiterated so that high sticking does not occur. Players must be forewarned about head butting and stopped from pushing their hands or elbows into an opponent's face.

Protective Equipment. Perhaps the most interesting development in the protection of hockey players in recent years has been the design of face masks and mouth guards. The incidence of fractures of the nose, jaw, and upper facial area; lacerations and abrasions of the eyebrow, cornea of the eye, lips, and forehead; and loss of teeth as a direct consequence of high sticking, reckless play, puck contact, or being blind-sided requires the production of a helmet or mask that can prevent or reduce such injuries. Sometimes the use of a helmet restricts peripheral vision of the wearer, causes tunnel vision, or other sight problems. The compulsory use of mouthpieces should be enforced. Wearing face masks will probably contribute to the reduction of serious facial injury and introduce the element of better stick technique into the game. Where players do not feel that they are vulnerable to penetration, they will probably compete more aggressively. The better the protection, the less injury will occur. When the helmet/mask is well designed, individually fitted, and does not impede the players' vision, it should be required whenever there is practice or competitive play.

Recreational Teams. As more young persons become actively engaged in ice hockey, the number of injuries will mount—unless proper precautions are taken by those nominally in charge of such activity. Spontaneous or pick-up games that occur on natural ice or in the back yards of residences will never be brought under control of any authority, except by the parents of participating youngsters. Where sponsoring agencies field an ice hockey team either through a public recreational service department, private organization, school system, or college, the need for instruction, coaching/supervision, warnings, and the use of protective equipment must be part and parcel of the activity. Failure to abide by the common sense precautions necessary to safeguard participants may result in serious injury and, perhaps, allegations of negligence. As in all such activities where body contact is part of the game, the assumption of risk doctrine will apply. The only exception made will be in terms of the age of the participant.

Standardization. A number of organizations concerned with the development of protective equipment and facility design have attempted to test the effectiveness of certain pieces of equipment for their safety capacity. The Amateur Hockey Association of the United States, the American Society for Testing and Materials, and the Hockey Equipment Certification Council have become increasingly aware of injuries caused by lack of protective gear as well as by the style of play involved in ice hockey. Much still remains to be done. However, everyone who is involved in improving the quality of protective equipment in order to reduce injury is constantly attempting to devise pads, gloves, guards, and masks that will sharply cut or eliminate the risk of injury to players. In the final analysis, it is player behavior, style of play, and certain illegal techniques such as spearing an opponent that can undo all of the promotional advances that safety practices introduce.

NOTES

1. Communication to F. J. O'Dea, Esq., Attorney at Law, 16 August 1976.
2. Communication to J. E. Riehl, Esq., Attorney at Law, 4 September 1978.
3. *Maine Statutes Annotated.* Title 26, 488 (Supp., 1978).
4. *Sunday v. Stratton Corp.* 136 Vt. 293, 390 A. (2d) 398 (1978).
5. *Sabi v. Brechenridge Lands, Inc.,* 255 F Supp. 602 Colo. (1966).
6. *Olsen v. Hansen,* 299 Minn. 39, 216 N.W. (2d), 124 (1974).
7. *Ujifusa v. National Housewares, Inc.,* 24 Utah (2d), 219, 469 P. 2d 7 (1970).
8. *Recreation Vehicle Act,* Section 1, 1977 (State of Utah).

13
Gymnasia, Stadia, Courts, and Special Facilities

Areas that supply physical spaces for particular forms of recreational activity include the golf course, stadium, zoological park, gymnasia, and other indoor facilities for active games and sports. These facilities may often be found in the kinds of places previously described in chapters 6, 7, 8, and 9. However, there appears to be some tendency to acquire separate sites for some of the facilities, especially zoos and golf courses. Some notable exceptions are Griffith Park in Los Angeles, which contains both a golf course and a major zoo, or some of the Westchester County parks in New York State that combine golf courses, swimming facilities, recreational buildings, and other special features. There is no standard plan for the location, acreage, or comprehensiveness of different recreational facilities that can be provided in one place or in many different places. Some communities can afford diverse recreational areas and facilities and provide them to their constituent public. Other communities are less well endowed and may have few buildings or park areas and no special facilities. In whatever way recreational opportunities are provided to clientele, whether by public or private organization, certain problems pertaining to health and safety hazards are well known and must be alleviated to prevent or reduce accidents, injuries, and potential litigation.

GOLF

The game of golf offers unlimited opportunity for young and old alike to get out into the open air, enjoy physical activity (unless golf carts are used), indulge in a bit of fanaticism, or simply play a leisurely game in a relaxed and noncompetitive atmosphere. Golf may be as demanding and frustrating as the golfer will permit, or it can be an easy, sociable, and carefree experience. How intensively and skillfully the game is played depends, for the most part, on what the player wants to achieve.

Unfortunately, golf is a game that requires hitting a small ball with a special club along a fairway to reach a cup. In the process, human nature being what it is, and chance or probability always operating, the likelihood of someone being injured is possible. It is the incidents and injuries that arise from the playing of golf that are now addressed. Of course, many players may go through a lifetime of play and never become involved in any litigation, but there are also numerous cases on record where individuals have been severely injured, some permanently disabled, as a consequence of being hit by an errant ball or club. With mechanized golf carts available for carrying the indolent to the next tee, there is also the very real danger of pedestrians being hit by unthinking drivers.

One must appreciate the nature of the game of golf. In order to cause the ball to travel in the desired direction for any distance, a certain amount of skill and coordination are required. Professional players have developed their skills to a high degree and are able to smash long drives, chip, or putt with devastating accuracy. But even a golfing professional sometimes mishits a ball with dire consequences for spectators, other golfers, and his or her scores. However, the average golfer, who does not get the hours of practice that are necessary for proficiency of play, may not have developed the precision of timing and coordination of motion necessary for smooth stroking and accuracy. Even some slight variation of grip, stance, swing, or posture may mean that the golf ball will fly off in a hook, slice, or tangent with great speed. It is these pulled strokes or mishits that lead to litigation. No player has ever reached such perfection of play that on occasion the hit ball does not make an erratic pattern during flight. With most players, this is a common occurrence.

Courts appreciate the fact that the golfer may not be able to have control of the ball after it is hit and that most novice golfers will hit balls in directions about which they have never imagined. Therefore, it is unlikely that golf related injuries due to balls hitting other players or spectators will be the basis for a liability suit, unless the golfer did not take the last clear chance to warn of impending danger to a person or persons in the way of a hit ball. This concept is part of the potential plaintiff's case where contributory negligence or assumption of the risk doctrines apply. In the game of golf, let us say that a spectator or another player has negligently placed himself in the way of an errantly hit ball. Even if contributory negligence could be proved, the injured party may still obtain redress if it can be shown that the defendant had the last clear chance to avoid injuring plaintiff. If the defendant does not take advantage of the last clear chance and warn the potential victim, then the defense of contributory negligence will be invalid and liability will be found on the basis of the defendant having created an unreasonable risk that was not eliminated.

There can be little question that those who either play golf or are spectators on a golf course know that balls are hit hard and travel with sufficient velocity to cause injury if a vulnerable body part is struck. Thus, players and spectators assume the risk of being hit by errantly traveling golf balls. This is a foreseeable danger. It is only when a golfer does not deliver a warning to others, after hitting a badly stroked ball or a longer drive than originally anticipated, that negligence may be inferred. Even here, there is some question as to whether negligence can be shown when a warning is not given.[1] The nature of the game precludes a golfer from knowing who is in a danger zone at the moment of hitting the ball.

There is a factor of unreasonable risk that is not part of the game. Where individuals fail to follow the established rules of play or game etiquette, it is possible that recovery for injuries will be likely. The ordinary and inherent risks of the game are assumed by all who play or observe it. However, there are risks that arise as a result of inappropriate behavior or failure to abide by the well-known and recognized rules of the game.[2] Thus taking practice swings in a crowd,[3] playing a third ball while others are on the course searching for the first two lost shots,[4] employing a vicious or dangerous person,[5] permitting one group to start before a previous group has had time to get out of range,[6] all constitute liability.

ZOOLOGICAL PARKS, GAME FARMS, AND WILD ANIMAL RESERVES

Most people think that viewing wild animals in enclosures is the most fascinating of exotica. The great cats, large mammals, and reptiles of all colors, shapes, and sizes elicit awe, fear, and excitement. Small wonder then that the best of the animal exhibits draw an increasing number of people to their environs each year. Unfortunately, as the cost of keeping wild animals has risen, so have the entry fees that patrons must pay. It no longer is a matter of a few cents to gain entry, but of several dollars for young and old alike. Not only has the cost of maintaining the animals skyrocketed, the cost of separating the animals from the public, for the protection of both, has also climbed rapidly. The modern zoo has a combination of open sequestered areas as well as fenced and barred enclosures in which animals may be observed.

With increasing patronage and relatively limited space for the animals to be housed, zoos have become somewhat congested. Spectators may now choose how they will view animals, either by riding a bus, tram, or tandem carts drawn by a tractor or some other engine. Naturally, the most used method of transportation is walking. Vehicles share the traffic arteries with pedestrians. As with any close conjunction between vehicles and walkers, some accidents are bound to occur. Today's zoo transportation must accommodate the physically disabled as well. These may be in wheelchairs, on crutches, or using canes. Sometimes the disability is blindness. For these persons, special spaces have been added to the vehicles and accessibility has been dramatically enhanced to provide barrier-free opportunities. Some zoos have also constructed special viewing platforms so that patrons may observe animals.[7]

Vehicular Problems

The most immediate and obvious problems occur upon entry into the vehicle. For some reason, zoo patrons feel that they must hang out of the sides of the conveyors or they will miss the sights and sounds. Some passengers are constantly putting their hands and arms through windows or standing up while the vehicle is still in motion. In order to prevent accidents to passengers, zoo officials have prominently placed signs in easily seen locations at the vehicle boarding areas that request passengers to refrain from behaving in ways that might cause injury to themselves or others. Passengers are asked not to stand in moving vehicles and not to place portions of their body outside and are directed to notice emergency doors. Furthermore, a sound system has become an integral part of the vehicle. This system is used by the driver or guide to describe the areas of the zoo to be visited, provides an on-going narrative of the animals as they are observed, and warns passengers to conduct themselves so that they will be safe and avoid injury.

Zoos have become very cautious about loading and unloading passengers on their tour vehicles. Not only is a ticket taker stationed at the entrance to the vehicle, to lend assistance or give directions if necessary, but signs are posted that remind the passengers to embark carefully. All this effort has not been wasted. Although there are still a few injuries to passengers because of contributory negligence, there are almost no injuries that involve negligence on the part of zoo personnel. If collisions occur between a zoo vehicle and pedestrian, it is almost assured that the pedestrian suddenly decided to cross the road at an inappropriate time, did not first look to see if a vehicle was approaching, or exhibited some other thoughtless behavior that ended with injury. For the most part, however, zoo vehicles travel well-marked routes, are brightly colored, may have their own sound effects, travel quite slowly

Tree house designed for safe patron viewing.

(although faster than a walking pace), and thereby prevent accidents to pedestrians even when the latter are irresponsible.

Patron Behavior Problems

The greatest single problem that zoos and other animal exhibits have are patrons who refuse to follow posted rules and regulations, are rowdy, drunk, malicious, irritating to others, or display behaviors that are inappropriate for the zoo environment. Most zoo patrons are content to follow whatever regulations are necessary for their own safety and that of the animals and zoo property. There are a few individuals who urgently feel that they can best express themselves by vandalism of property and brutality against the animals.

Vandalism has taken the form of spray painting walls, windows, and walkways. It includes such activities as breaking sanitary fixtures, knocking out lights, breaking windows, cutting through fences, and, in some extreme cases, breaking into animal cages. In one recent incident, a young boy smashed a glass case holding poisonous tropical snakes and stole one of the vipers. He was promptly bitten and had to be taken to a hospital for antisnake venom treatment. For the most part, vandals are almost never apprehended and continue to do irreparable damage to property thereby raising the cost for zoo operations for the rest of the population.

There are other malicious souls who take immense joy in hurting or destroying animals. There are many cases on record of missiles being hurled at penned in deer or other fauna so that the animals are bruised or their bones are broken. Sometimes people actually shoot the animals with air pistols, bullets, or arrows. Invariably, these attacks are against the most benign and defenseless creatures. In less ferocious instances, some people merely irritate the animals. The San Diego Zoo treats this latter behavior in a humorous way by posting signs that request the patron not to annoy any animal with every synonym that can be used for the word "annoy" in hopes that the message will come across. Youths are particularly noted for this form of conduct. On occasion adults may be caught at pestering. The more intelligent and capable animals respond to annoyance by retaliating against their persecutor. At least one chimpanzee at the Los Angeles Zoo has learned to wait patiently for the annoyer to step closer to the moat, which separates the animals from the people, and then hurls dung or stones at the offender—a most salutary lesson.

Despite all of the warnings that are signed, verbal, or signaled, people persist in coming as close to the animals as they can get and putting their hands and arms through the bars of cages. The Los Angeles Zoo has reported several instances of zoo patrons being bitten by monkeys under these circumstances. Sometimes mentaly ill persons insist upon climbing into cages with the most ferocious of animals for whatever irrational impulse they may have. The Central Park Zoo ejected one such individual twice because that person attempted to climb into the cage of a polar bear. The polar bear is the largest carnivore. Apparently this person succeeded sometime during the night when the zoo was closed. His partially devoured body was found the following day in the bear's cage.[8] If a person wants to commit suicide and is determined enough, there is little that zoo officials can do to prevent such incidents. Locks, bars, gates, and moats notwithstanding, the dedicated self-killer will eventually find a way to fulfill his death wish.

Parents have been observed on occasion holding their infants over the open enclosures of large wild animals and playing catch with their child. Everybody has a good time unless, of course, the baby is accidentally dropped. Warning signs request that zoo patrons not reach over the enclosures, even when they are separated from the animals by sufficient space and water filled moats. It is not known what motivates these "parents" to behave with such recklessness, unless they do not appreciate how foolish is their conduct. The most that zoo officials can do is admonish the people or request that they leave the grounds.

Zoo patrons who carry portable stereo sets with them and loudly play them on zoo grounds have been well controlled. Staff persons simply have to request that the stereo be shut off or that it be put into safe storage at the entrance. While cameras may be permitted in zoos, flashbulb use is prohibited. Where this rule is violated, zoo staff offer the offender an alternative of not using the flash or having it confiscated.

While zoo officials and their staff may be able to contend with most of the

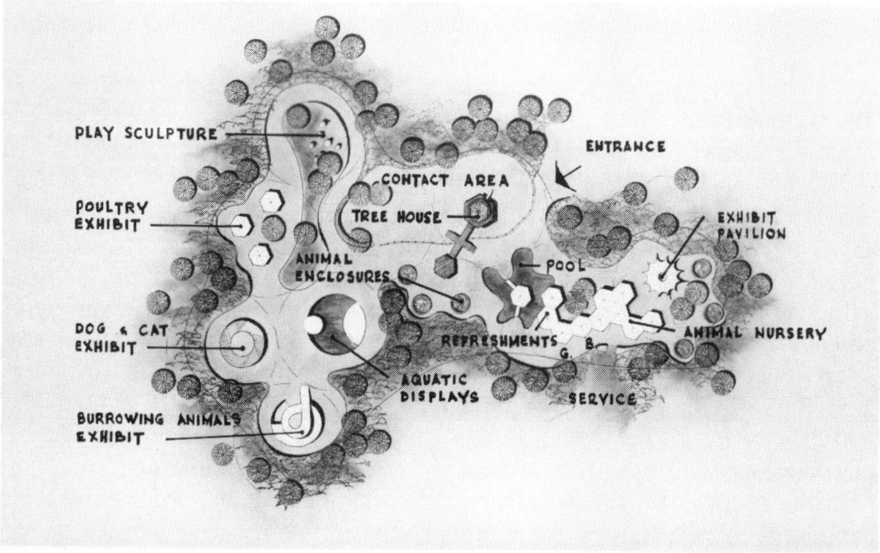

Children's zoo plan—designed, safe contact.

human problems that continuously crowded facilities receive, there are some behavorial situations that require police support. Drunk and disorderly patrons may require police escort out of the zoo environs. Sometimes assaults and thefts occur at the zoo. After all, the zoo is accessible to all kinds of persons. Police posts unobstrusively established within the zoo grounds may enable quick apprehension of muggers and others who break the law. Zoos also have their own fire fighting equipment and trained fire fighters to handle emergencies. Modern zoos have also established first aid stations as part of their security service to the public who throng to the wild animal exhibits.

GYMNASIA, COURTS, AND WEIGHT-TRAINING ROOMS

Essentially, gymnasia are designed to be integral parts of larger structures, usually field houses, recreational centers, or school buildings. The gymnasium is a large room of a height, width, and length able to accommodate at least one and often two or three full-sized basketball courts. The gymnasium is laid out in such a manner as to be able to fulfill the function of several teaching stations simultaneously. Therefore, many volleyball games may be played at one time, badminton courts may be set up, a variety of weight-training equipment can be present (a Universal or Nautilus machine, perhaps a rowing machine), as well as gymnastic equipment. Among the latter will be permanently fixed climbing ropes, swinging and still rings, and floor locks for the erection of uneven parallel bars, high bars, and attachments for safety belts for use with the trampoline. Additionally, other gymnastic equipment that is moveable, such as parallel bars, horse, hurdle, and balance beam will round out the gymnastic paraphernalia. Combat sports can also be organized in the gymnasium.

The Gymnasium

The gymnasium is the locus of many different recreational and fitness activities. It is also the facility that is used by schools, camps, recreational service departments, and private clubs or associations for instructional purposes, exhibitions, and competitive physical activities. The gymnasium is sufficently large that it may serve a multipurpose function. Thus, a variety of physical activities may be performed simultaneously without undue or any interference between them. However, when competitive activities are operated, it may be that only one game can be played at a time or the gymnasium will have to be set up so that three or four games of the same kind will be played at once, for example, basketball, volleyball, or badminton.

In the event of a gymnastic, wrestling, or other combat sport contest or exhibition, it is usual for the entire gymnasium to be taken over so that participants can compete and spectators may watch. Among the uses for a gymnasium will be that of tumbling and gymnastic classes and competitions. This means that the entire gymnasium will be given over to that activity for instruction, practice, or demonstration. The facility will then be cleared of all other but the equipment necessary for gymnastics.

Gymnastics and Tumbling. Gymnastics is a sport for individuals who want to combine strength, speed, and agility with aesthetic form. It is an exhibition of power and grace when performed by highly skilled persons. It is unquestionably an activity that lends itself to recreational use as well as physical education. In its incipient form it may be observed in the monkey bars, climbing devices, swings, slides, rings, and seesaws that abound on playgrounds everywhere. In its developed form gymnastics requires flying rings, still rings, side horse, parallel bars, high bar, uneven parallel bars, balance beam, mats of various thicknesses, trampoline, and vaulting horses. Such equipment can be found in middle or secondary schools, the gymnasiums of agencies such as the YMCA and Jewish Community Center, colleges, universities, athletic clubs, and some health clubs.

The space needed for participation in gymnastics depends upon the numbers of participants and the type of activity involved. Typically, the gym-

A well-designed gynasium showing multiple use, clearly marked courts, illumination, and spectator seating.

nasium will be of sufficient size to house the activity comfortably. The essential criterion is that the area be large enough to permit whatever instruction or practice is required with maximum safety conditions extant. The element of safety is the only limitation insofar as the area of participation is concerned.

The activity is well suited to recreational use because it does not necessitate an organized group, club, team, or association to allow participation. The interested person may utilize whatever facilities are available and accessible without having to wait for some organized group to form. Another attractive feature is that the individual may choose whatever stunts or skills are most interesting and satisfy some personal needs or reach desired goals. Gymnastics is a year-round activity. It is not limited to the gymnasium, but may be performed in the outdoors as well. Gymnastic camps and general recreational programs invariably feature some aspect of gymnastics and tumbling.

The incident recounted below is particularly valuable because it contains so many elements of what could be termed supervisory neglect. There are instances of alleged poor or inadequate instruction, more students in the gymnasium than could reasonably have been expected to receive adequate supervision for the type of activities engaged in, failure to prepare pupils and equipment properly to help prevent injuries, and failure to take into account the physical prowess and experience of the pupils. The facts in this case, as presented by statements made by plaintiff, a witness, and investigative reports, schematics of the gymnasium, and supply catalogues were as follows in *Goodwalk v. Board of Education of Clark County:*

> The plaintiff was a twelve-year-old seventh grader male student at the KHK School on 14 February 1979. Plaintiff was injured during his participation in a required physical education gymnastics class that took place during the school year in the latter part of January and the beginning of February 1979.
>
> Plaintiff had been taking gymnastics for approximately two weeks and to that time he had not received extensive instruction concerning precautions to be taken or safety techniques. On occasion, the physical education instructor, Mr. C, did demonstrate a particular exercise on the gymnastic equipment. Thereafter, the students were permitted to perform such exercises and any others that would affect their ultimate grade for the course. At no time did the physical education teacher undertake any intensive form of instruction with respect to the individual devices (apparatus) on which the students practiced. Among these devices were high bar, low bar, side horse, parallel bars, tumbling mats, and ropes. Furthermore, the instructor stressed that the program was required, that students were free to design their own gymnastic program, and the difficulty of the program would be reflected in the grade that they received. No exercises were recommended to beginners and none were prohibited as being those necessitating greater experience.
>
> On 14 February 1979 shortly after the start of the physical education class, plaintiff went to the high bar to practice certain exercises. The instructor was on the other side of the gymnasium. Plaintiff hung on the high bar and

began to swing back and forth. He was unable to sustain his grip, fell off the bar, and struck his head and right side on the mat underneath the bar. He sustained traumatic subluxation (incomplete or partial dislocation) at C-2 and a right parietal (top and side) fracture of the skull. He was totally incapacitated for approximately four months and partially incapacitated for another one and a half months during which time he was directed to wear a soft cervical collar. Thereafter he returned to school. His physician's diagnosis was guarded because he (plaintiff) could develop an instability of the spine at the C-2 level.

It is well known by all who are familiar with gymnastic instruction that great care should be exercised in maintaining safety on the high bar. Since the bar is fairly high off the floor and the activity involves swinging on and around the bar, supported most of the time only by the hands, the danger of falling can be great. Thus, there is required close adherence to safety rules. In many cases the stunts do not progress gradually so each one must be thoroughly learned before proceeding on. It is highly important that the stunts be tried in an orderly progressive manner. The instructor should always be at hand to assist the performer through the learning stages of the stunts. The following list of safety rules are generally recognized for working the high bar:

a. Check apparatus for solidity and maintenance.
b. Use plenty of mats around the bar for safety and dismounting purposes.
c. Always use bar chalk (carbonate of magnesium) on the hands.
d. Keep the bar clean.
e. Always have at least one spotter while learning new stunts to prevent slips or falls. Two spotters are preferred with one of them being the instructor.
f. In working on an adjustable bar, work low at first and gradually increase the height.
g. It is advisable to work the bar only for short periods due to fatigue build-up and friction on the hands.

Spotting in gymnastics is defined as the manipulation of the performer either by direct use of the hands or by means of a belt tied around the waist of the gymnast. The objective of spotting may be to prevent injury, to assist the gymnast in performing his skill, or both. A safety spot in gymnastics is designed to prevent falling. To execute a safety spot, the instructor or spotter must first determine where the fall might occur and place himself in that position. Then he must determine how he will grab or hold the performer to allow for maximum control of his body. In all spotting techniques by hand, the spotter should grab or hold the upper body of the performer whenever a spot is required. The purpose of this technique is to keep the head and shoulders off the mat, since these are most delicate parts of the body.

Good spotting technique is not easily learned. It requires a great deal of practice and an understanding of gymnastic moves. When spotting by hand, certain techniques are most helpful. The first one is to stand close to the performer. Regardless of the hand placement on the performer, one cannot properly assist or hold the gymnast up if one is more than half an arm length away. Many times, the spotter's arms and body are in direct contact with the gymnast. A second technique is to be at the right place at the right time; anticipate the fall and be there before it happens.

Paying close attention to the task is another technique of extreme importance. Many times classmates will be looking around the gymnasium or paying attention to some other activity when their performer is ready to attempt a move.

Instruction on the horizontal bar should always begin with a few comments on safety. Safety instruction should include the following three points: grip, chalk, and spotting. Both instructor and pupil should practice spotting. When spotting, the spotter should know what the performer is about to do and the possible mishaps that might arise.

It is highly recommended that a rotating safety belt be obtained with the horizontal bar. This belt is designed to couple around the bar and rotates on a ball bearing surface with the performer. Even if the performer's hands slip from the bar, he cannot fall. For a small amount of money expended the safety factor is thus assured and can reach almost fantastic proportions.

Supervision is one of the critical elements in safety. Ordinarily there are two kinds of supervision, general and specific. General supervision means that one is giving overall direction to the activities going on, while specific supervision requires the instructor to be with a participant, directly supervising the activity. Among the general guidelines for supervision are the following:

1. Develop a plan of supervision by rotating, observing, and communicating.
2. Inspect equipment, watch for potential problems, and anticipate errors.
3. Make sure that every assistant has proper credentials and competency.
4. Keep people alert and motivated and under a controlled type of discipline.
5. Observe individuals from a physiological and psychological point of view, knowing when fatigue is setting in or when activities are being performed irregularly.
6. See that participants know the rules and also follow them.
7. Oversee from a nearby moving position and not from a sitting or distant spot.
8. Understand that a single teacher will reach a hazard level if too many pieces of equipment are used at one time.

Selection of mats should be made with five factors in mind: (a) the gymnastic activities planned, (b) the ages and fitness of the participants, (c) the nature of the gymnasium and the apparatus, (d) the continuing effectiveness of the mats themselves, given proper installation, care, and maintenance, and (e) requirements or standards devised by authoritative bodies. Good judgment must also be used. For example, a mat suitable for floor exercises is inadequate for landing from a high bar; a mat approved for competition may be unsafe for beginners; and a safe mat may become unsafe through abuse or neglect.

A basic mat is used beside and under apparatus. A Base Filler Mat fits around the base of certain apparatus. A Landing Mat is used in the landing areas for horizontal bars so it contains both firm and soft cushioning material. Special mats are used to provide additional safety and reassurance for young children and beginners. These usually contain only soft spongelike cushioning material.

Mats and protective equipment are not the complete answer to eliminating or reducing injuries. It is more important that falls be prevented rather than to assume that they will occur. Careless progression or escalating learning at the expense of control and ability cannot be safeguarded by additional mats. Absolute mat requirements cannot be set for every situation, but the difference between resiliency and shock absorbancy should be understood by the instructor. In a gymnasium, mats should never be idle. There is always a place for additional mats. Mats are not fail-safe. Nothing can substitute for proper instruction, spotting, and good common sense in the teaching of gymnastics.

> In the face of these well-known standards and practices it is apparent that the instructor of record, Mr. C., was remiss in regard to certain essential elements required for complete gymnastic instruction in that he failed to act in a reasonable and prudent manner befitting a professional person by exercising foresight so that injury to the plaintiff could have been prevented.
>
> It appears the rudimentary instruction given to students concerning the various stunts and exercises to be performed on the different pieces of apparatus available in the gymnasium class was insufficient. Moreover, it seems that there were too many different pieces of apparatus made available for use in consideration of the size of the class, some twenty-five students, and the fact that Mr. C was the only instructor for the males. A class of about twenty-five female students, under the supervision of a female teacher, was also operating in the same gymnasium simultaneously. Specific supervision could not have been given to pupils on such hazardous equipment as the high bar if general supervision was also mandated.
>
> It does not now appear that Mr. C exercised good judgment in providing every pupil with basic spotting techniques. Every student should have been given spotting techniques when guarding of any kind was needed. The fact that these were twelve-year-old, quite immature individuals, should have made the difference in terms of the measures taken to insure that sound safety practices were followed. It would have been necessary for Mr. C to explain what dangers to watch out for and then place the beginner with an experienced spotter to learn exactly how to stand and how to serve the performer best. Since Mr. C was the only experienced spotter available, there is some doubt as to whether the crucial instruction was adequate to meet the need.
>
> No spotters were at hand when the boy used the high bar. Plaintiff's peers,

who were supposed to spot, apparently were preoccupied with other things when he used the high bar. The instructor was on the other side of the gymnasium and may have been sitting down at the time of the accident and injury. He neither saw nor was able to safeguard the plaintiff during the time when the injury occurred. Had Mr. C been spotting for the boy or providing specific supervision, the accident would have been prevented.
It seems likely that Mr. C was remiss is not utilizing the full protection provided to him and available on the day of the incident. Crash or Landing Mats were available for use. However, such mats were not utilized. In fact, only one thin mat, whose cushioning capacity was disclaimed by the manufacturer, was in use at the time. Had the Landing Mat been used, it is probable that the extensive injuries suffered by plaintiff could have been minimized or avoided. No sound reason for such lack of protection for the plaintiff can be found.
It seems likely that the use of the boy's peers as the only spotters was an error. It is obvious that most twelve year olds do not have a sense of responsibility, and their attentions are easily distracted. With a spotter who knows little or nothing about a skill being attempted, the possibility of slips and falls is likely, particularly with a serious injury resulting. That this happened in just this manner is proof of the foregoing statement. Failure to conform to even minimal safety standards operating in the instruction of a gymnastics program in a physical education class was the proximate cause of the injuries that the plaintiff suffered. Mr. C, the physical education instructor, failed to provide the necessary learning environment wherein every pupil in that class would have learned how to spot others for all stunts where guarding was necessary. This is borne out by the fact that although other pupils were present at the apparatus, they were positioned behind the performer and could not have assisted even if they were prepared to do so. It is the instructor's responsibility to see that assigned spotters do their share.
Failure to utilize maximum mat protection, despite the fact that such Landing or Crash Mats were available for use indicates a lack of good judgment on the part of the instructor.
Having too many pieces of apparatus in use simultaneously, which effectively prevented specific supervision and personal hand spotting by the instructor, certainly contributed to the injuries suffered by plaintiff. The instructor failed to note the physiological and psychological state of the plaintiff. Mr. C did not think much of the plaintiff's skills or attitude and should have provided him with greater support or maximized assistance. He knew that chalk should have been used and failed to make certain that his students actually used the magnesium for the activity. This substandard teaching situation was potentially dangerous and ultimately led to one pupil's injury. Failure to foresee the need for protective matting, sound progressive instruction, sound and consistent spotting, and safety instruction for apparatus and tumbling use and failure to provide specific supervision was an irresponsible act and directly contributed to the accident and injuries received by the plaintiff.
Such substandard instructional practices deviate remarkably from acceptable gymnastic teaching techniques and practices widely recognized and advocated throughout the physical education and gymnastic safety field.

The case was settled out of court. Plaintiff received monetary redress, but the defendant did not admit any error.[9]

COMBAT ACTIVITIES

Almost without exception, the law holds that individuals who engage in mutual combat activities do so knowing the risks that they have assumed. Therefore, it is unlikely that actions will be initiated against third parties, unless it can be unequivocally shown that malicious intent to hurt or gross or flagrant negligence was instrumental in the injury received or that some unforeseen and unreasonable risk was the proximate cause for any injury encountered by any combatant. Among the combat sports are those of boxing, wrestling, judo, karate, other martial arts forms, and fencing and its variations.

Boxing

Of all the combat activities performed for competitive purposes, only boxing has achieved the worldwide notoriety that it enjoys and is the only activity in which striking the opponent is a chief purpose. Boxing has been perennially popular among spectators as entertainment and as a way for economically poor individuals to obtain an income and has been used as a recreational activity in inner-city agencies supported by newspapers and popularized by television and other media. Boxing on an amateur competitive basis is still a part of some intercollegiate programs as well as world boxing events and the Olympic Games.

While other sports and games have certain inherent risks to participants, no other activity has as its sole purpose the deliberate striking of an opponent as hard and as often as can be accomplished within a three-minute period. Although amateur boxing promoters continually state that the primary objective in the activity is not to knock the opponent out, that is precisely what is attempted every time a match is organized. A knockout or causing contracoup (brain concussion) is the only sure way that one contestant can be declared a winner over the other. In matches where the judges' decision must be relied upon, it remains for the eventual winner to pummel the opponent as hard as can be done even if no knockout can be obtained. In the process, a variety of facial fractures may occur, eyes and eyebrows are subject to laceration and scarring, hands may be damaged, and other bones can be broken. The worst effect is the brain damage that accrues by being hit around the head and face too many times. It is possible for such injury to take place despite the wearing of a protective head guard. The courts have consistently held that mutual combatants have no basis for recovery for injuries received based upon the doctrine of the assumption of obvious risks involved and to the extent that they result from ordinary and inherent risks of the activity.[10] Anyone who boxes knows, or should know, that there is great likelihood of physical injury in spite of great skill, strength, speed, or protective gear worn. There is always the possibility that an opponent will make solid contact with some portion of the anatomy during the contest and sufficiently disable the competitor so that the exhibition will be called off. Every boxer knows that some injury is to be expected. It is the unexpected or unreasonable risk that courts will find actionable.

If competitors are mismatched by size or weight, if the protective equipment is of poor quality or in poor condition so that protection is not afforded, if the individual has not been properly or adequately coached or instructed in amateur competition, if the arena is improperly constructed, not sufficiently padded, or has a slippery surface, if spectators throw objects into the ring thereby injuring the contestants, any of these constitute an unreasonable risk. For the most part, however, the very nature of boxing makes the activity one of great risk. It is the only contact sport where the paramount objective is to hurt the opponent so badly that the competition will have to be stopped. Recreational service departments would be well advised not to support or lend organizational assistance to such a dangerous enterprise regardless of the clamor for it. For every physical value that boxing is supposed to contribute to the participant, there are other activities that can do as well without placing the life or health of the participant in jeopardy.

Wrestling

Amateur competitive wrestling is a body contact sport that is designed to develop physical fitness, speed, strength, and sportsmanship. It is used as a developmental activity in physical education classes in schools and for intramural competition and also finds a place in some recreational programs. Under no circumstance may a wrestler force a body part into an unnatural position. No strangle holds, arm locks, arm bars, or any hold that is used to punish the opponent may be used. While participants may grasp four fingers in an effort to break a hold, it is illegal to grasp the thumb and bend it back or do the same to one, two, or three fingers. No contestant may lift an opponent off the mat and bring that person to the mat with unnecessary roughness. A contestant who lifts an opponent free of the mat is responsible for the safe descent of that person.

Any intentional striking, gouging, kicking, butting, elbowing, or other malicious act, even in the heat of competition, is illegal and looked upon with the utmost contempt. Thus, to the best of the supervisor's ability, whether the title is coach, teacher, or trainer, such tactics must be prevented. The sport of wrestling may provoke few serious injuries and is considered to be relatively safe as far as most combat activities are concerned. The most common injuries that do occur are strained muscles and mat burns. Such incidents may be considerably reduced by making sure that participants are in excellent physical condition, are thoroughly warmed up before any practice or match is permitted. Mat burns can almost be eliminated if wrestlers wear protective clothing or tights that can cover the legs. Close fitting tank tops may also be worn to prevent burns on the upper back, shoulders, or chest. Head gear, protecting the skull and ears is optional, but it should be worn to prevent ear bruises.

Wrestling mats should be of plastic foam material, thoroughly cleaned and disinfected prior to use, and of a sufficient size to extend at least five feet beyond the actual wrestling area in every direction. The mat itself is at least a one-inch-thick ensolite material, covered by a plastic or rubber envelope. Periodic airing and sterilization with an antiseptic solution will maintain the desired hygienic condition and prevent infections from occurring if open wounds result. The typical mat size is twenty-four by twenty-four feet, although the mats may be larger.

Although wrestling strategy consists of using selected offensive and defensive maneuvers in order to gain leverage advantage and finally pin the opponent, this activity does not have to be dangerous to participants. In fact, except for minor injuries, wrestling produces fewer serious injuries than most other contact sports. Perhaps the most serious damage that will accrue to the poorly conditioned participant will be knee injuries to ligaments or tears in the menisci in extreme cases. Even these injuries can be significantly lessened if wrestling technique is practiced, physical conditioning is mandated, and all contestants are enjoined never to exert pressure against the normal range and direction of joints.

Fencing

Among the combat sports, fencing has a universal appeal. It combines grace, agility, speed, and poise with hand-eye coordination. Essentially, fencers attempt to score points and win a match by touching the opponent with one of three weapons. Épée, sabre, or foil are the instruments used. The body must be touched in terms of the target areas that are legal for the weapon used.

Protective clothing and other gear is designed to provide maximum safety for the participants as well as freedom of movement. Fencing attire consists of a padded jacket of sufficient strength to prevent injury to the upper body due to touches with the foil or slashes with the épée or sabre. The glove for the hand holding the weapon offers a tight fit and is padded to prevent minor cuts or bruises to the hand or fingers. The glove almost always has an extension that securely fastens to the sleeve of the jacket thereby preventing blade entry up the arm. The mask is made of wire mesh with a metal framework. It contains a big attachment at the lower edge providing optimum protection to the face and neck. Leather padding on the sides and top offer protection from sabre cuts. Flatheeled rubber soled shoes complete the garb.

Fencing class is for thrust and parry maneuvers that require split-second timing and mastery of the fundamentals of the activity. Basic movements must be taught and repeated over and over again until the fencer can execute the move rapidly and correctly. Instructors must explain the tactics and strategy of fencing, provide opportunity for the participant to practice, and then permit contests to take place under controlled conditions. Fencing is a very safe activity. Although injuries have occurred, these are almost always due to weapon breakage at a critical moment or by thoughtless behavior on the part of one or both of the contestants who may engage without wearing appropriate clothing or masks. Fencing is an excellent activity for physical education, intramural, recreational, and varsity athletics. The etiquette of fencing is such that all participants know and clearly recognize certain signals to discontinue, call touches on themselves, and other gestures of good sportsmanship. Surely the nature of the activity carries some inherent risk, but this can easily be negated by proper instruction and the maintenance of the equipment used. If injuries are to be avoided simple application of common sense and adherence to the rules will suffice.

Other forms of combat follow the same legal principles and rules for safe practice. They require competent instruction, sufficient warnings about the inherent risks of the activity in clear and understandable language for all who want to participate, and emphasis upon good physical conditioning, progressive skills, and adequate areas where the activity may be conducted without obstructions or congestion. Participants must wear whatever protective matting, clothing, or other gear that is necessary to protect them from injury. Failure to enforce this, particularly in the presence of a supervisor, may result in allegations of negligence if an individual is injured. Supervisors must always enforce whatever safety rules or regulations are recognized in order to prevent undue injury to participants.

Reiterated warnings about not following prescribed routines or safety procedures can be a significant defense in the event of participant injury. Of course, any person who participates in combat activities assume the risk of potential injury. Redress fcr injury sustained in the engagement of combat sports will be more likely if there is injury from nonanticipated sources or behaviors that are not an accepted aspect of the activity. Thus, failure of equipment, protective clothing, and gear; faulty construction of the building in which the activity occurs; spectator aggression; incompetent instruction or coaching; and failure to provide first aid or medical attention as necessary may constitute the basis for litigation.

INDOOR RACQUET GAMES

All racquet games have common elements. Some kind of ball is used; an extension of the arm and hand is utilized to propel the ball against the wall, walls, or through the air; two or more people can practice or compete during a game; and points are scored when an opponent cannot return the ball in the air before it bounces on the floor twice. All of the racquet games are derivatives of handball. There are specific rules and tactical changes because the racquet adds a dimension of greater speed and striking power. Among the indoor racquet games are squash racquets, paddleball, racquetball, and handball. The latter is included because the arm and hand are used as a racquet would be. Many of the movements, strategies, and ball handling effects are similar or identical. The essential difference is the length of the racquet used, the capacity of the ball to rebound with greater or lesser velocity, the weight of the ball, and the size of the ball. All indoor racquet games are played within the confines of an enclosed court, the walls of which are blank and smooth. One variant is three-wall paddleball. Some of the newest courts are constructed of clear plastic that permits excellent spectator viewing.

The greatest dangers in racquet games are the confined space in which two, three, or four players are competing or practicing with a rapidly moving relatively hard ball and the swinging or stroking of paddles, racquets, or arm and hand that can seriously injure another player or oneself if uncontrolled. For purposes of this text, it will probably suffice to recount the hazards and safety techniques of one racquet game. Since racquetball has become so popular in recent years, particularly with the advent of private racquetball clubs, intramural play in educational institutions, and tournament play recorded among recreational service departments, its inherent risks and the procedures to be taken to alleviate such dangers can be the exemplar for all kinds of racquet activities.

As with all activities that require instruction, the major necessity is that learners must receive proper instruction concerning the game at hand and the concomitant skills that are appropriate for successfully participating. One other subject must be reviewed by any supervisor or instructor and that is to warn learners of potential dangers to themselves and others. Personnel who are employed to teach, coach, or supervise activities that require instruction must provide detailed warnings about the dangers of the activity. Furthermore, personnel need to be familiar with the most up-to-date safety techniques concerning the activity. Agency administrators should monitor the pertinent staff member's knowledge of the activity and lesson plans for adequate conditioning of participants, lead-up, and progression of the activity to be taught. Emphasis should be placed on possible injuries that might accrue if appropriate skills and techniques are not used.

Of paramount importance is for instructors to point out all foreseeable risks inherent in the activity. These could include the dangers of collision with walls or other players, being struck by flying balls traveling at great speed, or being hit by equipment or hands or arms of others. In some activities, overstroking with a forehand may lead to painful injuries that are self-imposed as the racquet or paddle strikes the opposite arm or leg during the follow-through. Unless individuals are in good physical condition, there is always the possibility for strained muscles, sprained joints, stretched or torn tendons and ligaments, or bruises, lacerations, dislocations, or fractures. All foreseeable hazards should be explained, demonstrated, and reiterated whenever there is an instructional period. Methods for avoiding such risks and positive safety procedures should be taught.

Instructors should be cognizant of the latest safety precautions and methods concerning the activity supervised, coached, or instructed. The need for maintaining safe distances when a learner is practicing a swing or stroke, for example, the use of protective gear when available, the need for proper attire, and the necessity for equipment to be well maintained are part of this responsibility.

Physical conditioning and progressive sequences have a significant part to play in preventing accidents from occurring. Individuals should be required to sustain a degree of physical fitness that permits them to participate in the activity without undue stress. If the activity requires cardiovascular and pulmonary efficiency, then the participant must be warned about activity participation prior to developing a level of conditioning that will contribute to health rather than precipitate death. Activities that require the mastery of simple movement before attaining a high degree of skill in more complex movements have to do with progression. Learners must be taught at a pace and within the limit of their current capacity and skill development. It is inconsistent with competent instruction to expect a beginner to be knowledgeable about advanced skills. This is valid for all lead-up or sequential skills that rely upon a simpler form before more complicated skills are acquired.

Racquetball

The game of racquetball is played within the relatively small area of a court where player movement is continuous, racquets are swung at close quarters, and a rubber ball can be hit powerfully enough to drive it with great velocity. All of these elements combine to make racquetball a potentially dangerous activity. Participants must be made aware of the facts that any one of these aspects. confined space, rapid movement, equipment used, and constantly changing positions, can lead to serious injury. Collision with wall, or other players, being struck with the racquet or ball, and inflicting self-imposed injuries are all potential problems in racquetball. The force of a swinging racquet can be great enough to fracture a bone, put out an eye, or cause abrasions or concussions, depending upon which part of the body is hit. The ball can also inflict injury to eye, nose, mouth, or any portion of the body that it contacts during flight to the front wall. During the course of play the action may be so strenuous that participants perspire profusely. Sweat may collect in droplets on the floor of the court and cause a slip that could produce, not only a fall, but torn ligaments, tendons, and other damage.

It is not beyond the realm of possibility that racquetball has the potential to produce conditions that can result in injuries including: blindness, bone fractures, joint dislocations, concussion, neck and/or spinal cord injury, loss of teeth, deep tissue injury, and surface cuts and bruises. Any of these injuries can occur as a result of forceful contact between a player and the ball, racquet, wall, or other player, or slips and falls. Nor are these injuries farfetched. All of these injuries result from uncontrolled and unskillful play. There does not have to be any malicious attempt to hurt an opponent. The normal course of play, if not restricted by court courtesy and common sense, is fully capable of producing such serious injuries that they can be permanently crippling. Yet, all of these adverse conditions can be overcome.

Competent instruction teaches the player the rules of the game, proper court position, and game tactics. This, in itself, reduces the necessity for constant movement and lessens the danger of contact. Game etiquette calls for the hitting participant to call a "hinder" on the opposing player. This means that the receiver has positioned himself in such a way as to obstruct the hitter's swing or to prevent the ball from progressing directly to the front wall. Hinders indicate lack of sufficient space to play the ball. Competent instruction not only explains the conditions that produce hinders but also attempts to demonstrate that hinders, the bodily interference between ball flight and front wall or room for opponent racquet use, are basically putting oneself at risk of being struck. Participants should always be instructed to call a hinder rather than hit an opponent with either ball or racquet. Being hit by the ball or racquet is not always the fault of the nonhitting participant. On occasion, the player striking the ball may wildly swing and send the ball in a direction not intended. Glancing blows may also cause erratic flight, and then the nonhitting participant may be struck by the ball despite court position and knowledge of the other player's position.

WEIGHT LIFTING, WEIGHT TRAINING, AND FITNESS

The physical fitness passion has reached astounding proportions. People of all ages are recognizing that physical fitness activities can do much to maintain good health and prevent premature death through cardiovascular or pulmonary inefficiency. All of these activities can add luster to life, but there are also negative aspects to these activities when they are not properly instructed or when inappropriate activities are offered to persons who are either not capable of carrying them out or where such activities may be detrimental to life and health.

Foreseeability and standard of care play a vital role in any question of negligence that may arise as a consequence of death or injury to a participant in a school or recreationally related fitness or weight-training program. It is not sufficient to be reasonable and prudent in terms of the ordinary person. Instead, if someone is claiming professional competence, then that person will be held to a standard of care that the professional, not the layman, is supposed to deliver. All programs of this nature should have standardized procedures that both instruct and warn potential participants about the possibilities of risk involved in participation. Activities that are strenuous to begin with should not be given to individuals unless they have been examined by a physician and declared to be capable of engaging in the activity. Even when programs pretest the would-be participant, there is always the danger that the test itself may produce a condition that jeopardizes the health and safety of the performer.

Instructors and other supervisors of fitness and weight-training activities should be certified by some professionally recognized association that can attest to the person's competence. Presumably this can be shown in terms of courses taken, laboratory experiences performed, and other practical and theoretical knowledge gained in fitness testing situations.

Typically, indoor fitness and weight-training activities are conducted in gymnasia. Usually weight training is assigned to a separate room immediately adjacent to the gymnasium, and all activities that are conducted in the gymnasium will be a contributing part of the fitness program. Whether a private club, school, or recreational service department conducts these activities makes little difference. Of necessity, those who are in charge of activities must demonstrate competence, be certified or registered with a professional association, and have the correct equipment if testing is to be performed before potential participants are permitted to engage in activities. Generally acknowledged procedures and examinations should be used to screen recreators and students. Potential dangers from participation should be carefully explained to all. It would be better if printed warnings and instructions could be handed out as a routine procedure. Finally, emergency plans must be carefully devised, organized, and operated in the event of need.

STADIA

The stadium is a specialized structure primarily designed for the exhibition of competitive, highly organized sports and games. It is typically constructed as a part of a larger institution, such as a high school or college or as part of a recreational complex. It may also be a single facility operated commercially by a community and leased for professional contests and other presentations. It is intended to serve many thousands of people who come to watch whatever event is scheduled. The largest stadia may have a seating capacity of eighty thousand to one hundred thousand spectators. Permanent seating facilities and sufficient parking space for private automobiles and buses, as well as amenity services are all incorporated within the confines of the stadium's site. The stadium structure is almost always enclosed by high fencing or walls. Some stadia have some permanent seating and temporary bleachers erected for the type of contest offered. Stadium seating may be enlarged by adding temporary bleachers. Very small stadia may be contained within three to five acres. Some stadia require twenty to forty acres that incorporate the main structure, outlying parking areas, walk-ways, and other access points to accommodate all the spectators, participants, concessionaires, and security forces necessary to maintain the facility.

The stadium is constructed so that it may have a quarter-mile running track, traditional track and field areas, a football field, soccer field, or baseball diamond, or it may be arranged for boxing, wrestling, religious services, or other game and sports contests. The newer stadia have sanitary facilities, locker rooms for participants, showers, training rooms, and emergency medical facilities provided within the structure. If such associated facilities are not built into the stadium, then a separate building immediately adjacent to the stadium must be available for these purposes.

Stadia must be constructed according to whatever building and fire codes are applicable. Probably, the greatest danger to spectators at stadia is fourfold: (1) coming into contact with high velocity objects used in the sport or game, (2) being physically abused by another spectator or the victim of

Typical multi-use stadium showing football/soccer field and quarter-mile running track. Spectators are well removed from playing areas.

robbery,[11] (3) being physically abused by a player, and (4) being injured in consequence of a stadium structural deficiency or failure.

There is always a risk that spectators will be injured if they are hit with thrown, kicked, or batted balls, pucks, or other objects. Spectators may be struck by players who do not confine their enthusiasm to the field, but overrun sidelines and continue into the stands. Spectators have been injured when racing cars have skidded out of control and disintegrated on the track while spewing flying parts and flaming gasoline and oil onto those seated too closely to the action. An injured spectator will undoubtedly seek redress against those whose actions lead to the injury. In such instances, the courts will determine whether negligence on the part of the stadium operators was the proximate cause of the injury or whether common knowledge of the risks associated with being a spectator at a stadium event precludes recovery.[12] The assumption of risk that spectators invite by being present at an arena where erratically hit or thrown balls may strike them does not mean that unreasonable risks also bar recovery. There are certain risks that no spectator shall have to assume. These are the risks that are not accepted as common knowledge, part of the appurtenances of a game, or ordinary in occurrence. These are risks that occur because of failure on the part of the stadium operator to meet his/her duty of care.

Duty of care varies with the individuals who are on the premises at any given time. Thus, patrons or invitees are invited onto the premises in order to participate in some way, usually as a spectator at a scheduled event. The highest standard of care must be provided to those individuals who fall under this designation. Individuals who have the consent of the operator to be on the premises to conduct some enterprise, e.g., concessionaires, are called licensees. A lesser standard of care is owed to these persons. Finally, there are individuals who enter the premises without the consent or knowledge of the operator. Nothing is owed to the trespasser unless the operator had prior knowledge of the trespasser's presence. In that case, the trespasser would be considered as having the same status as a licensee.

The primary duty owed to the spectator is to provide a safe place. This means that the stadium operator will be liable for conditions at his facility that cause physical injury to spectators. The liability exists if the condition of the facility poses an unreasonable threat of harm that the spectators will not ordinarily perceive or insure themselves against. Stadium operators are responsible for maintaining their premises in a reasonably safe condition. This also means that they must supervise the conduct of those at the facility in order to prevent accidents and possible injuries.

A fundamental aspect of the stadium operator's duty is to make thorough and timely inspections of the facility in order to ascertain the suitability for the use of invitees. Such routine inspections may reveal unsafe conditions that must be repaired at the earliest possible time and prior to the occupancy of spectators. If thorough inspections are not carried out regularly or if performed, are done improperly, and unsafe conditions are neither determined nor corrected, the operator will be charged with failure to offer the necessary standard of care that was required, and allegations of negligence will become the basis of an action against the stadium administrator. This is typical in instances where bleachers collapse.[13]

Spectators assume that they are safe when entering a stadium for their expected entertainment. In fact, most spectators never even think about any potential danger that they might be in when coming into a highly congested place. They simply believe that whoever operates the stadium has performed competently, that the structure meets all relevant codes, that it is sound, and that any safety deficits have either been repaired or that appropriate warnings are conspicuously posted so that patrons will be safeguarded.

It is unlikely that patrons will be allowed to recover for injuries received from being jostled or even assaulted by other patrons. These are not unreasonable risks and probably attend any spectator event where thousands of people are in close proximity, excited by the witnessed activity, or behaving in ways that are less than mature. Therefore, spectators are held to have assumed the risk of injury caused by nonnegligent factors.

AMUSEMENT PARKS

An amusement park is a special facility that houses a number of mechanical rides, side shows, eating places, and other entertainments that are designed to draw large numbers of people to its environs. Disneyland and Disney World are just the tip of a great commercial iceberg that rehabilitated itself after a long period of decline. Most of the great amusement parks are in private ownership. However, there are some notable exceptions such as Rye's Playland administered by Westchester County in New York and other municipally operated or county organized properties.[14] For the most part, the traditional amusement parks and the newer theme parks contain a variety of entertaining attractions including rides of all kinds. Many of the traditional amusement parks may be found in the traveling carnivals, tent shows, midways, and leased arrangements made at state and county fairs. The traditional amusement parks are often poorly maintained, drab, run-down, and seedy affairs. It is to these latter facilities that most of the unsafe conditions attach and to which greater attention must be paid.

So many accidents and serious injuries have occurred at these places that the United States Consumer Product Safety Commission wants the power to investigate accidents at the permanent amusement and theme parks throughout the country. But the traditional amusement parks are the ones with the greatest number of accidents and injuries, and these, together with the traveling shows, have had the least amount of supervision by state and local authorities insofar as inspection of facilities, maintenance of property, and conformity to state and local building and fire codes are concerned.

Fewer than half of the states at this writing have any regulations concerning the safety of patrons at these places, but many are moving toward them. California and Oregon call for annual inspections. Texas requires one million dollars of insurance for any amusement park operation. New York is going to pass new rules governing the commercial enterprise of amusement parks. The reason for this intense interest by the states is the result of the more than twenty-five thousand people who have been injured since 1981 at amusement parks. More than fifty people died in consequence of injuries received in accidents at these parks or shows.[15]

Almost without fail, traditional amusement park operations have been maintained inadequately or improperly. Cables holding cabins, chairs, or cockpits have been allowed to fray or disintegrate, cars have been derailed at crucial points, bolts have not been inspected and machinery has broken apart. All of these incidents have taken their toll of spectators and patrons.[16] Now government has become aware of the safety problems that are part of theme and amusement parks that use mechanical contrivances to attract their paying audiences. Legislative calls have gone out for the power to regulate such places, for routine and unannounced inspections to be made by state personnel, and for standards to be set up or maintained concerning the owners of park properties to perform as common carriers.[17]

NOTES

1. *Schmidt v. Orton,* 190 Neb. 257, 207 N.W. (2d) 390 (1973).
2. *McWilliams v. Parham,* 273 N.C. 592, 160 S.E. (2d) 692 (1968).
3. *Carroll v. Asken,* 119 Ga. App. 224, 166 S.E. (2d) 635 (1969).
4. *Getz v. Freed,* 377 Pa. 480, 105 A (2d) 102 (1954).
5. *Country Club of Jackson v. Turner,* 192 Miss. 510, 4 So. (2d) 718 (1941).
6. *Slotnick v. Cooley,* 166 Tenn. 373, 61 S.W. (2d) 462 (1933).
7. "Three People Slightly Injured," *New York Times,* 28 December 1981, p. 16.
8. "Man Killed," *New York Times,* 27 September 1982, sec. 2, p. 3.
9. Communication with Joseph Triarsi, Esq., Attorney at Law, 15 December 1982.
10. *Rosenweig v. State,* 5 App. Div. 2d 293, 171 N.Y.S. 2d 912 (1958), aff'd, 5 N.Y. 2d 404, 158 N.E. 2d 229 (1959).
11. Jay S. Shivers and Joseph W. Halper, *The Crisis in Urban Recreational Services* (East Brunswick, N.J.: Associated University Presses, Inc., 1981), 107.
12. F. Harper and F. James, *The Law of Torts,* 3 vols (Boston: Little, Brown & Co., 1956).
13. *Miratsky v. Beseda,* 139 Neb. 229 N.W. 94 (1941).
14. "Playland Ride Shut After Accident," *New York Times,* Tuesday, 10 July 1984, Region section, p. 86.
15. "Woman Flung to Death From Roller Coaster," *New York Times,* Monday, 9 July 1984, Around the Nation section, p. A8.

16. "Man Injured in Fall From Roller Coaster," *The Hartford Courant,* 10 July 1983, p. B8.
"Girl Chokes to Death After Riding 'Spider'," *The Hartford Courant,* 19 July 1983, p. B6.
"$20 Million Settlement Reached in Fair Death," *New York Times,* Wednesday, 23 May 1984.

17. Jeannye Thorton, "When Parks' 'Scare Rides' Run Wild," *U.S. News and World Report,* 20 August 1984, p. 66.

14
Aquatic Areas, Facilities, and Activities

Any natural or man-made area that fronts an ocean, bay, river, or lake that can support some form of waterborne activity may be defined as an aquatic area. Especially is this true of water systems that are developed as the result of dam construction so that water is empounded. These man-made lakes serve as primary recreational areas for swimmers, boaters, and fishermen. The natural waterfront of the seas, estuaries, inland seas, and lakes have always been great recreational resources. All forms of aquatic activity probably account for more participation than any other form of recreational experience. Additionally, countless swimming pools, both public and private, as well as hot tubs, spas, and the like have become commonplace in recent years. Marinas, boat launching ramps, and a number of commercial enterprises that rent equipment for aquatic use round out the variety of facilities that have direct impact upon the number of potential recipients of water related services or those who frequent aquatic areas for experience on, in, or under the water's surface.

While it is beyond the scope of this text to discuss the instructional aspects of the kinds of recreational activity usually performed at aquatic areas or facilities, there is the underlying assumption that those who do participate must have the skill to do so. Anyone who wants to swim, dive, sail, boat, fish, or surf must have the ability to swim as well as the knowledge required to participate in the activity of choice safely.

BEACHES

All beaches are not alike. Some front on lakes while others are washed by the tidal currents of rivers or oceans. Each type of beach will offer splendid opportunities for recreational activity in the water. However, unseen dangers often develop as a result of wind direction, current flow, and any barriers that have been constructed to protect the shoreline or to serve as piers for promenades, fishing, or docking purposes.

Among surf hazards are riptides, undertows, and heavy surf. A riptide is a strong current flowing from shallow water near the shore out to sea. The outgoing current is probably caused by heavy surf cutting channels and holes in the sandy bottom. Waves sweeping up the sloping beach will recede faster and in greater volume at a point where the water flows into a channel or hole. Riptides may be recognized by the action on incoming waves. The riptide tends to flatten the wave in its path while producing larger waves on each side. The water in riptides is generally discolored from the sand being churned up. The same action is also observed where water is flowing through a hole created by the heavy surf. The current tends to move to the far side of the hole and return in a circular motion, instead of continuing out to sea. Riptides may also be caused by groins or piers or any obstruction extending out into the surf, thereby hindering a lateral current that is carrying loose sand. Obstructions may cause a buildup of a sand bar or cut holes and channels.

An undertow is prevalent on any beach where there is a tidal flow or wave action. It is particularly treacherous on steep slopes or at or near high tides. Water flow or waves thrown up on the beach return seaward with great force beneath oncoming waves. This condition is particularly dangerous to unsuspecting people, especially small children playing at the water's edge, since the surge of water backward toward the sea can carry the individual down and seaward.[1]

Heavy surf that breaks close in becomes dangerous in terms of the weight and force of the water on any object. A wave can build up and smash down upon a bather in shallow water, knocking the person down and tumbling him about. Heavy surf breaking out away from the beach generally causes currents and riptides creating a dangerous condition when there are occasional lulls. During these lulls, a riptide may sweep a bather out into or through the breakerline, after which the surf may start crashing again.

Jetties, breakwaters, piers, and pilings may create dangerous conditions due to prevailing wind patterns and the currents. It is not uncommon to have wind patterns that ran obliquely to the shore. In such situations, ocean currents flow against the obstruction in circular movements or eddies. There is a strong undertow created by wind, water, and the obstruction so that a swimmer or boater is in danger of being dashed against the jetty or other construction. In order to break free of such a current, it is best to maneuver around the jetty with the current escaping from any whirlpool effect on the opposite side. Sand bars are built up by the action of waves and currents. Sand bars are not stationary and tend to move as the action of the wind causes directional changes of current. Sand bars become parallel breakwaters tending to hold water against the shore. When the water builds up enough force, it smashes through the bar at its weakest point. This permits the empounded water to run out through the break creating a strong current through the bar. The current rapidly dissipates once the bar is crossed.

The Lifesaving Program at the Beach

Every beach that fronts an ocean that is operated for the recreational enjoyment of patrons should be safeguarded by a well-conceived lifesaving service, operating equipment, and other vessels or supplies useful in rescue work. The selection of lifesaving equipment and the type of water craft used will depend upon the location of the beach, water conditions, and the personnel assigned the responsibility of lifeguarding and beach operation. The operation of beaches requires the development of a comprehensive lifeguarding program, the assignment of competent persons to lifeguarding positions, the daily practice of lifesaving and physical fitness exercises, knowledge of crowd control, the use of appropriate equipment, and the standard practices of first aid.

The lifeguard program requires an individual who is thoroughly prepared in lifesaving and water safety skills. Naturally, the first requisite is that the lifeguard be able to swim well. Although there are nonswimming rescues, all lifeguards must be competent swimmers and demonstrate their lifesaving skills in simulated rescue operations in order to pass the typical examination offered by those who operate public and private beaches. As with other areas of recreational service, the individual lifeguard must recognize his responsibilities and understand that any substandard deviation from acceptable practices that results in injury or death to a patron of the beach could initiate litigation proceedings both for the beach operator as well as the lifeguard.

Depending upon the nature of the beach and water area to be covered, it may be feasible to utilize lifelines and anchors to designate swimming areas. If such lines are used, they will be secured by anchors of sufficient weight to keep the line taut despite any number of swimmers clinging to the rope. The beach end will be secured by a buried anchor.

Rescue vessels such as rowboats, catamarans, and heavy surfboards should be available both for routine patrolling of the water and for rescuing those in trouble. Routine patrols are usually established just beyond the lifelines. The patrol is maintained by rowing parallel to the lines and holding a stationary position for a few minutes before retracing the route. Where there are no lifelines, the patrol should be on a course parallel to the beach (shore), especially when swift tides or currents are running. This use of patrol boats at regular intervals puts the vessels out in the water where they can immediately come to the aid of any swimmer who requires assistance. Other watercraft may be stationed ashore. These shore stations permit the vessels to be placed in positions, usually on heavy wooden rollers for quick launching in the event that a swimmer ventures too far out for a swimming rescue to be attempted.

On beaches of extensive length, telephones become an important factor in the available lifesaving equipment. Telecommunications puts the lifeguards in immediate contact with the main lifeguard station, the beach manager's office, the local medical unit, or police post. Telephone and/or radio hookup between the main lifeguard station and any rescue vehicles or powered rescue craft should be part of the lifesaving procedure. The faster injured persons can be attended to, the greater the probability that injuries will be restricted and less complicated by excessive time lapse between rescue and medical attention.

Lifeguard Rotation Schedules

Beaches, pools, and lakefront operations may vary insofar as opening and closing times are concerned, but it is very likely that some facilities will start their operations at 8:00 A.M. and close down at 11:00 P.M. This means that at least three shifts of guards must be employed to provide proper coverage of the waterfront or aquatic facility area. Morning hours of operation, except on weekends, will probably serve children, with few adults present. As the day wears on, more and more patrons will participate at the facility. Peak loads will occur during the hottest part of the day, between 11:30 A.M. and 4:00 P.M. This capacity use will differ among localities. Previous experience and recourse to whatever attendance records are maintained will supply information on which lifeguard assignment may be based.

Assignment of guards should be such that there is sufficient coverage at all times, with the greatest coverage, i.e., the number of lifeguards on station, being during the heaviest concentration of use at the aquatic area. Lifeguards should be scheduled so that one shift begins work when the waterfront is open. A second shift should report for duty at noon, and the last shift reports at 2:00 P.M. Each shift is on duty for nine hours, with a one-hour break for lunch or dinner. The maximum number of guards will be on station during the heaviest periods of patron use.

Guards may be scheduled for early, late, or midwatch assignments on a permanent basis, or there may be installed a rotating assignment so that each guard serves at least one week in each shift category. For those who request permanent late shifts, a more rapid rate of rotation through the other shifts may be achieved. Rotation of scheduled breaks for guards will be instituted during normal periods of operation. Depending upon the patron attendance at a facility, guards may stand down from duty after every 1½ hours for fifteen minutes or take a five-minute break after each fifty-five minutes of duty.

A typical rotation plan for pool guards, for example, may move each guard to another station at intervals of one-half-hour duty at each station. Thus, each guard serves at a fixed station, while two guards are assigned walking stations around the periphery of the pool. After three successive moves, one guard takes a fifteen minute rest. Since the guards come on duty at staggered intervals, the full compliment of guards always permits one to be on a break period throughout the course of the pool day. Such break periods are initiated only when all three shifts have reported in and there is maximum coverage available.

For lakefront and beachfront operations, regularly rotating scheduled breaks for guards will be instituted during days of normal attendance in order to guard the beach properly and to keep beaches and lakefronts open at all times. Where sufficient lifeguard staff is employed, two-man posts may permit one guard to stand down for five minutes after a fifty-five minute period on duty. Where the routine has been accepted in the minds of beach or lakefront users, the beach may be cleared five minutes before the hour for break periods by guards. In this way, lifeguards will obtain sufficient respite from the normal activities required of them and continue to be vigilant in the performance of their duties and responsibilities.

Lifeguard Training

Beach operations vary in extensiveness and are determined by waterfront accessibility and presence of beaches along the oceanfront. Whether publicly or privately operated, lifeguard training programs are essential if the beach operator is to escape charges of negligence. Beaches that are open for public or invitee use carry the responsibility for providing some sort of lifesaving capability. When individuals are invited to participate in aquatic activities, there are inherent dangers that can be mitigated only by thorough preparation and the expectation that individuals will behave inappropriately. The inability to swim or use other aquatic skills that are called for, the suddeness of being overwhelmed by a crashing wave, pulled down by a strong undertow, or hurled into a jetty may cause panic and submersion of even competent swimmers. This is the basic reason for having lifeguards standing by.

Lifeguard training begins with the recruitment and enrolling of trainees in some lifeguard preparatory course provided over a four-to-six-month period. The course is devoted to the following schedule:

1. Lifesaving techniques. This includes all of the procedures for swimming and nonswimming rescues. It encompasses water approaches to those in trouble, holds, releases, and carries. It offers instruction in rescue techniques from water craft as well as the use of torpedo bouys, lifelines, reels, and a variety of ring bouys or tubes.
2. Training also requires the daily workout of potential lifeguards by building up stamina through lap swimming of up to one mile each day.
3. The course also deals with first aid procedures, especially that of resuscitation of inhalator, pulmotor, or mouth-to-mouth techniques.
4. Crowd control. This topic is covered through lectures and demonstrations by supervisory personnel. Discussions concerning the management of people so that they do not get in the way of rescue work as well as the control of behaviors that are undesirable on the part of patrons

are treated in this section of the course. Emergency procedures and signals are also learned.
5. Employee discipline. This concerns the appearance, punctuality, conduct, and the rules and regulations governing the employees' behavior while serving as a lifeguard.
6. The use and maintenance of all lifesaving equipment. This part of the course deals with the care and handling of all of the rescue and guarding equipment and facilities that will be used by the lifeguard during the time of employment. The various watercraft to be used, their characteristics as rescue vessels insofar as water conditions are concerned are thoroughly explained. Additionally, the use of lines and reels for heavy surf rescue; the placement of life lines, anchors, and bouys; the use of lifeguard towers and scuba and air hose diving gear may also be covered in terms of care of equipment and its use.
7. A written examination as well as an oral test plus a practical demonstration of lifeguard and first aid skills completes the course. Those who successfully pass the course are given numerical grades of qualification. A list of candidates is developed based upon the grade received in the training course. If the candidate accepts employment, a beach assignment is than given by the employing organization.
8. A waterfront manual may also be issued to employees. Especially is this done in smaller departments where fewer than fifty lifeguards are employed at various waterfront locations. The larger the department, the less likely is it that printed manuals will be distributed. This is probably unfortunate, because manuals can accurately spell out the details of the lifeguard position without equivocation. Then there is no excuse for poor performance in the sense that the employee could have forgotten some of the rules, regulations, and procedures for maintaining a safe beach.

The Lifeguard Manual

Organizations that employ lifeguards would do well to publish and distribute a manual covering all of the personnel policies, behavioral expectations, rules, regulations, personal appearance, emergency procedures, characteristics of the various waterfronts at which lifeguards are assigned, and other topics that are considered to be significant in maintaining the safety of patrons. The typical manual offers the following material and information for use by lifeguards:

1. Organizational chart of the division. This provides a schematic of the line and staff arrangement of authority and responsibility between the lifeguard and superiors.
2. General instructions concerning seasonal personnel. This material provides information about employee conduct, responsibilities to the department/organization, and any activities that require police action.
3. Specific rules for employee conduct. These are detailed requirements

to which the lifeguard will conform. They deal with conduct while on duty, days off, uniforms, manners toward patrons, rule and regulation enforcement, use of alcoholic beverages or drugs, making required reports to supervisors, lost and found turn-in, and other activities a lifeguard would ordinarily be requested to perform.

4. Public relations. The subject of providing patrons of the beach with prompt and courteous service is reflected in this section of the manual. It may also deal with the providing of information to news media, conformity to organizational policies, and offering factual information to those who ask about the organization or the operation of the beach.
5. Emergency procedures. This topic covers such diverse information as fire information, fire fighting, contact with local fire stations, fire classification, and any extinguishing procedures and equipment provided by the organization. Additionally, there will be a section devoted to accident and injury cases. This will specify what information is to be gathered, what forms are to be used, and how to file a situational report of the type, place, time, and consequences of the accident. There will be information given for the use of resuscitation devices.
6. Employee duties and functions. A detailed statement concerning each position that the organization enrolls for beach operation is given in this section. This material deals with the precise daily activities that should be undertaken by the particular employee. This may range from a general statement concerning management of the beach or waterfront to the patrolling of the beach or waterfront sector assigned to the lifeguard.
7. Rules and regulations governing patron conduct. This will be a detailed statement of the organization and operation of the waterfront facility for aquatic and other recreational use by patrons. It often refers to whatever local or state ordinances or legislation permits the control of waterfront areas to governmental agencies or may refer to the power of corporations as owners of property in the event of private operation. These regulations govern such diverse matters as hazardous objects brought to the beach, swimming in certain areas, prohibition of certain activities or behavior, sanitary code violations, hours of waterfront operation when the public is permitted to use the beach or water area.
8. In-service training procedures. This section covers the need for continuous first aid practice, physical conditioning drills, and emergency signals and procedures for use under any given type of accident, including submerged victim search techniques.
9. Records, reports, and forms. There may be materials added to the manual dealing with appropriate records, reports, forms, and filing procedures to be taken in the event of accident, injury, or drowning. There may also be illustrative materials concerning time sheets, requests for supplies, and other necessary equipment.
10. Priority items. Of supreme importance is the statement that prevention of death is the primary object of the waterfront program. Second priority will be given to the prevention of serious injuries. This requires constant vigilance on the part of lifeguards so that foolish or intempe-

rate behavior will not result in injuries from diving or swimming where there are obvious hazards, e.g., rocks, cliffs, wharf, jetty, or other obstructions. Finally, the prevention of minor accidents that can occur because patrons do not pay attention to rules or regulations. This requires the prevention of the use of hard objects in swimming areas.

The utilization of a manual of this type can clearly spell out organizational needs and concerns with regard to beach operation. Manuals call for particular safety objectives to be met by lifeguards and other beach supervisors; provide detailed statements concerning how, when, and where emergency procedures will be used; call upon employees to adhere to the basic guidelines that have been established by the agency so that risks to personal safety on the part of patrons and employees will be reduced, if not completely eliminated; and enumerate the responsibilities that personnel have in carrying out their duties.

The manual has another useful effect. It prevents any misunderstanding as to what an employee should or should not be doing during the course of each day on the job. It explains the need to perform in specific ways and concentrates the reader's attention on important subjects that every waterfront safety program requires. In short, the manual is designed as a primary safety guide for organizational employees and may be utilized as a standard against which employee conduct may be compared. It will also serve as a useful piece of evidence in any alleged case of negligence to show that the organization has developed a well-conceived and logical plan of action to safeguard the health, welfare, and safety of patrons. Adherence to the manual of procedures can be the surest way to prevent accidents from occurring. If accidents do occur, the practices developed in the manual may prevent a tragedy and will assuredly be used to refute any claims of substandard practice on the part of employees.

The Lake Waterfront Program

Unlike ocean beaches or riverfront beaches, the lakefront aquatic program probably does not have to worry about tides, currents, and whirlpools. Except for extremely windy days, it is rare that excessively high waves will ever become a problem. For those few days, it is well to shut down the lakefront operation. Any public or private organization may operate a lakefront aquatic program. Communities that are situated on a lake, private youth or adult camps, hotels, spas, and resorts may all own a lake, lease or rent lake frontage, or operate aquatic programs on lakes that are near enough to their property to make such use feasible.

Depending upon the age group to be safeguarded and the objective of the waterfront operation, aquatic activities and the physical layout of the swimming, boating, or diving area, the waterfront will be patrolled. As in all organized or free play aquatic activities, lifeguarding becomes a question of prevention rather than rescue.

Camps, by their very nature, operate waterfronts on both an instructional and recreational basis. The camp, at the very beginning of the season, needs to segregate the campers into several groups. These represent swimming and diving skills ranging from novice to advanced. Campers who cannot swim at all are provided with the necessary instruction in shallow water areas. Intermediate and advanced swimmers are provided with swimming and diving areas that afford them opportunities to practice skills, gain stamina and strength, and learn lifesaving and water safety techniques.

The lakefront aquatic program may or may not have a beach from which to work. If there is a beach, almost always man-made by removal of trees and the dumping of sand on the area to be converted to the strand, the waterfront director will assign counselors to lifeguard and to instruct during the time that each counselor's group has an aquatic activity period. The waterfront staff typically consists of a director and an assistant, with counselors holding lifesaving and water safety instructor's certificates designated as instructors for the various groups that use the lake. There may also be small craft specialists employed by the camp to further supplement the waterfront staff. If scuba diving and water skiing are also provided, other specialists may be employed, unless one or more counselors possess the skills necessary for instructional purposes.

The lakefront beach may be organized as is the oceanfront beach. There will be a crib area, set off by lifelines and bouys for nonswimmers and beginners. An intermediate swimming area will also be designated for those who can participate in swimming activities but who have not yet become sufficiently skilled to swim long distances or perform complicated strokes. An area will be set aside for advanced swimmers. These are persons who may be highly skilled swimmers and who will want to learn junior or senior life saving techniques or even earn water safety instructor's certificates—if they are old enough to qualify.

Where the nature of the lake does not permit direct access to the water from a beach or sloping ground, it may be necessary to construct a swimming dock. The layout of the dock may approximate a variety of shapes and sizes. A, double A (AA), H, I, L, M, T, F, E, Y, and enclosed docks are all commonly used. Docks should be constructed of durable material that can be permanently installed and be able to withstand the rigors of winter weather and freezing conditions without mishap. Many camps utilize temporary dock installations and remove the structures at the end of the camping season. While this may protect the structures from physical damage, it also promotes a certain amount of instability, maintenance, and possible hazards to camper safety.

In the illustration an M dock is used to define a lakefront aquatic facility. Campers may enter the dock from any one of three entry points. The beginner's area is clearly marked, and campers are directed to enter that area by counselors acting as lifeguards and other specialists who are available for swimming instruction. Intermediates are directed to the other section of the M under the same circumstances so that the two least skilled groups are served by a completely enclosed area with the shore at the fourth side. The depth of the water for beginners will not be greater than 3½ feet, while that for intermediate swimmers may be up to five feet. Advanced swimmers will be enabled to swim along the long side of the M, outside of the dock area, but within a section segregated by lifelines and attached to two floating rafts that are anchored approximately twenty-five yards from the ends of the dock. There will always be counselors in the intermediate and beginning swimming areas with campers. Counselors will serve as instructors and lifeguards. Lifeguard stations will be equipped with reaching poles and ring bouys. A constant boat patrol will be in effect during all swimming periods.

SWIMMING POOL OPERATION AND SAFETY

Without any question, swimming pools serve an extremely important part in contributing to the recreational enjoyment of most persons who want to learn how to swim or participate in the various phases of an aquatic program on a year-round basis. Except for outdoor swimming pools in climates that permit swimming in cold weather months, indoor pools satisfy the aquatic needs of persons of all ages throughout the year. Unlike natural bodies of water, which may contain a number of hidden dangers, swimming pools

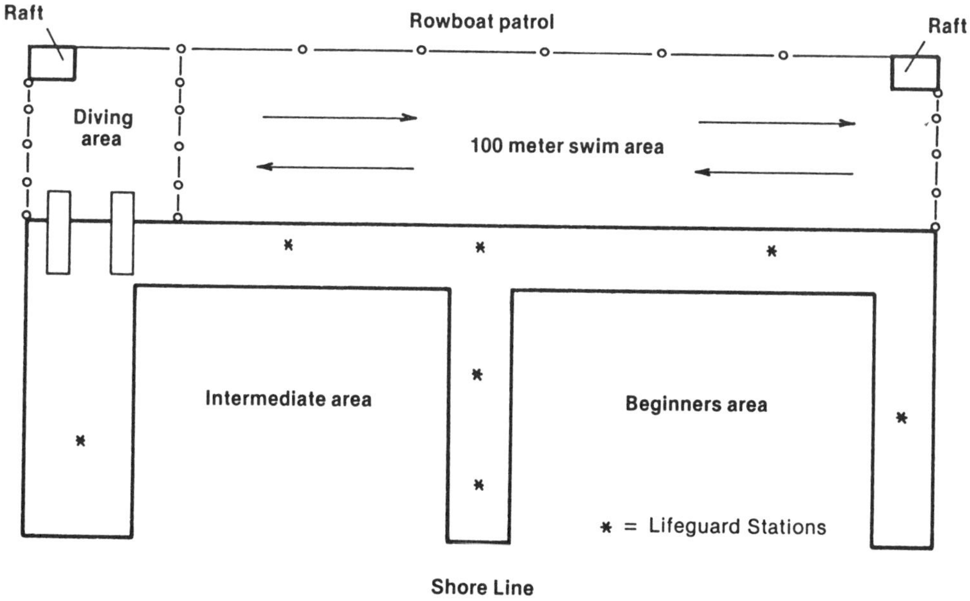

Lakefront aquatic dock for comprehensive safety coverage.

provide both clean water and visibility that should permit the safest kind of environment possible. Nevertheless, there are dangers to which swimming pools contribute. Among these are poorly planned, designed, and constructed facilities; poorly sited illumination fixtures; poor site location as to the pool itself; hazardous diving conditions; and a number of behavior related problems that add to the risks of swimming.

Pool Operation

Pools vary in size, shape, and use. Some public pools are of a standard rectangular shape, twenty-five yards long and sixteen yards wide. Such a pool might have one to three diving boards. The typical motel swimming pool is fewer than twenty yards long and proportionately reduced in width. It generally has only one diving board. Of course, pools may range up to several hundred meters long and half as wide with separate diving wells and the capacity for carrying a patron load of many thousands of persons each day. Under all of these circumstances, the need for pool behavior regulations, emergency procedures, and employed lifeguards is obvious.

The composition of the swimming pool staff varies from location to location without any standardized pattern manifested. The job assignments in pool operation are performed by persons with a number of different titles and responsibilities. At some pools, one worker will perform a number of different tasks, e.g., the pool manager or supervisor may also serve as head lifeguard and filtration plant operator. This is typical of small pool operations.

As the pool size increases and the potential patron carrying capacity gets larger, the need for increased numbers of pool staff to operate the facility also increases. The number of paid employees staffing a pool will depend, to a great extent, upon the type of pool, i.e., its use, bathhouse location, hours of operation, patron volume, pool shape, and the needs for specialized personnel for maintenance and/or filtration operation. The number of employees required to operate a pool fluctuates with conditions and size and may range from a low of one to a high of thirty in an extensive operation. Several kinds of workers may be employed. The essential personnel are lifeguards. Other workers may include such titles as pool manager, cashier, locker room attendant, filtration operator, and vendors of merchandise.

Lifeguard Staff

The patron volume, location of diving facilities, pool size, and shape tend to determine how many lifeguards will be needed for adequate patron protection. Small pools probably require only one guard. Pools between twenty-five and fifty meters in length and twenty-five meters in width with a separate diving well that are open to the public will require a complement of six lifeguards. As the pool size increases the necessity for additional guards also grows.

Pool Accidents

Slipping on wet pool decks or running and sliding constitute the most frequent causes of injuries associated with swimming pools. Pushing, fighting, or other reckless activity is the next greatest cause. Diving is the pool activity that will probably produce the most serious kind of injury. To be sure, there is always the likelihood that someone who cannot swim will slip and fall into the pool, that an individual will overestimate capability and become a submersion victim, or that a person could hurt himself by swimming into the wall of the pool.

For the most part, however, a serious and persistent error occurs in pool design that always builds in a dangerous condition that invariably leads to fatal or severe injury. The incorporation of improper dimensions and depth for safe diving from springboards and platforms creates an unacceptable hazard that can be easily avoided. Standards for the construction of safe diving wells in pools have been formulated by several national organizations.[2]

Adequate depth must be allowed for a diver reaching the bottom of a pool fifteen or more feet from the front end of the springboard. Thus the upward slope from the diving well must be slanted so that the diver will not come into traumatic impact with the slope. There must be sufficient distance between the diving board and the pool side—at least ten feet for one-meter boards and twelve feet for three-meter boards. Depth beneath the board and toward the pool wall on which the board is situated must permit sufficient depth so that divers are safe. All dimensions, especially those concerned with the distance that a diver traverses in the air with the assistance of a springboard, must be adequate to prevent sudden impact with the pool bottom.

SMALL CRAFT USE AND SAFETY

Almost all natural bodies of water and some artificial empoundments permit the use of small water craft for recreational purposes. A number of organizations may be engaged in the rental of, instruction concerning, or the selling of excursions in small crafts. Such organizations may be private, public, or agency camps; business enterprises that rent a variety of water vessels for use on an hourly, daily, weekly, or longer basis; and excursion oriented enterprises that take tourists and other enthusiasts on trips in powered and unpowered vessels. These latter activities may be with a traditional water craft, but they are almost always associated with white water

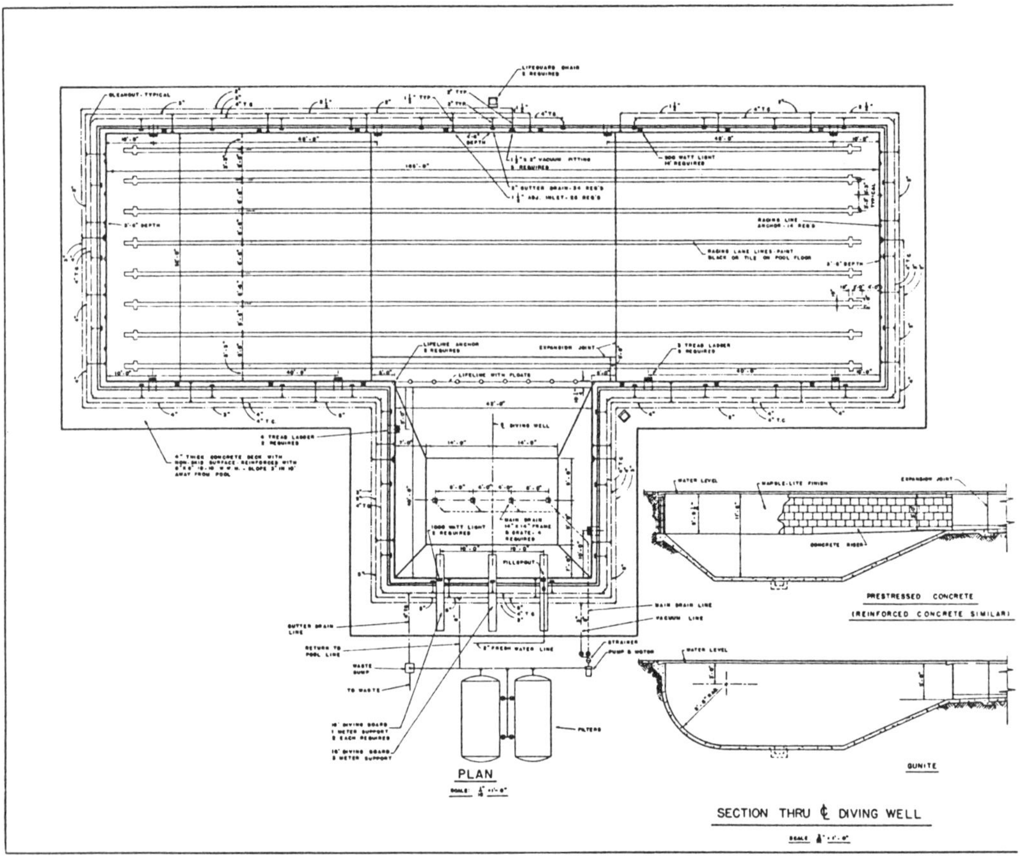

Good pool design shows adequate width and depth for diving well.

(rapids) conditions and relatively remote environments. Additionally, tubing or the use of large inner tubes as the vessel for floatation are used to convey a participant down a swiftly flowing stream, river, or white water course.

Small crafts are limited to rowboats, canoes, kayaks, and small sailboats. Although sailing is extremely popular along the seacoasts of the nation and in the inland regions where lake or river access permits it, only a small percentage of the population has ever learned to sail. Safety rules and regulations developed by the American Red Cross or the United States Coast Guard should be utilized to insure the safe handling of small crafts by any participant. In the following pages, material concerning the safety aspects and possible liability problems will be offered. The scope of the text does not permit the detailed coverage of instructional methods and types or vessels that can be utilized.

Boating

Rowing is the simplest and easiest form of boating that can be included within the small craft aquatic program. Rowboats, in a number of varieties, are used in ponds, lakes, coastal waterways, rivers, and wherever water is sufficiently deep to permit access. Rowboats provide a relatively safe means of transportation on waterways, even for the unskilled swimmer. Rowing requires little skill and can be mastered within a few minutes by the rankest novice. However, there are certain aspects of rowing that call for considerable skill, and these must be practiced under proficient supervision before the participant can excel.

For those who like to fish from a boat, rowing is a requisite skill that must be achieved before many fishing experiences can be undertaken. Rowing is one technique that can be utilized in rescue procedures from the water. Skilled boat handling must be used when attempting rescues from ocean surf. Rowing also calls for a high degree of skill if it is used for competitive purposes.

The hazards inherent in boating activities can be overcome if common sense is used and participants are alerted to the need for maintaining control. First of all, boaters should be qualified swimmers. While it is true that one need not be an excellent swimmer, it is just good judgment to be able to remain calm and be able to think logically in a frightening situation. The ability to swim may provide the margin of difference between survival and death. At the very least, a person who uses a rowboat should be able to maintain himself in the water. No rowboat should ever be overloaded with passengers. While rowboats may be able to accommodate a number of people simultaneously, it is always better to reduce the number of those who enter a a boat to a load that will avoid capsizing. The boat may be built to handle two or more passengers, but it is wiser to leave a space vacant than to risk the possibility of overloading the boat and causing it to become swamped. No

DON'T OVERLOAD—THAT COULD BE DISASTROUS.

Overloading contributes to the hazards of boating. *(Courtesy of the American Red Cross.)*

individual who uses a rowboat should ever engage in horseplay or rock the boat. These activities are fraught with peril and can result in capsizing or swamping the boat. Passengers should stay in their respective seats. If changes have to be made, the boat should be landed at the nearest shore. Changes in seating arrangements may be performed, if absolutely necessary, by trimming the craft at each stage of the transfer. That means that each person must move with the others in the boat so that it remains relatively steady. This is done by crouching so that a low center of gravity is maintained, thereby insuring that the boat does not capsize. As one individual moves from his place to another, the gunwales are grasped and movement is made toward the vacated seat. The rower shifts his weight to one side so that the passenger can slip into the seat beside him. The rower then vacates his seat and executes the same maneuvers to the passenger's vacated seat, while the new rower shifts his weight to the middle. One other common sense safety rule should be observed. If a boat is overturned or swamped, it will remain afloat even though it is awash. Passengers should stay with the boat, which will maintain their weight and continue to float until help arrives.

Canoeing

The canoe is generally looked upon as an extremely unstable craft by those who really do not know anything about its natural properties. The myth of unstability is readily scotched. In competent hands, the canoe is one of the safest and most seaworthy of all watercraft. Its extreme bouyancy makes it practically unsinkable; however, some precautions have to be taken in canoeing as in any other activity. The ability to swim is of paramount importance, but this skill by itself does not guarantee safety. Several other conditions must be met. Canoeing skills should be acquired before an individual is permitted to participate. This is particularly true for young campers or other novices who might want to be active on canoe trips. Safety procedures should be thoroughly learned by all who want to take part in canoeing, especially if such activity includes excursions to distant locations or days of travel.

Rafting and Tubing

Rubber rafts comes in all sizes and shapes and have been used successfully in different aquatic area situations. Typical is the six-person raft, although some rafts may be large enough for one person only. Of course, there are rafts that can accommodate ten or more people. However, unless the raft is motorized, it is unwise to load so many passengers aboard. This is of even greater importance if rafts are to be used for passage on swift streams and fast running rivers.[3] A rubber raft should be durable and easily mended in the

A basic safety procedure—stay with the overturned canoe.

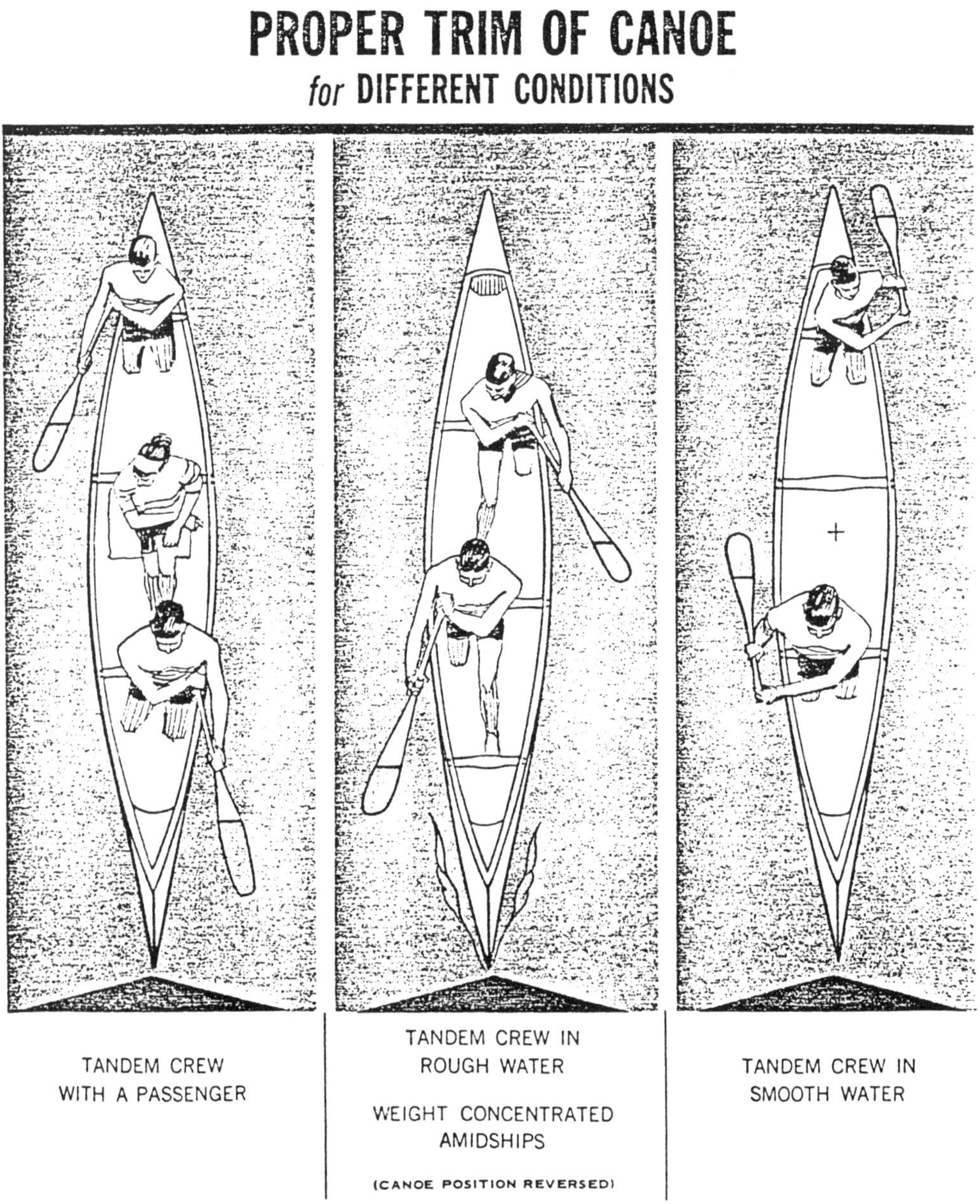

Lowering the center of gravity by kneeling in the canoe is far safer than sitting on the seats. ***(Courtesy of the American Red Cross.)***

PROPER TRIM OF CANOE
for DIFFERENT CONDITIONS

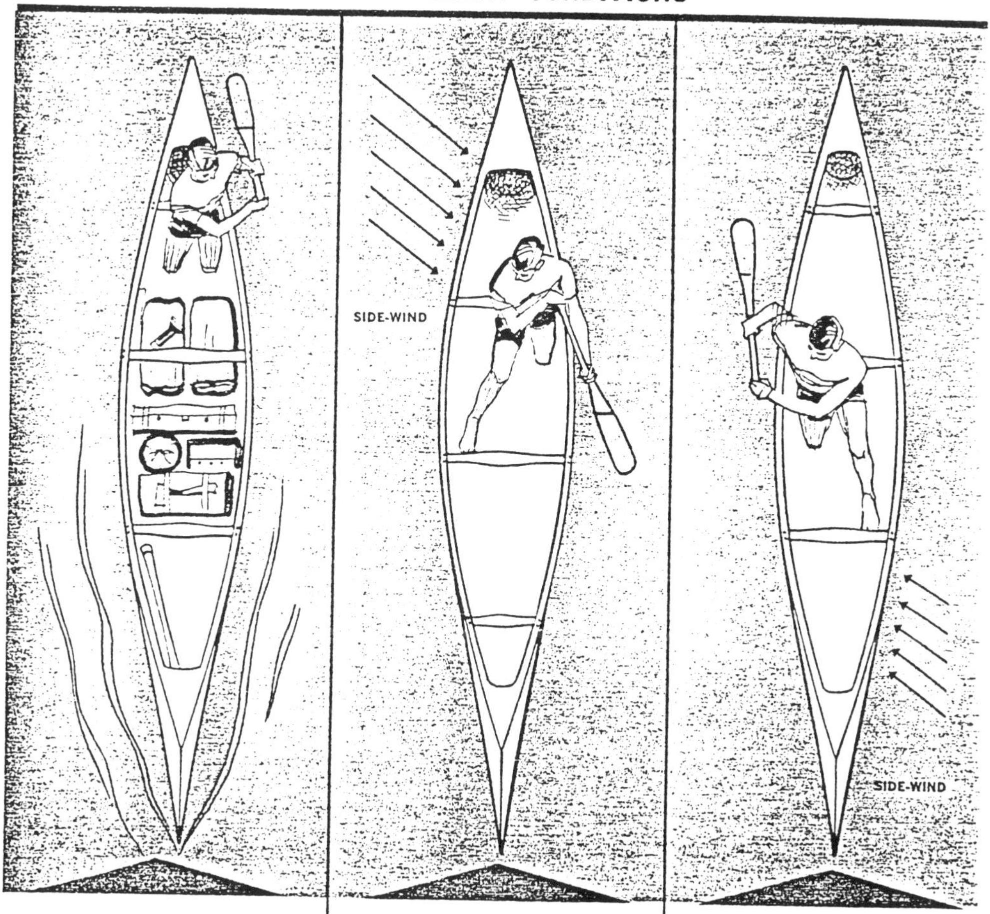

ONE MAN IN SMOOTH WATER, WITH DUFFLE ABOARD

ONE MAN IN A MODERATE SIDE-WIND OR A STERN-WIND

(CANOE POSITION REVERSED)

ONE MAN IN STRONG HEAD- OR SIDE-WIND, OR WHEN MAXIMUM MANEUVERABILITY IS NEEDED IN FAST WATER OR RAPIDS event of a tear in the fabric. It should contain no fewer than two separate inflation chambers. A lifeline will be strung around the outside of the raft. A lead line or painter will be attached to the front end of the raft.

All persons participating in rafting, whether as passengers or paddlers, should be equipped with proper flotation devices that will be worn at all times while riding the rafts. Repair kits should be carried in the raft so that in the event of damage to the craft immediate repairs can be made. Large rips in the fabric will have to be sewn before any patching can be attempted. Once the rip is sewn, the area around the damage can be roughed by using a file, sandpaper, emery cloth, or other such material so that patches can be glued on.

In rafts the best paddling positions will depend upon the size of the craft and the number of paddlers and/or passengers. It should be noted, however, that the best position for the paddler's protection will be sitting on the sides or pontoons of the raft. No paddler should kneel with knees on the bottom of the raft because the pliable skin of the raft could permit injuries to the paddler if the raft bottom were to strike some hidden object beneath the surface. No passenger or paddler should ever dangle his or her legs over the sides of the raft.

Tubes

Tubes have become something of a commercial venture in recent years. Local business persons may set up rental facilities along swiftly flowing rivers or where there are rapids and waterfalls. Tubing may be enjoyable, but it can also be quite dangerous to the uninitiated. There are no paddles with a tube. The passenger simply sits within the opening, casts off, and is carried downstream and through any rapids that are encountered. All tubers should wear a life jacket. The hazards of tubing in swift waters are probably greater than those for canoeing or rafting because there is no chance to steer a tube. Even the frantic efforts of hand paddling will be ineffective in changing direction or slowing a descent. The tuber is at the mercy of the stream.

Renters of tubes may find themselves defendants in a liability action against them if individuals are injured while tubing. The commercial operator of such a rental business should know the waterway that is being used and must inform the person who rents equipment of the likely hazards to be found. Furthermore, life vests or PFD's must also be supplied. Children and teenagers are most often found to be patrons of tubing activities. These are the very people who will take unnecessary risks and fail to wear a PFD. All that the renter can do is provide the equipment, instruct the person in the use of it, warn that the PFD must be worn, and then hope that the participant will follow directions. Of course, if the directions are also supplemented by threat of denying access to the tubes if PFD's are not worn, this may serve as a deterrent against unruly or substandard behavior.

Although the commercial renters of tubes cannot force tube users to wear protective gear such as high-top sneakers, knee pads, or helmets, they can promote such wear by notifying the tuber of any dangers that are known about the water course to be passaged. Organizations that can enforce protective gear use, e.g., camps, public recreational service departments, or other enterprises that have control over the behavior of their membership, must see that protective gear is worn. Furthermore, they also have the responsibility for knowing of any hazards that exist on any river that they intend for their members to use. They must also follow the same safety procedures for tubing as would be in effect for other small craft operations. While supplies and equipment could not be carried in a tube, supervisors must be placed in strategic locations along the waterway so that assistance can be rendered at any point where tubers might have trouble.

Skin and Scuba Diving

Skin diving is swimming underwater while breath-holding. Underwater movement is aided through the use of swim fins for the feet, a watertight mask for the face, and a snorkle device that assists breathing while the swimmer is focusing on objects beneath the surface. Scuba diving, on the other hand, requires a self-contained underwater breathing apparatus. This means that the diver is equipped with a mask, fins, air tank, and regulator.

Organizations that permit skin and scuba diving in swimming pools need not worry about the hazards that can be encountered underwater. Pool use for diving is probably best for instruction in both activities. In the pool, under certified personnel, participants are required to perform standard series of exercises and practices after undergoing a comprehensive physical examination to determine fitness for such programs. Obviously, the individual who wishes to participate must be a swimmer of some expertise, capable of continuous swimming for relatively long distances and able to participate in the rescue of another person. The skin diving course consists of a series of lectures covering the type of equipment used and the selection of apparatus. Maintenance of equipment, the aquatic environment that may be encountered, physical laws associated with skin diving including an understanding of gases bouyancy and the water medium itself are all part of the information given. Physiological problems in descent and ascent, first aid practices, and hazards that may be encountered are offered. Among the hazards may be marine animals that sting, pinch, bite, or puncture; tides; currents; waves; and underwater obstacles or potential traps. In addition there will be direct water instruction utilizing the skin diving equipment, communication system to be used, and a checking system developed to keep participants under close observation and skin diving instruction that develops underwater skills. All of these must be conducted under proper supervision by highly trained and competent persons. If the organization does not have a safe environment such as a swimming pool to use for its indoctrination and initial instructional activities, it must find other protected aquatic areas so that the program can be carried on with minimum possibility of danger to the participants.

Scuba diving requires an even more stringent application of safety rules and regulations to protect the health and welfare of participants. A more complicated and longer course of instruction is necessary because of the mechanical devices and techniques that must be learned. There will be familiarization with all necessary apparatus, including the purpose, construction, and maintenance of each item. Additionally, the fitting out of all equipment will be performed. Such methods as defogging the mask, equalizing pressure, use of safety equipment, and purging will be assimilated by participants prior to any water instruction. Once the basic understanding of scuba diving is accomplished, swimming tests will be administered to determine proficiency and lifesaving capability. Diving first aid is an important component of the scuba course and incorporates such measures as treatment for bleeding, shock, and a variety of wounds.

A regular first aid course should be a part of any scuba diving program. Diving physics will also be provided, particularly Boyle's Law on gases, buoyancy principles, and the various pressure effects, e.g., absolute, ambient, gauge, and atmospheric. In-water lessons will include water entry, communications, gear release and recovery, buoyancy problems, and the various pathological aspects that may be encountered because of depth, pressure, and the effects of gas. Thus, air embolism, emphysema, lung punctures, narcosis, oxygen poisoning, and decompression sickness will be explained in terms of causes, preventions, and cures. Decompression dives should not be permitted despite the fact that decompression tables may be provided to participants so that they may know now to avoid these dives.

Once the participants have been instructed in the use of the gear including regulators, tanks, and safety equipment, a continuation of in-water instruction and practice may be performed. Participants will be given instruction in such techniques as removing gear and donning gear underwater, buddy breathing, bouyancy practice, and all other necessary instruction so that safe scuba diving habits will be ingrained in each participant. Finally open water training dives will be attempted. Of course, it will be necessary for the instructor to ascertain any potential hazards that might be encountered in the open water areas. These will include currents, tides, or waves (if any), marine life that might be encountered, underwater obstacles present, and other hazards.

Body Surfing, Wind Surfing, and Board Surfing

Most, if not all, of the surfing activities will be conducted on beach fronts that are lapped by ocean water. Long swells and waves make the ideal medium by which all forms of surfing may be performed. There are, however,

Proper gear, appropriate instruction, and not diving alone are the keys to safety in scuba diving.

a number of organizations that sponsor surfing on lakes, rivers, and even in swimming pools where artificial waves are produced by wave-making machines. Essentially, the surfer simply positions himself in the ocean swell just before the wave begins to crest. The surfer then paddles vigorously into the wave until the body or board is travelling slightly in front of the breaking wave or "tube." By maneuvering body or board, the surfer is enabled to maintain momentum and ride the wave to shore. Body surfing means that waves are ridden without any equipment. The surfer simply swims onto the back of a wave, waiting for the crest, and then with arms outstretched and body arched, lets the water carry him onto the beach.

Board surfing is performed much the same way, except that the board becomes the craft on which the surfer rides instead of using only his body for the ride. The actual skill of board and windsurfing is beyond the scope of this book.

Wind surfing combines the surf board and a hand operated sail whose mast is seated in the board. The surfer manipulates the sail according to wind, wave, and tidal conditions while standing on the board.

Water Skiing

Water skiing is the adaptation of light ski-type equipment to water use. The skier is pulled along in the wake of a motor driven boat, either with inboard or outboard engine. Proper equipment including skis of a size and length associated with the weight of the user, ski tow ropes with handles or grips and a life jacket round out the equipment that can be used. Of course, a variety of ski types may be obtained for specific performance. Among the facilities required for the instruction of water skiing are a protected teaching area, boat mooring dock, and provisions for the maintenance of all equipment.

SAFETY GUIDELINES FOR NONSWIMMING FACILITIES

Among the facilities currently being used throughout the United States are spas and hot tubs as well as water slides. Such use may not be controlled by adequate legislation so that the health and safety of users are protected. Control of infectious diseases may become a significant factor if proper precautions are not taken in the design, operation, and maintenance of these facilities.

Spas and Hot Tubs

Spas and hot tubs may be utilized for any number of reasons including relaxation and therapeutic use or for social activities that may be carried on within the confines of the container. Neither spas nor hot tubs are for swimming and diving purposes because they are too shallow to support such activity. These pools are not drained, cleaned, and refilled after each use, but they are closed cycle water systems composed of water circulation, filtration, heating, and overflow systems. Sometimes a disinfectant system is also integrated into the water circulation system. In most instances, spas and hot tubs with installed heaters usually have automatic temperature controls. A public spa or hot tub can, depending upon its size, site, and carrying capacity accommodate from one to ten bathers.

The major categories of health and safety problems fall into a number of distinct groups: drug and alcohol abuse, water temperature, sanitation, and accessways. A real problem concerning hot tub or public spa use is the combination of drug use, drug abuse, and the temperature of the pool. In some instances fatalities have been recorded when users have fallen asleep as a result of accelerated dissemination of harmful chemical substances in the blood stream through the effects of hot water.[4] The high temperatures of the spas or hot tubs invariably contribute to a condition of drowsiness, and the victims have drowned. It is imperative that systematic and constant checking of patrons by operators must be given the highest priority if such incidents are to be avoided. As is true of almost any recreational use of any facility, the key element will be direct supervision of users of the facility. Moreover, patrons who insist upon using alcohol or drugs should be warned against possible fatal consequences. Persons who are obviously controlled substance users/abusers or inebriated should be prohibited from using the facility.

Infectious diseases may be spread due to the type of equipment employed in the hot tub and spa industry. If water conditions and safe disinfectant residuals are not properly maintained, serious risk to personal health could be the outcome. Hourly checking of temperature and water conditions for a safe level of disinfectant residuals is an essential practice and must be strictly enforced. Whatever local or state health codes that apply to the operation of public spas and hot tubs should be enforced by unannounced visits and inspections of the premises by authorized health department personnel.

Accessibility to public spas and hot tubs is a potential danger spot due to the wet and filmy condition of surfaces where patrons enter and exit from the facility. Falls resulting in serious injury could occur. To prevent such accidents, appropriate design, construction, and maintenance of the equipment should be mandatory. This requires that nonskid surfaces be installed; handholds, steps, or ladders must be planned so that they afford the safest means for entry and exiting the facility without great effort on the patrons's part. Materials utilized in the construction of these facilities should be of substances that are harmless to users and capable of fulfilling the design purposes for which they have been made. The facility should be constructed according to whatever local building code regulations are in effect as well as be engineered to provide a sound, long-lived structure that will safely carry the loads it is built to handle. The spas and hot tubs should be of a nontoxic, watertight, smooth, and easily maintained material for sanitary objectives. Other construction features will conform to appropriate heating and temperature requirements; electrical equipment codes; and water circulation system, filtration system, disinfectant and chemical procedures for sanitizing the water and all other associated areas, surfaces, and installations that have an effect upon the healthful and safe use of facilities.

Water Slides

Water slides or flumes are facilities that incorporate the exhilaration of a one-hundred-yard slide together with a curvilinear smooth-surfaced channel partially filled with flowing water that enables a patron to plummet downhill and end up in a 3 ½-foot-deep pool. Generally, sliders can plunge down a thirty-foot vertical drop in complete safety. There is no possibility of a slider falling off or out of the slide. Operators can easily supervise patron use so that any pushing or shoving and crowding is entirely eliminated. Furthermore, patron behavior can be carefully regulated so that reckless behavior that might cause accidents and injuries is not permitted. No equipment is necessary except the slide and water recirculating pumps as well as the appropriate disinfecting chemical to maintain a healthful water condition. Nevertheless, accidents sometimes occur.[5]

The water slide is constructed from slick fiberglass sections that are implanted in a cement bed that also carries the water pipes for recirculation. Approximately twelve hundred gallons of recirculating water rush down the chute every minute. The flowing water forms a stream several inches deep, and it is this combination of gravity, running water, and body weight that makes the slide an attractive and commercially successful venture. If the site location and preparation is well selected, a number of different slide configurations may be used to permit several slides simultaneously. When patron flow is efficiently handled almost five hundred sliders can be accommodated per hour. Patrons are controlled at the top of the slide by the operator's employee. A separate walkway is constructed from the lower pool to the top of the slide so that there is no danger of pedestrians encountering sliders at any time.

Fishing

Fishing falls within the category of a nonswimming aquatic activity, but there are instances when fishermen must know how to swim. Safety when fishing, either from a small craft, the shore, a pier, or while wading, is always governed by common sense and courtesy. Yet, it is not merely a matter of stating that common sense should be used by anyone participating in a recreational activity. That leaves too much to the presumption that everyone who engages in a recreational activity uses common sense. Unfortunately, as has been made abundantly clear, the facts show that this is not the case.

Organizations or institutions such as secondary school and camps, that promote a variety of fishing skills and activities make it a practice to insure that all participants have basic skills that are necessary if the activity is to prove enjoyable and safe. Educational or training institutions that have taken on the responsibility for teaching angling skills must provide adequate supervision, competent instruction, and appropriate equipment for participant use.

A number of instances have occurred where participants in fishing activities were badly hurt or blinded. These instances took place because one of the participants did not observe the simple safety rules that could have prevented the accident. In one instance, an adult wandered into an aquatic area where fly fishing was in progress. Despite signs warning hikers that they should not approach the area, this person ignored them and was hooked in the eye. There was no award for damage because no evidence could be shown that indicated that the fly caster had been negligent. Rather, the hiker had essentially contributed to his own injury.[6]

NOTES

1. Angus Phillips, "Swimmers Beware: Work With, Not Against, Rip Current," *The Hartford Courant,* Saturday, 7 July 1984, p. C7.

2. Dale Neuberger, "Common Design Errors in Aquatic Facilities," *Athletic Business* (October 1984): 88.

3. Philip May, "Proper Training Ensures Safety on Professional Raft Rides," *The Hartford Courant,* Sunday, 15 July 1984), p. F8.

4. U.S. Department of Health and Human Services, *Suggested Health and Safety Guidelines for Public Spas and Hot Tubs* (Atlanta, Ga.: Environmental Health Services Division, 1981), 1.

5. *Abee v. Stone Mountain Memorial Association,* Ga. 312 S.E. (2d) 142 (1983).

6. *Toca v. Rojas,* 152 La. 317, 93 So. 108 (1932).

15
Craft Facilities

Whether concerned with school shops, recreational craft rooms, camp craft activities, or culinary activities in kitchen like aras, there is a potential for danger both to instructor and participant. All environments that contain cutting, grinding, stamping, drilling, electrical, or chemical equipment can be hazardous. However, such facilities when properly equipped, arranged, and supervised, provide a relatively secure situation in which all persons of almost any age may enjoy themselves while learning new skills or improving upon those already learned.

CRAFT INSTRUCTION

The crafts instructor may be employed by public or private schools in grades ranging from one through twelve and on up to technical or vocational trade schools and colleges. Crafts instructors will also be employed by public and private recreational service agencies. Although the reasons for maintaining a shop program in schools vastly differ from those provided by recreational service agencies, the problems and outcomes are quite similar. The crafts instructor has the responsibility of caring for a wide assortment of tools, materials, and equipment for safe and effective operation. He or she must provide instruction in the safe use of all of the instruments with which pupils and participants work as well as information about the materials, activities to be performed, and equipment that will be necessary to acquire skill within the crafts program. In school oriented activities shop work is identified as being within the industrial arts program. Cooking and kitchen activities fall within the purview of the home economics department. All other craft activities are identified as something called arts and crafts. For purposes of this text, all references will be to crafts shops, instructors, and participants.

Despite maximum care, accidents can and do happen in the crafts shop. When these occur, the instructor, the employer, or both may be liable, depending upon a variety of factors prevailing at the time. It is only natural that craft instructors want to prevent any accidents from happening. First, such prevention safeguards the welfare of participants and supports the reason for the continuation of craft activities. Second, the instructor has a defensive purpose and that is to protect himself from liability. The third aspect is to protect the employing agency from having to face the onerous charges that usually result from litigation. For those reasons, instructors must become aware of the facts about the legal aspects of crafts shop accidents and injuries, work within the standards of care applicable for the prevention and reduction of accidents, and understand the conditions that would produce liability.

ACCIDENT-CAUSING SITUATIONS

There are a number of willful or completely spontaneous situations that may lead to accidents in craft activities. However, three major factors are particularly significant when it comes to the common causes of craft room injuries. Among these are: (1) hazardous conditions that concern machines, tools, and the arrangement of the facility itself; (2) careless performance that involves lowered standards of behavior than are normally thought to be acceptable insofar as safe practices are concerned; and (3) physiological inability or psychological deficiency on the part of participants. All of these factors may be a part of any sequence that results in an accident and injury. Sometimes these elements are associated. At least one of these conditions will always be found to be the proximate cause of accidental injury. Competent instructors must be alert to these elements, remove them or reduce their likelihood of existence, and thereby limit the possibility of future occurrences.

Equipment failure or environmental hazards will be rare if good maintenance practices are followed. The basic tenets of keeping the workplace free of debris and inspecting tools, machines, and other technological instruments for operating efficiency should preclude malfunction or other dangers to the participant. Nevertheless, unless good housekeeping practices are followed and enforced, craft-place conditions can deteriorate so that equipment failure or cluttered work space can produce an accidental injury. One example is the case of an adult vocational student who was enrolled in a shop class in order to augment his skills as a grinder. The injury occurred when the student switched on the multiple-speed grinder. The grinding wheel came apart causing serious injury to the user. It was determined that the machine was improperly guarded, and this was one of the facts that led to a judgment for the plaintiff.[1]

Psychological or physical disability may enter into unsafe behaviors. These include apathy resulting from poor attitudes, lack of ability to perform safely, insufficient knowledge about the activity in question, and physical and or mental disabilities. Legislation that has been enacted during the past ten years has far-reaching effects on those who may participate in craft activities. Federal Public Law 94–142 states, in part, "that appropriate education will be provided" to those with a variety of mental or physical disabilities. This means that more and more persons with some degree of mental retardation or physical disability will be taking part in crafts. To the extent that the disabled individuals can participate to the limit of their ability, they should be permitted to do so. However, supervision by the crafts instructor will have to be more intense and immediate than is usual.

Persons with defective vision, hearing loss, mental retardation, loss of hands or fingers, epilepsy, or other physical and mental problems that might prevent them from acting in a way to preserve their own welfare offer problems to crafts instructors that exceed the need for ordinary or higher care. Crafts instructors must be alerted to the nature of the mental or physical dysfunctions of these participants. This can be done if administrators, parents, and, in some cases, the individuals involved play the informative role in seeking appropriate solutions. Thus, the person suffering from psychomotor seizures can inform the instructor of the nature of his or her problem. Others will be more obvious. Whenever persons with physical or mental disabilities are participating in craft activities, an instructor competent to work with them should be on the job.

Probably the most insidious aspect of unsafe conditions relates to the adage, "A little knowledge is a dangerous thing." When participants are not given adequate information about the inherent dangers of certain crafts, particularly those dealing with electrical circuits, explosive mixtures, power machines, and the like, a sense of false security can be built up that evaporates upon accidental injury. Thorough indoctrination about accepted safety practices and fundamental instruction about tools, machines, and materials—not to mention specific craft skills—is essential. Insufficient information places the poorly informed participant in a situation that may merely dull an individual's precautions to hazards. This usually occurs when a person with poor skills tries to perform some activity that is quite above his or her level of ability. That this happens at all is part of the problem that is passed along by thoughtless instructors. The person who is charged with the responsibility of caring for others must be interested enough to provide complete information about the activity and all of its constituent parts. Preventing accidents lies with the development of proper attitudes toward safety as well as learning about the dangers that accompany complicated craft skills.

Safety Attitudes

Knowing about the cause and effect of accidents may reduce them, but one of the more salient features in eliminating accidents is in the development of sound attitudes toward safe practice. It is the instructor's responsibility to encourage positive attitudes to assist participants in acquiring a conscientious regard for safety principles and rules.

Among the devices that have been developed to prevent machine accidents are guards, mechanical safeguards, protective clothing, and improved illumination, ventilation, and visual aids to call attention to potentially dangerous conditions. All of these devices are rendered useless if an individual does not develop a positive approach to craft activities and the employment of these safety measures. A careless attitude or one that elicits the idea that the participant is immune to injury, regardless of his knowledge, skill, or work habits produces a set of expectations that will eventually culminate in an accident. Every opportunity should be taken by the instructor to lessen the vulnerability of participants to accidents by reiterating the necessity for an appropriate response to safety needs. If the participant learns to be reasonable in his or her approach to craft activities, serious attempts toward assisting individuals to recognize dangerous situations and to respond suitably can be made.

There seems little doubt that human error is probably the major cause of accidents. People do not always understand or accept this fact, because too many feel that nothing untoward can happen to them. This sense of indestructibility is nothing more than a poor attitude based upon a faulty premise. Many accidents occurring in craft facilities stem from ignorance, carelessness, or inattention to what one is doing. Of course, there may be other emotional stresses to which the individual is subjected at any given time that can produce substandard conduct. The attitudes that must be developed if participants are to perform in a safe manner in the crafts facility should be initiated early, reiterated often, and be correlated with successful outcomes. The potential participant can be significantly helped with regard to such attitudes by making him or her recognize the crippling injuries that lie waiting if careless work habits and inattention occur. Attitudes centered on personal responsibility should be encouraged at every contact that the craft instructor has with the participant.

Safety Training Techniques. The nurturing of safe attitudes can be promoted by exposing the learner to procedures that permit the participant to gain satisfaction from the activity while reducing the degree of risk involved. To ensure that participants understand these safety techniques, a training program is presented as soon as an individual enrolls for a session in crafts. In this way, the person quickly realizes that careful preparation and correct practice can virtually eliminate whatever inherent danger there is in craft activities.

1. The participant receives specific, comprehensive instructions in the correct techniques for performing craft activities.
2. The instructor will demonstrate the most suitable procedures one step at a time so that the participant readily understands why safety practices are necessary.
3. The participant is enabled to practice the procedures that he or she has

been shown, but receives close supervision until the requisite skills are completely mastered.

Strict Conformity to Safety Rules. When people have developed a modicum of skill, they tend to relax and take short cuts. Sometimes they actually remove the very safeguards or devices that are designed to protect them. Such risk taking is unacceptable behavior and must be corrected before an accident occurs. People are more readily persuaded to conform to safety regulations when they are explained than they are to adhere if coerced. To this end, the instructor must take every opportunity to impress upon the participant that personal alertness and following safe practices will result in greater satisfaction, self-realization, and enjoyment. Any deviation from safe conduct must be stopped before a set of circumstnaces is put in motion and eventuates in accidental injury.

The major objective of safety instruction is to insure safety and prevent injury to participants. Another reason is to forestall or minimize the possibility of litigation. Crafts instructors have been held personally liable for injuries to participants who were allowed to use power machines, work with corrosive fluids, potentially explosive conditions, or with tools about which they knew little. No participant should be permitted to operate any equipment in a craft facility unless he or she has been given the necessary instructions to do so. Anything less invites a suit if the person is injured. Naturally, the instructor's ability to defend against allegations of negligence will be immeasurably strengthened if it can be proved that the participant was given safety instruction.

School shop teachers probably have a better chance of protecting all concerned because they have a high degree of control over what students can use. Moreover, they can devise safety examinations as an integral part of the school shop program. Since every student must be exposed to safety instruction and take safety tests designed to evaluate how well pupils have assimilated equipment use and safe procedures, these tests could be decisive in acquitting a teacher of charges of negligence in the event of a mishap.

Safety tests may prove important not only because they contain written and permanent records of the student's understanding of craft techniques and safe practices, but because they also serve as significant aids in the overall instructional process. Written and practical tests should also be supplemented with visual reminders as well as continual demonstrations of techniques prior to each and every new operation. While it may not be possible for recreationists to give safety examinations in craft facilities, the use of audiovisual aids, posters, slogans, and other instructional means are available to them in trying to instill within participants the desire to use safe practices in all craft activities.

Safety instruction should be continuous for every group coming into the craft facility. It may be that the constant reiteration of safe practices and behavior is the determining factor that nullifies any allegation of negligence on the instructor's part if a participant is injured in an accident.

Fundamental Legal Consideration

The reader should, by now, be familiar with many of the principles of tort liability and the various doctrines that the courts consider when litigation proceedings are heard. However, it should be remembered that each state may enact legislation that defines certain school operations, such as shops, and provides immunity even where negligence on the part of teachers may be clearly shown. Other states may no longer give the protection of sovereign immunity for school related activities. To the extent that recreational services are controlled by legislation stemming from enabling acts, there may be no specific reference to such recreational activity as crafts in the laws of the state. Nevertheless, all states have tort laws on their books. Unless there are specific legislative enactments dealing with specified recreational activities, such recreational activities will be governed by the law of torts if and when incidents arise making litigation necessary.

A basic law controlling the association of participants and instructors demands the avoidance of negligent conduct that could result in harm to participants. The participants have a correlary duty to be alert for their own safety in accord with their age and maturity level. In order for the primary requirement to be met, the environment in which the craft activities occur must be designed to eliminate unsafe conditions or dangerous circumstnaces. Instruction of the best possible kind, so that participants may gain an understanding of the tools, materials, activities, safe practices, attitude formation, and skills necessary for the satisfactions to be derived from taking part in crafts is not only desirable, but constitutes a legal mandate. Promulgation and application of safety rules, regulations, and practices in all craft environments are absolutely necessary. When participants are made aware of the need for safe performance and recognize their own responsibility to adhere to whatever safety practices are required, there will be less likelihood of contributory negligence or behaviors that cause accidents. The instructor should be a role model for participants. He or she should consistently conduct activities in ways that represent reasonable and prudent behavior and, therefore, safe performance.

Actions Brought—Case Illustrations

Craft instructors have specific responsibilities to their charges. Whether the instructor is supervising a recreational department crafts facility or teaching a shop class in a school, the degree of care criterion is always constant. Shop teachers and recreational craft instructors assume a level of responsibility for the safety and well-being of those in their charge because of assigned duties that go with the position. Injuries to pupils in school shops have been well documented and are instructive because they serve to provide a better understanding of the forces that interplay. For this reason, several court decisions in liability cases have been selected to explain the elements that are necessarily considered in arriving at a decision for fixing blame and reparations.

> Under the supervision of a shop teacher, plaintiff and other pupils were dismantling an automobile to prepare a cut-away model. The auto top was cut off, and plaintiff and others were attempting to bend the top before disposing of it. Plaintiff was holding a jagged edge of the top when another pupil suddenly jumped onto the top. The plaintiff's hand was badly cut by this unexpected action. The teacher was close by when the mishap occurred, instructing other pupils. Plaintiff's parents claimed negligence on the teacher's part in failing to supervise in a proper manner the activities of pupils who were taking the automobile apart at the time of the accident.
> The trial court directed the jury to return a verdict for the teacher and the school district. The parents appealed from this judgment, and the lower appellate court reversed the decision of the trial court. Then the defendants appealed.
> The state supreme court held that the test of negligent conduct was what a reasonable and prudent person would or would not do under the circumstances. Before liability could be imposed for an act, the prevision of a reasonable person must be able to recognize risk of harm to another. To state that the teacher in this case had to anticipate the action of a pupil who caused the accident and somehow to prevent it amounted to making it the responsibility of the school teacher to anticipate the many unexpected acts that occur daily in and about schools and on school property. The court held that neither teachers nor school districts should be subject to such claim. Furthermore, the court did not believe that there was an invocable legal doctrine or principle that could lead to such a result.
> The state supreme court overturned the opinion of the lower appellate court, and the judgment of the trial court was affirmed.[2]

In another instance, a fifteen-year-old boy sued the school district and his shop teacher for damages for injuries when a replica of a Revolutionary War cannon made to scale in the school machine shop accidentally fired.

> The boy took his model cannon home and proceeded to load the cannon with the powder from a shotgun shell. He successively loaded the weapon with powder, rag wadding, shot, and more wadding. He then worked the powder mixed with match heads into the touchhole with a thin pointed instrument. Almost instantly the cannon fired blowing off two fingers from one hand as well as a part of the palm and wrist.
> The jury verdict was for the defendants. The plaintiff appealed, and the appellate court held that the teacher failed to warn the pupil of the dangers involved in loading and firing the cannon. This was sufficient to constitute proximate cause of injury. The teacher was declared negligent, and the school district liable for payment of damages to the injured plaintiff.[3]

Environment

The physical layout and construction of the crafts shop as well as its location in a building can contribute to the safety or unreasonable risk of participants. Physical conditions start with whatever structure houses the crafts shop and includes those safety features that are designed into the facility. These physical attributes concern form, function, housekeeping, equippage, and arrangements of the spaces, work places, storage areas, and security features that live up to the standard for supplying an environment that is safe, healthy, and suitable for the kinds of activities to be carried on.

Poorly planned facilities containing cramped spaces, insufficient ventilation, inadequate illumination, or other faulty arrangements can be the cause of accidents. Badly sited machinery, lack of clearly distinguished safety zones around machine locations, and proximity that gives rise to operator interference can be the basis for an accident. Inability to store dangerous materials, e.g., flammable liquids, caustics, acids, lack of provision for the storage of craft tools, poor construction of stock and supply facilities may be part of the problem that leads to accidents.

Conditions that retard the learning processes or are at an unreasonable level of risk to the health and welfare of those who participate cannot be permitted. Once such conditions are discovered, they should be corrected as quickly as opportunity allows. Those who are responsible for shop safety must remedy any defects immediately. No instructor can plead ignorance of defective equipment or inadequate facilities. It is the instructor's function to inspect the premises and everything in them prior to use. To do less, when there are dangerous conditions present is negligent.

Operating authorities are responsible for providing their craft shops with tools and equipment that, at a minimum, satisfy the safety standards of the state department of labor. Failure to provide safety equipment, for example, may be held to be negligence. After all, if industrial firms are required to furnish their employees with appropriate safety equipment, it appears likely that similar activities offered by schools and recreational service agencies should also provide such gear. To do less is tantamount to inviting unreasonable risk for participants.

For good management, the physical facilities of the crafts shop can be monitored through the use of a formal checklist. Each inspection of the facility and its contents should be checked off. Defects in tools, supplies, or pieces of equipment can be noted with written recommendations for their replacement or reconditioning and then transmitted to the proper authorities. This type of record keeping serves two important functions: (1) it brings notice to any faulty aspect of the shop, and (2) it serves as evidentiary material that plant and equipment maintenance was routine procedure in the event that allegations of negligence are brought should an accident occur.

Craft Facilities

Craft facilities are called by many names. Among the most common, depending upon where they are found, are shops, rooms, laboratories, studios, kitchens, or centers. Such facilities may be consolidated, that is, contain many different kinds of craft apparatus and equipment with which to work diverse activities simultaneously. Facilities may be highly specialized as well. The specialty shop may be designed for the printer's trade, a machine shop for automobile repair, automotive engines, or marine engines. It could be devoted to woodworking, metalworking, glassblowing, leather tooling, pottery making, electronics, drafting, or plastics. Some, one, or all of these craft activities, and others that do not require elaborate machines or tools, are capable of being operated within the confines of this physical setup.

Craft Room.The desirability for having a separate area organized as a craft room cannot be underestimated in any recreational or school operation. Typically, this room is designed for the younger child—between the ages of six and twelve—although the same kind of room can also be utilized for any age group depending only upon the kinds of activities offered. Usually, the craft room will contain work benches that can accommodate participants standing around them while at work. Along the walls will be located locked tool cabinets conveniently situated near work areas, a metal-lined and fireproof cabinet for paints and stains, wall benches with cabinet spaces for supplies, display shelves, and a sink with hot and cold water taps, kitchen, stove, and counter space. Additionally, several sewing machines, two jig saws, a power drill, a grinder, and a sufficient number of electrical outlets will round out the accoutrements.

The craft room is fully equipped with tools and simple machines to meet the diverse craft activity needs of those who participate in handwork. It is not arranged for specialty crafts of a major type, nor is it designed as a central craft establishment. The craft room is a modular facility that is probably duplicated in many locations throughout a community wherever the organizing agency operates a center or other building. Thus, schools as well as public recreational service departments may set aside spaces for craft rooms.

Flammable and Corrosive Liquids. Storage of flammable liquids and their proper use must be taught to all crafts participants. This is part of the responsibility of the crafts instructor. Moreover, adequate warnings about the dangers that accrue during improper use of such liquids need to be given. Liquids having a flash point, or temperature at which the liquid vaporizes sufficiently to produce an explosive mixture near the surface of the liquid, at or below two hundred degrees Fahrenheit, are flammable. Thus, gasoline, ethyl alcohol, lacquer, varnish, kerosine, turpentine, a variety of paints, etc., all may produce explosive mixtures that can be ignited by static electricity or some spark produced by switching on a light. Each of these liquids may be found in a craft shop. Storage should be in appropriate containers that are properly labeled. The containers should be stored in a locked metal cabinet and used only after instruction has been given and the craft activity is in session.

Corrosive liquids, such as acids and other chemicals, must be stored in glass containers, sealed, and made available only to those who have been previously instructed in their use. Pure sodium, for example, should never be stored in a way that might permit moisture to accumulate. When sodium is mixed with water, a destructive explosion could occur. Acids, which are perfectly safe when handled with care, are basic to such craft activities as etching metal. However, no instructor can assume that participants will always be careful in avoiding spills or dropping the container with the acid. Therefore, acid will be poured by the instructor into smaller containers for easier handling, and participants will be closely supervised when working with such material.

Craft Shop Location. For all practical intents and purposes, it is better that craft rooms and shops be located on the first floor of a building. This permits easy evacuation in the event of fire or explosion. It also makes easier the delivery of supplies, materials, and equipment to the shop area without infringing on other activity areas of the structure. An emergency access door also serves as the point of entry for the delivery of craft supplies.

Craft Room Safety. Very often craft activities are considered after a center building has been erected. Whatever space is left over from "more important" activities is assigned to crafts. Sometimes these areas are located in the least desirable part of the building. As craft activities have increased in popularity, the older craft rooms have become inadequate. Crowded work areas constitute a serious hazard in many older facilities. The instructor must assume responsibility for making the craft room as safe as possible by remodeling the area if necessary and making sure that sufficient illumination is provided so that any machine or activity area will be well lit for work. The conduct of regular inspections, daily if the activity is a daily affair, will bring dangerous conditions to the attention of administrators who are authorized to make whatever improvements are suggested.

Knowledge of Participants. The reduction of craft room incidents depends, to a large extent, on the instructor's ability to understand his or her clients, to anticipate any potential for unsafe acts, and to be aware of what must be done to ensure a proper attitude toward safe work habits. Crafts reach out to an extraordinarily varied clientele, different age groups, skill levels, degrees of experience, attitudes, and work patterns. Some will be unskilled and reckless, others will be methodical and cautious. There are those who exhibit sound judgment and others who are unreasonable when it concerns accomplishing some project.

Presenting Safety Precautions. The crafts instructor should make training in safety an integral part of every craft session. By correlating his or her instructions dealing with a particular activity to specific precautions where they apply, the instructor will help the participants recognize the importance of such safety measures. Every individual who enters the craft room to participate in some activity which requires the use of a machine must be taught the importance of using mechanical protective devices in operating

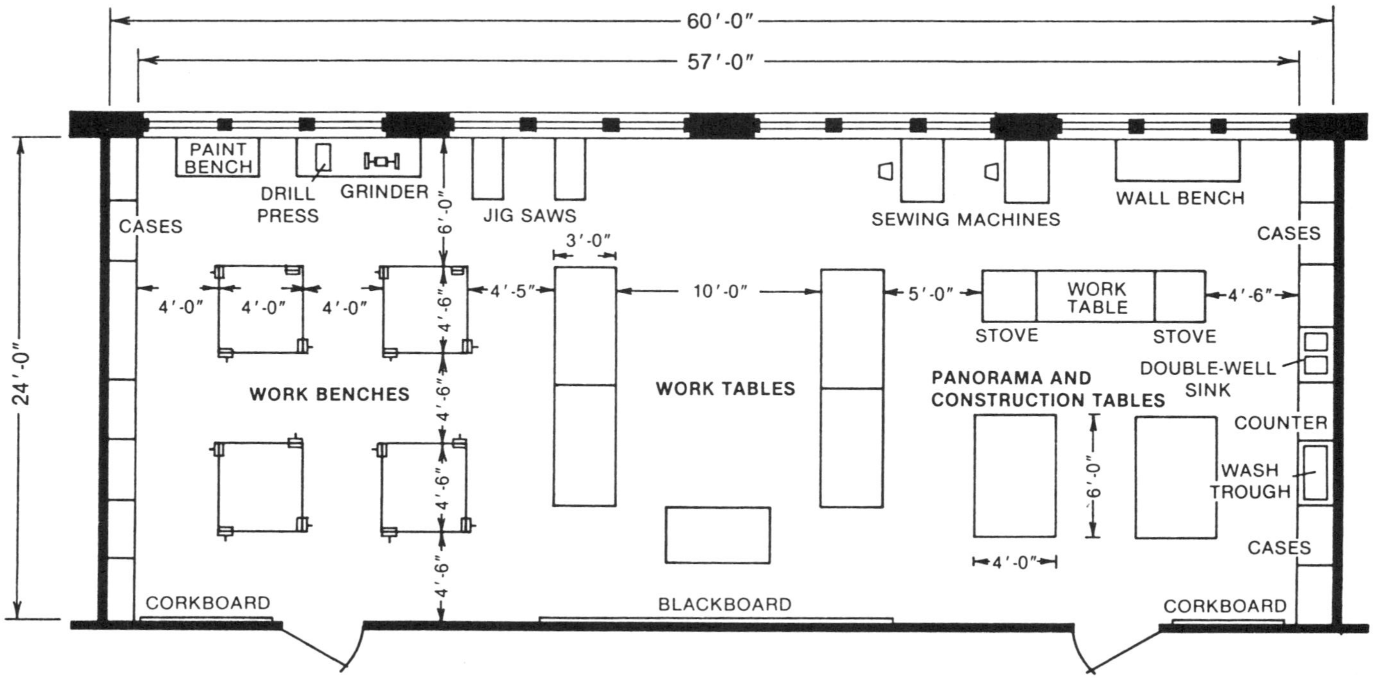

Well-designed elementary craft room.

the machine. The instructor will be responsible for showing all participants that ultimate limitations of human ability make guards a fundamental of safe performance.

Assisting people in the development of proper attitudes toward safe performance in the craft shop probably means not only adhering to standard rules and regulations governing machine and tool use, but also developing respect for the need to utilize protective coverings or guards. The crafts instructor should graphically describe the result of accidents that can occur if guards are not attached to whirling saws, crushing presses, or spinning drills. All participants must learn to avoid dangerous or substandard behavior before it ends in an accident and injury.

Among the precautions developed for all persons participating in the craft room activities will be those relating to: (1) appropriate clothing to be worn. Whatever safety equipment must be worn will be worn before participants can approach and/or operate a machine. Loose clothing should be removed or tied firmly. Perhaps, overalls or a shop apron should be worn to prevent material from being caught in a machine with disastrous consequences. (2) Most adults will not tolerate horseplay in a potentially dangerous area where they are working. However, young children and adolescents may very well indulge in rowdiness. This form of behavior must be prohibited. (3) Vigilance must be directed toward the prevention of careless work habits. Inadequate attention to safety must be corrected as soon as it is observed by the instructor. All machine guards must be in place. All machines must be turned off when not in use. Only those who have received instruction in the use of a given machine will be permitted to operate the machine. All others are not allowed to work on the machine. Machines must be set for optimum efficiency through proper adjustment. (4) Good housekeeping must prevail in the craft room. It is necessary that work places be swept periodically so that debris does not accumulate. (5) A daily inspection of the storage area is required. Examination of tools and power equipment must also be accomplished so that any defects can be noted and corrected. (6) All materials and stock must be stored in appropriate and locked containers. (7) Any fire hazards should be remedied immediately as they are detected. (8) Glass shards or fragments must be picked up immediately. (9) All electrical equipment should be checked for defects, and this is also true of cables as well. Any frayed or damaged electrical cords, sockets, or appliances should be replaced upon detection. (10) Fire extinguishers should be periodically checked and recharged as necessary. Instruction in fighting various types of fires should also be given to participants. Fire drills and evacuation of the room in the event of an emergency should be rehearsed. (11) Tool handling and use should receive the kind of instruction that will, with practice, produce a skilled user. All participants must be taught about tool selection. Since the craft room will have a supply of tools for use in all of the activities presented or desired, the participant must be informed about which tools are appropriate for which activities. Tool choice and condition will enable the participant to appreciate the following:

1. The right size tool for the job will be safer.
2. Keen-edged tools must be stored safely. Sharp tools are safer than dull ones.
3. Tools must be in good condition before they are used.
4. Never place a tool into a machine that is moving.
5. Never use a tool in a manner that will permit it to cause injury if it should slip.
6. Safety goggles must be worn whenever there is danger of chips flying.
7. Place material in vises or clamps if they must be held while working.

Instruction in the use of all tools must precede all activities in which such tools are to be used. The participant should be familiar with the properties of each tool and should learn how to work on material properly. Thus, the technique for using a chisel, brace and bit, jigsaw, or plane must be demonstrated, tried, and practiced with emphasis being placed as much upon the safe utilization of the tool as on the development of skill in handling the tool.

Adherence to the rules and regulations governing tool use and machine operation can prevent many accidents. However, the crafts instructor should augment these basic orders with careful, systematic direction in the appropriate use of each particular type of tool and machine with which participants will come in contact during the course of the activity. This means that instruction should cover the correct way to manipulate the tool when standing or sitting. The participant should be made to recognize certain dangers that could occur if proper procedures are not followed explicitly. If protective gear is designed to be worn, it should be worn. If the tool is supposed to be maintained in a sharp condition, it should be inspected for sharpness. Every aspect of tool or machine operation should be impressed upon the potential user so that the possibility of injuries will be lessened or eliminated. The instructor has the responsibility of providing the best type of guidance and instruction to those who want to perform in crafts activities. The instructor should carefully explain and demonstrate each feature and then closely supervise while participants practice. The crafts instructor of a recreational session has as much responsibility for the safe operation of the crafts laboratory as does the shop teacher in a school.

All-purpose Crafts Shop

The consolidated crafts shop may be located in a recreational center or in a school building (if some cooperative agreement has been worked out between the school system and the community recreational service department). The crafts program will include such major categories as metalworking, woodworking, electronics, automotive mechanics, graphics, plastics, ceramic arts, printing, and leather working. Of course, some school-based programs in industrial arts will also have forges, drafting studios, and other industrially oriented activities as well.

When there is a consolidated crafts shop, the need for a well-equipped plant is obvious. Only with modern and well-maintained equipment can participants be expected to work safely and effectively with tools, materials, and machines. Ceilings and walls of shops should be treated acoustically so as to reduce noise and make the shop an enjoyable place in which to work. Efficiency, interest, and safety can be heightened by using a variety of colors on machinery and also to signal dangerous areas, need for caution, or hazardous materials. Color schemes do much to call attention to combustibles, cutting edges, and requirements for special protective gear, as well as to improve interest and attention of participants.

Crafts shops should be well lighted. Craft rooms should have from twenty to thirty footcandles of illumination on the work bench tops. There should be one square foot of window glass to five square feet of floor space in a shop. The ceiling height of a crafts shop should be at least half the width of the room, and the tops of the windows should be about one-half the width of the room from the floor. The use of fluorescent lighting is probably best because it provides a well-difused light without glare. Fluorescent lighting is generally installed in parallel rows running the full length of the ceiling of the shop. The lights should be set so that each row can illuminate about one-third of the room from the adjacent wall.

The size of the community and the interest in recreational crafts of the population to be served will be the best indicators of whether a consolidated crafts shop (center) or a diversified number of specialty craft rooms or shops will be advisable. In large cities, it is likely that almost every high school and, perhaps junior high or middle school, will have some kind of shop facility. It may also be true that nearly every community recreational center will have some space set aside for crafts or have a craft room to accommodate the program.

The organization and planning of the recreational crafts activity is so important that several shop layouts have been described. Each craft shop is illustrated with a floor plan. The floor plan will be helpful to all those who expect to plan some form of recreational crafts activity as well as offer a visualization of the arrangement of the shop in terms of tools and equipment. These layouts have been designed to accommodate approximately twenty-four participants in a single session. If the program is operated eleven hours each day, it is possible to have at least 250 people taking part in some form of craft activity on a daily basis.

The Consolidated Shop. The community center with its crafts specialist can provide a relatively comprehensive crafts program by utilizing the shop plan presented. This shop has a separate planning room, a tool room, and a materials storage room. It is equipped to instruct in just about any craft activity that requires machinery as well as those activities that may be called

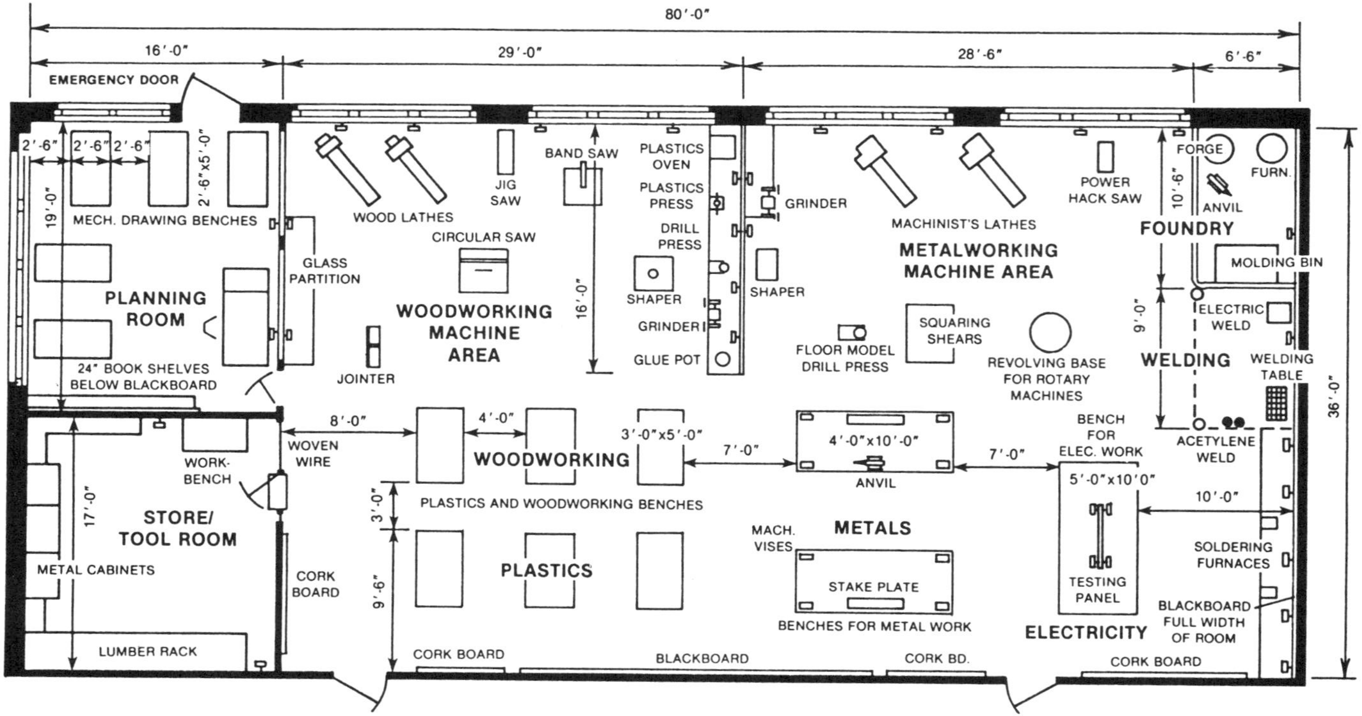

Consolidated crafts shop designed for safety.

handicrafts. The shop has a blackboard, corkboard, a wash trough, kitchen area, and ceramic area with kiln. This floor plan easily holds twenty-four participants and permits 120 square feet per person. It is equipped so that an individual who is interested may be able to spend one or more years learning about various craft activities and practicing them. The floor is wood except for the kitchen area which is tile. The ceramic kiln is situated so that the heat is allowed to escape through an exhaust hood. The shop is well supplied with electrical outlets and has two doors to the corridor and an emergency door leading to the outside. There is little doubt that such a room would be able to satisfy the most rigid fire safety code.

Tools and equipment will be of such variety and number as to require a separate storage space within the room. The tools will be displayed by size and shape, and attached to the wall by enclosed brackets that permit the tools to be taken down deliberately, but will not allow them to fall accidently. The tool storage space will be enclosed by heavy gauge floor to ceiling wire mesh. There will be only one entryway with an access way for the passage of tools and materials. This area will always be locked, unless the craft activity is in session and the instructor is giving out tools and/or materials. The tool storage area will be fully equipped for handicraft activities that would normally appeal to whatever age group the agency deals with at a given time.

Protective Devices. The entire concept of using safeguards is to prevent the machine user from coming into contact with any moveable part. These guards are built into the machine. If machine operation is not possible with safeguards as an integral component, then other mechanical devices are joined to the machine so that physical contact between operator and moving part is avoided. In order to insure operator safety, guards must be sturdily constructed, simple, dependable, easy to use, and never obscure the operation.

Safeguards are designed to reduce or eliminate the possibility of injury to one using the machine. Of course this can occur only if the safety device is in place. Moreover, the devices are incorporated in such a way that they function to stop the action of the machine if they are tripped. Thus, circuit breakers, fuses, and other expedients are employed to assure proper operation. Finally, it is the responsibility of the agency that purchases the power machines for use in the crafts program to make sure that the machines are equipped with controls that work at the command of the user. Starting switches should be positioned so that they cannot be activated by mistake. It may be necessary to design control switches so that only when pressure is applied the machine can function. Any lessening of pressure would automatically brake the machine. As with any mechanical device, they must be used if protection is to be obtained. However, despite safeguards, the attitude of the user is extremely important in cutting down on the possibility of accidents. Safeguards are not foolproof. Therefore, the machine user must never believe that because a machine has guards on it he or she can become less attentive in the certain knowledge that protection is assured.

Improperly guarded machines have contributed a number of accidental injuries in craft activities. Many of them have been in school shops, but not a few have been found in recreational service department craft rooms. The instructor's violation of good safety procedures was an important factor in one court's decision to grant plaintiff redress. The plaintiff injured his hand when using a power press without a guard in position. Evidence was offered in court to corroborate plaintiff's claim that the instructor used the press without a guard when demonstrating its use to participants. The department was held liable, and the crafts instructor was found negligent insofar as setting an example was concerned.[4] Many cases bear out the fact that agencies and their employees have a primary responsibility to their clients or participants to make sure that safeguards are always used and to act as models when providing instruction for safe work.

If an Accident Occurs

Despite precautions and vigilance, accidents do happen and injuries can ensue. Whenever there is an injury to a participant in a crafts activity, the instructor should be prepared to administer first aid—if necessary—and do whatever else is required to assist the injured party. Thereafter, the instructor must see to the stability of the other participants in the session. There are certain basic steps that any crafts instructor should take in the aftermath of an accidental injury. Of paramount importance is the health and welfare of the injured person. The instructor must determine the nature and extent of any injury received and then provide appropriate care. There are many injuries that require immediate first aid until the services of a physician can be substituted. In other instances only a minimal amount of aid can be given to the injured party.

When a participant has suffered an injury, the immediate concern is to find out precisely the severity of the injury. Once this is determined the application of first aid that is essential to the survival of the person or to minimize the trauma of the injury should be effected. Simultaneously, superiors should be notified and, if medical assistance is deemed necessary, it should be sent for at once. If the participant is seriously injured, next of kin should be notified and arrangements should be made to transport the individual to a hospital emergency room. Whatever first aid is necessary should be given, but nothing should be done that is questionable or beyond the competence of the instructor to perform.

Supervision

As always, a key element in the prevention of accidental injuries will devolve upon the instructor. The responsibility for supervising a group of people who are engaged in a variety of craft activities requires vigilance and concern for the welfare of everyone who participates. Regardless of the age and maturity of participants, instructors of craft activities would do well to use the highest degree of care in carrying out their functions. Any potential danger to the safety of those who participate that can be foreseen comes under the aegis of the instructor. By observing proper supervisory duties, the instructor will probably avoid accidents which might be prevented along with allegations of negligence.

Novices desiring to learn new skills in a crafts facility cannot acquire such skills unless they have an opportunity to practice with the tools, equipment, or machines that normally are employed in the activity. At some point, the participant is going to have to operate a dangerous piece of equipment. Craft activities can be graded according to the age and maturation of the participant so that children will not be subjected to the danger of operating power machines before they are ready to do so. Other activities, equally satisfying and enjoyable, can be substituted until age and maturity provide the necessary hand-eye coordination, and the proper attitude toward safe practice has become ingrained. However, for older youth and adults, tool and machine use is vital to participation. This is the point where supervision reaches its apogee. Although recognizing hazardous situations that surround equipment use, the instructor must provide proper information so that participants will avoid potential dangers. Supervision based upon extreme alertness comes into play.

There is no reason, in the ordinary course of work, why an instructor should be absent from the crafts facility when a session is in progress. Despite favorable court decisions or where governmental immunity precludes plaintiff recovery for damages received during such absence, an instructor who leaves a session unsupervised will probably be judged to have been negligent if an accidental injury occurs due to lack of supervision. There can be no question, especially among youth, that unsafe behaviors including practical jokes and other forms of horseplay are likely to increase in an instructor's absence. Such conduct invariably leads to reduced alertness and carelessness with a high probability of accidental injury. Even adults may shortcut certain safety precautions if they are skilled, and the absence of the supervisor reinforces poor habits. There is no substitute for adequate supervision unless it is in the person of another supervisor, of equal training and competence. Absence will evoke a presumed assessment of negligence under the basic principle of tort law that against the probability and gravity of risk of harm must be balanced the utility of conduct.[5] If, for any reason, a crafts instructor is called away from the session, it is highly desirable to obtain a substitute or else shut off all power machines and lock them.

Contributory negligence was denied by a court as a defense for the recreational department when a youthful participant had part of his hand cut off by the whirling blade of a circular saw in a woodworking shop. The accident occurred when, during the absence of the instructor who was called to the main office in the building, another participant turned on the switch operating the saw as the plaintiff was trying to extricate a piece of wood that had jammed the saw. The court found for the plaintiff and ruled that, but for the negligence of the instructor by being absent from the room, the plaintiff would not have been injured by a third party's action. Additionally, it was observed that by being absent the instructor could not determine whether or not the machine was being used properly.[6]

Good supervision and the operation of well-planned safety instruction can materially help the crafts person to successfully defend against any allegation of negligence. Plaintiff, a young adult, filed suit against the crafts instructor and the municipal recreational service department for loss of a hand while working on a metal shearing machine in that section of the shop designated for metal working. The court, in deciding for the defendants, ruled the department and the instructor not liable for the injury to the participant because he had been given detailed and repeated instructions in the safe operation of the equipment, the machinery was color coded to indicate its dangerous nature, and there were appropriate signs and notices posted regarding use of the equipment.[7]

The degree of care exercised, or lack of care due to absence or negligence, is demonstrated by a person's behavior and is typically given to a jury for decision. No publication of standards of conduct or regulations can be applied to make sure that a recreationist's performance (or a teacher's conduct) will guarantee that he or she will be free of liability. Moreover, there is no rule that can preserve a person from making errors. The instructor of record must assist all participants in recognizing that the agency has tried to provide a safe environment for their craft experiences and that they have a responsibility to behave in a safe manner. The crafts instructor who makes a conscientious effort to foresee potential risks and who is alert to possible dangers will be in the best possible position to care for the safety of those in his or her charge as well as protecting his or her personal interests.

NOTES

1. *Severson v. City of Beloit* 167 N.W. 2d 258 (1969).
2. *Morris v. Ortiz,* 437 P. (2d) 652 Supreme Court of Arizona, 16 February 1968.
3. *Calandri v. Ione Unified School District of Amador County,* 33 Cal. Rptr 333. District Court of Appeal, Third District, California, 22 August 1963.
4. Severson v. City of Beloit, Wis., 167 N.W. 2d 258 (1971).
5. Fowler V. Harper, *The Law of Torts* (Indianapolis: The Bobbs-Merrill Company Publishers, 1933), 164–65.
6. *DeBenedittis v. Board of Education,* 271 A.D. 886, 67 N.Y.S. 2d 31 (1946); also *South Ripley Community School Corporation v. Peters,* 396 N.E. 2d 144 (1979); *Taylor v. Kelvin,* 121 N.J.L. 142, 1a.2d 443 (1938). Cf *Herman v. Board of Education,* 234 N.Y. 196, 137 N.E. 24, 24 A.L.R. 1065 (1922); and *Meyer v. Board of Education,* 9 N.J. 46, 86 A.2d 761 (1952).
7. *Kiser v. Snyder,* 205 S.E. 2d 619, 21 N.C. App. 708 (1974).

16
Organized Camps

Although fifty-five million people participate in some form of camping in the United States each year, only eight million persons actually engage in residential camping. Day camping accounts for several million more enthusiasts. Organized camping is a deliberately planned, nature oriented, recreational experience designed to enable the participant to live in a setting that encourages environmental appreciation, a variety of outdoor learning skills, and opportunities to form associations in a democratic framework. All aspects of organized camping have distinctive characteristics. First, there is a permanent facility with adequate and appropriate structures from and through which camping takes place. Secondly, qualified persons are employed to supervise campers placed in their charge. Thirdly, all aspects of health, safety, and the well-being of campers is enhanced by competent administration. Finally, all camping activities revolve around group living situations. It is in the latter context that the individual learns to accommodate himself to the need for accepting responsibility as a member of a group.

CAMPING TODAY

While the American Camping Association (ACA) has become the mainstay for advancing the camping movement and, in the process, has become the chief advocate for improving the health, safety, and personnel standards throughout the field, there are still substandard operators at work, and they function on such a low level that campers are endangered just by being at their facilities. Even in very well-run camps accidents can and do happen. For the most part, these accidents are spontaneous and unforeseen occurrences for which nobody can be prepared. However, there are occasions when the best intentioned camp administrators or their agents permit themselves a momentary lapse with disastrous results. In the most notorious instances, campers have been killed because those in charge failed to act in a reasonable and prudent manner. Camping accidents run the gamut from mild poisonings from noxious weeds to death by drowning. Camps operate in every state, often located in remote areas, not within easy traveling distance to treatment centers, or have programs that send campers out on trips that have a high degree of risk for the participant. All of these factors promote the possibility of serious injury and health hazards from infectious diseases or tainted food and water supplies to life threatening situations that could result in some catastrophic outcome.

The following report, from an insurance company's files, dramatically illustrates the kinds of circumstances that may occur:

> A fourteen-year-old boy went to a camp in Norwich, New York. On the date of the incident he was playing baseball. Counselors were present to supervise the various activities taking place. A sudden storm arose. It was anticipated that there would be lightning and the counselors decided that it would be best to send the campers to their bunks. This camper returned to his bunk.
>
> While the camper rested on his bed in the cabin, a lightning bolt struck the ground approximately three feet from his bed. Burn area and a hole was discovered where the bolt had struck. Immediately after the lightning bolt struck, this camper had trouble breathing. His friends tried to give him mouth-to-mouth resuscitation. They sent for the camp nurse who came and called for an ambulance that took him to the local hospital.
>
> Although he was worked on for ninety minutes by the hospital staff, he could not be resuscitated and was declared dead. There were no marks on the child's body. It was surmised that electricity could have passed through the boy's body. The local sheriff thought that death might have been caused by fright because of the proximity of the lightning strike to the child. To date, no legal action has resulted from this incident. Neither the camp nor the insurance company is actively pursuing the matter because they feel it will never come to trial.
>
> Additionally, the insurance company attorney pointed out that every state has a statute for wrongful death of from one to three years. It is not the usual statute where a child has to reach eighteen years of age before the statute of limitations begins to expire. The attorney was of the opinion that if an action were to be brought in this case it would be that of wrongful death. The statute of limitations (two years in New York) has already expired.[1]

Attempts at Standardization

The efforts of the American Camping Association to upgrade the field of camping can be documented by the examination of its national standards that it developed for camps dealing with personnel, program, facilities of all types, management, health and safety procedures, and other operational features by which a well-administered camp may be judged. Camps that desire certification from the ACA, indicating to prospective clients that high standards are maintained, are visited by ACA specialists and rated. If the camp meets the proclaimed standards, it is entitled to advertise its rating. The visitation program has taken the camping industry an exponential step forward in its professional growth. Other services of ACA include public relations and education of the public toward camping values and good camping practices, encouraging research, lobbying for legislation favorable to camp interests, performing consultive services, developing leadership courses, providing a placement center for camp personnel, and conducting conferences, workshops, and institutes. Naturally, it is concerned with the wide dissemination of successful practices and methods of camp management. It continually attempts to raise the criteria by which camps operate. It unceasingly calls for professional conduct in the administration of all camps and tries to gain maximum counselor competence and effectiveness.

Several state governments, notably New York and Connecticut, have developed camping legislation that controls all organized camping within the respective borders of their states. This legislation is aimed at making sure that camp administrators and other employed personnel are certified to perform in the most skilled and knowledgeable manner possible. Legislation is directed to the number of campers a camp may accommodate in terms of camper-to-counselor ratio, health, safety, accident reporting, medical services available to the camp, water sources, refrigeration units for keeping food, and other regulatory techniques that are designed to safeguard campers from potential harm.

CAMPING SAFETY CONCERNS

Since all camps are situated in the outdoors, there are likely to be natural hazards that must be recognized by camp administrators. Electrical storms, hidden ravines, dead standing trees, various poisonous plants, stinging and biting insects, venomous reptiles, or dangerous animals all contribute to the attraction and risk of the outdoors. There are also artificially contrived dangers from carelessly thrown matches, man-made wells, sharp tools, and a number of activities in which injuries may occur.

Many accidents, which could easily be avoided if proper care was taken, often occur at camp. Camp records and regulatory agency books are full of reports of camper related injuries that need not have happened. Factors immediately involved in accidents can be eliminated without difficulty if the camp administrator requires adherence to certain safety policies. The physical plant of the camp should be free of attractive nuisances. Broken glass, rusty nails, tools, equipment, and other devices that tend to attract children and create hazards should be removed. Machinery must be properly stored. Dangerous substances such as lead-based paint, insecticides, or caustic chemicals must be stored in secure places.

Perhaps the instruction of campers and staff in routine safety precautions is the best possible solution to the safety problem. It is essential that all persons residing at or participating in any camping situation know standard safety measures and act accordingly. Because camps deal, for the most part, with immature children, such safety lessons must be reiterated at every opportunity.

As in all things at camp, the counselor is the chief functionary to whose supervision the safety of the camper is entrusted. Through reasonable and prudent actions the counselor is the camp's most important line of defense against accident-causing injuries and camper infraction of safe conduct. The counselor stands in the same relationship to the camp as the teacher does to the school. In almost all ways the two functions are similar and the liability is the same. Among the specific areas that have special meaning for the safety of campers and the adequate management of the modern camp are: activities such as crafts, the waterfront, rifle or archery range, horseback riding, out-of-camp trips, and the various sport and game activities. Additionally, concern for the safe handling of food, a potable and protected water supply, sanitary facilities, medical assistance, transportation, shelter, and maintenance operations require close attention and sound practices so that risks are reduced or eliminated. In these efforts the camp manager may insure that avoidable incidents leading to injury or fatality will be under control.

Campcrafts and Shop

The workshop may have some tools, chemicals, and power equipment that should be used only when adequate instruction has been given and under the immediate supervision of a specialist competent to handle them. Rules and regulations governing the crafts shop will deal with tool use, equipment and materials storage, fire safety, and proper behavior.

Campers participating in campcraft activities must receive instruction in the correct methods for use of axes, knives and fire. Axes must never be left lying around. They should either be stored in some locked container or secured with the rest of the tools in the shop. Knives are handled in the same manner. Campers must be drilled in the proper stance, swing, and cut of axes or hatchets. Holding the knife and utilizing it for cutting purposes need to be taught. Use of fire building for protection, warmth, or food preparation should be preceded by instruction in how to start, maintain, and put out fires, and which type of fire is most effective for cooking, baking, heating or drying. Above all, campers must be shown how to extinguish fires and prevent destruction of themselves, others, or property by uncontrolled fires.

Aquatic Areas

Aquatic safety standards have been devised for the operation of different water activity facilities by the American National Red Cross. Long and practical experience has been the determinant of their water safety programs. Water safety personnel are the major elements in the minimalization or elimination of aquatic area hazards. Competent personnel assigned to direct and control swimming and boating activities are the surest means for the prevention of avoidable accidents. When well-trained personnel are given responsibility and authority to set up rules and conduct for aquatic facility use, the dangers to campers are nearly insignificant. Whether the camp has access to a lake, river, ocean, or private swimming pool makes little difference. Safety rules, equipment, and camper checking systems must be initiated and enforced. Of course, waterfront personnel must also check the aquatic facility. They must investigate water source bottoms for weeds, muck, drop-offs, and potholes. They must protect campers against strong currents or tides when applicable. They must be alert against rocky outcroppings and pier pilings. In fact, if such dangerous conditions exist, it is their responsibility to bring them to the attention of the camp manager and recommend discontinued use of the area until such hazards are eliminated. If this cannot be performed, then recourse to other water facilities must be effected.

The waterfront or aquatic staff will be supplemented by counselors who may be skilled in diving, swimming, and water safety instruction. Necessary equipment to prevent drowning may include bouys, rings, tow ropes, long aluminum poles, inhalator devices, and a lifeboat, surfboard, or catamaran for water rescues. However, the best preparation for prevention of water accidents will be highly competent staff. Aquatic facility regulations apply to all those who use the area. These rules range from a restriction on night swimming, except under certain supervised circumstances, to the length of time any camper is allowed to be continuously in the water during a given swimming period. Aquatic safety is also concerned with instructional performance and the recreational and competitive swimming phases of aquatics. No part of the waterfront should be open to the chance of any user becoming the victim of an unforeseen hazard.

All forms of boating, whether rowing, sculling, canoeing, or sailing will be subject to strict rules and regulations governing the use of small craft, availability of personal flotation devices, skill of users, and previous instruction received by the camper. Only those campers who have been given instruction in the care and handling of small craft are to be permitted such use. Boating safety rules as promulgated by the American Red Cross or the United States Coast Guard should be adhered to without exception.

The Rifle Range

Range safety procedures are determined by the specialist in charge of this activity. Specific rules for the instruction of campers and all those who use the range must be strictly observed. No individual shall participate in shooting activities unless a qualified and authorized specialist is present. All weapons will remain under lock and key until an organized range activity is scheduled. No one will be permitted to bring a personal pistol or rifle to camp. All bullets will be accounted for, and each expended shell will be counted and deleted from the inventory of rounds. This practice will reduce or eliminate the possibility of accidents. When campers are on the range, National Rifle Association safety regulations should be in effect. Rifles will always be pointed up into the air and down range when not actually being fired. No loaded weapon will ever be pointed anywhere except at the target. Assistant instructors will be assigned to each shooter to assure that this rule is carried out. Orders by the range instructor will be complied with instantly. Before any firing is allowed, participants must be thoroughly indoctrinated in safety precautions, told how to hold their weapons, and given detailed instruction on aiming, positions, and firing. Range safety signals will be well known and recognized by all range users.

Shooting accidents and accompanying injuries can be eliminated. However, there are situations where inappropriate activity results in tragedy. One incident concerned a twelve-year-old boy who attended a camp located on Peach Lake in New York.

> The camp offered riflery as one of its activities. A rifle range was constructed away from the normal flow of traffic. The equipment consisted of a single shot .22 caliber rifle with bolt action. Rifles were placed on firing line mats with the bolt open, chamber clear, and with the bolt in an upright position.
>
> The campers were then instructed to take a prone position. Each camper was issued five rounds. Target shooting then commenced. Rifles were loaded on command of the counselor-in-charge. When the campers were ready, they were given permission to fire.
>
> One of the campers was issued an old Winchester whose bolt continuously jammed due to the weapon's age. A counselor-in-training went over to assist the camper. The CIT picked up the rifle and in doing so turned it slightly to obtain a better view of the bolt. The rifle fired and wounded the camper in the leg. A major artery was severed. Subsequently, the camper's leg had to be amputated.
>
> The case was settled for $95,000. That was done on the basis that the camp's insurance was for $100,000 coverage. Although the insurance company's attorney settled the case with the claimant's attorney, the former knew that a monetary settlement would have been greatly augmented had the case actually gone to trial.
>
> The responsibility for utilizing an old and poorly conditioned rifle clearly rested with the camp. The camp discontinued riflery as an activity in the aftermath of the incident.[2]

The Archery Range

Archery ranges should be relatively isolated, well-marked, and protected so that stray arrows will do no damage to persons or things. The shooting range should be banked at the area of the archery butts. This prevents loss of arrows and also eliminates the possibility of injury to a person inadvertently walking behind the targets. All archers must be cautioned about stepping over the shooting line while others are shooting. This is not only a courtesy lapse but also very dangerous. The archery range supervisor must make this rule clear and enforce it.

Overdrawing can be dangerous because the arrow might be shot into the hand. This can be avoided by making sure that all arrows are of a length suitable for the individual archer's draw. All archers must be instructed to keep their arrows toward the target butts when shooting. The commands of the range supervisor must be obeyed instantly. If a cease-fire is ordered, all archers, at whatever draw they have, should immediately relax the draw and unnock the arrow. The wearing of protective gear is mandatory for all archers. This may include a forearm guard and finger or hand guards.

Examination of bows, bowstrings, and arrows for signs of wear from friction or deterioration should be performed before any shooting occurs. Injuries from snapped bows can be avoided if appropriate inspection of tackle is made. Arrows that have unaligned feathers or shafts that are warped are potentially dangerous and cause inaccuracies in shooting. Care of equipment will, in most cases, prevent damage or injury and permit better shooting performance. Although there is no one organization that sets nationally recognized instructor standards or certification, a number of archery associations publish archery standards that may be used as guides. The National Field Archery Association is one such organization.

Sports and Games

Minor injuries such as bumps, bruises, and small cuts may occur from time to time during the course of the numerous physical activities that are or can be conducted at camp. These simply cannot be prevented. They are part of the normal course of activity and are to be anticipated. However, it is the uncommon or major injury that happens that is to be avoided if it is foreseeable. Numerous accidents of major import do occur because of carelessness, inattention, or some other lapse of good judgment. Camp records, insurance claims, and lawyer's files are repleat with the incidents that have tainted the camping season. Some injuries have been severe enough to permanently disable the victim; others have been fatal. That is why it is so important for counselors to be especially vigilant and be chosen for competence and intelligence.

Among the cases that have developed due to serious injury of a camper, the following appear to be instructive:

> A fourteen-year-old boy from Texas attended a baseball camp at Glassboro State Teacher's College in New Jersey. The youth attended batting practice while wearing eyeglasses, which were prescribed for his poor eyesight. The counselor, a college graduate and certified physical education teacher, was pitching to the boy at a speed he thought appropriate for this camper to hit. The camper did hit several balls and felt that he could hit pitches at this

speed. On the final pitch, the camper hit a foul tip, causing the ball to rebound from the bat and strike him in the face shattering his eyeglasses. He sustained severe eye injuries, and subsequently was medically evaluated as being legally blind.

In Texas, glasses are permitted to be sold and dispensed without shatterproof glass. If the eyeglasses had been shatterproof, it is unlikely that the injury would have occurred.

This kind of accident is foreseeable. If campers are wearing glasses and a baseball is being pitched at them, there is every reason to believe that foul tips could result in glasses being knocked off or broken. However, it is not foreseeable to have known that the camper, in this case, had on glasses that were not shatterproof.

The attorney for the defendant felt that the liability was somewhat questionable, but thought that it favored the camper in this instance. If the case had gone to a jury, the camper would have gotten a verdict. Under these circumstances defendants settled the case out of court for a total sum of ten thousand dollars.[3]

In another incident, an eleven-year-old boy was a camper at a camp located in Gilford, New York. While he was playing football, the ball was thrown to the camper and may have hit him in the chest, although this was not ascertained. The child died almost immediately.

It was subsequently learned that the boy had a congenital cardiac problem. The heart was ruptured at the time of the accident. It is unclear as to whether the football caused the injury. It was thought that this had not occurred. Rather, the attorney for the company that insured the camp believed that the boy's heart "simply ruptured and he died."

No action was ever brought against the camp as a result of this incident. The insurance company's files were closed without payment of any kind. The insurance company's attorney made the point that if, in fact, the child did have some heart defect, it should have been brought out prior to admission to camp so that proper precautions could have been taken.[4]

Horseback Riding

Qualified instructors must be responsible for the supervision and direction of horseback riding in camp. Basic instruction for beginners, as well as advanced instruction, requires a capable person in charge. An enclosed ring may be used for novice riders; trails and open fields serve the more experienced riders. All campers must be able to demonstrate sufficient control of the mount before being allowed to proceed to the next stage of advancement.

The careful instructor will, to the best of his or her ability, attempt to match available horses to the rider's capacity and present level of skill. The stabling of horses is another important factor if this program is to be a successful one. Where camps maintain horses on their own property, stables must be located a far remove from campers' eating and sleeping facilities so that noissome odors and potential health problems will be avoided. Stable areas will be well drained and cleaned regularly, and the animals' food supply will be protected from vermin or insect infestation. All riding equipment will be maintained in good condition and inspected on a daily basis.

Although no nationally recognized organization exists for the certification of horseback riding instructors, a number of riding schools do exist, and some are associated with institutions of higher education. These latter agencies offer courses in horsemanship.

Water Supply

A dependable supply of potable water sufficient to supply fifty gallons of water per person per day shall be available. Where pit or chemical toilets are used, this figure may be reduced to thirty gallons per person per day. It is probable that primitive camps may not have a water supply. Whenever water is obtained from other than an approved public water system, the following restrictions about the sources will be in order:

1. Wells. All ground water sources shall be located at safe distances from sources of contamination such as pit privies (twenty-five feet), sewer or septic tank (fifty feet), subsurface sewage disposal field or seepage pit (one hundred feet), or cesspool (150 feet).
2. Wells shall not be dug in areas subjected to flooding, unless the casing protrudes substantially above known flood levels or an adequately sealed submersible type of pump installation is used.
3. Construction. All wells shall be provided with an impervious casing that can exclude subsurface and ground waters that are contaminated or thought to be contaminated. If dug wells are constructed, there shall be no construction joint within ten feet of the surface. Dug wells may not draw water from the strata into which sewage is being discharged.
4. All pumps situated over the well will be mounted on the well casing, a pump foundation, or a pump stand, so that the top of the well is effectively sealed. Where the pump unit is not located over the well, the casing shall be finished above floor level and a watertight seal shall be provided between the well casing and discharge piping.
5. Openings into the casing for air pressure relief, for sounding, introduction of gravel, or for other purposes required in operation of the well may be permitted, but must be closed above floor and high water levels. These openings will be protected against any intrusion by caps, screens, or down turned "U" bends as suitable.
6. All new wells shall be properly disinfected and the water produced shall evidence satisfactory bacterial quality prior to service. A sample tap shall be made on the discharge line close to the pump for purposes of collecting water samples for analysis.
7. Springs. A spring shall not be used if sources of contamination are situated where they would be above the spring or in the path of the ground water flow toward the spring. At no time should a spring be situated nearer than two hundred feet to an up-stream potential source of contamination.
8. Springs, as supply sources, will be developed with the pumping mechanism contained within an enclosure having a sealed cover. This will prevent the entrance of contaminating elements.

9. Stream/rivers. No stream/river sources will be used unless they are treated.
10. Stored water will be kept in impervious tanks protected against surface drainage. No storage tanks shall have any connection with a sewer. All tanks shall have watertight covers and all openings shall be covered with corrosion-resistant screens capable of excluding pests.
11. Distribution system. The water supply lines shall not have any pipe connection with questionable water supplies. All plumbing fixtures and other equipment connected to the water supply will be constructed and installed so as to safeguard the water supply from contamination through cross-connections or back siphonage.[5]

Food Service

The food service is one of the chief concerns of any camp administration. The practical aspects of food procurement, storage, preparation, and service for mass feeding involve a series of steps that are determined by the camp's location. For this reason, every camp will have its own built-in problems. There are however, general procedures that can be applied to almost any camp. The kitchen staff needs modern equipment and must have proper working and living conditions. A fair wage will insure employment of competent staff. Good food service requires the employment of an expert dietician who is competent in dealing with hiring kitchen staff, formulating their respective duties, and supervising their functions.

A balanced diet should imply a palatable and satisfying diet. The food service director must provide food that is well cooked, tasteful, and appealing to the appetite. Guided by his or her knowledge of what foods are essential to the health of all persons at camp and the quantity that will be consumed at each meal, the dietician can order a basic amount of food. Naturally, the quantity of various food types to be maintained will be regulated by the availability and quality of the storage and refrigeration units.

In organizing a camp food program, attention must be given to state and local health regulations for food preparation areas and food handlers. In nearly all states, a food handler's license is required. This license certifies the healthy state of the food handler's condition concerning freedom from tuberculosis, venereal disease, skin infections, and the like. Camps themselves should make health examinations compulsory for all food handlers.

Dishes and utensils should be sanitized in ways that absolutely eliminate the possibility of food poisoning. This means that all dishes, pots, pans, and utensils must be subjected to rigorous cleansing with sufficient detergent and scalding water to insure cleanliness. If the camp does not have an automatic dishwasher, it is necessary to insure all dishes and utensils are scraped clean of food particles, immersed in hot water (at least 125 degrees Fahrenheit) with detergent, dipped into water of at least 150 degrees Fahrenheit, and then stacked on a carrier and immersed in scalding or boiling water. After air drying, the dishes and utensils may then be stored in cupboards, chests, or other protected places free from potential infestation by insects, rodents, or mildew.

Garbage Disposal

Garbage and refuse from all parts of the camp should be collected each day and dumped so that sanitary conditions prevail. Kitchen garbage may be disposed of by having it hauled away to dump or burning sites far from the camp's location. Commercial haulers may be used or the camp may have to have its own dump truck. In any case, garbage from the kitchen and dining rooms will be disposed of after each meal. Adequate garbage cans must be available so that whatever waste is generated can be easily removed. The camp's sewer system will be utilized to get rid of waste water. When the camp location does not permit the installation of a sewer system, then other methods must be found to conform to existing state and local regulations. Garbage can cleaning and storage sites and waste water disposal areas must be effectively screened, cleaned, and maintained so that odors, insects, varmints, and other pests can be eliminated as potential health hazards.

Transportation

The safe conveyance of campers and staff to and from camp is of great importance to all camp operators. If the camp uses automobiles, trucks, or buses to transport campers and staff anywhere, it should adhere to legal restrictions or regulations concerning the operating conditions and maintenance of the vehicles. Even if governmental regulations are absent, the camp should maintain a high standard of vehicular operating efficiency.

All staff personnel who are responsible for operating camp transportation vehicles must be physically capable of such responsibility. They must have the skill, qualifications, and knowledge required for the possession of a state license that certifies the holder to be in compliance with existing codes for the operation of such equipment. The camp must have some logical plan to follow during the transportation of campers and staff. There must always be adequate supervision present to maintain control and assure common standards of safety. There should always be a ratio of one counselor to each eight campers. The counselors and the campers must be instructed in the procedures of evacuating vehicles in the event of accident or necessity.

> A transportation incident occurred when a newly employed counselor was given responsibility of transporting campers from one activity area to another. A van-type vehicle was used. The counselor overloaded the van with too many campers and then proceeded to drive down a secondary road away from the campsite. Evidently, the counselor lost control of the van when he steered the vehicle off the road. One of the tires hit a soft

shoulder and caused the van to overturn. There were a number of severe injuries experienced by the campers among which were several fractured skulls, broken bones in other parts of the body, and serious scarring of faces and backs.

In commenting on the accident, the insurance company's attorney stated that the driver of the van was a young person who did not appear to have a great deal of experience and did not use good judgment in transporting all of the campers in one van. Accidents of this type happen quite often when too many children are loaded into a van and seat division is very poor. The van load should be restricted to a limited number of children transported at any given time. Passengers should be seated, must be wearing seat belts, and instructed to behave properly when the van is in motion.

In this instance, it wasn't the inappropriate behavior of the campers that caused this accident, but the improper driving of the counselor. Because of the severity of the injuries and the facts surrounding the injuries, the camp was sued, in addition to a negligence action, for punitive damages, and the insurance policy did not cover punitive damages. The insured may be held liable for the amount of money that the jury can award to the plaintiffs if the punitive allegation is substantiated. Punitive simply means that negligence is so gross that the jury should punish the driver of the vehicle or the owner—in this case, the camp.[6]

When a camp provides transportation for campers, it will assume responsibility for a child between the place of pickup and the camp, and from departure until met by the parents or a person designated by the parents.

Camp Maintenance

The physical plant of a modern camp represents considerable investment. For this and obvious safety reasons, the structures and equipment used by campers and counselors should be given the best possible care so as to retain good condition, effectiveness, and long life. Good maintenance means that potential hazards from equipment or facilities in disrepair will be eliminated. The camp site and all structures within it are to be kept clean and in good repair, and no artificial contrivance that could cause injury can be permitted to create potential danger. Maintenance deals with power sources, water supplies, mechanical devices, structures, equipment, and garbage disposal so that both a safe and healthy situation exists.

Vehicular Access

A camp system, if the grounds are extensive enough to warrant one, should provide access from the highway to the administration area. While there is really no need for automobile traffic within the confines of the camp, there are vehicular needs that must be considered. Access should be open from the administrative center to the mess hall, kitchen, and infirmary. These areas should be easily traversed by car, truck, or ambulance. The camp itself should not be open to vehicular traffic. Road spurs should lead from the camp parking lot near the administrative center to the rear of the mess hall and kitchen. Another spur should lead to the infirmary. These roads should permit access by food supply and emergency vehicles.

Fire Prevention and Control

Regardless of location, the camp administrator must take every precaution possible to prevent fires in the camp or during out-of-camp activities. Whenever proximity permits, the camp administrator will contact the nearest local fire department or other fire fighting agency in the vicinity and make sure that fire fighting apparatus will be available on call.

All camp staff personnel will undergo fire fighting drills and become prepared to assist in avoiding or controlling fires. Fire safety and preventative measures, as well as evacuation procedures, will be undertaken by all personnel.

Every camp facility should have wall-bracketed soda-acid fire extinguishers, and these can be supplemented by smaller hand-held foam extinguishers. Where water pressure is sufficiently high, hoses can be supplied at the most critical or potentially critical points. A fire extinguisher should be placed in the kitchen, crafts shop, infirmary, maintenance facility, or wherever combustibles are stored. Extinguishers should be of a type designed to combat the particular kind of fire that might occur. Thus, oil, gasoline, or grease fires would require foam, while wood would respond better to water or sand.

All camp staff should be concerned with fire prevention and control. The program of fire safety should be given detailed consideration and practice during precamp staff training. At this time, each of the camp's counselors should be instructed as to the actions to be taken by them to evacuate campers safely, transportation methods or routes from the site of the fire, fire fighting practice, and other information that they need to know in order to reduce or eliminate the threat of fire in camp. Fire drills for campers will also be a mandatory preparation together with any fire signals or alarms so that all who need to can respond while campers are kept safe from harm.

Health Services

Inseparably associated with camper safety are the health services supplied by the camp. In well-operated camps every measure is taken to insure healthful living conditions that, by extension, mean safe living. Any compromise with standard health care procedures immediately makes the camp suspect in the eyes of competent health authorities.

The organization of the health services at camp depends upon certain variables such as length of camp period, permanence of camp structures, age group involved, and nearness to treatment centers and/or medical assistance. While it is unlikely that every camp will have a resident physician, every camp should have a medical consultant. Some kind of contact for a physician-on-call must be established for health service continuity and effectiveness. Every residential camp must have a nurse in residence. The nurse will be the chief health officer of the camp if a physician is not in residence. Nurses have specific responsibilities that are defined by law; their duties will be further amplified by the orders of a resident or contracted physician.

The camp health program starts with a camper health certificate. This requirement is met when a camper obtains a physical examination from a licensed physician not more than two weeks prior to the opening of camp. Every person employed by the camp is also subject to this rule, and in some states, the Department of Health may be responsible for the publication of health care standards that all personnel must meet if they are to be employed. The health certificate will be received by the camp's administrator, turned over to the medical staff for appraisal, and then filed in the employee's or camper's personal records. The health certificate provides such information as medical history, specific illnesses, injuries, surgery, vaccinations, physical disabilities or deficiencies, special diet or medication needed, and a statement by the examining physician that the individual is free of infectious disease or illness at the time of the examination. For the campers there should be a statement that the camper is capable of participating in normal camping activities.

The health program at camp involves all personnel and campers. Counselors will cooperate with health care personnel to insure daily inspection of campers to determine health status or injuries sustained within the previous twenty-four hours. All campers will have adequate rest and nourishment, as well as appropriate exercise, and will maintain personal hygiene at a high level. This will be supervised by counselors who must be certain that campers practice a basic health regimen. This means that hot soap showers will be taken, teeth brushed, and face and hands washed before eating and after using toilet facilities.

The handling of food by employees will be supervised by the dietician or other qualified food service director. Proper health and sanitary precautions will be taken to store and handle food to prevent spoilage, waste, and the transmission of contaminants that cause infectious disease.

Sanitation

State and local health departments publish sanitary codes relating to the operation of summer camps. These codes should be consulted to determine whether the sanitary arrangements of the camp are adequate, efficient, and effective. This procedure is particularly necessary to safeguard a pure supply of drinking water. Public health personnel may be requested to inspect the sewage disposal system, garbage handling and refuse disposal, latrines and toilet facilities, waterfront area, and sources of swimming water. Drinking water, originating at the camp, even when certified safe, needs to be tested at its source each week. Although some administrators feel that this is unnecessary, the health of everybody connected with the camp can depend upon such inspections.

Counselors on Duty

A formal routine and rotating system whereby at least one and preferably two counselors are given the responsibility of patrolling or making rounds of the camp grounds at night insure protection against prowlers, fire, or the consequence of unexpected storms that might cause damage to structures. Counselors may be given compensatory time off the following day of the night they were on duty.

Whenever there is an incident at camp that could have been prevented, the fault will invariably lie with poor human judgment, either on the part of the staff or the campers. Lack of common sense, failure to adhere to regulations concerning safety practices, or disregard of camper infraction of certain basic safety policies are the primary causes of dangerous accidents. A basic safety plan should be devised to cover all activities, environmental hazards, and the human factor of imprudent behavior or unsound judgment. No contingency should be overlooked in forming the most comprehensive safety program for the camp. There is no excuse for negligence in camp; the lives of too many people depend upon the alertness and responsibility of the staff. By anticipating possible dangers; inspecting the buildings, structures, and grounds for hazards; and putting a logical plan into effect to prevent damage and injury, accidents will be reduced to a minimum.

NOTES

1. Communication with Jesse Farrow, Rhulen Agency, Inc. (Insurance), 29 March 1982.
2. Ibid.
3. Ibid.
4. Ibid.
5. R. G. Rice, ed., *Safe Drinking Water: The Impact of Chemicals on a Limited Resource* (Alexandria, Va.: Lewis Publishers, 1985). Also, U.S. Department of Health, Education, and Welfare, Public Health Service, *Water Supply and Plumbing Cross-Connections—Hazards in Household and Community Systems* (Washington, D.C.: Governing Printing Office, 1962).
6. Communication with Jesse Farrow, Rhulen Agency, Inc. (Insurance), 29 March 1982.

17
Maintenance of the Physical Plant for Safety Purposes

The upkeep of recreational areas, facilities, and equipment has an obvious outcome in presenting a clean, attractive, and stimulating environment to those who participate or spectate. Of equal importance is the fact that sound maintenance management can be a vital factor in the prevention or reduction of accidents to all who frequent recreational places. With regular maintenance operations areas, equipment, and facilities will keep up with visitor load. In consequence, optimum use of such areas will be possible without the deterioration that might accompany heavy traffic. Whether of the indoor or outdoor variety, recreational areas and facilities can be environments where people may find a healthy, safe, and inviting condition. There is little question but that maintenance operations will be a significant cost element in the planning and administration of the physical plant. Nevertheless, without routine and special maintenance to effect cleaning, repairs, replacements, or refurbishment consequent risks will mount along with decay of the premises. This in turn, could create serious environmental health hazards for all concerned.

Maintenance Programs

Maintenance of recreational places is of vital significance to the safety of participants and spectators alike. When a structure is built, an accessway constructed, or a beach developed, the management is obliged to maintain it—regardless of the size, space, or nature of the facility. This includes bridges, roads, paths, stairwells, emergency doors, and any other device, tool, or apparatus that is incorporated into the physical plant of the organization. The basic presumption by nearly all who enter the premises of an institution, agency, or voluntary association is that the facilities are properly maintained insofar as their expected use is concerned. Participants rightly assume that authorities have taken care of the premises so that they are safe for use. The attention of most participants and spectators is on the activity in question, not on the place where it is performed.

The chief objectives of maintenance are determined to be as follows:

1. To extend the useful life of property. This includes all premises, tools, facilities, structures, paraphernalia, equipment, or materials.
2. To maximize the availability and accessibility of all premises and whatever contents are to be used for participation or observation.
3. To insure the carrying capacity of all facilities.
4. To have available and ready for use all equipment that contributes to the safe enjoyment of activity.
5. To insure that all emergency equipment is operational and available for use when needed.
6. To insure the safety of all users of the premises.

In order to carry out these objectives every organization that has contact with people for the express purpose of delivering or supplying recreational services at varied sites and areas must perform certain maintenance practices on a routine basis, keep records that deal with such practices, and then regularly monitor all units of the physical plant on a formal and informal basis. There are a number of methods that can be used to determine whether or not facilities are well maintained and ready for participants. Among these are formal inspections and informal or nonstandardized observations. Both aspects can be of considerable significance to the safety of all if they are developed with the cooperation and support of the work force involved.

Formal inspections are performed on a routine basis by supervisory personnel. Records are kept at a central administrative office for easy reference concerning schedules and pending files so that regularly all elements of the physical plant are checked. When any safety deficit is noted, it is either corrected immediately or brought to the attention of those who can authorize whatever repairs or replacements are necessary. Such inspections are also a preventive measure in that they can inhibit accelerated deterioration of structures and facilities by catching minor problems before they escalate.

Informal or nonroutine maintenance is performed by all personnel on the staff. This really means that every employee has a responsibility for observing those aspects of the physical plant with which he or she comes in contact. All employees should be aware of and recognize any potential hazards that might develop in sections where they work and report any deficiencies in structure, equipment, or other assets. The use of maintenance report forms can greatly facilitate accurate reporting as well as officially notify administrators of real or suspected safety problems. In this manner the manager will be informed of any problems in the making or actually present and do something about them. Because the safety of recreators and others who attend agency functions is a primary concern in carrying out the organization's legal requirements, every employee must be instructed to note and report hazards. The premises on which recreational activities or other learning takes place must be as safe as possible, without destroying the inherent enjoyment of activities, and all facilities must be in reasonable condition for use.

Maintenance records are also excellent documentation for demonstrating the extent to which efforts are made by an organization in maintaining its premises for the safety of those using them. Maintenance inspection records can show that regular monitoring of all facilities and areas is performed, that deficiencies are noted, and corrective actions are taken in a timely manner.

Preventive Maintenance. Part of every maintenance program should be given over to the prevention or inhibition of deterioration of the physical plant and its contents. This means that maintenance personnel are constantly employed to forestall excessive wear and expensive repairs. The objective of preventive maintenance is to obtain the longest life from the premises and assets owned and operated by the agency. A basic requirement is attentive planning and scheduling so that minor repairs and replacements can be made before greater damage or deterioration occurs.

Preventive maintenance may do much to offset the failure rates of tools, machines, equipment, and apparatus that might prove dangerous to users. Outside preventive maintenance can retard or eliminate the erosion, breakup, or washout of roads, bridges, paths, and other facilities. Steps can be taken to shore up, fill in, or channel water (where necessary) so that accessory facilities do not become the source of accidents. With relation to buildings and other structures, attention must be paid to the care of mechanical parts, roofs, floors, accessways, hallways, and surfaces that take heavy contact. It can be just as important to make sure that a roof on a field house is well maintained so as to prevent leaks as it is to resurface outdoor court and game areas. Filling in potholes in an athletic field may prevent a participant from twisting an ankle or breaking a leg. Stopping leaks before they occur may prevent a participant from slipping, falling, and experiencing some traumatic occurrence that could result in litigation. Preventive maintenance is part of a sound managerial policy. Preventing physical plant deficiencies may do much to reduce the risk that is inherent in nearly every feature of recreational activity.

Safety Maintenance. It is the responsibility of any agency serving a clientele to provide premises that are safe for use. The capacity of a building or other structure to support hundreds or thousands of persons assembled to participate in or watch activities requires facilities that are designed to be safe and maintained that way. Daily inspections of activity areas and the facilities themselves may be accomplished by maintenance personnel and recreationists who are assigned to instruct or supervise specific activities or facilities. More formal, regular, and standard inspections may be performed by managerial teams or designees. No inspection should be superficial. Accidents, their cause, and nature should be recorded and analyzed so that steps can be taken that will eliminate the source—if the injury was produced by the physical failure of property. Sometimes, employees are oblivious to the existence of hazards despite their exposure to in-service training and continual requests for awareness. When this happens, an accident will eventually occur because an unfortunate coincidence of time, place, behavior, and the uncorrected danger will come together. In many instances, maintenance personnel performing a routine job may be the only ones in contact with an existing or potential hazard. If they fail to take corrective action and simply leave the hazard, there is almost a certainty that a patron will blunder into it with disastrous results. The following case is an example of this particular situation, coupled with other factors in a suit for alleged negligence:

> Richard Diodato, a thirty-one-year-old man, employed by the Boise Cascade Company at its Moonachie plant, attended a company picnic and outing at Cooper River Park on 21 September 1974. The park is a component of the Camden County Park Commission that operates them in order to provide recreational services to the public.
>
> A softball game between the Pennsauken Branch and the Moonachie Branch of the company took up much of the day's activities. The softball game occurred at the park on the other side of Cooper River, fronted by North Drive, approximately two miles from the picnic area.
>
> At about 2:30 P.M. a picnic was held in the vicinity of Saginaw Lodge, a pavilion at the park. A variety of recreational activities were engaged in by the participants, including a game of catch.
>
> Sometime around 4:00 P.M. Richard Diodato and another company employee participated in a spur-of-the-moment foot race to the edge of the river bank directly in front of the pavilion, and both entered the water. Richard Diodato used a flat racing dive entry from a running start and Al Rinaldi jumped into the river feet first. Both entered the water without first having stopped running.
>
> Richard Diodato struck a partially submerged object, probably with the lower part of his face at a point just below his mouth, was knocked unconscious by the impact, and sustained a fracture of his spinal column at C5. The result of the injury left Richard Diodato a quadriplegic, i.e., paralyzed from the chest downward. The object with which Diodato impacted was a fifty-five-gallon, blue painted oil drum that the Camden Park Commission utilized for trash cans.
>
> Richard Diodato was pulled unconscious from the river and subsequently taken to the hospital where his injury was diagnosed and he was given medical treatment. Mr. Diodato had never before been to Cooper River Park and has not returned there since the day of the accident.
>
> It was noted that when Diodato was at Cooper River Park on the day in question, there were no warning signs posted either forbidding entry into the river or signs indicating that swimming was prohibited. Furthermore, the permit that enabled the company to hold its picnic and outing at Cooper River Park carried no written notification of any prohibitions against using the river waters for swimming, diving, or other aquatic activity. The following facts seem to be pertinent:
>
> 1. A Camden County Park Commission trash can, dumped into the water of Cooper River by person or persons unknown, was the direct cause of the injury suffered by Richard Diodato when he came into violent contact with it after attempting to dive into the Cooper River on 21 September 1974.
> 2. Although personnel of the Camden County Park Commission were

required to maintain the Cooper River Park, including the Cooper River, by cleaning the area whenever trash, rubbish, or other garbage was placed on the grounds or found in the river, the fifty-gallon drum trash can was permitted to remain in the river adjacent to the bank for at least one year prior to the day of the accident.

3. Park personnel were supplied with a row boat by which they could remove inappropriate articles and other debris from the river. Despite this equipment, the trash can was not removed from the river.
4. There is little doubt that maintenance workers of the commission observed the trash can on numerous occasions as they either mowed the grass near the river bank or otherwise cleaned the area. Although the workers were required to pick up debris or other obstructions from the river park personnel failed to act in accordance with park administrative directions and left the trash can in the river where it became the dangerous condition that caused the injury to Diodato.
5. Insofar as the facilities of the Cooper River Park are concerned, the following commonly accepted planning and safety promotional principles in the field of recreational service apply: Improvident behavior on the part of participants or users of public recreational service facilities has required those employed within the field of recreational service to establish certain safety standards to guard people against their poor judgment. For these reasons, it is generally considered standard practice to post those areas that are either unsafe or that are to be prohibited from use. At no time were any signs posted that would have prohibited swimming in the river. Furthermore, no rules, regulations or maps were provided by the park commission to any of its permittees informing them of prohibitions on the use of the river waters for swimming purposes. In fact, no rules or regulations for use of the park were supplied to the Boise Cascade Company during the time of its request for the use of Cooper River Park.
6. Most people consider the park and recreational facilities and areas under public jurisdiction to be safe. The public assumes that operating authorities have acted in ways that omit any hazardous areas or spaces within the confines of a park or other recreational place. The public also presumes that warnings about dangerous or prohibited areas, by well and frequently displayed notices, will be posted for protection purposes. Furthermore, written rules and regulations describing prohibited areas are distributed to those who utilize public recreational areas. Ordinances that have been passed regulating the use of public recreational facilities are typically posted at recognized entrances of public recreational places so that potential patrons may be made aware of dangerous conditions and are able to avoid them. The posting of clearly readable signs of warning at frequent intervals at specific sites from which potential users are to be prohibited or restricted has been a standard practice to insure the safety of patrons.
7. The operational authorities of Cooper River Park, the Camden County Park Commission, have continuously administered the facilities that people in the vicinity and region use for recreational purposes. Among

the facilities is Cooper River, a nontidal waterway in the area of Saginaw Lodge, whose rise and fall is controlled by a dam. There has been a constant and recognized problem with the use of the river for aquatic purposes, including swimming, over a period of years. This is born out by the numerous citations and reports filed by the Camden County Park Police concerning park patrons' use of the river.

8. The park commission has known about the use to which the river's waters are put. While some aquatic uses are permitted, there are no signs or visible warnings prohibiting other uses. Although there is a Park Ordinance, passed in 1941, that states that "no person shall bathe, wade, or swim in any park waters, except at such times and in such swimming or wading pools as the Commission may designate," and despite the fact that park employees have on numerous occasions directed persons who have been swimming to leave the river, indications are that park authorities have known about the use that patrons regularly make of the river's waters, i.e., for swimming purposes. Additionally, "no swimming" warnings were posted on the stone boating docks, according to one park employee's testimony, but for some inexplicable reason the practice of posting was discontinued. The fact that there have been numerous cases of swimmers and other users being directed to leave the river by park employees requires that the Camden County Park Commission operators take cognizance of the park's accessibility to the public. This means that any dangerous or prohibited areas of the park must be properly posted to protect against use or entry by an unwarned public. The Camden County Park Commission had a higher responsibility than merely keeping their 1941 ordinance in an office file. The ordinance itself should have been conspicuously posted at all entryways to the park and distributed to permittees when permission was granted by the park authorities to utilize any portion of the park's facilities. In order to maximize safety of park users, the Camden County Park Commission should have posted any and all areas that authorities wanted to restrict from public use.
9. It is well within reason for the Camden County Park Commission to have stenciled, painted, or in some other manner installed restrictive warnings at regular intervals on the stone docks, at the various pavilions, on fire places, or with emplaced signs of an appropriate nature at entryways to the park or along the bank of the river. The failure to replace warnings that had once appeared on the stone docks does no justice to the commission. They still have the responsibility for posting such areas if, indeed, the park commission wanted to prohibit the use that custom has made prevalent, i.e., as an aquatic facility in which swimming periodically occurred.
10. Park employees were under orders to maintain the Cooper River Park by, among other functions, picking up trash on the grounds and cleaning up the Cooper River by ridding the river bed of debris and other obstructions. The park commission failed to make sure that this responsibility was performed adequately. Consequently, an obstruction

continued to exist in the river for at least one year. By neglecting to post the area in question, failing to warn off potential users, failing to conform to its own administrative directives, the Camden County Park Commission did not act in a reasonable and prudent manner in its operation and administration of an area within a recreational facility under its jurisdiction.

11. The Camden County Park Commission failed to set up any policy in recognition of the fact that over the years many warnings had been given to users of the Cooper River for swimming and wading therein. If the commission was serious about the desire to prohibit such aquatic use of that particular water area, it should have taken specific steps, outlined or confirmed by a detailed policy statement, concerning the denial of access to that waterway to potential users. The Camden County Park Commission's assertion of concern for the prohibition of use of the river for swimming may be challenged insofar as no real effort has ever been made to establish or initiate policy dealing with the public's use of Cooper River. When a waterway is admittedly open for use for some aquatic activity, e.g., boating, fishing, sculling, etc., it is difficult for the public to know what activities are not permitted unless there are specific messages indicating activity restriction. No such warnings or prohibitions were provided by the park commission in recent years. The commission may be legitimately questioned as to whether it ever really intended to prohibit such use of the area when, according to Camden County Park Police records, there was never any attempt to fulfill the letter of the ordinance by imposing penalties upon those who entered into the river for other than boating or fishing purposes. In other words, the ordinance was not carried out nor is there any indication that any definite statement of policy was issued covering such use by the commission. The commission's own "Safety Committee" keeps no records, does not or did not discuss aquatic problems of safety that existed at the Cooper River Park despite knowledge of same, and, in fact, never met for any reason between 1972–74. Furthermore, it can be observed that the Camden County Park Commission substantially deviated from normal standard of practice established in the field of recreational service by failing to operate under a clear and unequivocal policy that would have mandated the full implementation of the ordinance automatically and would have officially defined park personnel functions so that potential users would have to be warned away from the river.
12. The number of incidents responded to by park police from December 1973 through 21 September 1974 were 222 in number, with not less than fifty instances of swimming in the river. These conditions should have prompted the park commission to formally deal with such continuing problems through the issuance of policy. Failure to write such policy and reliance upon an ordinance that might be unknown by potential users constituted a significant breach of responsibility on the part of the Camden County Park Commission, if, in fact, it really was concerned with the prohibition of swimming and other uses at Cooper

River Park. Moreover, failure to post conspicuous prohibitory notices to insure compliance deviates substantially from accepted practices in the recreational service field with regard to such matters.

13. By omitting the posting of signs, notifications, or restrictions of use at various points along Cooper River and specifically at sites where prior knowledge of aquatic problems had occurred, the Camden County Park Commission failed to act responsibly and in accordance with well-established field practices for the protection and safety of its patrons.
14. By failing to maintain Cooper River Park in an appropriate manner consonant with standards of maintenance established throughout the field of recreational service, the Camden County Park Commission substantially deviated from recognized park practices of maintenance that are well known and published.[1]
15. By failing to assume the responsibility for the degree of care necessary to insure the health, safety, and welfare of its patrons, the Camden County Park Commission did not act in a reasonable and prudent manner in carrying out its functions. By permitting a dangerous condition to exist at one of its facilities, failing to foresee the probability of an accident caused by the presence of the obstruction in the river, although having prior notice of it over a lengthy period of time, failing to maintain its facility in a way that would have been appropriate, and failing to fulfill those safety obligations with which it was charged; the Camden County Park Commission operated in ways that substantially deviated from recognized standards of practice in the field of recreational service and materially contributed to the conditions that resulted in the injuries to Richard Diodato.

Subsequently, Mr. Diodato was awarded a substantial payment for injuries received.[2]

In-Service Maintenance Staff Training

Just as there is the necessity to orient and educate maintenance personnel about their functions and responsibilities concerning upkeep, cleanliness, and repair of the physical facilities that compose the organization's property, so too is there a need for periodic training for job and patron safety. Maintenance is primarily concerned with preserving the outdoor environment as close to its original state as is possible. It is also concerned with the prolongation of the physical assets such as buildings, structures, apparatus, equipment, tools, and other material whose durability can be enhanced through regular repair, refurbishment, or replacement of worn or used parts. Such activity generally has to do with the places on which organized activities are provided as well as those areas where self-directed experiences assume a dominant role. At each of the sites, maintenance is responsible for the appearance of property. Thus, public relations becomes one of the functions of the maintenance operation. Attractiveness, cleanliness, and a healthy environment promotes good will and stimulates participation and support. There is another aspect of maintenance management, however, that, while an integral part of public relations, takes as its major objective the provision of a safe environment for all users. It is this function that requires reiteration until safety habits become instilled within all staff personnel. Safety training may be divided into two components: job-related risks and environmental hazards, either internal or external, that accompany the development of premises designed for recreational purposes.

As general policy, each maintenance worker will receive approximately one hour of safety training each month. This training can be in the form of group instruction with visual aids, informal supervisory conferences, or any practical method of communicating safety information. The maintenance division of the organization will establish a written schedule concerning the program, instructors, places, and amount of time allocated to in-service safety training. Among the topics to be included for attention at some time during the year and depending upon the need as determined by operating personnel are:

1. Vehicle operation and safety.
2. Equipment/machinery operation and safety.
3. Chemical safety.
4. Explosive handling and safety (where applicable).
5. Lifting and reaching, hoists, and cranes.
6. Use of ladders, scaffolds, and staging.
7. Storage areas.
8. Flammable and combustible liquids.
9. Gas cylinders.
10. Protective clothing and equipment.
11. Fire prevention.
12. Electricity.
13. Traffic control, warning signs, and devices.
14. First aid.
15. Patron safety.
16. Safety consciousness.

The division will always engage qualified instructors who, when appropriate, have certificates or licenses that attest to their expertise for instructing such classes. Such in-service safety training should do much to promote appropriate attitudes and awareness on the part of the maintenance workers. This latter aspect becomes extremely significant in eliminating or reducing environmental safety hazards, not only for the organizational work force, but for the patrons who participate or spectate at agency areas and facilities. Maintenance workers should become aware of actual or potential hazards that they might observe during the normal course of their daily functions. Maintenance workers have an obvious responsibility for checking on the condition of indoor and outdoor apparatus, playground devices, equipment, and field surfaces, as do recreationists. However, maintenance workers can perform an invaluable service to the organization and its patrons by accomplishing their functions and noticing potential dangers that, if not corrected in time, might lead to serious accidents and injuries.

Fencing and Locking

Although the development of security measures for the premises of an organization rightly belong to administration, the maintenance division will, no doubt, be called upon to install and keep such equipment in good condition. Lock and key security is maintained by distributing keys only to those personnel with a need to have them. Except for specifically responsible management personnel, no single individual will be given keys to all locks. While there may be master keys for a number of locks within one facility or structure, no one key will open all of the locks necessary for securing far-flung premises operated by the typical recreational service department, school system, camp, club, or other association.

Security can be maintained within a building by having internal gates or doors under lock to prevent an intruder from making much headway even after an outer entryway has been penetrated. A series of reinforced steel gates at strategic locations within corridors leading to offices, activity rooms, or specialty shops may do much to frustrate the trespasser and prevent vandalism. By assigning keys to personnel, knowing which employees have keys in their possession, and making the employees responsible for the loss of keys, greater security can be obtained. Maintenance personnel can do much to assist in reducing accidents to facility users by checking locks to assure that equipment, tools, and rooms are secured. If a key is lost, it may be necessary to change the lock.

Fencing, while a security measure, is more often designed to assure the safety of area users, screen off unsightly places, direct pedestrian traffic, and prevent accidents by prohibiting access to environmentally hazardous areas. Fencing may be installed through the use of man-made or natural materials. Where strength, durability, and prohibition of access is paramount, then chain-link or some other metallic form will be preferred. When aesthetic conditions are desired, then natural substances, bushes, plants, or water barriers may be used.

In some instances, the use of earthen berms topped with a variety of plantings may provide the necessary protection to divide activity use, direct patrons to different sections of the premises, or prevent access to areas that place the individual at risk. Fencing requires regular inspection to forestall attempts at cutting, bending, or damaging metallic barriers. Natural materials, while being selected for their aesthetic appearance, can be tough, hardy, and prevent access by being interlocking or growing thorns or other sharp projections that will discourage entry attempts.

Any kind of fencing should be scheduled for routine maintenance that can offset the deterioration that often accompanies long-term use. Plantings should be well maintained and cultivated to provide maximum protection. Other barriers must be monitored so that breaching in vulnerable places is prevented. Some form of fencing is desirable in minimizing access to surroundings that are hazardous or in preventing persons from gaining entry to places where equipment is kept. The unsupervised use of equipment or apparatus may lead to serious accident and injury that fencing should help to ameliorate.

Fire Protection

All recreational buildings and other structures must conform to state and local fire codes. Beyond that, however, the departmental safety plan must include a fire safety program. The fire safety program requires regular and periodic inspections to determine potential hazards and the presence of adequate fire fighting equipment to extinguish various kinds of fires. Together with fire retarding doors and emergency exits, sprinker systems, alarms, and anticipated escape routes, the fire safety plan has to include all personnel who are employed at the site or who can be expected to answer an emergency call. Maintenance personnel will probably respond to such fire problems first. Therefore, they must know how to check on all fire fighting equipment, know how to use the equipment, and have the skill to recharge extinguishers that require it. Moreover, it will be a maintenance function to check all such equipment on a monthly basis to determine its correct placement, accessibility, visibility, and operational capacity. Fire drills and the use and handling of hoses are also a part of maintenance personnel responsibility.

Signs

All informational and warning signs are the direct responsibility of the maintenance division of an organization. While signs and symbols used to communicate with participants and spectators may be authorized and designed by other department members, it is part of the maintenance division's responsibility to make sure that signs and bulletin boards are kept up, replaced, repaired, or cleaned. Sometimes, a maintenance person may become aware of an environmental hazard that should be posted. By transmitting such information through the proper channels, the sign will be installed and may prevent someone from getting hurt.

Surely, signs should be attractive, compatible with the environment in which they are used, functional, and simple. The single most important issue concerning the use of signs is that they have a direct bearing on preventing accidents and keeping patrons safe. Posted warnings can reduce the number of incidents that would occur if no sign was present. If people are informed that a danger exists and it is pointed out to them, it is likely (but not inevitable) that they will try to avoid the hazard. Some people refuse to be warned. There is little that authorities can do about persons whose attitude toward their own safety is one of indifference. If signs are prominently posted at locations where the greatest number of people are going to be informed or if specific hazards are posted, then the standard of care owed to the invitee is performed.

Vandals occasionally steal, destroy, or mutilate signs. Where this occurs, the sign should be replaced or repaired as quickly as possible. The message that has been printed on a background may blur or disappear over time; periodic maintenance inspections can be performed to determine whether such obliteration is taking place, and the signs can be repainted or renewed.

Illumination

Lighting can be an effective method for reducing potentially dangerous areas. Stairwells inside buildings, steps leading from a building to a path or walkway, sport and game facilities intended for night use, all may be made safer for users through adequate and efficient lighting. Maintenance will be responsible for the replacement of nonoperational lights, domed lamps, light poles, or the electrical connections that operate such equipment.

Strategic illumination may be assistive in preventing criminal elements from committing assaults on the persons of park users during evening hours. By lighting up exteriors of buildings and structures, vandals and others who might use the cover of darkness to transgress against the rules and regulations of acceptable conduct may be discouraged.

Night lighting for recreational activities of all kinds provides the assistance necessary for play to take place and probably prevents accidents that could occur because participants were not able to see balls, bats, clubs, or other paraphernalia normally utilized in a variety of sport and game activities. The maintenance of effective lighting can prevent minor nuisances and major injuries. Maintenance personnel must be alert to any damage or malfunctioning of illuminating equipment, supplies, and materials so that they function in a manner that was intended. The whole enterprise is thereby geared toward the safety of all who participate in any organizational activity, entertainment, or performance.

NOTES

1. Robert E. Sternloff and Roger Warren, *Park and Recreation Maintenance Management* (Boston: Holbrook Press, 1977), 18–19.
2. Communication with William D. McGovern, Esq., Attorney at Law, 16 November 1977.

Epilogue

What are the major principles that may be understood from the foregoing material? Any organization involved in the provision of recreational services to patrons must be ready with plans, policies, procedures, and programs designed to educate, inform, and guide activity behavior so that accidents are either discouraged or reduced in number and severity. Every element of the organization (personnel, places, material, and activities) should be prepared and designed to sustain the safety of all who come into contact with the agency. This means training programs for all personnel with specific emphasis on potential environmental and inherent hazards to be found in nearly every recreational activity. Wherever the organization sponsors, organizes, administers, or supervises an area, facility, or activity, it must actively prevent foreseeable dangers from becoming injuries. This may be performed when agency personnel are alerted to potential hazards and enjoined to fulfill their employment responsibilities which are concerned with the safety of recreators.

Good judgment or common sense, based upon an analysis of safety hazards and the sources of accidents that produce injuries to recreators, may mitigate a great deal of sorrow and loss. By taking reasonable action in a timely manner, recreationists can prevent most serious injuries from happening. It is unreasonable to think that all injuries will be prevented, particularly in those instances where individuals acting wholly on their own bring themselves into needless exposure to risk.

Prudent action on the part of recreationists in the development of policy and routine procedures for the guidance and supervision of recreators can prohibit behaviors that all too frequently lead to the disablement of the person simply trying to have a good time.

The standard of care necessary for the safety of all those who are patrons of a recreational service organization requires that competent personnel be employed, that such personnel involved in the instruction of activities provide warnings about the potential for accidents as well as the techniques for obtaining skills in the performance of activities. Where equipment is supplied by the organization, it must be of the highest quality. Continual inspection of the environment, supplies, materials, and equipment in or with which recreational activities occur is mandatory so that any deterioration, fault, or failure may be corrected before it contributes to an injury.

Emergency measures and contingency plans known to all employed personnel and ready for operation when necessary are also a significant part of a safety program. Each employee should know what to do and how to do it during times of exigency. Current techniques should be studied and incorporated into the emergency plan as new and proved methods are published or otherwise recognized.

Accurate records should be kept of the maintenance program, emergency plans to counteract natural or man-made disasters, and accident reports—including their causes and disposition—so that safe practices and procedures can be assimilated. Moreover, such record keeping will document the organization's commitment to safety.

Appendix
General Safety Policies

I. The following general safety policies are to be implemented:

A. Fire control

1. Fire extinguishers will be placed in all maintenance buildings, employee and guest residences, and system vehicles. At least one additional extinguisher will be kept available in the facility office. All such extinguishers should be of the ABC type.
2. The system may request that the State Fire Marshall or representatives inspect all structures at least annually. These inspections will be thorough and should check for proper storage of combustible fuels, exposed live electrical wires, adequate attic ventilation, and other items that might give rise to fire.
3. The system will work for acquisition of pumper fire trucks. Supervisors will insure that designated employees are trained in the proper use of fire trucks and related equipment.
4. Where fire hydrants exist, proper tools for opening the hydrant will be readily available.
5. Specific fire fighting hand tools will be kept available in each park. Included will be hard hats, fire rakes, and fire flaps. In large parks such tools will be kept in various strategic locations, possibly include some backpack water tools, and be well maintained. The primary use for such tools will be as containment aids for small fires until help arrives. Other hand tools or equipment may be suggested by the park commission.

B. First aid

1. All recreational places will be required to keep a first aid kit in all appropriate vehicles, in all maintenance buildings, in the facility office, at all organized swimming areas, and at other areas as deemed necessary by the supervisors. All first aid kits will include the items listed as part of the twenty-four-unit kit mentioned in the American National Red Cross book *Advanced First Aid and Emergency Care*. Also, a snake bite kit will be included in all first aid kits. All first aid kits will be accompanied by the book *Standard First Aid and Personal Safety*. In addition,

each facility will keep a copy of the book *Advanced First Aid and Emergency Care* in the office. Both books are publications of the American National Red Cross and will serve as the official first aid reference books for the system.

2. An emergency telephone number list will be posted in every vehicle, in the facility, and in all other structures used by system employees and visitors. Included on the list will be the telephone numbers of local fire departments, local police department, rescue squad, and ambulance service. Attached to the list will be a clear map indicating the fastest route to the nearest hospital. However, park personnel will not transport injured persons to the hospitals unless there is no other option by which serious injury or death can be prevented. Local ambulance service will be used for such transport whenever possible.
3. All supervisors and assistants may be required to complete the American National Red Cross Standard First Aid Multimedia Course. Refresher courses may be required annually. Supervisors and assistants would in turn be responsible for training and informing other staff members of proper first aid practices.
4. Special emphasis will be placed on proper practices for emergency situations involving heat stroke, heat exhaustion, shock, heart attack, artificial respiration, and broken limbs. First aid procedures for each of these cases will be found in *Advanced First Aid and Emergency Care*. Special training in these areas may be encouraged by the system.
5. Properly trained, system employees will be encouraged not to hesitate in administering first aid to seriously injured persons especially when death or permanent injury seems a real possibility. If professional medical care is readily available, however, it should be sought first. In cases where professional medical care is not available, properly trained employees will administer the first aid appropriate for the situation.

C. Law enforcement

1. All supervisors and assistants will be given basic training in proper law enforcement procedures. The system will seek cooperation from the Game and Fish Commission, State Police, or other law enforcement training agencies that may be able to provide guest speakers or training instructions to system employees operating parks, beaches, or reservations.
2. All personnel will rely as much as possible on professional law enforcement personnel to handle or assist with enforcement problems on system property. Supervisors and assistants will actively pursue good personal relations with local and state law enforcement agencies. Supervisors will provide for ready contact with the nearest law enforcement agency in case of emergency.

D. Traffic control

1. Road surfaces will be maintained as well as possible. Where road conditions are poor and guardrails are missing, special note will be made in all facility safety inspections, and corrections will be made as soon as possible.
2. Regulatory signs will be posted for the speed limit along with stop signs, yield signs, and various other warning signs. All center lines will be painted as needed. All signs will be placed in visible locations, consistent with information given by other signs in the area and consistent with practices in cities and counties throughout the state. Warning signs such as "watch for bicycles," "pedestrian crossing," and "slippery when wet" will be used wherever the need dictates.
3. Traffic flow will be improved wherever possible by looping traffic through the facility on one-way roads. This, however, will not be practical in most parks because of their layout.
4. Scenic pull-offs will be well marked and advance roadway signs will indicate the distance to the pull-off area as well as warn of cars entering the traffic flow. This is especially important where the road is curving. Pull-offs will provide a large enough parking area so cars leaving the site do not have to back onto the roadway.

E. Water quality

1. All system facilities will have water supplies provided in parks or other areas tested for quality at least once per month. If a park has more than one water supply, each will be tested. Water samples will be taken from various locations throughout the park so that points where contamination may occur can be isolated.
2. All drinking fountains will be inspected periodically to make sure debris and food articles are not lodged in the fountain basin near the drain pipes. Wire mesh will cover all basin drain pipes. Drinking fountains will be checked especially closely in campgrounds and picnic areas.
3. Water quality tests will be periodically made of swimming lakes and streams throughout the system. Such tests of swimming areas will be conducted at least monthly in the summer season with preseason tests conducted prior to the opening of the swimming areas.
4. If in any case water tests show unsatisfactory results or harmful contaminants in either the drinking water or the swimming areas, steps will be taken to restrict use until an acceptable water quality level has been re-established.
5. All water quality tests will be conducted by the Department of Public Health. The water samples may be delivered to their office whenever necessary.

II. Personnel safety

Safety practices are to be a part of the daily job for all system personnel. The requirements covered in this section include safety requirements to be observed by employees using equipment that could become a potential hazard if safety rules are not applied.

A. Training

1. All supervisors and assistants will be required to have thorough training in the safety areas covered. Specifically, this includes first aid, fire control, and law enforcement. Refresher courses for first aid, fire control, and law enforcement for supervisors and assistants will be required annually. Training for supervisors and assistants will be handled through an annual in-service training program that will be arranged by the central office. This training will be provided during off-season periods. It will last from three to five days and will include guest speakers, question and answer sessions, and physical practice of the principles learned.
2. Supervisors and assistants will be responsible for giving or arranging for training to be given to members of their staff for first aid and fire control. This will be coordinated or arranged through the central office. Each facility will be required to hold a monthly safety meeting with all supervisors in which training can be reviewed, questions can be answered, and problems can be discussed.
3. Special lifeguard training sessions will be held prior to the start of each summer season. These sessions will review general lifesaving techniques and the safety policy of the system. All lifeguards hired by the system will be required to attend. A similar annual training session will likewise be adopted for horseback riding facility employees.
4. Maintenance personnel should be dressed to perform their function adequately and safely and at the same time present a good image to the public. Items of clothing that are likely to become entangled in equipment should be avoided. It is the responsibility of the maintenance supervisor to see that clothing worn by crew members is within safety standards and will not compromise safety regulations. Park Rangers and all personnel who operate potentially dangerous equipment will be issued a pair of safety glasses or goggles and a hard hat. Each employee to whom these items are issued will be required to wear them and be responsible for their care. Employees must furnish their own work shoes, normal work gloves, and normal work clothes.
5. The facility supervisor or safety officer/coordinator will teach safety courses to all personnel. When new employees (seasonal, temporary, or permanent) are hired, a thorough knowledge of safety requirements within the facility must be part of their

indoctrination course. Permanent employees should receive refresher courses during the off-season months. Safety meetings for all employees should be held by the supervisor or safety officer/coordinator, at least once each month. No employee should be permitted to miss three successive meetings without authorization from the supervisor.

6. Safety rules and regulations will be posted in each working area. The employee's immediate supervisor or safety officer/coordinator must be certain that all employees are familiar with the posted safety rules and regulations.
7. It will be the responsibility of each system employee to report any possible safety hazard or violation of safety procedure to his or her immediate supervisor or to the safety officer/coordinator.

B. Equipment safety

1. The operation of equipment is a major responsibility of all grounds maintenance personnel. By exercising safety measures at all times, they can avoid a great number of accidents. The following guidelines should be posted as constant reminders for all equipment operators:
   a) Know the situation and equipment.
   b) Avoid potentially dangerous situations.
   c) Let others know what to expect, where a safety hazard is present.
   d) Do not try to exceed the equipment's capability.
   e) Do not exceed your own capability.

   The maintenance supervisor will be responsible for maintenance and service on all equipment that would constitute a potential safety hazard.
2. No employee will be allowed to use any item of equipment until he or she has received complete operation and safety instructions from the maintenance supervisor, or safety officer/coordinator. The manufacturer's recommended safety precautions for every type of equipment should be observed.
3. Employees operating equipment will be cautioned to remain alert at all times for any safety hazard they may encounter. They will be expected to use good judgment and adhere to safe operational procedures.
4. Protective clothing and, in particular, eye and head protection must be used when operating certain items of equipment. All protective shields must be left in place on equipment and not removed during operation for any reason. Electrical circuits must be securely fastened in the *OFF* position when repairing or installing electrical service.
5. Essentially, all work area dangers can be reduced by good safety practices. On-the-job accidents can be reduced by good, safe work methods. Specific safety guidelines for maintenance personnel include the following:

a) All personnel must use safety equipment that is provided according to the instructions for its use. Safety equipment is provided to reduce the probability of on-the-job accidents.
b) Orderly and uncluttered work areas reduce the potential for accidents. All crew members are responsible for maintaining a neat and well-organized work area.
c) Anything that draws the worker's attention away from the job at hand is a threat to everyone in the area. Therefore, horseplay and the use of alcoholic beverages or illegal drugs are prohibited at the work site and during working hours.
d) The simplest and safest vehicle, piece of equipment, machinery, electric circuit, or work procedure can be very dangerous when used by an unqualified person. Only authorized and qualified personnel should use, operate, inspect, or work on items requiring special knowledge, skills, and abilities.
e) The biggest safety hazard on a work crew is the person who is skilled and unfamiliar with safe operational procedures.

III. Administration of system safety program

A. Facility safety officer
The facility safety officer is required to coordinate safety efforts in the facility and make periodic inspections. The inspections will be in addition to the daily inspections made by other employees as mentioned in other sections. The safety officer is responsible for filing all accident reports and personally investigating all personal injuries and property damages within the facility. If the safety officer is not the supervisor or assistant, the safety officer is required to receive the same safety training required of supervisors and assistants. The safety officer will be continuously watchful for possible hazards and work to have such hazards corrected. The system actively encourages the safety officer to seek as much additional training as possible.

B. Accidents are preventable
Accidents do not happen without cause. The identification and elimination of accident causes are essential to accident prevention.

C. Causes of accidents
Theoretically, preventable accidents may be traced to antecedents or causes originating in the heredity and early environment of individuals. These beginnings may further be said to manifest themselves in unsafe personal characteristics that allow an individual to perform an unsafe act or overlook or tolerate an unsafe condition. Therefore, unsafe acts and conditions may be considered the immediate cause of any accident. Usually, unsafe acts and conditions can be anticipated, readily identified, and

eliminated almost immediately upon discovery. System accident prevention efforts, therefore, are aimed at removing unsafe acts and conditions.

D. A safety inspection inventory
The safety officer will use the system's own book of guidelines during safety hazard inspections. When a hazard is identified, the action or condition needed to correct it is obvious. The things that must be carefully screened tend to fall into twenty-four broad categories. *For any given area, not all of these categories necessarily apply, nor are all of equal importance.*

1. *Atmospheric surroundings:* Hazardous conditions of dust, gases, fumes, sprays, etc.
2. *Chemical substances:* All liquids and solids that are toxic in nature.
3. *Containers:* All objects for storage of materials, i.e., barrels, boxes, bottles, cans, etc.
4. *Conveyor systems:* Any system that transports materials to or from operations or processes.
5. *Electrical conductors and apparatus:* Wires, cables, switches, controls, transformers, lamps, batteries, fuses, etc.
6. *Engines and prime movers:* Sources of mechanical power, excluding electric motors, i.e., steam engines, gas engines, etc.
7. *Elevators, escalators, and man lifts:* Require no further explanation.
8. *Fire-fighting equipment:* All fire-fighting equipment, plus sprinklers, fire plugs, etc.
9. *Guards and safety devices:* All removeable and fixed guards and safety devices or attachments excluding personal protective apparel.
10. *Hand tools:* Equipment that is held or carried when in use.
11. *Hoisting equipment:* Cranes, derricks, power shovels, dredges, air hoists, hydraulic jacks, etc.
12. *Flammables and explosives:* Require no further explanation.
13. *Machinery and parts thereof:* Power equipment that processes or modifies materials, i.e., agitators, grinders, forging presses, pulverizing machines, drilling machines, etc.
14. *Materials, raw or processed:* Materials and supplies essential to production of finished product, excluding materials elsewhere classified.
15. *Mechanical power transmission systems:* Shafts, bearings, gears, pulleys, drums, cables, belts, sprockets, ropes, chains, etc., when used to transmit power.
16. *Overhead structures and equipment:* Any structural part or equipment that may fall from above.
17. *Personal protective apparel:* Goggles, gloves, aprons, leggings, boots, etc.
18. *Pressure vessels, boilers, and pipes:* Objects subject to internal pressure from compression of liquids or gases.

19. *Pumps, compressors, blowers, and fans:* Objects that move or compress liquids, air, or gases.
20. *Shaft ways, pits, pumps, and floor openings:* All types of openings into which persons may stumble or fall.
21. *Walking or standing surfaces:* Floors, aisles, stairs, platforms, ramps, roads, scaffolds, ladders, etc.
22. *Warning and signal devices:* Direct communication systems such as radios, telephones, buzzers, bells, lights, flags, etc.
23. *Vehicles and carrying equipment:* Trucks, cars, motorized carts, and nonmotorized equipment for transporting materials.
24. *Miscellaneous:* Other potentially-hazardous objects or conditions that do not fall into the above categories. Five categories have been developed for efficiency.
    a) Guards (protective shields)
        (1) Missing or inadequate guards against being struck
        (2) Missing or inadequate guards against contact
        (3) Missing or inadequate guards against being crushed
        (4) Missing or inadequate guards against falling
        (5) Lack of or faulty support, bracing, shoring, or guying
        (6) Missing or faulty warning or signal device
        (7) Missing or faulty automatic control device
        (8) Missing or faulty safety device
    b) Structural defects and material characteristics
        (1) Sharp-edged, jagged, splintery, or serrated conditions
        (2) Worn, frayed, cracked, broken conditions
        (3) Slippery conditions (for gripping or walking)
        (4) Dull, irregular, mutilated conditions
        (5) Uneven, rough, pocked, or with holes
        (6) Decomposed or contaminated conditions
        (7) Flammable or explosive characteristics
        (8) Poisonous characteristics (by swallowing, breathing, or contacting)
    c) Functional defects
        (1) Susceptibility to breakage or collapse
        (2) Susceptibility to tipping or falling
        (3) Susceptibility to rolling, sliding, or slipping
        (4) Leakage of gases, fumes, or fluids
        (5) Excessive heat, noise, vibration, fumes, or sparking
        (6) Failure to operate
        (7) Erratic or unpredictable performance
        (8) Lack of adequate electrical grounding
        (9) Operation that is too fast or too slow
        (10) Low voltage leaks
        (11) Signs of excessively high or low pressure
        (12) Throwing off of parts, particles, or materials
        (13) Standard indications of need for special attention
    d) Ventilation, illumination, or noise
        (1) Noxious fumes or gases
        (2) Flammable or explosive fumes or gases

(3) Insufficient illumination
(4) Excessive glare from light sources
(5) Hazardous dusts or atmospheric particles
(6) Hazardous temperature condition
(7) Excessive noise

e) Storage, positioning, and arrangement of materials
(1) Improperly secured against sudden movement such as falling, slipping, rolling, tipping, or sliding.
(2) Unsafe storage that permits easy contact by men or equipment.

It is obvious that these conditions do not include every possible hazard.

E. Accident investigation and reporting

Thorough investigation of accidents is essential to an effective safety program. Positive corrective and preventive action cannot be formulated from conjecture, hearsay, or opinion. The efficiency of the action depends upon the adequacy of the facts, the correctness of the interpretation, and the appropriateness of the remedy selected. Complete factual reports are to be written by personnel investigating an event. Evidence of unreported accidents may require action to prevent recurrence. Every accident occurring within the system will be investigated to determine the causes and to formulate measures to prevent recurrence. The facility supervisor will determine whether the accident is reportable to the central office. The initial investigation should be made at the scene as soon as possible to obtain facts concerning conditions at the time of the accident and to obtain witnesses' statements while events are fresh in their minds. A common mistake made by investigators is to investigate the injury or damage and not the accident. Each accident must be investigated to determine where, what, when, how, and why it happened.

Personnel who are charged with the responsibility for accident investigation will find the following guides helpful to their task.

1. Get to the scene. Investigators should arrive at the scene as soon as possible after the accident has been reported to obtain facts quickly and while they are still fresh.
2. Interview the injured. Injured persons will be interviewed, if conditions warrant, to determine causative factors. Permanent or temporary physical and mental characteristics that may have contributed to the accident will be noted, and the extent of injuries will be reported.
3. Interview the witnesses. Witnesses will be interviewed to obtain their versions of the accident. On-the-spot witnesses often provide information that eventually establishes the causes of the accident. For best results, allow each witness to tell what happened, in his own way. Investigators should distinguish between biased and unbiased witnesses.

4. Obtain physical evidence. Physical evidence helps to determine the cause of the accident. Mechanical defects will be noted and measurements taken of distances or dimensions. When necessary and for further reference, photographs should be taken of the scene and other outstanding evidence. The extent of all damage will be recorded.
5. List other evidence. All other evidence will be recorded. This includes weather conditions or traffic signal locations, if the accident involves motor vehicles or the adequacy of lighting and machine operating speed if it is an industrial accident. Proper consideration should be given to work surfaces, machine condition, and adequacy.
6. Accurately record data. Information gathered in all investigations will be accurately tabulated for transfer to standard accident report and summary forms.
7. Recommend Corrective Actions. The most important outcome of any accident investigation is the determination of cause factors and implementation of suitable corrective measures. Appropriate action for hazard elimination will be expeditiously recommended to responsible persons.

Bibliography

Bird, Frank E., Jr., and Robert E. Loftus. *Loss Control Management*. Birmingham, England: Royal Society for the Prevention of Accidents, 1981.

Brown, Robert, ed. *Boater's Safety Handbook*. Seattle: Mountaineers-Books, 1982.

Ferry, Ted S. *Safety Management: Planning Manual*. Santa Monica: Merritt Publishers, 1982.

Firenze, Robert J. *The Process of Hazard Control*. Dubuque, Iowa: Kendall-Hunt Publishing Co., 1978.

Hipskind, Verne K. *Personnel Safety for Public Employees*. Springfield, Ill.: Charles C. Thomas Publishers, 1965.

National Safety Council. *Public Employees Safety Guide: Parks and Recreation*. Chicago: National Safety Council, 1974.

Peterson, Dan. *Safety Management: A Human Approach*. Huntington, N.Y.: Aloray Inc., 1975.

Strasser, Maryland K., and James Aaron. *Fundamentals of Safety Education*, 3d ed. New York: The Macmillan Company, 1981.

Index